A Content-Based Grammar

Third Edition

mosaic one

Patricia K. Werner

with contributions by

Lida R. Baker
University of California, Los Angeles

Mary Curran
University of of Wisconsin, Madison

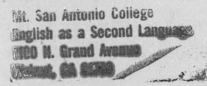
Mt. San Antonio College
English as a Second Language
1100 N. Grand Avenue
Walnut, CA 91789

The McGraw-Hill Companies, Inc.

New York St. Louis San Francisco Auckland Bogotá Caracas Lisbon
London Madrid Mexico City Milan Montreal New Delhi San Juan
Singapore Sydney Tokyo Toronto

This is an EDI book.

McGraw-Hill

A Division of The McGraw-Hill Companies

Mosaic One
A Content-Based Grammar

1 2 3 4 5 6 7 8 9 0   DOC DOC   9 0 9 8 7 6

ISBN 0-07-069576-8
ISBN 0-07-114512-5

This book was set in Times Roman by Monotype Composition Company. The editors were Tim Stookesberry, Bill Preston, Steve Vogel, and Caroline Jumper; the index was prepared by Jeanine Briggs; the designers were Lorna Lo, Suzanne Montazer, Francis Owens, and Elizabeth Williamson; the production supervisors were Patricia Myers and Tanya Nigh; the cover was designed by Francis Owens; the cover illustrator was Susan Pizzo; the photo researcher was Cindy Robinson, Seaside Publishing; illustrations were done by Rick Hackney and Michelle Margelli.

R. R. Donnelley & Sons Company, Crawfordsville, IN, was printer and binder.
Phoenix Color Corporation was cover separator and printer.

Library of Congress Catalog Card Number: 96-75306

Grateful acknowledgment is made for the use of the following:

Photographs: *Page 1* © Frank Tapia; *22* © AP/Wide World Photo; *31* © Bryce Flynn/Stock, Boston; *65* © Patricia Werner; *96* © UPI/Bettman; *103* © Comstock; *147* © AP/Wide World Photo; *169* © Fujifotos/The Image Works; *172* © Spencer Grant/Monkmeyer Press Photos; *179* © Comstock; *211 (left)* © The Bettmann Archive; *(right)* © Alan Carey/The Image Works; *217* © Ken Robert Buck/Stock, Boston; *220, 238* © Patricia Werner; *243* © John Elk/Stock Boston; *252* © Kopsrein/Monkmeyer Press Photos; *263* © Bachmann/Stock, Boston; *272 (left)* © Stern/Black Star; *(right)* © AP/Wide World Photo; *273 (left)* © The Bettman Archive;

(continued on page 474)

Contents

CHAPTER **three**

Relationships **65**

Verbs (2)

CHAPTER four

Health

Modal Auxiliaries and Related Structures

High Tech, Low Tech

The Passive Voice

CHAPTER **six**

Money Matters   *179*

Nouns and Noun Modifiers

CHAPTER **seven**

Leisure Time   *217*

Gerunds, Infinitives, and Other Verb Forms

CHAPTER eight

Creativity   263

Compound and Complex Sentences (1)

CHAPTER **nine**

Human Behavior   *309*

Adjective Clauses and Related Structures

Contents

Together on a Small Planet   421

Noun Clauses

Appendixes   457

Preface
to the Third Edition

The Mosaic One Program

The Mosaic One Program consists of four texts and a variety of supplemental materials for intermediate to high-intermediate students seeking to improve their English language skills. Each of the four texts in this program is carefully organized by chapter theme, vocabulary, grammar structures, and where possible, learning strategies and language functions. As a result, information introduced in a chapter of any one of the Mosaic One texts corresponds to and reinforces material taught in the same chapter of the other three books, creating a truly integrated, four-skills approach.

The Mosaic One program is highly flexible. The texts in this series may be used together or separately, depending on students' needs and course goals. The books in this program include:

- **A Content-Based Grammar.** Designed to teach grammar through content, this text introduces, practices, and applies grammatical structures through the development of high-interest chapter topics. This thematic approach motivates students because they are improving their mastery of grammatical structures and vocabulary while expanding their own knowledge.

- **A Content-Based Writing Book.** This text takes students step-by-step through the writing process—from formulating ideas through the revision stage. Writing assignments progress from paragraphs to essays, and students write about interesting, contemporary subjects from the sciences, social sciences, and humanities that are relevant to their current or future academic coursework.

- **A Listening/Speaking Skills Book.** This text teaches learning strategies and language functions, while maintaining a strong focus on both listening and speaking. Each chapter includes a realistic listening passage on an interesting topic related to the chapter theme. Short conversations also provide comprehension practice, while a variety of speaking activities reinforce use of language in context.

- **A Reading Skills Book.** The selections in this text help students develop their reading skills in a meaningful rather than a mechanical way—enabling them to successfully tackle other academic texts. The three readings per chapter come from a variety of authentic sources, such as textbooks, magazines, newspapers, interviews, and so on, and are accompanied by pre- and post-reading exercises, including skimming, scanning, making inferences, paraphrasing, and group problem solving.

Supplemental Materials

In addition to the four core texts outlined above, various supplemental materials are available to assist users of the third edition, including:

Instructor's Manual

Extensively revised for the new edition, this manual provides instructions and guidelines for using the four core texts separately or in various combinations to suit particular program needs. For each of the core texts, there is a separate section with answer keys, teaching tips, additional activities, and other suggestions. The testing materials have been greatly expanded in this edition.

Audio Program for Mosaic One: A Listening/Speaking Skills Book

Completely re-recorded for the new edition, the audio program is designed to be used in conjunction with those exercises that are indicated with a cassette icon in the student text. Complete tapescripts are now included in the back of the student text.

Audio Program to Accompany Mosaic One: A Reading Skills Book

This new optional audio program contains selected readings from the student text. These taped selections of poems, articles, stories, and speeches enable students to listen at their leisure to the natural oral discourse of native readers for intonation and modeling. Readings that are included in this program are indicated with a cassette icon in the student text.

Video/Video Guide

New to this edition, the video program for Mosaic One contains authentic television segments that are coordinated with the twelve chapter themes in the four texts. A variety of pre- and post-viewing exercises and activities for this video are available in a separate Video Guide.

Mosaic One: A Content-Based Grammar, Third Edition

Rationale

Designed to teach grammar through context, the text introduces, practices, and applies grammatical structures through the use of thematic material on topics such as health care, relationships, economics, and creativity. This thematic approach allows students to work with real language that conveys information—

not mechanically produced unrelated sentences. In *Mosaic One: A Content-Based Grammar,* form and content are never separated: What we express and how we express it are the combined focus of the text.

Chapter Organization and Teaching Suggestions

The text is organized by grammatical structures and by themes. It begins with diagnostic and review material that is optional; later chapters introduce more complex structures. The chapters are divided into grammar topics, many of which include related subtopics. In general, each grammar topic represents one to two hours of class work with one to two hours of homework. The earlier chapters (diagnostic and review) should be completed as quickly as possible, and parts of them can be omitted entirely. Later chapters need more class and homework time.

All chapters begin with a general introductory passage that introduces the content and previews the key structures included in the chapter. Each grammar topic within the chapter opens with a brief passage that highlights specific structures covered in that section. The topic openers can be used to introduce key vocabulary and to make sure the students have a general understanding of the content. They can be covered with the class as a whole, or they can be used as homework assignments, timed readings, or listening comprehension exercises.

All structures are presented in boxes that include general rules and examples. Also included when necessary are notes on particular usages and variations, spelling, punctuation, and pronunciation guidelines, and exceptions to the general rules. Grammar explanations can be assigned as homework, or they can be covered briefly in class. We do not recommend long, detailed presentations in class.

Every topic includes a variety of exercises and activities that are sequenced to progress from more-controlled to less-controlled practice of the target structures. Most exercises can be used for either oral or written work; they can be done as a class, in pairs, in small groups, or as homework. Three types of exercises are clearly labeled: **Rapid Oral Practice, Error Analysis,** and **Review. Rapid Oral Practice** and **Error Analysis** exercises are included periodically to focus on common problems. **Review** exercises appear frequently throughout the text, recycling previously studied material and integrating it with newly practiced material. In addition, Chapters Four, Eight, and Twelve each include an entire section devoted to review.

Finally, every chapter offers a wealth of speaking and writing activities found in sections called **Using What You've Learned.** The activities range from mini-dramas and language games to debates, discussions, formal presentations, and compositions. These activities are optional, but we recommend using as many as possible. They are designed to encourage the use of target structures and vocabulary in natural, personalized communication. Moreover, they help to form a bridge between the controlled, structured language of the classroom and real-life language outside the classroom.

Flexibility

Students come to a course with varying skills, attitudes, needs, and time available for study. Likewise, ESOL courses vary greatly in length, number of contact hours, and focus. Therefore, *Mosaic One: A Content-Based Grammar* includes more material than may be necessary for many courses. If you do not want or have time to cover all the material in the text, be selective. Cover the structures that the majority of your students have the most difficulty with, and omit the structures that most already have command of. You may also want to omit diagnostic or review material, reading passages, and activities. Of course, the extra material can be assigned to those students who need additional work with given structures, or the material can be used as the basis for quizzes and exams. However, we heartily encourage using as many of the activities as possible. They are stimulating and lively ways of allowing students to communicate more authentically within the classroom.

New to the Third Edition

1. **Streamlined Design.**   The two-color design and revised art program make this edition more appealing to today's students. It is also more user-friendly because many directions have been shortened and clarified, exercises and activities have been numbered, and key information has been highlighted in shaded boxes and charts.
2. **New Chapter Theme on Crime and Punishment.**   The new edition features an entirely new theme for Chapter Ten: Crime and Punishment, which covers *hope, wish,* and conditional sentences. In addition, themes for several other chapters have been broadened to include new content.
3. **Review Sections Every Four Chapters.**   While many structures are periodically recycled and reviewed throughout the text, the third edition provides even more systematic integration through special review sections in Chapters Four, Eight, and Twelve. These review sections have a variety of cumulative exercises that can be used in class, for homework, or as the basis for quizzes.

4. **Focus on Testing.**   These new boxed features in every chapter are designed to help students prepare for standardized grammar and usage tests like the TOEFL. Most chapters have a short **Focus on Testing** box that highlights structures covered in the particular chapter. However, Chapters Four, Eight, and Twelve have slightly longer boxes that include test items on structures from a variety of chapters. Through repeated exposure to and practice with this standardized test format, students will gain more confidence and experience less anxiety in actual test-taking situations.
4. **Reference Appendixes.**   All key reference material—including spelling rules and irregular forms, irregular verb forms, verbs + gerunds and/or infinitives, special uses of *the,* and so on—has been consolidated in special appendixes, making it easier to find.

Acknowledgments

A very special thanks to Maria Pace and Stella Blanco for their help during the completion of this book.

Our thanks to the following reviewers whose comments, both favorable and critical, were of great value in the development of the third edition of the Interactions/Mosaic series:

Jean Al-Sibai, University of North Carolina; Janet Alexander, Waterbury College; Roberta Alexander, San Diego City College; Julie Alpert, Santa Barbara City College; Anita Cook, Tidewater Community College; Anne Deal Beavers, Heald Business College; Larry Berking, Monroe Community College; Deborah Busch, Delaware County Community College; Patricia A. Card, Chaminade University of Honolulu; José A. Carmona, Hudson County Community College; Kathleen Carroll, Fontbonne College; Consuela Chase, Loyola University; Lee Chen, California State University; Karen Cheng, University of Malaya; Gaye Childress, University of North Texas; Maria Conforti, University of Colorado; Earsie A. de Feliz, Arkansas State University; Elizabeth Devlin-Foltz, Montgomery County Adult Education; Colleen Dick, San Francisco Institute of English; Marta Dmytrenko-Ahrabian, Wayne State University; Margo Duffy, Northeast Wisconsin Technical; Magali Duignan, Augusta College; Janet Dyar, Meridian Community College; Anne Ediger, San Diego City College; D. Frangie, Wayne State University; Robert Geryk, Wayne State University; Jeanne Gibson, American Language Academy; Kathleen Walsh Greene, Rhode Island College; Myra Harada, San Diego Mesa College; Kristin Hathhorn, Eastern Washington University; Mary Herbert, University of California, Davis; Joyce Homick, Houston Community College; Catherine Hutcheson, Texas Christian University; Suzie Johnston, Tyler Junior College; Donna Kauffman, Radford University; Emmie Lim, Cypress College; Patricia Mascarenas, Monte Vista Community School; Mark Mattison, Donnelly College; Diane Peak, Choate Rosemary Hall; James Pedersen, Irvine Valley College; Linda Quillan, Arkansas State University; Marnie Ramker, University of Illinois; Joan Roberts, The Doane Stuart School; Doralee Robertson, Jacksonville University; Ellen Rosen, Fullerton College; Jean Sawyer, American Language Academy; Frances Schulze, College of San Mateo; Sherrie R. Sellers, Brigham Young University; Tess M. Shafer, Edmonds Community College; Heinz F. Tengler, Lado International College; Sara Tipton, Wayne State University; Karen R. Vallejo, Brigham Young University; Susan Williams, University of Central Florida; Mary Shepard Wong, El Camino College; Cindy Yoder, Eastern Mennonite College; Cheryl L. Youtsey, Loyola University; Miriam Zahler, Wayne State University; Maria Zien, English Center, Miami; Yongmin Zhu, Los Medanos College; Norma Zorilla, Fresno Pacific College.

CHAPTER **one**
New Challenges

in this chapter

Introduction

Chapter One is a review chapter. It covers some basic structures and grammatical terms, and it looks at some special challenges involved in adjusting to life in a new language and culture. While you are reviewing the grammar topics in the chapter, you will have a chance to get to know more about your classmates: about their ideas, their backgrounds, and their cultures.

The following passage introduces the chapter theme, New Challenges, and raises some of the topics and issues you will cover in the chapter.

Studying a New Language and Culture

Learning to communicate in another language can be very difficult and frustrating at times, but it can also be one of the most rewarding experiences of your life. Being able to communicate in another language will open doors for you to experience a world of new people, places, and ideas. It will offer you a look at cultures from every part of the earth. And if you have the opportunity to live in another culture, the experience will show you many things—above all, about your own culture. It will reveal cultural similarities and differences that you had never noticed in the past. In addition, the experience can also show you a great deal about your own personal beliefs, attitudes, and perceptions. Within a short time in another culture, you will find that you begin to learn a great deal about yourself and your own country and culture.

getting to know your class

Learning always involves asking questions. Why don't you begin by finding out some information about a new person in your class or about someone you haven't talked with for a while? In pairs, ask each other for the following information, forming complete questions about each item.

1. Name — (What . . . ?)
2. Age and date of birth — (How old . . . ? When . . . ?)
3. Hometown (country) — (Where . . . ?)
4. Native language — (What . . . ?)
5. Reason for studying English — (Why . . . ?)
6. Length of time studying English — (How long . . . ?)
7. Education (major, occupation, or plans) — (What . . . ?)
8. Family (single or married) (brothers, sisters, children) — (Are you . . . ?) (Do you . . . ?)
9. Interests (sports or hobbies) — (What . . . ?)
10. Any special information to share (travels, accomplishments, goals) — (What . . . ?)

After everyone has finished, introduce your partner to the class. Begin your introduction by saying:

I would like to introduce my friend. . . .

Review of Basic Sentence Structure

Setting the Context

What did you expect before you came here to study? Have your experiences been different from your expectations? Read the following passage. It was written by an English language student from Switzerland. As you read, compare his ideas to yours.

How My American Stay Affected Me

When I left Switzerland, my life changed completely. I had not known what I should expect or how I would be affected in education, sophistication, and personality through my stay in the United States. Coming from a small country and not having traveled outside of Europe, I was not exactly what people would call a sophisticated man. Now I believe that I am a little more aware. Not only did I learn about the United States, but I also learned tremendously about other fascinating cultures. Most of all, I learned to understand and to accept other cultures. Living in a new country and learning about new cultures has been, I believe, the most important experience in my life.

5

Daniel Pfister

discussing ideas Write three things you expected before you came here to study. Then choose a partner. Take turns discussing your expectations of life here. Have your experiences so far been different from your expectations? If so, how?

A. Parts of Speech

Every sentence in English is made up basic building blocks, the *parts of speech.* You should be familiar with these: adjective, adverb, article, conjunction, noun, preposition, pronoun, and verb.

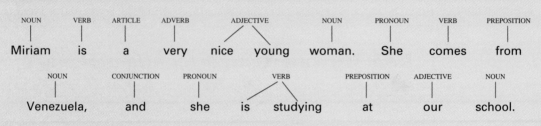

| NOUN | VERB | ARTICLE | ADVERB | | ADJECTIVE | NOUN | PRONOUN | VERB | PREPOSITION |
| Miriam | is | a | very | nice | young | woman. | She | comes | from |

| NOUN | CONJUNCTION | PRONOUN | VERB | PREPOSITION | ADJECTIVE | NOUN |
| Venezuela, | and | she | is studying | at | our | school. |

B. Kinds of Sentences

A sentence is a group of words that expresses a complete idea. There are four kinds of sentences. Each includes at least one subject and one verb. The chart gives some examples.

	examples	notes
Questions	What is your name? Are you a student?	A question asks for information or for a "yes" or "no."
Statements	My name is Miriam. That's a beautiful name.	A statement gives information or opinions.
Exclamations	What a lovely name you have! We won the World Cup!	An exclamation expresses surprise, pleasure, or other emotions.
Commands	(you) Tell me about yourself. Have a seat, please.	A command tells what to do. The subject "you" is understood.

 **exercise 1** Tell whether these sentences are questions, statements, exclamations, or commands. Identify the part of speech of each italicized word.

<blockquote>
example:
adjective   noun
| |
What's *your name*?   question
</blockquote>

1. *My* name *is* Anton.

2. Tell *me* your *last* name.

3. *If you* really *want* to know, it's Boxrucker.

4. What *an unusual* name you *have*!

5. Are you *from Switzerland*?

6. I've *always* wanted to go *there*, *but* I've *never* had *the opportunity*.

7. Switzerland is *a beautiful, mountainous* country *in* the heart *of* Europe.

8. The *capital* is Bern, *and its other* important cities *are* Geneva and Zurich.

 # C. Subjects

The subject is normally the most important person, place, thing, or idea in the sentence. Subjects can take several forms: nouns, pronouns, phrases, and clauses.

	examples	**notes**
Noun or Pronoun	**Miriam** comes from Venezuela. **She** is from Caracas.	A noun names a person, place, thing, or idea. Pronouns replace nouns.
Phrase	**Many Venezuelan students** are studying in the United States. **To study in the United States** can be expensive. **Studying in the United States** can be expensive.	A phrase is a group of related words. Infinitive (*to* + simple form) or gerund (*ing* form) phrases can be used as subjects. These and other verb forms are covered in Chapter Seven.
Clause	**How long they stay in the United States** depends on many things.	A clause is a group of related words that includes a subject and a verb. Dependent clauses are covered in Chapters Eight to Twelve.

D. Verbs, Objects, and Complements

Some verbs tell what the subject does. These verbs can be transitive or intransitive. Intransitive verbs do not have objects, but transitive verbs *must* have objects. Another group of verbs are linking verbs; they connect the subject to the complement. A complement is a noun, pronoun, adjective, or verb form that describes the subject. Common linking verbs include: *be, appear, become, feel, get* (when it means *become*), *look, seem, smell, sound,* and *taste.* The chart gives some examples.

	examples	notes
Intransitive Verbs	Miriam **travels** often.	An intransitive verb is complete without an object.
Transitive Verbs and Objects	When she travels, she always **buys** souvenirs.	A transitive verb *must* have an object. It is incomplete without one.
Direct Object	She bought her daughter **a sweater.**	Direct objects answer the questions *who(m)?* or *what?*
Indirect Object	She bought **her daughter** a sweater.	Indirect objects answer the questions *to/for who(m)?* or *what?*
Linking Verbs and Complements	Miriam **is** a lawyer. She **seems** happy with her work. It **appears** to be an interesting job.	Information that describes the subject follows linking verbs. Remember that adverbs cannot be used as complements after linking verbs. *example:* Correct: *He seems happy.* Incorrect: *He seems happily.*

 Find the subjects, verbs, objects, and/or complements in the following sentences. Underline each subject once and each verb twice. Circle objects or complements.

example: Every year, thousands of foreign students begin university studies in North America.

1. Most of these students have studied some English before coming to an English-speaking country.

Mosaic One • Grammar

2. Many already read and write English fairly well.

3. A major difficulty for all new students, however, is to understand and speak English.

4. Making phone calls or understanding directions can be difficult.

5. Many Americans use a lot of slang.

6. Each part of the country has variations in vocabulary and pronunciation.

7. Nevertheless, after the first few weeks, most new students will notice tremendous improvement.

8. All of a sudden, English becomes a lot clearer and easier!

E. Pronouns and Possessive Adjectives

Subject Pronouns	I	you	he	she	it	we	they
Object Pronouns	me	you	him	her	it	us	them
Possessive Adjectives	my	your	his	her	its	our	their
Possessive Pronouns	mine	yours	his	hers	its	ours	theirs
Reflexive Pronouns	myself	yourself yourselves	himself	herself	itself	ourselves	themselves

 exercise 3 Complete the sentences here and on the next page by using appropriate pronoun forms.

example: When we communicate, each of __us__ speaks two distinct languages.

1. We express _____ with _____ bodies as well as with _____ words.

2. People's movements often communicate more than _____ words.

3. Each culture has _____ own body language.

4. Arabs often move very close when _____ want to communicate.

5. A Japanese woman will tilt _____ head to the side when _____ is confused or puzzled.

6. Germans may feel uncomfortable when someone stands or sits close to _____.

7. When an American businessman is doing business, _____ tries to keep eye contact with _____ client.

8. You can learn more about _____ own body language by observing _____ as _____ talk with others.

 F.

Sentence Types

Sentences can be simple, compound, complex, or a combination of compound and complex.

	examples	notes
Simple	Sukariati arrived from Indonesia last week.	A simple sentence has at least one subject and one verb.
	Sukariati's sister and brother are living here now.	A simple sentence can have a compound subject.
	Her cousin wanted to come, too, but couldn't.	A simple sentence can have a compound verb.
Compound	Sukariati began her classes yesterday, and she likes them a lot.	Compound sentences are sentences joined by a comma and a conjunction: *and, but, or, so, nor, for,* or *yet.*
Complex	Muljati, who is originally from Jakarta, has lived in the United States for some time. She chose to live in California because she liked the climate.	Complex sentences are sentences joined by connecting words such as *who, that, because, after, while,* and so on. These are covered in Chapters Eight to Twelve.

exercise 4   Label the subject(s) and verb(s) in each of the following sentences. Tell whether the sentences are simple, compound, or complex. If the sentence is compound or complex, circle the connecting word.

                      V   S   V

examples: Have you met Kunio Takahashi?   *simple sentence*

                    S   V

                   Kunio is one of the most interesting people (whom)

                  S   V

                   I have met here.   *complex sentence*

1. My friend Kunio is from Tokyo, Japan.

2. He has studied English in the United States for a year, and now he hopes to study at an Australian university.

3. Because Kunio wants to study both English and veterinary science, he has applied to schools in the United States and Australia.

4. Is he working on an undergraduate or a graduate degree?

5. Kunio already has his bachelor's degree.

6. He will get his master's degree, and then he will begin a doctoral program.

7. What did he study as an undergraduate?

8. I'm not really sure.

9. Why don't you ask him when you see him again?

10. He's so busy enjoying American life that I never see him!

exercise 5    **Error Analysis.**   Indicate whether the following twelve items are complete or incomplete sentences. If the sentence is incomplete, tell what is missing and add words to correct it.

     example: Learning a new language.
                    Incomplete. It needs a subject and a complete verb.
                    She is learning a new language.

       Or: *It needs a verb and a complement.*
                    Learning a new language is challenging.

1. Is difficult.

2. Learning a new language can be frustrating.

3. Lots of vocabulary.

4. Body language is different from culture to culture.

5. The experience of life in a new country very exciting.

6. Another language will open doors for you.

7. To experience a world of new people, places, and ideas.

8. Cultures from every part of the earth.

9. Think about the similarities and differences across cultures.

10. The experience can show you a great deal.

11. You will learn a lot.

12. You will meet.

Using What You've Learned

Separate into groups and reread the passage "How My American Stay Affected Me" on page 3. Take a few minutes to discuss the ideas and then analyze the passage. Find the subject(s) and verb(s) in each sentence. Then choose one or two sentences and label the parts of speech in each.

Separate into groups and read the following passage together. First, discuss the ideas in the passage and your opinions about them. Then, analyze the passage. Find the subject(s) and verb(s) in each sentence. Note whether the sentences are simple, compound, or complex.

NEW CULTURES

Culture hides much more than it reveals. Strangely enough, what it hides, it hides most effectively from its own members. Years of study have convinced me that the real job is not to understand foreign culture but to understand our own. I am also sure that all you ever get from studying foreign culture is a token* understanding. The ultimate reason for such study is to learn more

---

token superficial, not in-depth

about your own system. The best reason for experiencing foreign ways is to generate a sense of vitality and awareness—an interest in life that can come only when you live through the shock of contrast and difference.

Adapted from Edward T. Hall, *The Silent Language*, p. 30

TOPIC **two**
Word Order of Modifiers

Setting the Context

previewing the passage

In English, word order is important. Is word order important in your language? How does it differ from English word order? As you read the following passage, think about your own language.

Order

*T*he laws of order are those regularities that govern changes in meaning when order changes. "The cat caught the mouse" means something obviously different from "The mouse caught the cat." Order is used differently in different languages and cultures. While order is of major importance on the sentence
5   level in English, this is not the case in some languages.

    Order also has great importance in other parts of cultural systems besides language: order of birth, order of arrival, order in line to get tickets. Order applies to the courses of a meal. Consider what it would be like to start dinner with dessert, then switch to potatoes, hors d'oeuvre,* coffee, salad, and end with
10   meat!

Adapted from Hall, pp. 132–133

---

hors d'oeuvre   (French) appetizers, small snacks before a meal

 discussing ideas Work in pairs or small groups. Try to find people who have different first languages. Take turns comparing your first language to English. How important is word order in your first language? Is it similar to or different from English? Can you give some examples?

A. Adjectives

One or more adjectives can modify a noun. Usually, no more than three adjectives are used to describe the same noun. The chart gives examples of the usual order of some descriptive adjectives.

number	quality or characteristic	size	shape	age	color	origin	noun
a	beautiful			new	green	Italian	suit
three		big	long		red		pencils
some	expensive			old		oriental	carpets
five	different	small	round		gold		rings

B. Adverbs

Adverbs modify verbs and adjectives. Many adverbs are formed by adding -*ly* to related adjectives (*quick* → *quickly*). In general, adverbs cannot come between a verb and a direct object.

	subject	verb	object	adverb	adjective (complement)
Modifying Verbs	Our teacher They I	speaks answered drank	 the question the hot tea	**slowly.** **quickly.** **politely.**	
Modifying Adjectives	John The test Linda	is was seems		**very** **extremely** **terribly**	tired. difficult. unhappy.

Some adverbs are used to express time or frequency. These usually come after the verb *be* or the first auxiliary verb but before the main verb. In questions, they usually come after the subject. Other expressions come at the beginning or end of sentences. The chart on the next page gives some examples.

	subject and auxiliary verb or *be*	adverb	main verb (+ object or complement)	adverb, phrase, or clause
Adverbs of Time	Mr. Jones was Dr. Gill will I will		sick give the test see you	yesterday. today. tomorrow.
Adverbs of Frequency	We are The train I have Do you	**seldom** **always** **never** **usually**	late leaves been good study English	to class. on time. at math. at home?

Note: See Chapters Two and Three for more information on adverbs of frequency and other time expressions.

C. Adverbials

Adverbials are words or groups of words that act like adverbs—that is, they modify verbs and adjectives. The chart gives some examples. Notice the word order of the different adverbials.

subject	auxiliary verb	main verb	indirect object	direct object	adverbial of direction/ place	adverbial of manner	adverbial of frequency/ time
The men		ride				on the bus	every day.
We		carried		our books	to school	in backpacks	this morning.
Bob		brought	me	those shoes	from Italy		last summer.
You	can	go			to work	by train	on weekdays.
I	couldn't	speak		Spanish		fluently	until this year.

 Add the information in parentheses to the following sentences.

> **example:** Traveling is an amazing experience. (in foreign countries, always)
>
> *Traveling in foreign countries is always an amazing experience.*

1. Travel can be tiring but rewarding. (very, extremely)

2. You will learn about cultures. (a great deal, foreign)

3. The problem is the language. (most, difficult, often)

4. Travelers who don't speak the language have difficulties. (sometimes, in foreign countries)

5. It is easier if you speak the language. (much, of the country, fluently)

6. If you don't speak the language, however, it is helpful to know some words and phrases. (fluently, extremely, useful)

7. Travel guides to foreign countries have sections that list words and phrases. (usually, special, important)

8. People in foreign countries are happy even if you only try to speak a few words. (usually, very, of their language)

 Circle the correct word from each pair to complete the following paragraph. As you make each choice, think about why the other possibility is wrong. The first one is done as an example.

DISTANCE AND COMMUNICATION

In interpersonal (communicate /(communication)), people in almost every
                                        1
culture recognize four (different / differently) distances: intimate, personal,
                                    2
(society / social), and public. Intimate distance occurs in a very (close /
         3   4
closely) relationship such as between a mother and a child. Personal distance
lets good friends talk closely but (comfortable / comfortably). Social distance
                                                      5

is used at parties or other gatherings. Public distance (concerns / concerning)
more formal situations such as between a teacher and a student.
6

These (fourth / four) types of distance exist in all countries, but the amount
7
of distance (usual / usually) depends on the culture. At a party, for example, a
8
Canadian may sit several feet away from you, while (a / an) Arab may sit very
9
near you. (Your / Yours) awareness of the other (culture / culture's) use of dis-
10   11
tance can often help you communicate better with (its / it's) people.
12

exercise 3   **Error Analysis.**   The following sentences have errors in word order. Find the errors and correct them, as in the example.

example: Many North Americans (speak rapidly English.)
            Correction: Many North Americans speak English rapidly.

1. It is difficult often to understand Americans.

2. That Italian new student has with English some problems.

3. He went yesterday to a restaurant, but he couldn't understand the waiter.

4. The waiter spoke very rapidly English.

5. The student ate at the restaurant a hamburger.

6. He paid money too much.

7. The waiter realized this and returned immediately the money to the student.

8. Some people always are honest, but other people take frequently advantage of situations like that.

9. Problems with communication interpersonal can from speaking come, but they can come from also differences in body language.

10. The gesture Italian for "Come here" looks exactly almost like the gesture North American for "Good-bye."

exercise 4 Work with a partner. Make complete sentences by putting the following groups of words in correct order. As a help, the first word in each sentence is capitalized.

> **example:** important / of / our / Our / part / bodies / an / are / language
> *Our bodies are an important part of our language.*

1. expressions / often / Our / people / a / deal / facial / tell / great

2. contact / important / also / Gestures / are / eye / and

3. cultures / use / frequently / some / very / gestures / in / People

4. from / only / them / People / occasionally / North / use / America

5. look / people's / into / some / cultures / People / from / directly / other / eyes

6. Americans / other / not / keep / contact / North / with / constant / do / eye / people

Using What You've Learned

 **activity 1** The following paragraphs are incomplete. Add your own descriptive words or phrases and then add an ending to the composition.

Visiting a(n) _____ country can be a(n) _____ experience. Sometimes there are _____ problems, especially with _____. People _____ have difficulties because _____. They may feel _____, or they may become _____

_____

_____

When I went (came) to _____, I had (didn't have) problems because _____

_____

_____

_____

 **activity 2** Have you had any problems understanding the body language of people from other cultures? Have you misunderstood someone's gestures or facial expressions? Write a short paragraph about your experience. Include as much description as you

can. When you finish writing, exchange papers with another student. How were your experiences similar or different?

1. Test your skill at "reading" body language! With a partner, visit a place where you can observe people. Choose two or more people in a group to watch. Stay far enough away that you cannot hear the people's conversation and try not to let them know you are watching. Notice their physical appearance and body language—their gestures, facial expressions, posture, their physical distance from each other, and so on. What can you guess about the people?

2. Each partner should complete a chart like the following. (Add more information if you like.) After you have finished, compare your charts. Are your guesses the same?

	PERSON 1	PERSON 2	PERSON 3
Male or female			
Approximate age			
Occupation			
Level of education			
Current mood (sad, happy, angry, and so on)			
General personality type (talkative, outgoing, quiet, shy, stubborn, modest, conceited, and so on)			
What is the relationship of this person to the other(s)?			
Why did you make these guesses? What gave you clues?			

3. In class, form small groups and talk about your experiences. How many different kinds of body language did you notice? Did people interpret this body language the same way?

activity 4

In pairs or small groups, role-play one or more of the following situations. You can also create additional situations if you wish. As you talk, try to give as much description as possible: shape, size, color, height, weight, and so on.

1. You've just arrived at an international airport in the United States. You have been waiting at the baggage claim for your luggage, but nothing has arrived. Go to the baggage claim counter and ask for help. Describe your luggage and the contents in detail.

2. You are at an international airport in Canada. You are supposed to meet the sister of your friend and drive her into the city. You can't find anyone who looks like her. Talk to the airline personnel and ask for help. Describe your friend's sister in detail.

3. You left your jacket at school during orientation, and you are trying to find it. You have gone to the lost and found to ask for help. Describe your jacket in detail.

4. You had bought a car soon after arriving in the United States. You parked it downtown while you were shopping. Your car (and its contents) has been stolen. You have gone to the police for help. Describe your car and all the things that were in it in detail.

TOPIC **three**

The Principal Parts of Verbs and Verb Tense Formation

Setting the Context

previewing the passage

What is culture? How much does our culture influence us? Edward Hall says that the most basic and obvious parts of our culture are often the parts that influence us the most. As you read the following passage, try to decide what he means by this. What are some of the most basic parts of your culture? Do they influence you a great deal?

What Is Culture?

Cultures are extraordinarily complex, much more so than TV sets, auto-mobiles, or possibly even human physiology. So how does one go about learn-ing the underlying structure of culture? Looking at any of the basic systems in a culture is a good place to start—business, marriage and the family, social

5   organization—any will do.

Culture is humanity's medium; there is not one aspect of human life that is not touched and altered by culture. This means personality, how people express themselves (including shows of emotion), the way they drink, how they move, how problems are solved, how their cities are planned and laid out, how transportation systems are organized and function, as well as how economic and government systems are put together and function. However, it is frequently the most obvious and taken-for-granted and therefore the least studied aspects of culture that influence behavior in the deepest and most subtle ways.

10

Adapted from Edward T. Hall, *Beyond Culture*, p. 106

discussing ideas

In the first paragraph, Edward Hall gives three examples of basic cultural systems: business, marriage and the family, and social organization. Discuss one of these examples (or one of your own) with another classmate. How is U.S. or Canadian culture different from your own culture concerning business, marriage, the family, and so on? What is the biggest cultural difference you have noticed between these countries and your own?

A. The Principal Parts of Verbs

All tenses and other verb constructions are formed from the five principal parts of the verbs.

infinitive	simple form	past form	past participle	present participle
to walk	walk	walked	walked	walking
to play	play	played	played	playing
to run	run	ran	run	running
to write	write	wrote	written	writing
to be	be	was/were	been	being
to do	do	did	done	doing
to have	have	had	had	having

The modal auxiliaries—*can, could, may, might, must, ought to, shall, should, will,* and *would*—are not included here because each has only *one* form, the simple form. (See Chapter Four.)

B. Verb Tense Formation: Regular Verbs

	examples			notes
Simple Form	**COMMANDS** Stand! Be seated!	**SIMPLE PRESENT** I walk. She walks.	**SIMPLE FUTURE** I will walk. She will walk.	The simple form is used to form commands, the simple present tense, and the simple future tense. It is also used with modal auxiliaries.
Past Form	**REGULAR VERBS** I walked. She walked.			The past form is used for the simple past tense. Regular verbs are the simple form + *-ed*.
Past Participle	**PRESENT PERFECT** I have walked. She has walked.	**PAST PERFECT** I had walked. She had walked.	**FUTURE PERFECT** I will have walked. She will have walked.	The past participle is used to form the present, past, and future perfect tenses and all passive voice forms.
Present Participle	**PRESENT CONTINUOUS** I am resting. She is resting. We are resting.	**PAST CONTINUOUS** I was resting. She was resting. We were resting.	**FUTURE CONTINUOUS** I will be resting. She will be resting. We will be resting.	The present participle is used with the verb *be* to form all continuous tenses.
	PRESENT PERFECT CONTINUOUS I have been resting. She has been resting.	**PAST PERFECT CONTINUOUS** I had been resting. She had been resting.	**FUTURE PERFECT CONTINUOUS** I will have been resting. She will have been resting.	

exercise 1   Change the following sentences to the singular. Add *a* or *an* and change pronouns when necessary. Use *his* or *her* instead of *their.* If you do this exercise orally, give the spelling of the singular verbs. Notice the different ways the *-s* ending is pronounced.

example: Children begin to learn about culture at an early age.

A child begins to learn about culture at an early age.

1. Children pick up cultural rules quickly.

2. Children rely on their parents.

3. Children watch and imitate their parents.

4. Parents convey a great deal nonverbally, as well as with words.

5. Children learn their society's rules of time, distance, and order.

6. For example, American parents teach children promptness.

7. If children miss the bus, they get to school late.

8. Eventually, the children try to be on time.

exercise 2 Fill in the blanks with the past tense of the verbs in parentheses to complete the passage. If you do this exercise orally, give the spelling of each past tense form. Notice the different ways the -ed ending is pronounced.

1. Margaret Mead ____studied____ (study) island people in the South Pacific.

2. She first _____ (visit) the isolated Manus tribe in 1928.

3. The Manus _____ (agree) to let her live among them.

4. They _____ (permit) her to record their day-to-day life.

5. The isolation of the Manus tribe _____ (stop) with World War II.

6. The United States government _____ (ship) supplies and soldiers through these islands during World War II.

7. This contact with another culture _____ (affect) every aspect of Manus life.

8. After the arrival of U.S. soldiers, incredible changes _____ (occur) on the islands.

9. Margaret Mead _____ (travel) to the islands again in 1953 and _____ (observe) many changes.

10. She _____ (notice) that the Manus _____ (dress) in Western clothes, _____ (cook) Western food, and _____ (carry) transistor radios.

Margaret Mead

exercise 3 Complete the passage by filling in the blanks with the present continuous tense of the verbs in parentheses. If you do this exercise orally, give the spelling of each present participle.

1. Today, social scientists ___are studying___ (study) the influence of American television in foreign countries.

2. Many believe that American television _____ (cause) cultural change.

3. Stations around the world _____ (carry) American programs, movies, and commercials.

4. Changes _____ (happen) worldwide because of television.

5. Some people believe that American TV _____ (create) a world culture.

6. Through television, people everywhere _____ (get) regular "lessons" in American culture and values.

7. Some countries _____ (control) the number of American programs on local stations.

8. Others _____ (begin) to eliminate American shows entirely because they feel the shows _____ (threaten) their own culture.

9. Few countries _____ (succeed) in eliminating all shows, however.

 C. # Verb Tense Formation: Irregular Verbs

> Irregular verbs appear often in both spoken and written English. You should know the forms of these verbs *without* consciously thinking about them. The following exercises give you a brief review of some of the more common ones, and Chapters Two and Three include more practice.
>   See Appendix One for a complete list of irregular forms.

exercise 4 Complete the story by filling in the blanks with the past tense of the verbs in parentheses. If you do this exercise orally, give the spelling and pronunciation of each verb.

ADJUSTING TO A NEW CULTURE

When I _____left_____ Brazil to live in the States, I _____ I
                1 (leave)   2 (know)

would probably experience "culture shock," but I really _____ no
                                                              3 (have)

idea what culture shock actually _____.
                                      4 (be)

I _____ through several different stages during my stay, and for
      5 (go)

a long time I _____ that these stages _____ unique to me.
                 6 (feel)   7 (be)

Finally, I _____ to discuss my feelings with other foreign students,
               8 (begin)

and I _____ that our "stages" _____ along similar lines.
          9 (see)   10 (run)

At first, we all _____ thrilled about everything "new." Then,
                       11 (feel)

problems _____—with transportation, money, housing, and so
              12 (arise)

on. All of us _____ at that point we suddenly _____
                   13 (say)   14 (become)

exhausted and frustrated—with the language, the people, with everything. I

almost _____ home! Luckily, I didn't because things _____
           15 (go)   16 (get)

better in a short time. Soon, I _____ that I _____ people
                                    17 (find)   18 (understand)

better. I _____ more and more used to my new way of life, and this
              19 (grow)

helped me relax. I _____ a lot of nice people, and I _____
                       20 (meet)   21 (make)

some very good friends after that first "crisis." Later _____ a
                                                            22 (come)

second crisis, though, and finally real "adjustment." Well, I still haven't

gone back to Brazil. . . .

exercise 5 Fill in the blanks with the past participles of the verbs in parentheses. If you do this exercise orally, give the spelling and pronunciation of each verb.

RETURNING TO YOUR OWN CULTURE

People who have _____spent_____ time in other cultures often talk about
                      1 (spend)

"reverse culture shock." If you have _____ your country for more
                                          2 (leave)

than a short tourist trip and then have _____ back home, you may

3 (go)
have _____ it.

4 (feel)

What is "reverse culture shock"? Well, imagine the following: You've

_____ adjusted to a new culture and you've _____ to

5 (become)   6 (grow)
enjoy life in it. You've_____ new friends and have _____

7 (make)   8 (have)
a great variety of new experiences. Then it's time to leave, and you're sad, but

you're also very excited about going home. Arriving home is "wonderful"!—

seeing all the friends and relatives you hadn't _____, eating all the

9 (see)
special foods you hadn't _____, reading the newspapers you hadn't

10 (eat)
_____, hearing music you hadn't _____ in such a long

11 (read)   12 (hear)
time. But then, after you've _____ home for a few weeks, perhaps,

13 (be)
things may not seem so "wonderful." You may become critical of your home

country; you may not like certain things or ideas. Your city may have changed,

and people may have changed too. Or, perhaps in your eyes, you've changed

and they haven't changed at all.

This is the process of readjustment. It's a difficult period, and many people

experience it after the initial excitement of coming home has _____

14 (wear)
off. Fortunately, it doesn't usually last as long as adjustment to a new culture

does.

Using What You've Learned

activity 1

In small groups, reread the passage "What Is Culture?" on pages 18 and 19.
First, discuss the ideas expressed in the passage and then analyze it. How many
of the five different forms of verbs can you find? Underline them. Are all the verb
forms used as *verbs*? Or do some function as other parts of speech (adjective, and
so on)?

activity 2   In groups or as a class, read the following and discuss the questions below.

EACH LANGUAGE HAS ITS EXCEPTIONS

    At least fifteen hundred languages are spoken in the world, and some linguists estimate that as many as eight thousand languages may exist. Even though most languages seem very different, there are some interesting universal aspects of language. The following cartoon illustrates one: Every known language seems to have exceptions to its "rules"!

1. What is wrong in the cartoon?
2. What exceptions or irregularities exist in your language? Do there seem to be as many as in English? Why do you think English has so many "special cases"?

TOPIC **four**

An Overview of the Tense System

Setting the Context

previewing the passage   How important is time in your culture? How important is the concept of time in your language? What differences have you noticed between the way people express time in English and in your own language?

Time

Time is a core system of cultural, social, and personal life. In fact, nothing occurs except in some kind of time frame. A complicating factor in intercultural relations is that each culture has its own time frames in which the patterns are unique. This means that to function effectively abroad it is just as necessary to learn the language of time as it is to learn the spoken language.

5

From Edward T. Hall, *The Dance of Life*, pp. 3–4

discussing ideas

Work in pairs or small groups. Try to find people who have different first languages. Take turns comparing your first language to English with regard to tenses. Does your language have a system of tenses? If so, is it similar to the English system? If not, how does your language express time? Can you give some examples?

FRANK AND ERNEST   **By Bob Thaves**

FRANK AND ERNEST reprinted by permission of Newspaper Enterprise Association, Inc.

The Tense System

Developing a sense of time in English, as well as a sense of order, is essential to your mastery of the language. The following exercises are designed to give a brief review of the tenses and their time frames *before* you study each tense in more detail.

Note that each tense will be covered in detail in Chapters Two and Three. The passive voice will be covered in Chapter Five. How the tenses Interconnect in complex sentences will be covered in Chapters Eight, Eleven, and Twelve.

exercise 1 Work with a partner. Underline the verbs in the following sentences. Tell the time frame that each expresses (past, present, past to present, or future). In sentences with two verbs, explain the relationship of the verbs by time (earlier, later, at the same time). Then indicate the tense of each.

> *past time*   *past to present time*
> (simple past)   (present perfect)

example: Emilda <u>was born</u> in Switzerland, but she <u>has spent</u> very little of her life there.

1. While Emilda was growing up, her parents moved frequently.

2. By the time she was ten, she had already lived in Europe, Africa, and North America.

3. She would speak French with her father, Italian with her mother, and English at school.

4. As a result, she speaks three languages fluently.

5. She's been living in Iowa for the last ten years.

6. During this time, she has become accustomed to life in the United States, but she misses her family.

7. She is planning a trip to Europe to visit her parents.

8. She'll be leaving on September 20.

exercise 2 The following passage is a story about an Iranian student's first few days in the United States. Complete the story by circling the appropriate verb form from the pair in parentheses. As you make each choice, try to decide why the other possibility is incorrect. The first one is done as an example.

THE RESTAURANT

Before I (left / had left) for the United States, my father (was warning /
                    1   2
had warned) me, "Every foreigner (has / is having) problems in a new country."
                                                              3
But I (told / was telling) myself, "Ali, you (will have been / will be) different.
                4   5
You (don't have / won't have) problems in the United States. By the time you
                    6
(arrive / arrived), you (will have learned / will be learning) enough English
        7   8

28   Mosaic One • Grammar

to understand everyone!" So I (made / have made) my preparations, and on
January 2nd I (flew / had been flying) to Boston.

Of course, I (have had / have) many problems since I (arrived / was arriving) in the United States. Some of the funniest ones (occurred / occur) during
the first few days after my arrival. English (was not / had not been) as easy as
I (was thinking / had thought). But I (was making / made) a friend, and I
(was having / would have) a good time.

During those first few days, the most comical experience (was / was being)
our first night out in a Boston restaurant. My friend (spoke / was going to
speak) no English, but I (thought / would think) that I (knew / was knowing)
a lot. Before we (went / have gone) to the restaurant, we (had promised / used
to promise) each other that we (would speak / spoke) a lot of English. And, we
(were going to listen / listened) carefully so that we (learned / would learn) a
lot!

After we (had arrived / were arriving) at the restaurant, we (sat / had sat)
down, and the waiter (was giving / gave) us menus. While I (was trying / had
tried) to read mine, my friend (was staring / used to stare) blankly at his. He
(understood / understands) nothing! The waiter (came / was going to come)
back, and we (ordered / were ordering). Still staring blankly, my friend (pointed /
would point) to the first three items on the menu. The waiter (seemed / was
seeming) surprised and (asked / was asking) "(Is / Will . . . be) your friend
sure?" I (was answering / answered) "My friend (will be / is) sure. I (have /
will have) the same." The waiter (was saying / said) "Okay. . . . If you (want /
are wanting) that, you (have gotten / will get) that. Foreigners . . . "

(Imagine / To imagine) our surprise when the waiter (came / had come)
back with six dishes: two bowls of tomato soup, two bowls of cream of
mushroom soup, and two bowls of clam chowder!

Ali Mohammed Rooz-Behani

exercise 3

Error Analysis. Many of the following sentences contain errors because the verb tenses and time expressions do not correspond. Discuss the sentences and suggest possible corrections. Put a check (√) next to sentences that are correct as they are. The first one is done as an example.

1. After Andrea ~~studied~~ *had studied* in Argentina, she ~~had come~~ *came* to Canada.

2. She has finished her studies in Argentina in 1993.

3. Andrea had been buying her ticket before the exchange rates changed.

4. Andrea said that she was going to stay in Canada for a year.

5. While she lived in Toronto, she was working on her master's degree.

6. She has received her degree three months ago.

7. Since she finished her degree, she travels around the country.

8. She wants to visit as many places as possible.

9. She is staying in Montreal since last week.

10. Next week, she will be leaving for South America.

Using What You've Learned

activity 1

When and where were you born? Where did you live while you were growing up? Where did you go to school? What did you study? Have you ever worked? What are you doing now? What special hobbies or interests do you have? What are some of your plans for the future?

Briefly tell or write a short autobiography. If you choose to tell it, work in small groups and take turns. Be sure to include any important events from the past and present, and any plans for the future. When one person finishes, the other group members may ask questions if they have any.

If you choose to write, write three paragraphs—one each for past, present, and future events. When you finish, exchange autobiographies with another classmate.

activity 2

In small groups, take turns talking about your own experiences in adjusting to life in a new language and culture. Share some of your stories—funny ones, sad ones, embarrassing ones, happy ones. Later, write your story and, if possible, make a class collection of "memorable moments" you have had.

Looking at Learning

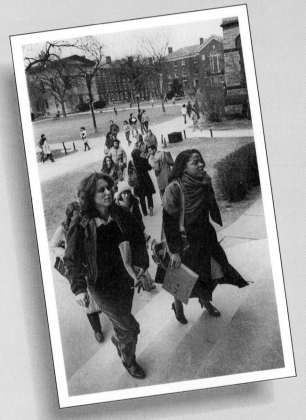

Introduction

Chapter Two reviews uses of auxiliary verbs—*be*, *do*, and *have*—and covers the present tenses—the simple present, present continuous, present perfect continuous, and present perfect. More information on the present perfect tense is given in Chapter Three, and modal auxiliaries are covered in Chapter Four. Much of this chapter is review, and you may not need to study everything in detail.

The following passage introduces the chapter theme, Looking at Learning, along with information and issues you will cover in the chapter.

The Diversity of Education in the United States

While you are studying English, you are probably thinking about other educational possibilities, for now or for later. If you are currently living in the United States or planning to go, you will find an incredible variety of alternatives for study.

5   In terms of higher education, over 3,200 colleges and universities with four-year programs operate in the United States. They employ more than 650,000 teachers and administrators and teach 13.7 million students, over 400,000 of whom come from outside the United States. These colleges and universities range in size from 500 students to more than 55,000 students at one campus.

10   Some charge over $15,000 annual tuition, while others charge as little as $450 per year.

If you're thinking about a shorter program, there are around 1,300 community colleges in the United States. Community colleges are different in three ways: They offer two-year (not four-year) degrees only; they normally have both

15   academic and vocational/technical programs; and they are relatively inexpensive. The average tuition nationwide is around $600.

Even the most academically oriented people enjoy other pursuits, however, and the educational system recognizes this. So, if you've always wanted to study Italian, auto mechanics, bowling, watercolor painting, or windsurfing,

20   there's a school for you. Many cities and towns have programs in adult education, and most universities offer "extension" programs that involve a very wide variety of courses for credit or for enjoyment.

discussing ideas   How does the education system in the United States compare with the one in your native country? Can adults return to school at different times? Are part-time programs available? Is it possible to take a variety of classes for enjoyment or personal enrichment?

TOPIC **one**

Auxiliary Verbs

Setting the Context

previewing the passage Are you planning to do further academic work in English? If so, you probably have many thoughts on your mind. Have you asked yourself some of the following questions?

Studying at a North American College or University

"**W**hat is the college system like? Is the Canadian system the same as the U.S. system? I hope I'm not going to have many problems in adjusting. What is the system for grading? I don't understand it. What kind of exams are given? Is it difficult to graduate?"

5   "Will I be able to understand my professors? There'll be a lot of homework, won't there? Should I buy a tape recorder to tape classes?"

"Have I applied to enough schools? I've sent in everything—transcripts, test scores, letters of recommendation; why haven't I heard anything yet? There isn't much time."

10 "What kind of English test scores do I need to get into academic courses? Do I have to take other entrance exams? All colleges give their own English placement tests, don't they?"

"When should I take the TOEFL test? How long does it take to get the scores?"

discussing ideas Can you answer any of the questions in the passage? What other questions, issues, or problems have occurred to you?

A. Statements, Yes/No Questions, and Short Responses

With *do*

examples		notes
Affirmative Statements	**Negative Statements**	The simple present and past tenses use forms of *do* in questions, negatives, short responses, and tag questions. The verb *have* follows the same patterns when it is a main verb in these tenses. See Appendix Two for more examples.
We study a lot.	They don't study a lot.	
Maria has a lot to do.	He doesn't have a lot to do.	
Yes/No Questions	**Possible Responses**	
Do you study a lot?	Yes, I do. No, I don't	
Does she have a lot to do?	Yes, she does. No, she doesn't.	

With *be, have,* and Modal Auxiliaries

examples		notes
Affirmative Statements	**Negative Statements**	Sentences with continuous and perfect tenses, modal auxiliaries, and the verb *be* as a main verb all follow the same pattern for formation of questions, negatives, short responses, and tag questions. See Appendix Two for more examples.
We are studying.	They aren't studying now.	
Maria can help.	Ming can't help.	
Tomas has left.	Ali hasn't left.	
Yes/No Questions	**Possible Responses**	
Are you studying now?	Yes, I am. No, I'm not.	
Can Leah help?	Yes, she can. No, she can't.	
Has Alfred left?	Yes, he has. No, he hasn't.	

 **Review.** Many Americans use incomplete questions in conversation. Form complete questions from the following by adding auxiliary verbs and subjects.

example: Working hard?
           Are you working hard?

1. Have a lot homework?
2. Need some ideas for your paper?
3. Finished writing it?

4. Already typed it?
5. Want me to proofread it?
6. Have to hand it in today?

7. Going to campus soon?

8. Your roommate say when she was coming back with the car?

9. Want a ride?

10. Ready to leave now?

 **exercise 2**

Review. Working in pairs, make short conversations using the information in parentheses in items 1 to 5. After you have completed this the first time, change roles or work with a new partner to practice it again.

example: A: I saw Tomoko last night.
Have you seen her recently? (see her / recently)

B: **No, I haven't. Is she still studying biology?** (still / study biology)

A: **No, she isn't. She's studying botany now.** (botany)

B: **Do you have her phone number? I'd like to call her.** (phone number / call)

A: Sorry, **I don't.**

1. A: I ran into Professor Sommer yesterday.

_____ (see him / recently)

B: No, _____ (still / teaching beginning German)

A: No, _____ (German literature)

B: _____ (schedule / make an appointment

with him)

A: Sorry, _____

2. A: I saw Brenda the other day.

_____ (run into her / recently)

B: No, _____ (still / study accounting)

A: No, _____ (finance)

B: _____ (e-mail address / send her a message)

A: Sorry, _____

3. A: I got a card from your old roommate yesterday.

_____ (hear from him [her] / recently)

B: No, _____ (still / go to the University of

Massachusetts)

A: No, _____ (Boston College)

B: _____ (address / write)

A: Sorry, _____

4. A: I had lunch with Tony last week.

_____ (talk to him / recently)

B: No, _____ (still / take classes at the community

college)

A: No, _____ (work at a bank)

B: _____ (phone number / call)

A: Sorry, _____

5. A: I saw Miki this morning.

_____ (call her / recently)

B: No, _____ (still / write textbooks)

A: No, _____ (novels)

B: _____ (address / visit)

A: Sorry, _____

B. Information Questions

Information questions ask *When? Where? Why? How? How often?* and so on. As in yes/no questions, an auxiliary verb normally precedes the subject in information questions. See Appendix Two for more examples.

question word	auxiliary verb + negative	subject
when	do	you have class?
	did	you have class last semester?
where	will	you take classes?
	are	you going to take classes?
	have	you taken classes?
	had	you taken classes before enrolling here?
why	are	you late?
	weren't	you on time yesterday?

Common Question Words

how	. . . asks about manner
how . . . like	. . . asks for an opinion
how + adjective or adverb	
how cold (fast, old, and so on)	
how far	. . . asks about distance
how long	. . . ask about length of time
how many	. . . asks about quantity (count nouns)
how much	. . . asks about quantity (noncount nouns)
how often	. . . asks about frequency
what	. . . asks about things
what . . . be (look) like	. . . asks for a description*
what + noun	. . . asks for specific details
what color (country, kind of, size, and so on)	
what time	. . . asks for a specific time
when	. . . asks about time (specific or general)
where	. . . asks about place
which + noun	. . . asks about a specific person, place, and so on
which book (city, one, person, and so on)	
who(m)	. . . asks about people
whose	. . . asks about ownership or possession
why	. . . asks for reasons
why . . . not	. . . gives suggestions

*Note: *What does he look like?* asks for a physical description. *What is he like?* asks about qualities or characteristics (*nice, fun, serious,* and so on).

exercise 3 Complete the following twelve questions by adding appropriate question words.

       example: _____Why_____ are you leaving?

       Because I have to study.

1. _____ did you leave home this morning?

At 8:30.

2. _____ did you get to school today?

By bus.

3. _____ did you take?

The express bus.

4. _____ are you going later?

To the library.

5. _____ don't you study at home?

Because it's too noisy.

6. _____ roommates do you have?

Three.

7. _____ do your roommates make noise?

Almost every night.

8. _____ do you live with?

Two Americans and one foreign student.

9. _____ do you pay for rent?

$200 a month.

10. _____ is your apartment like?

It's large but it's old.

11. _____ is it to campus from there?

Three blocks.

12. _____ does it take to get there?

About fifteen minutes.

C. Information Questions with *who, whose, which,* and *what*

In some information questions, the question word replaces part or all of the subject. Auxiliary verbs are *not* used, and the order of the subject and verb does *not* change.

	examples	notes
Question	**Who** teaches that class?	*Who* is used only with people. It normally takes a singular verb, even if the answer is plural.
Response	Dr. Johnson.	
Question	**Who** teaches that class?	
Response	Dr. Johnson and two teaching assistants.	

	examples	notes
Question	**Whose** class has a lot of reading?	*Whose* replaces a possessive noun or pronoun.
Response	Dr. Johnson's class.	
Question	**Which** art class has the most work? **Which** (one) has the most work?	*Which* can be used with or without a noun. It normally refers to one or more people, places, or things familiar to the speaker.
Response	Art 210.	
Question	**What** makes the class so difficult?	*What* is generally more informal than *which*, and it usually refers to one or more people, places, or things unfamiliar to the speaker.
Response	The amount of homework.	

exercise 4   Complete the following questions by using *who, what, which,* or *whose.*

example: _Who_ is your roommate this semester?

I have three. Miki, Mary, and Anni. One is from Canada, one is from Spain, and one is from Poland.

1. _____ is the Canadian?

Mary is.

2. _____ roommate is from Spain?

Anni is.

3. _____ is the most difficult thing about foreign roommates?

The problems with language. We speak four different ones.

4. _____ accent gives you the most difficulty?

Mike's accent. It's very strong.

5. _____ roommate brought that great stereo?

Anni did.

6. _____ mother came to visit last week?

Miki's mother, Bakka.

exercise 5   In pairs, alternate asking appropriate questions and giving the following answers.

example: Q: How often do you study at the library?

A: I usually study there once or twice a week.

1. Q: _____

A: After school, from about 3:30 to about 5:00.

2. Q: _____

A: Walk down three blocks, turn right, and you will see it on the left.

3. Q: _____

A: Because it is quieter than my apartment.

4. Q: _____

A: It's about five blocks from my apartment to campus.

5. Q: _____

A: I have three roommates right now.

6. Q: _____

A: He is the tall one with the glasses.

7. Q: _____

A: My other roommate has brown curly hair and a moustache.

8. Q: _____

A: He usually rides his motorcycle.

 **exercise 6** **Rapid Oral Practice.** First, make short questions for the following answers. Some answers can have more than one question. Then, work in pairs. Take turns asking and answering the questions.

example: A: **When?** B: At 3:00.

1. A: _____ B: On Monday.

2. A: _____ B: At the library.

3. A: _____ B: Ann and Mary.

4. A: _____ B: Mary's.

5. A: _____ B: Three times a week.

6. A: _____ B: For two semesters.

7. A: _____ B: 10:00.

8. A: _____ B: The red one.

9. A: _____ B: Four hours.

10. A: _____ B: Fifty miles per hour.

11. A: _____ B: Because I want to.

12. A: _____ B: Size 12.

13. A: _____ B: That one.

14. A: _____ B: Twenty-two years old.

15. A: _____ B: English class.

D. Negative Yes/No Questions

Negative yes/no questions often show a speaker's expectations or beliefs. A negative question can mean the speaker hopes for a yes answer but realizes a no answer is also possible. If the speaker is sure of a no answer, he or she can ask a negative question to show anger or surprise. Note that contractions must be used in negative questions.

examples		
Asking for Information	TEACHER:	"You look confused. **Didn't you study?**"
	STUDENT:	"Yes, I did, but I didn't understand the homework."
Showing Surprise or Anger	TEACHER:	"This paper has a lot of misspelled words! **Didn't you use your dictionary to check the spellings?**"
	STUDENT:	"No, I didn't. I'm sorry."

First change the following questions to negative questions. Then work in pairs and take turns asking and answering the questions. As you practice, vary the tone of your voice. Ask some of the questions to get information, and ask other questions to show surprise or anger.

example: Are you going to the library?

A: (*surprised*) **Aren't you going to the library?**
B: **Well, no, I'm not. I'm too tired.**

1. Are you going to study tonight?
2. Did you buy your books?
3. Have you finished your work?
4. Are you reviewing for the quiz?
5. Have you turned in your assignment?
6. Can you come with us?

In pairs, take turns making requests and responding to them. Using the example as a model, respond with appropriate negative questions.

example: A: Could I borrow your lab manual? (you / buy one)
B: **Didn't you buy one?**

1. Could I borrow your notes from the lecture? (you / go to class)
2. Could I borrow your dictionary? (you / have one)
3. How can I get in touch with Dr. Mills? (her phone number / be in the directory)
4. Could you lend me some money? I'm broke. (your check / arrive)
5. Let's go to a movie tonight. (you / need to study)
6. I don't feel like studying. (you / be worried about your grades)

First, use the following statements to make negative questions with *why*. Then, work in pairs, taking turns asking and answering the questions.

example: I'm not going to study.

A: **Why aren't you going to study?**
B: **I'm not going to study because I've got a headache.**

1. I didn't go to class today.
2. I haven't finished my homework.
3. I don't like rock music.
4. My cousins can't come to visit this weekend.
5. We aren't going to go to the party.
6. My roommate didn't pay the rent.
7. I didn't return your books to the library.
8. You shouldn't buy that car.
9. We don't want to practice more questions!

exercise 10 **Error Analysis.**   Many of the following sentences contain errors. Circle the error and correct it, or indicate that the sentence contains no errors.

> **example:**   Why (he didn't come) to the party?
>
> Correction: Why didn't he come to the party?

1. Have I to do all the homework for tomorrow?

2. Which sweater did she buy?

3. Who did call you?

4. Where he is studying now?

5. Why you don't come to visit us more often?

6. Whose car are you driving?

7. Who told you that?

8. Did not she mail the package?

9. How often you do have classes?

10. Whose book this is?

11. Did you not study economics?

12. How long time does it take you to get to school?

exercise 11 **Review.**   Complete the conversation here and on the next page using appropriate forms of the verbs *be, do*, and *have*. Use negative forms and contractions and add pronouns when necessary. The first two are done as examples.

TOSHIO: Excuse me, Jim. __Am__ I interrupting you? __Do__ you have a few minutes?
                                    1   2

JIM: Sure, _____ _____. I was just about to take a break. What _____ the
                3   4   5
problem?

TOSHIO: I _____ understand this paragraph. I've looked up all the new words,
             6
but I still _____ understand the ideas. What _____ the paragraph means
               7   8
to you?

JIM: Let me see the passage. . . . Why _____ you write all those notes? Oh,
                                          9
they're definitions, right? You looked up a lot of words! How long _____
                                                                      10
it take you to read this? _____ it boring to read using a dictionary all the
                             11

time? Sometimes it _____ better to guess the meanings of words. A
dictionary _____ always help.
       13

TOSHIO: I know. My English teacher tells me not to use the dictionary all the time.

         I guess I have a bad habit. When I read, I stop at every new word. By the

         the end, I _____ remember any of the ideas.
               14

JIM: _____ you gone through this paragraph without stopping?
    15

TOSHIO: No, I _____.
        16

JIM: Let's do it together. Then, we'll go back and look at the details.

Using What You've Learned

activity 1

Silently read the following description of good readers. As you read, observe yourself. Do you use any of the techniques mentioned in the passage? Do you read the same way in your native language and in English?

After reading, separate into small groups. Take the most important ideas from the passage and write a short questionnaire about reading skills to give to your classmates. Use yes/no questions. Exchange questionnaires with another group. While you are completing the questionnaire, share ideas on how to improve both your reading speed and comprehension in English.

A GOOD READER

A good reader reads fast and understands most of what he or she reads. Although each person is different, most good readers share six characteristics.

1. Most good readers read a great deal. They make time for reading and spend two full hours, three to four days a week, reading.
2. Fast readers look for the main ideas in their reading. They don't waste time and effort on unimportant details.
3. Good readers practice comprehension by reading more and more difficult material.
4. Fast readers plan their time for reading. Like students with assignments, good readers give themselves time limits, saying, "I want to finish this book by tomorrow. How much time can I spend?"
5. Good readers set goals. (To set a goal, they may read for fifteen minutes for quick understanding, then count the number of pages read and multiply by four. This gives them a number of pages to try to read each hour.) Steadily, they increase these goals.
6. Fast readers concentrate. They do not let outside distractions or daydreams interfere with their reading.

activity 2

Read the following cartoon "Real Life Adventures." What is happening in it? Can you understand the general idea even though none of the questions in the cartoon is complete?

After reading the cartoon, work in pairs. Write a dialogue for the cartoon using complete questions and statements instead of the shortened forms.

REAL LIFE ADVENTURES by Gary Wise and Lance Aldrich

WISE/ALDRICH

IT IS?
WOW.
IT DOES?
WOW.
HOW MUCH?
WOW.
IT WILL?
WOW.
HOW LONG?
WOW.
HOW MUCH?
WOW.

There's always more wrong with your car than you thought.

REAL LIFE ADVENTURES © 1995 GarLanCo. Reprinted with permission of Universal Press Syndicate.

TOPIC **two**

The Simple Present and Present Continuous Tenses

Setting the Context

previewing the passage

Many new students spend their first few days on a campus getting lost! Have you had any interesting, funny, or not-so-funny experiences learning your way around?

Getting Around

TOSHIO: Excuse me. Could you help me, please? I'm new here and I don't know my way around campus. I'm looking for the undergraduate library.

CONNIE: Sure! It's not too far from here. In fact, I'm going that direction in a few minutes. Do you mind waiting a little while? I need to speak to a professor, and she normally stops at her office around this time.

TOSHIO: Thanks, take your time. I appreciate your helping me.

CONNIE: So, you're new here. Where are you from?

5

TOSHIO: I'm from Kobe, Japan. I'm studying English, and I'm taking two undergraduate courses this semester.

10 CONNIE: Are there many Japanese here? I hardly ever meet foreign students.
I'm majoring in philosophy, and foreign students rarely take classes in
the department. In general, foreigners choose business or science
majors, right?

TOSHIO: Like me, for example. I'm doing work in computer science.

15 CONNIE: Oh, here's Dr. Johnson. I'll be right back. . . .

discussing ideas   Have you had any interesting, funny, or not-so-funny experiences learning your
way around a new place? Share some of them with your classmates.

A. The Simple Present Tense

The simple present tense often refers to actions or situations that do not change
frequently. It is used to describe habits or routines, to express opinions, or to
make general statements of fact. The simple present can also be used to refer to
the future.

uses	examples	notes
Facts	Alan and Lu **are** professors at the university. Alan **works** in the physics department. Lu **teaches** music.	Time expressions frequently used with this tense include: *often, every day, from time to time*. Questions with *When . . .?* and *How often . . .?* are also common with this tense. See the following pages for more information on time expressions and their placement in sentences.
Routines	Lu **has** classes every day. Alan **doesn't have** classes on Tuesdays or Thursdays.	
Opinions	**Do** they **enjoy** their work? Lu **enjoys** her classes very much. Alan **doesn't like** to teach.	
Reference to the Future	Next year, Alan **has** a sabbatical. He **doesn't teach** next year.	

Note: See Appendix One for spelling rules for verbs ending in *-s*. See page 21 for practice on
pronunciation of *-s* endings.

exercise 1   **Review.**   Give the *he* or *she* form of the following verbs in the present tense. Then list them according to the way the *-s* ending sounds in each: *s* (walks), *z* (runs), or *ez* (watches).

1. carry
2. establish
3. reply
4. watch
5. go
6. employ
7. laugh
8. bet
9. worry
10. box
11. fly
12. do
13. collect
14. argue
15. stay

exercise 2   Form complete sentences from the following cues. Use the simple present tense and pay attention to the spelling and pronunciation of the *-s* endings.

> **examples:**   be an exchange student
>
> **Toshio is an exchange student.**
>
> live in a dormitory
>
> **He lives in a dormitory.**

1. be Japanese
2. come from Kobe, Japan
3. live with an American roommate
4. have several hobbies
5. enjoy sports, music, and cooking
6. not like American food very much
7. not go to the cafeteria very often
8. study at the library once or twice a week
9. play tennis almost every day
10. not be a very good student
11. miss his family
12. enjoy life in the United States

exercise 3   Now tell about yourself. Answer the following in complete sentences using the simple present tense.

1. What are three facts about yourself?
2. What are three things that you like (to do)?
3. What are two things that you don't like (to do)?
4. What are three things that you do every day?
5. What are two things that you do not do every day?

B. Adverbs of Frequency and Other Time Expressions

Expressions such as the following are frequently used with the simple present tense. Many of these expressions also appear with verbs in the present and past perfect tenses.

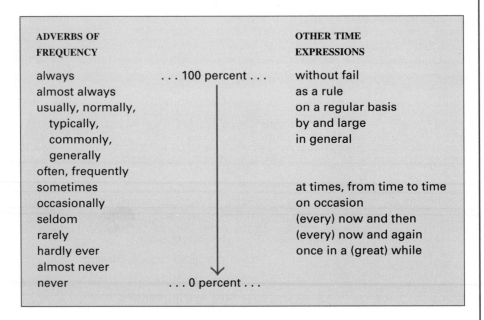

ADVERBS OF FREQUENCY		OTHER TIME EXPRESSIONS
always	. . . 100 percent . . .	without fail
almost always		as a rule
usually, normally,		on a regular basis
typically,		by and large
commonly,		in general
generally		
often, frequently		
sometimes		at times, from time to time
occasionally		on occasion
seldom		(every) now and then
rarely		(every) now and again
hardly ever		once in a (great) while
almost never		
never	. . . 0 percent . . .	

Placement of Adverbs of Frequency

Adverbs of frequency and several other one-word adverbs can be placed before the main verb in a sentence. They usually follow auxiliary verbs and *be* used as a main verb. *Ever,* meaning "at any time," is often used in questions and negatives. Longer time expressions are normally placed at the beginning or the end of a sentence.

examples	
In Statements with One Verb	We **usually** go to the university on Mondays.
	My roommate **almost always** finishes early.
	I **seldom** finish my work before 6:00.
In Statements with Auxiliary Verbs and be as the Main Verb	Our classes are **generally** interesting.
	I don't **always** enjoy them, however.
	We have **occasionally** skipped classes.

	examples
In Questions	Are you **ever** late for class?
	Do you **usually** get to class on time?
Longer Expressions with Verbs in All Tenses	**As a rule,** we get to the university early.
	I'm late **every now and then.**

 **exercise 4**   Quickly reread the conversation "Getting Around" on pages 45 and 46. Underline all the time expressions and explain their placement.

> **example:**   In fact, I'm going that direction <u>in a few minutes.</u>
>
> Longer time expressions usually come at the beginning or the end of the sentence.

exercise 5   In pairs, take turns asking and answering these questions. Then add a few original questions. Give complete answers.

1. What is something that you always do every morning?
2. What is something that you never eat for breakfast?
3. What is something that you seldom wear?
4. Who is someone that you occasionally write to?
5. Who is someone that you hardly ever see now?
6. What is something that you generally do on weekends?

 **exercise 6** Complete the following passage with the simple present forms of the verbs in parentheses. Add time expressions when indicated. *Note that there are no blanks for the time expressions: you will have to decide on their placement.* Then, in groups or as a class, compare your answers. Some sentences will have more than one possible answer. The first one is done as an example.

1. In many countries around the world, young people __almost always stay__

1 (stay / almost always)

   at home until they get married. Universities _____

2 (not provide / in general)

   dormitories, and students _____ their own apartments. In the

3 (have / rarely)

   United States and Canada, however, young people _____

4 (move / frequently)

   away from home after high school. Most universities _____

5 (offer / by and large)

   housing facilities, and most college towns _____ a variety of

6 (have / typically)

   rooms, apartments, and houses for rent.

2. In many countries, there _____ a great deal of "distance" be-

1 (be / normally)

   tween teachers and students. Students _____ teachers by their

2 (call / never)

   first names, for example, or _____ personal problems with them.

3 (discuss)

   In the United States and Canada, on the other hand, teachers _____

4 (be / sometimes)

   _____ quite open and friendly. They _____

5 (encourage / often)

   students to be informal with them.

3. In many parts of the world, students _____ to

1 (not choose / as a rule)

   interrupt their studies. They _____ without breaks because

2 (continue)

   it _____ easy to reenter a university after leaving for a

3 (be / seldom)

   semester or two. In contrast, students in the United States and Canada

   _____ time off to travel, to work, or to make decisions about

4 (take / frequently)

   their lives.

C. The Present Continuous Tense

The present continuous tense describes actions or situations in progress at the moment of speaking. This includes activities that are happening right now and current activities of a general nature. In some cases, it can also refer to the future. As a rule, the present continuous tense is used for activities that are temporary rather than permanent.

uses	examples	notes
Activities at the Moment of Speaking	Sandy **is studying** in the other room right now. Jim **is working** on the computer. I'm **proofreading** the report.	Time expressions frequently used with this tense include: *now, at the moment, still, today, nowadays, these days,* and expressions with *this (this morning, this week, this year).*
Current Activities	Sandy **is majoring** in economics. She **isn't taking** many courses this semester.	
Reference to the Future	Sandy **isn't taking** classes next semester. **Is** she **going** to Europe instead?	

Note: See Appendix One for spelling rules for the *-ing* ending.

exercise 7  **Review.** Add *-ing* to the following verbs, making any necessary spelling changes.

1. study	**5.** write	**9.** begin
2. occur	**6.** open	**10.** change
3. travel	**7.** plan	**11.** swim
4. insist	**8.** happen	**12.** heat

exercise 8  Form complete sentences from the following eight cues. Use the present continuous tense and pay attention to the spelling of the *-ing* endings.

examples: not study right now

Toshio's not studying right now.

play tennis again

He's playing tennis again.

1. have fun in the United States
2. get a lot of exercise this semester
3. play tennis tonight and tomorrow night
4. not study very much

5. not do very well in school
6. fail one course
7. enjoy himself
8. plan to study more next week

 Now tell about yourself. Answer the following in complete sentences using the present continuous tense.

1. What are three things that you are doing right now?
2. What are two things that you are not doing now?
3. What are two things that you are doing this quarter (semester)?
4. What are three things that you are not doing this quarter (semester)?

D. Verbs Not Normally Used in the Continuous Tenses

The following verbs are seldom used in the continuous tenses, *except* in certain idiomatic uses or in descriptions of a definite action.

verbs of feeling or thought		examples	notes
appreciate	mind	He **doesn't understand** the problem.	These verbs are rarely used in a continuous tense; the verbs with an asterisk (*), however, sometimes appear in the present perfect continuous tense. The verbs *think* and *consider* occasionally appear in the present continuous tense, also.
be	miss	We **need** to talk about it.	
believe	need	I **think** that is a good idea.	
consider*	prefer	We **prefer** to talk later.	
dislike	recognize		
hate	remember	*Compare:*	
know	think*	We **have been considering** another possibility.	
like	understand		
love	want*	I **am thinking** about several other possibilities now.	
mean*			

verbs of perception		examples	notes
appear	seem	This apple **looks** good.	These verbs sometimes appear in a continuous tense in the description of a specific action or in certain idioms.
hear*	smell	It **tastes** delicious.	
look	sound		
see*	taste	*Compare:*	
		I **am looking** at the apple now.	
		I **am tasting** the apple now.	

verbs of possession	examples	notes
belong to cost have* own possess	We **own** a car. It **belongs** to my brother and me. He **has** the car today. *Compare:* He's **having** a great time. I**'m having** dinner with him tonight.	These verbs almost never appear in continuous tenses, except for the verb *have.* In idiomatic use, *be having* has several meanings, including "be experiencing" or "be eating, drinking,"

 **exercise 10** Complete the passage here and on the next page with simple present or present continuous forms of the verbs in parentheses. The first one is done as an example.

COMPUTERS AND EDUCATION

Computers ___are causing___ a new revolution on university campuses
            1 (cause)

today. At this moment, students throughout North America _____
                                                            2 (edit)

term papers on computers. They _____ statistics. They
                                  3 (calculate)

_____ reports. They _____ new products—all on
    4 (write)   5 (design)

personal computers.

Today's computer revolution _____ a major force on campus.
                               6 (be)

In fact, students who _____ computers _____ that they
                         7 (not own)   8 (feel / often)

_____ at a disadvantage. In many cases, they _____
    9 (be)   10 (have)

to borrow one or pay for time at a computer center. Personal computers

_____ very common, and throughout North America certain
    11 (be)

colleges and universities _____ students to buy their own.
                             12 (require / now)

Some educators _____ today's emphasis on computers. They
    13 (not like)

_____ the importance of computer literacy, but they _____
    14 (recognize)   15 (not believe)

in doing everything by computer. Most students _____ the com-
                                                    16 (prefer)

puter, however. As psychology student Kevin McFarley says, "Right now, I

_____ a project for a statistics class. I _____ calculating
    17 (complete)   18 (not mind)

statistics manually. Without the computer, though, this project would take

weeks to finish. At this moment, the computer _____ some calcu-
                                                    19 (do)

lations that would take me two weeks to figure. How can a human being

compete with that?!"

Using What You've Learned

activity 1

In pairs or in small groups, learn a little more about lifestyles in your classmates'
cultures. Take turns describing some of the following.

1. a typical grandmother or grandfather in your culture
2. a typical teenager in your culture
3. a typical weekday for a typical family
4. a typical weekend
5. a typical holiday or special event such as a wedding
6. a typical house or apartment

As you share your ideas, be sure to include information or opinions about
changes that are taking place in your culture.

activity 2

Read Exercise 5 on page 49 again. In pairs or small groups, discuss the differences
in your personal habits based on the questions in the exercise. For example,
what kinds of things do you do every morning? Think about your daily life in the
United States or Canada compared to that in your home country. How are your
personal habits different? What other differences have you noticed between your
personal life now compared to when you lived in your home country?

The Present Perfect Continuous and the Present Perfect Tenses

Setting the Context

At many schools, student advisors get together with foreign students periodically to see "how things are going" and to help answer questions or solve problems the foreign students may have. The following is one of a series of brief orientation talks for foreign students.

Exams

"**G**ood morning, everyone. It's nice to see you again. Well, let me get started. Up to now, we've been dealing with basic needs—registering, finding housing, buying books, and so on. But you've all lived here for a while now and you've begun to learn about 'the system,' so it's time to talk about some upcoming

5 realities—exams.

"Many of your instructors have been giving quizzes since classes started. Quizzes are much shorter and simpler than exams, though. You can expect two major exams in most of your courses: a mid-term and a final exam.

"The two most common types of exams are objective tests and essay tests.

10 Objective tests have traditionally been true/false or multiple choice. Individual instructors may use other types of questions, however. Essay tests involve writing paragraphs or short essays about a topic. In some cases, your instructor may tell you the topics in advance or may give you a choice of topics to write about.

"Any questions so far? No? Then, let's look at some sample exams. . . ."

What is the difference between quizzes and exams? What kinds of exams are common in North American universities? Have you taken exams in any academic classes?

A. The Present Perfect Continuous Tense

The present perfect continuous tense describes actions or situations that developed in the past and have continued to the moment of speaking. This tense often implies that the action or situation will continue in the future. Without time expressions, the present perfect continuous refers to a general activity that began in the past and has continued to the present. With time expressions such as the following, this tense stresses the duration of an activity.

	examples	notes
Actions and Situations that Began in the Past and Have Continued to the Present	How long **have** you **been studying** English? I**'ve been studying** English for six years. My brother **has** also **been taking** English since he was in high school. Lately, he **has been complaining** about his classes.	Time expressions frequently used with this tense include: *for* + period of time, *since* + beginning time, *all morning* (*day, week,* and so on), *lately, so far, to date, up to now, until now.* Questions with *How long . . . ?* are often used with this tense.

Note: See Appendix One for spelling rules for the *-ing* ending. See pages 52 and 53 for a list of verbs not normally used in the continuous tenses.

exercise  In pairs, ask and answer questions based on the following cues, using the example as a model.

example: computer / interesting / learn to program in BASIC

> A: **How has your computer class been going? What have you been doing in it?**
> B: **It's an interesting class. During the last few days we've been learning to program in BASIC.**

1. psychology / interesting / do experiments with rats
2. economics / confusing / study World Bank policies
3. German / hard / memorize irregular verbs
4. physics / interesting / learn about Isaac Newton
5. botany / enjoyable / plan a field trip
6. statistics / boring / calculate probabilities
7. Chinese history / informative / read about the Cultural Revolution
8. grammar / fascinating / review verb tenses

In pairs, take turns asking questions and responding to them. Using the following cues and the example as a model, form questions with *How long . . . ?* and answers with *for* or *since*. You may give long or short answers.

example: work on that report / early this morning

      A: **You look tired! How long have you been working on that report?**
      B: **Too long! I've been working on it since early this morning.**

1. study / 6:30 A.M.
2. research that term paper / three days
3. do homework / midnight
4. practice your presentation / early this morning
5. memorize German verbs / more than two hours
6. type that report / late last night
7. calculate those statistics / dinnertime
8. review English grammar / over six hours!

In pairs, take turns asking questions and responding to them. Form logical questions using *How long . . . ?*

example: A: You're still in school!

         How long have you been working on your degree?

      B: I've been working on my master's degree for about three years.

1. A: I didn't know that you were a jogger.

     _____?

     B: Well, I've been running about three years. I run two miles each day.

2. A: I didn't know that you moved.

     _____?

     B: We've been living in Cambridge for two months.

3. A: It's still raining! What a shame. I come to Boston, and the weather is terrible.

     _____?

     B: For almost a week.

4. A: I didn't know that you could play the guitar.

     _____?

     B: A long time. Since I was in elementary school.

5. A: Did you know that Alfonso is an expert in karate? He has his black belt.
     B: You're kidding! I never would have guessed.

     _____?

6. A: Did you know that I'm writing a book? I'm almost finished with it.
     B: Really? That's great!

     _____?

B. The Present Perfect Tense

In some cases, the present perfect tense can also describe actions or situations that developed in the past and that have continued up until the moment of speaking. It implies that the action or situation will continue in the future. A time expression, such as those listed below, is used to give this meaning with verbs such as *begin, expect, hope, live, study, teach, wait,* and *work.* In addition, this use of the present perfect tense occurs frequently with verbs not normally used in the continuous tenses.

Note that, in other cases, the present perfect tense usually refers to actions or situations that occurred at an unspecified time in the past. Chapter Three covers that use of the present perfect tense.

	examples	notes
With for, since, and Other Time Expressions	We'**ve worked** hard for several weeks. I'**ve studied** a lot since the beginning of the semester. Our teacher **hasn't taught** here for very long.	Time expressions that give this meaning of the present perfect tense include: *for, since, so far, till now, to date, up to now.*
With Verbs Not Normally Used in the Continuous Tenses	We **haven't understood** everything in class. The class **has seemed** difficult. The homework **has been** complicated.	Remember that the following nonaction verbs are occasionally used in the present perfect continuous: *consider, mean, think, want.* See page 52.

Note: See Appendix One for spelling rules for the *-ed* ending and for a list of irregular past participles.

 **exercise 4** Quickly reread the passage "Exams" on page 55. Then answer the following questions.

1. What tenses are used in lines 2 to 4? What time frames are expressed? What time expressions are used?
2. What tense is used in the first sentence of the second paragraph? What is the time frame? What time expression is used? Compare this time expression to the one in line 3. How are the expressions different in terms of meaning and structure?

 **exercise 5** Answer the following questions in your own words. Use *for, since,* or other time expressions in your answers.

1. How long have you been in this country?
2. How long have you lived in this city?

3. How long have you studied English?
4. Have you understood everything in your classes so far?
5. Up to now, which class has seemed the most difficult?

 exercise **6**   Complete the following with present perfect or present perfect continuous forms of the verbs in parentheses. Use contractions when possible. Mark all cases where both forms are possible and try to explain any difference in meaning between the two tenses. The first one has been done as an example.

Dear Susan:

I _____'ve meant or 've been meaning_____ to write you for weeks, but I
               1 (mean)

_____ much time! My classes _____ much
  2 (not have)   3 (seem)

more difficult this semester, and I _____ able to do anything
                                 4 (be / not)

but study. I _____ dropping one course, but so far I
          5 (consider)

_____ which one. To be honest, I _____ all my
  6 (not decide)   7 (enjoy / really)

classes up to now, and I _____ all the work.
                     8 (not mind)

    It's funny . . . Until now, I _____ science courses, but
                   9 (hate / always)

this semester I _____ to change my mind. Physics class
            10 (begin)

_____ my best. We _____ Newtonian physics for
  11 (be)   12 (study)

the past few weeks and I _____ so many interesting things.
             13 (learn)

Of course, I _____ everything, but my teaching assistant
      14 (not understand)

_____ me extra help. I _____ that a lot. Perhaps
  15 (give)   16 (appreciate)

that's why my attitude about science _____.
               17 (change)

    Along other lines, everything _____ fine here. And, how
                  18 (be)

_____ you _____? How _____ things
  19 (do)   20   21 (go)

_____? I _____ of you a lot. Please give my
  22   23 (think)

best to everyone.

                                  Love,

                                  Molly

exercise  Complete the following passage with simple present, present continuous, present perfect, or present perfect continuous forms of the verbs in parentheses. In some cases, more than one answer is possible. Add adverbs when indicated. Pay attention to their position in the sentence.

FOREIGN STUDENTS IN THE UNITED STATES

For over two hundred years, the United States has been ___*has been*___ a

1 (be)

center of study for foreign students. Since World War II, however, the foreign

student population _____ substantially, and today between 400,000

2 (grow)

and 450,000 foreign students _____ U.S. universities. Recently, the

3 (attend)

growth rate _____ to slow, however.

4 (begin)

The Far East _____ the greatest numbers of students in the

5 (have)

United States, and China _____ the list with over 70,000. Malaysia

6 (lead / usually)

and Korea together _____ around 75,000 students annually.

7 (send)

Who _____ these students? In general, over 70 percent _____

8 (be)　　　　　　　　　　　　　　　　　　9 (be)

males, and around 80 percent _____ single. Over two-thirds of these

10 (be)

students _____ for their education through personal or family funds.

11 (pay)

Less than one-third _____ scholarships or sponsorship from com-

12 (receive)

panies or organizations.

What _____ these students _____? In terms of ma-

13　　　　　　　　　　　　14 (study / usually)

jors, business _____ the largest numbers—about 20 percent of the

15 (attract)

total foreign student population. This _____ a new trend, however.

16 (be)

Only a few years ago, engineering was the most popular subject among foreign

students, but since 1984, enrollment _____ somewhat. Now, engi-

17 (decline)

neering students _____ up only 17 percent of the total foreign

18 (make)

student population. In contrast, enrollment in business and management

courses _____ since 1969.
           19 (increase)

    Why _____ business _____ so popular? Interestingly,
              20   21 (become)

large numbers of foreign students _____ to business schools even
                                        22 (apply)

though an MBA costs, in total, around $50,000. Perhaps because the dollar

_____ weaker in recent years, business schools _____
     23 (grow)   24 (seem)

more affordable today. Even the most expensive U.S. business schools

_____ record numbers of applications nowadays, and Harvard
     25 (receive)

Business School, for example, _____ a foreign student population
                                   26 (expect)

of at least 15 percent.

Using What You've Learned

Visit your student advisor or your local library to get information on a school or university that interests you. You can find out about academic studies, or you can look into other types of programs such as vocational/technical, adult education, or university extension programs. The school can be located in your own area or in another part of the country.

    Using the information you gather, prepare a brief report for your classmates. Be sure to include the following information:

- Admissions requirements
- Tuition and other costs
- Starting dates and length of program
- Description of course(s) or major(s)

Types of Standardized Tests

Testing is a major feature of academic life. Two basic types of tests exist: subjective and objective. Subjective questions can have a variety of answers, but objective questions have only one correct answer. As an international student or professional, you are probably familiar with objective English proficiency tests such as the TOEFL.

Below, you have examples of some of the kinds of questions asked on objective tests. Later, in Chapters Three to Twelve, you will have short practice exams that are similar to the TOEFL. In each of those, you will find reminders about common problems with the structures covered in the particular chapter. Use the exams to help you clarify any areas that you don't understand well and to learn which structures you need to study more.

True/False: Write *T* for true statements and *F* for false statements.

1. __T__ The simple present tense is used to express facts, opinions, and habits.

2. _____ The present prefect tense is used with actions at a specific time in the past.

Correct/Incorrect: Write *C* for correct statements and *I* for incorrect statements.

3. __I__ John is appearing to be angry.

4. _____ This is unusual because he generally seems quite happily.

Cloze: Complete the following by adding the correct word(s).

5. How _many_ people did you invite to the party?

6. _____ book is that on the table? It's Mary's.

Multiple Choice: Circle the correct completion for the following.

7. We _____ your help.
   a. appreciate really
   b. are really appreciating
   c. really are appreciating
   d. really appreciate

8. She _____ here since she was eight years old.
   a. lives
   b. has living
   c. has lived
   d. has live

Error Analysis: Circle the letter below the word(s) containing an error.

9. Since the mid-1980s, the number of international students <u>who</u>

A
<u>are studying</u> engineering <u>has</u> <u>been declined</u> somewhat.

B   C   Ⓓ

10. In many countries, young people do not own <u>generally</u> their own

A
apartments because the cost of housing is high and <u>because</u>

B
parents <u>prefer</u> their children <u>to stay</u> at home.

C   D

CHAPTER three

Relationships

Introduction

This chapter covers the past and future tenses and gives you more information on the present perfect tense. It also covers the expressions *used to, would*, and *was/were going to*. Some of this chapter will be a review for you, and you may not need to study everything in detail.

The following passage introduces the chapter theme, Relationships, and raises some of the topics and issues you will cover in the chapter.

Families Past and Present

Exactly what is a family? In the past, the traditional American family consisted of a working husband, a wife at home, and children. Responsibilities were clearly divided: While the husband was earning a living, the wife was caring for the home and raising the children. Of course, there were exceptions, but this concept of the family was the general rule until the 1960s.

5

Since the 1960s, however, the family has become more diverse, fragile, and changeable. Americans have accepted differing concepts of families, including single-parent, blended, two-paycheck, interracial, childless, and commuter families.

10

Nowadays, when people talk about their families, their descriptions vary greatly. One teenager described her family structure as "a dad, two moms, two sisters and a brother, and a baby on the way, eighteen cousins, four-and-a-half grandmas and five grandpas, five uncles, and eight aunts." (Her "half"-grandmother is a step-grandparent.)

15

Some critics believe that the American family has suffered greatly because of all the changes in society. According to these critics, the family had been much stronger before it began to struggle with issues such as divorce, working wives and mothers, gay couples, feminism, and unmarried relationships. Today's strongest critics feel that the traditional nuclear family will not be

20

society's basic unit in the twenty-first century.

Nationwide, however, most Americans believe that the family is going to survive. In fact, almost all major surveys in recent years have found that, in spite of what the critics say, the American family is as strong as it has ever been. For most Americans, the family continues to provide their deepest source of satis-

25

faction and of meaning in life. Thus, although today's family is different from what it used to be, it seems to be thriving.

discussing ideas

Is there one "typical" family type in the United States today? Was there in the past? In your native country or culture, is there a "typical" family? If so, what is it like?

TOPIC **one**
Past Verb Forms (1)

Setting the Context

previewing the passage

What made you the way you are? Some people believe your position in your family is a major factor. Do you agree?

Where Do You Fit?

Are you the oldest or youngest child? Are you in the middle or an only child? Many psychologists believe that your position in your family helped to shape you and your relationship to others. As a newborn, you quickly developed a relationship with your parents and later, while you were growing, you formed relationships with your siblings. According to psychologists, your birth order affected how your parents and your brothers and sisters reacted to you and treated you. That is, you and they behaved in certain ways depending on your position in the family. All of this strongly influenced your development, and in turn, influences you as an adult: what you think about yourself now and how you react to and treat others.

(line number 5 appears in margin)

discussing ideas

Think about your own family. Do you believe your birth order affected you and your brothers and sisters? In what ways?

A. The Simple Past Tense

The simple past tense describes actions or situations that began and ended in the past.

uses	examples	notes
Past Actions	Martin **grew** up in the country. Later, he **lived** in a small town. When **did** he **move** to the city? He **bought** a farm two years ago.	Time expressions frequently used with this tense include *ago (two weeks ago, a month ago today), in the past, in 1985 (in March)*. Sequence expressions are also used: *first, then, later, finally*. These often begin or end sentences. Adverbs of frequency normally come before the verb.
Past Situations or Conditions	He **didn't like** life in a large city. He always **preferred** the country.	

Note: See page 68 for spelling rules and pronunciation notes for *-ed* endings. See Appendix One for a list of irregular verbs.

Spelling Rules for *-ed* Endings

1. If the simple form of a verb ends in *-y* after a consonant, change the *-y* to *i* and add *-ed.*

    examples: try / tried   carry / carried   knit / knitted

2. If the simple form of a verb of one syllable ends in one consonant after a vowel, double the last consonant (except *x*) and add *-ed.*

    examples: plan / planned   stop / stopped

    Note: The letters *w* and *y* at the end of words are vowels, not consonants.

    examples: row / rowed   play / played

3. If the simple form of a verb ends in an accented (stressed) syllable, follow the rule above for one final consonant after one vowel.

    examples: permit / permitted   prefer / preferred

4. If the simple form of a verb ends in *-e,* add only *-d.*

    examples: tie / tied   change / changed

5. Add *-ed* to the simple form of all other regular verbs.

    examples: want / wanted   ask / asked   belong / belonged

---

Pronunciation Notes

The *-ed* ending is pronounced three ways, according to the ending of the verb:

- */id/* after *-d* and *-t* endings.

  examples: existed, knitted, needed, wanted

- */t/* after voiceless endings.

  examples: cooked, helped, talked, washed, watched

- */d/* after voiced endings.

  examples: argued, danced, listened, lived, played, sewed

Quickly reread the passage "Where Do You Fit?" on page 67. Underline all the regular verbs in the simple past tense. Then group the verbs below according to the pronunciation of the -ed ending.

/t/	/d/	/id/
helped		

exercise **2**
Review Add -ed to the following verbs, making any necessary spelling changes. Pronounce the past forms aloud, emphasizing the various pronunciations of the -ed ending. List them according to pronunciation: t (washed), d (changed), id (waited).

1. need	**5.** travel	**9.** permit	**13.** cry
2. study	**6.** paint	**10.** wrap	**14.** play
3. insist	**7.** hope	**11.** occur	**15.** clean
4. rob	**8.** agree	**12.** stop	

exercise **3**
Complete the passage with the simple past form of the verbs in parentheses. Include adverbs when indicated, and pay careful attention to spelling. The first one is done as an example.

THE FIRST BORN*

Mary __was__ was Bob and Dorothy's first child. When Dorothy
    1 (be)
_____ pregnant, the couple immediately _____ to
    2 (become)   3 (begin)
prepare for the baby. They _____ shopping for baby furniture and
                                4 (go)
_____ toys and playthings. Dorothy _____ little clothes
    5 (buy)   6 (make)
and blankets. And when Baby Mary _____ into the world, the
                                      7 (come / finally)
happy parents _____ in love with their precious child. They
                    8 (fall)
_____ pictures of Baby Mary's first smile, step, and birthday party.
    9 (take)
At bedtime, they _____ and _____ her and _____
                      10 (sit)   11 (hold)   12 (tell)
her little stories and _____ her books and _____ her
                            13 (read)   14 (sing)
lullabies. They _____ up in an instant if they _____ her
                      15 (wake)   16 (hear)
cry during the night. They _____ letters and _____ cards
                                17 (write)   18 (send)

_____

*Interestingly, over 50 percent of U.S. presidents and 21 of the first 23 astronauts were oldest children.

to friends and relatives detailing every little thing Mary _____.
19 (do)

In fact, her parents _____ Mary their complete attention. That is,
20 (give)

until her sister, Cathy, _____ born two years later. . . .
21 (be)

Complete the passage with the simple past form of the verbs in parentheses.
Include adverbs when indicated, and pay careful attention to spelling. The first
one is done as an example.

YOUNGEST CHILDREN

Jane _was_ the youngest of Dorothy and Bob's children. Because of her
1 (be)

special position as the "baby of the family," Jane _____ lots of at-
2 (get / always)

tention. Her mother _____ her often, her father _____
3 (carry)   4 (hold)

her on his lap, and her brothers and sisters _____ turns watching
5 (take)

her. All the neighborhood children _____ with her and _____
6 (play)   7 (teach)

her games and songs and stories. Everyone _____ her.
8 (spoil)

As parents, Dorothy and Bob _____ more relaxed and experi-
9 (be)

enced by that time, so they _____ so much about every sniffle and
10 (not worry)

whimper. Because of this, Jane _____ up in a freer, more easy-
11 (grow)

going environment with fewer rules. Jane's parents _____ her to do
12 (permit)

many things at a younger age, but at the same time, they _____ as
13 (not demand)

much help from her. This _____ problems between Jane and her
14 (cause / often)

siblings. "When I _____ her age, I _____ the house, I
15 (be)   16 (clean)

_____ the dishes, I _____ the floor, I _____
17 (wash)   18 (sweep)   19 (scrub)

the bathtub, and I _____ clothes." These _____
20 (iron)   21 (be)

common complaints in their household.

Jane _____ all the characteristics of youngest children. She
22 (develop)

_____ an optimist and _____ good things from life. She
23 (become)   24 (expect)

_____ rules _____ for other people, though—not for her.
25 (think / frequently)   26 (be)

Sometimes, she _____ her own intellect and _____ to
27 (doubt)   28 (go)

other people for help or advice. Of all the siblings, Jane _____ the
29 (be)

most lighthearted and playful.

Mosaic One • Grammar

B. The Past Continuous Tense

The past continuous tense describes actions in progress in the recent past (a few moments before the moment of speaking) or at a specific time in the past. It is often used to describe or "set" a scene.

uses	examples	notes
Events in the Recent Past	Mary, we **were** just **looking** for you. Oh! You startled me! I **was taking** a short nap.	The following time expressions are frequently used with this tense: *a few minutes (moments) ago, at that time, then, just, still.*
Events at a Specific Time in the Past	A year ago now, we **were living** in the Back Bay. At that time, I **was still working** at the bank, and my wife **was taking** classes.	
Description of a Scene	It was a beautiful summer evening. We **were** all **sitting** and **talking** on the front porch. Dad **was playing** the guitar, the boys **were singing**, and I **was watching** the stars.	

Note: See page 52 for a list of verbs not normally used in the continuous tenses. See Appendix One for spelling rules for verbs with *-ing* endings.

 **exercise 5** Use the past continuous tense to answer the following questions in complete sentences.

1. What were you doing two hours ago?
2. Where were you living a year ago?
3. What were you doing when you decided to come to this school?
4. What were you thinking about a moment ago?
5. What was your classmate, _____, doing a few minutes ago?
6. What were you doing the day before yesterday?
7. What was your teacher doing at this time yesterday?
8. What were you studying two weeks ago?

 **exercise 6** These passages describe scenes from the past. Complete them with the past continuous forms of the verbs in parentheses. Pay attention to the spelling of the *-ing* endings. The first one is done as an example.

1. I have a special memory of Christmas when I was five years old. My aunts,

   uncles, and cousins <u>were visiting</u> us. I _____ my beautiful new
                 1 (visit)   2 (wear)

   red dress. We _____ around the Christmas tree, and everyone
                      3 (sit)

_____ Christmas presents. I _____ one big present
4 (open)   5 (watch)

near the corner of the room. Then my mother took me over to that present.

It was for me! It was the most beautiful dollhouse I had ever seen!

2. I have a special childhood memory of a summer night when I was seven

or eight. My mom and dad and my sisters _____ on the front
                                          1 (sit)

porch. The sun _____ , and the sky _____ red and
                2 (set)   3 (become)

golden. My sisters _____ on the porch swing, and my mother
                    4 (swing)

_____ in her rocking chair. Our dog _____ on the
5 (rock)   6 (lie)

steps. My father _____ his guitar and _____.
                 7 (play)   8 (sing)

Everyone _____ to him. He loved to sing, and he had a won-
         9 (listen)

derful voice. I felt so happy and peaceful and secure. That night is one of

my best memories.

 ## when and while

When and while are frequently used to connect two past actions. Chapter Eight
includes more information on these connecting words.

	examples	**notes**
while	He was watching TV **while** I was doing the dishes.	*While* may connect two past continuous actions that were occurring at the same time.

	examples	notes
when *or* **while**	John was talking to the man at the door **when** his mother phoned. **While** John was talking to the man at the door, his mother phoned.	*When* or *while* may connect a simple past and past continuous action—*while* + the action in progress or *when* + the action that interrupted it.
when	**When** the doorbell rang, John answered it.	*When* may connect two simple past actions; *when* comes before the action that happened first.

exercise 7  Complete the passages with the simple past or past continuous forms of the verbs in parentheses. The first one is done as an example.

This morning everything went wrong at the Peterson household.

1. I ____wanted____ to get up early this morning, but I _____ to
        1 (want)   2 (forget)

    set the alarm. So I _____. When I _____ up, my
                   3 (oversleep)   4 (get)

    brother _____ a long shower. So I _____ to wait for a
            5 (take)   6 (have)

    long time. While I _____ my bike to school, I _____
              7 (ride)   8 (get)

    a flat tire. I _____ my first class, and I _____ late for
          9 (miss)   10 (be)

    my second class. It _____ a good morning.
            11 (not be)

2. I _____ up very early this morning and _____ the
        1 (wake)   2 (leave)

    house while everyone else _____. I _____ the bus at
                3 (sleep / still)   4 (catch)

    6:45 in order to get to work early. I _____ the newspaper on the
             5 (read)

bus, and I _____ attention to the traffic when suddenly a car
6 (not pay)

"_____" a red light and _____ the bus on my side.
7 (run)   8 (hit)

When the car _____ into us, I _____ off my seat,
9 (crash)   10 (fall)

_____ my head, and _____ my arm. What a day!
11 (cut)   12 (break)

exercise 8 Using the simple past and past continuous tenses with *when* and *while*, tell a story using the following information.

example: This morning everything went wrong for Dave Peterson too.
           At 8:30 A.M., Dave woke up late and took a two-minute shower.
           While he was getting out of the shower, . . .

8:35 A.M.	wakes up late
8:36–8:38 A.M.	takes a shower
8:39 A.M.	gets out of the shower
8:39 A.M.	falls on the floor
8:39–8:40 A.M.	shaves
8:40 A.M.	cuts his face
8:40 A.M.	throws the razor on the floor
8:41–8:42 A.M.	gets dressed
8:42 A.M.	tears a hole in his shirt
8:43 A.M.	finds a new shirt
8:44 A.M.	makes coffee
8:45 A.M.	pours the coffee
8:45 A.M.	spills coffee on his shirt
8:46–8:47 A.M.	looks for another clean shirt
8:47 A.M.	hears the doorbell
8:47 A.M.	runs to the door, but no one is there
8:48 A.M.	loses his temper
8:48 A.M.	goes back to the bedroom
8:50 A.M.	lies down and goes back to sleep

Using What You've Learned

Do you have clear memories of a particular time in your childhood or youth? Perhaps you remember a series of events, pleasant or unpleasant, such as Dave Peterson's. Or, perhaps it was a party, a celebration, a trip, or an accident. Briefly tell your story by answering the following questions. You may want to add other details.

1. How old were you?
2. Where were you living (staying, and so forth)?
3. What happened?
4. Where were you doing when this happened?
5. What were other people around you (family, friends, and so forth) doing when this took place?
6. How did you feel?
7. What did you do?
8. What did others do then?
9. What was the result?

"The Family Circus" is a daily cartoon in the United States. Billy is the oldest child in the family. He has a bad habit of going places *indirectly*. Follow his path, telling step by step where he went and what he did. Use the simple past tense. Add articles and other words as needed.

example: **Billy got off the school bus. He got into a soccer game.**

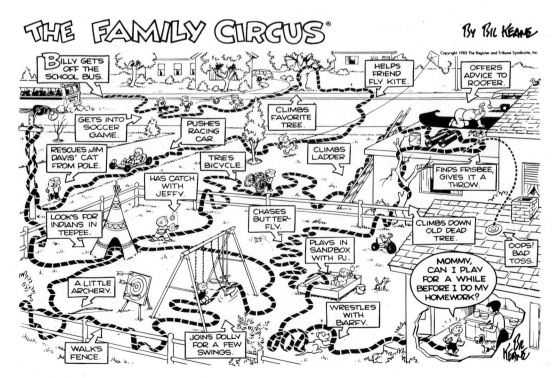

activity 3

The passage "Where Do You Fit?" on page 67 discusses birth order. Edward Hall's passage on page 11 in Chapter One also mentions that order of birth can be an important aspect of culture. Take some time to give your own perspectives on birth order.

First, separate into groups according to birth order—that is, all students who are the oldest should work together, students who are the youngest together, only children together, and middle children together. If you a twin or a triplet, move from group to group!

In your groups, take turns discussing what it was like to grow up as the oldest, youngest, second, and so on. Do you believe your order of birth is an important factor in your development? In your culture in general?

TOPIC two

The Present Perfect Tense with Unspecified Past Time

Setting the Context

previewing the passage

In the United States, men's and women's roles have been changing. In some cases, husbands have taken over household tasks and child care while wives work. Is this happening in your country too?

Househusbands

Bob Johnson is a househusband. For the past five years, he has stayed home with their three children while his wife, Sarah, has gotten up early and gone off to work at a large law firm downtown. Their situation is not unique, though. Bob and Sarah have been doing what many American couples have been doing in re-

5 cent years: They've been changing roles.

What has Bob's life been like? On a typical day, he prepares breakfast, helps the children dress, and makes sure the older children are safely on the school bus. By the time the children come home from school, he has already finished all the household chores—cleaning, shopping, and laundry. There's usually

10 some time to play with the children for a while before Sarah comes home. Then the family eats dinner together, a dinner that Bob has prepared.

Before he became a househusband, Bob worked as a teacher. He really liked his job, but he says that he hasn't missed it. He is surprised to find how much he has enjoyed his time with the children. He says that being the "prime

15 parent" has been one of the most rewarding experiences of his life.

discussing ideas

Househusbands have become more and more common in the United States. Is this true in your native country? Would you like to have a family arrangement such as this? Why or why not?

A. The Present Perfect Tense

Chapter Two included information on use of the present perfect tense in a past-to-present time frame. It has a more common use, however. The present perfect tense frequently refers to an event that happened (or did not happen) at an unknown or unspecified time in the past. It also refers to *repeated* past actions. *No specific time* is given with these statements. When a specific past time is used, the verb is in the past tense.

uses	examples	notes
Events at Unspecified Times in the Past	**Have** you ever **gone** to Austria? I **haven't** ever **been** there. I**'ve visited** Germany, though. *Compare:* I **went** there last year.	Time expressions frequently used with this meaning of the present perfect include: *already, ever, recently, still, yet (how) many times,* and so on.
Repeated Actions at Unspecified Times in the Past	How many times **have** you **visited** your sister? I**'ve been** there five times. We**'ve called** her twice this month. *Compare:* We **called** her last week.	

Note: See Appendix One for a list of irregular past participles and for spelling rules for the *-ed* ending of regular past participles.

 **exercise 1**

Reread the passage "Househusbands." Then answer the following questions.

1. What is the time frame of the second sentence? What verb tense is used? Is a time expression used? Is a time expression necessary for this time frame?
2. What is the time frame of the fourth sentence? What verb tense is used? Is a time expression used? Is a time expression necessary for this time frame?

 **exercise 2**

Read the following pairs of sentences. In each pair, one sentence has a past meaning (a completed action) and one has a past-to-present meaning (still in progress). Write past (P) or past-to-present (P-T-P) for each.

example: P   I've been in New York.
P-T-P I've been in New York since Friday.

1. _____ **a.** I've lived in Boston.

   _____ **b.** I've lived in Boston for ten years.

2. _____ **a.** We've been making some changes.

_____ **b.** We've made some changes.

3. _____ **a.** She's worked in that law firm since June.

_____ **b.** She's worked in that law firm.

4. _____ **a.** I've studied for the test.

_____ **b.** I've been studying for the test.

5. _____ **a.** Gabriel has taught algebra.

_____ **b.** Gabriel has taught algebra since 1988.

B. *already, (not) ever, just, never, recently, still,* and *(not) yet*

These adverbs are frequently used with the present perfect tense.

	examples	notes
Questions	Have you **ever** read that book? Have you **already** read the book? Have you read it **already**? Have you read it **yet**?	*Ever* must come before the past participle. *Already* can be used before the past participle or at the end of the sentence. *Yet* is generally used at the end of the sentence.
Affirmative Statements	I've **already** read it. I've **just** read it. I've read it **recently**. I've **recently** read it.	*Already* and *just* come before the past participle. *Recently* can come at the end of the sentence or before the past participle. It is sometimes used to begin the sentence.
Negative Statements	I have **never** read it. I haven't **ever** read it. I **still** haven't read it. I haven't read it **yet**.	*Never* generally comes before the past participle. *Not ever* must come before the past participle. *Still* must come before *have* or *has*. *Yet* is generally used at the end of the sentence.

 Go around the class in a chain, asking and answering questions about the following.

examples: meet a movie star

    A: **Have you ever met a movie star?**
    B: **Yes, I have. I met Jane Fonda once! She gave me her autograph.**

    be in a submarine

    B: **Have you ever been in a submarine?**
    C: **No I haven't. In fact, I've never even seen one.**

1. be in a hurricane (earthquake, or other natural disaster)
2. lose your wallet
3. buy a car
4. have an accident
5. get a speeding ticket
6. have a flat tire
7. read a novel in English
8. be on television
9. write a poem
10. fall asleep in a class
11. play chess
12. find a buried treasure
13. fly a small plane
14. ride a camel
15. take the TOEFL test

 Reread the last paragraph of the opening passage "Families Past and Present" on page 66. Then look at the comparison in the second sentence. It compares the American family in the past to the American family in the present. What structures are used?

 Form complete sentences from the following cues. Use the example as a model.

example: Mrs. Hyzer / strict

    Mrs. Hyzer is as strict as she has ever been.

1. John / thin
2. I / tired
3. Alfonso / overworked
4. Miki / absentminded
5. Drew / easygoing
6. Erika / interested in sports
7. Ivan / elegant
8. Charles / kind

 In spoken English, we often reduce sentences with *as* by using *ever* and omitting the rest of the sentence. Repeat Exercise 5, giving the shorter form. Use the example as a model.

example: Mrs. Hyzer / strict

    Mrs. Hyzer is as strict as ever.

exercise 7 In pairs, take turns making statements and responses. Complete each conversation by adding a sentence that uses *already*.

example: A: Don't start the washing machine! I haven't put all my clothes in yet!
   B: **Sorry! I've already started it.**

1. Don't put the broom away. I haven't swept the floor yet.
Sorry! . . .

2. Don't wax the floor. I haven't washed it yet.
Sorry! . . .

3. Don't walk in the kitchen. The floor hasn't dried yet.
Sorry! . . .

4. Don't mail those bills! I haven't signed the checks yet.
Sorry! . . .

5. Don't throw the newspaper away! Your father hasn't read it yet.
Sorry! . . .

6. Don't start painting the walls. I haven't washed them yet.
Sorry! . . .

 Complete the passage with the present perfect form of the verbs in parentheses. Use *still . . . not* or *not . . . yet* when indicated.

PROCRASTINATORS

My friend Larry is always procrastinating. For example, he _____
1 (live)

in his apartment for a year now, but he _____ any furniture. He
2 (not buy / still)

_____ to study at the university for a long time, but he _____.
3 (want)   4 (not register / yet)

His hair _____ so long he can barely see, but he _____ it
5 (grow)   6 (not get / still)

cut. He _____ books he borrowed from me for over three months,
7 (keep)

and he _____ them. I _____ several messages for him on
8 (not return / still)   9 (leave)

his answering machine, and he _____ me back. I know what he will
10 (not call / yet)

say when I finally talk to him. "Tomorrow, I'll do it tomorrow." Those are his

favorite words.

Using What You've Learned

Play a game of "Find Someone Who Has . . ." This is a two-part game. First, on a piece of paper, write three things that you have done: "I've climbed a mountain," "I've been to India," and so on. Do not show this to your classmates. Your teacher will collect the papers and make a list to distribute another day.

For the second part, your teacher will distribute the list. Walk around the room and ask your classmates, "Have you . . . ?" When you find the person who has done that, ask him or her to sign the paper. The first student who gets signatures for each item wins the game.

Are you a procrastinator? Have you written to your family lately? Have you been to the language lab? Have you done your laundry yet? You still haven't paid your rent? List five things that you planned to do during the past month but still haven't done. Then, in small groups, compare your lists. How many of you are true procrastinators?

Consider the current trends in your culture concerning changes in the family and in the roles of men and women. When did these changes begin? How have they developed? Have changes taking place in the United States affected your country?

In pairs or in small groups, compare some of the changes that have been taking place in your societies. Then choose one member of your group to give a brief summary of your discussion to the entire class.

TOPIC **three**
Future Verb Forms

Setting the Context

previewing the passage

What will your family be like in the future? What kind of families will your children and your children's children have?

Family Life in the Next Century

What are snapshots of a family gathering in 2050 going to look like? Probably, they will show a majority of elderly people and not too many infants. This is because, overall, Americans will be living longer, but they will be having fewer children. Just consider that people age sixty-five and older constituted only

5

11.3 percent of the U.S. population in 1980. In 2050, those sixty-five and older will make up 22 percent of the country. And in the 1950s, the average family had 4.8 children, compared with 1.3 children today. In fact, the average American has more parents living than children. If trends continue, the "face" of the United States will change a great deal. It will be older and much more wrinkled!

Can you explain the last two sentences of the passage on page 81? What is the "play on words" with the word *face*?

A. The Simple Future Tense

The simple future tense expresses intentions, and it can be used to express requests, promises, offers, and predictions.

uses	examples	notes
Intentions	I'll **try** to be home early tonight.	Time expressions such as the following are often used with future forms: *this afternoon (evening), tonight, later, in a while, in the future, in September, in 1995,* and so on.
Offers and Promises	I'll **help** you with the housework in a little while. Thanks. Then I **will make** you a special dinner!	
Predictions	With your help, we**'ll finish** by 10:00.	
Requests	**Will** you **promise** to help?	

The following are predictions researchers have made about the future in the United States. Add *will* to form complete sentences. Then discuss whether these predictions may be true for your native country, also.

example: American divorce rates / remain high
American divorce rates will remain high.

1. Fifty percent of marriages / end in court

2. A majority of people / marry more than once during their lives

3. Some couples / get divorced and remarried three or four times

4. Different concepts of the family / exist

5. The traditional nuclear family / not be the most common type of family in the United States

6. People / change jobs and careers several times during their lifetime

7. Universities / be filled with "aging" students

8. Many people / earn four or five different college degrees

B. Other Forms Used for the Future: *be going to*, Present Tenses with Future Meaning

	examples	notes
be going to	**I'm going to be** home no later than 7:00. What **are** we **going to have** for dinner?	*Going to* is often used to express specific future plans or intentions. It is used frequently in conversation and is often pronounced *gonna* or *gunna*. In some cases, *will* and *going to* are interchangeable, but *will* is preferred in formal English.
Present Continuous	I **am serving** dinner at 7:30. The guests **are coming** around 7:00.	Both the present continuous and the simple present can be used to express future time. Normally a time expression or the context indicates that the action or situation is in the future. Verbs of movement such as *go, come, arrive,* and *leave* are often used in present tenses, even when they have future meanings.
Simple Present	Dinner **is** at 7:30. We **leave** for the movie at 9:00.	

 In pairs, take turns asking and answering the following questions.

1. Will you see your family (boyfriend, girlfriend, best friend) soon?
2. When are you going to call them (him, her) next?
3. Will the call be long distance?
4. Will it be expensive?
5. When are you going to write your next letter to your family (best friend, and so forth)?
6. Is anyone coming to visit you soon?
7. When do the guests arrive?
8. What are you planning to do with them?

Complete the passage with future forms of the verbs in parentheses. The first one is done as an example.

WORK LIFE AND HOME LIFE

Technology has already changed the world of work, and in the near future improvements such as video-conferencing, fax machines, and the Internet

_____are going to make_____ it even easier for people to work from their homes. In
         1 (make)

general, people _____ less tied to an office. Work _____
                    2 (be)   3 (have)

a more international focus and _____ round-the-clock attention.
                                      4 (need)

Therefore, it _____ even more difficult to separate work and home
                  5 (become)

life.

Changes in the nature of work combined with changes in the work force

_____ about major changes in company policies. Because women
      6 (bring)

now constitute nearly half of the work force, corporations have already

become more dependent on female workers. Because of this, opportunities for

females to advance _____, and company policies _____
                          7 (increase)   8 (become)

more "family friendly."

In the future, gender inequality _____. With more and more
                                     9 (disappear / hopefully)

women in fields once dominated by men, the gap between male and female

wages _____. When this happens, power balances _____
           10 (close)   11 (change)

not only at the office, but also in the kitchen. When both sexes have equivalent

jobs and paychecks, it _____ the woman who works "the second
                            12 (not be / always)

shift" of housework after hours or who stays home when a child is sick. In

addition, women _____ child custody in a divorce as often as they
                     13 (not receive)

do now.

C. The Future Continuous Tense

The future continuous tense normally refers to actions that will be in progress, often at a specified time, in the future.

uses	examples	notes
Actions in Progress in the Future	Can you imagine! At this time tomorrow we**'ll be landing** in London! Yes, but at the same time next week, we**'ll be flying** home.	These time expressions are often used with the future continuous tense: *at this time next week* (*month*, and so on), *at that time* (*at 3:00*, and so on), *the day after tomorrow, a week* (*year*) *from today.*

Note: See page 52 for a list of verbs not normally used in the continuous tenses. See Appendix One for spelling rules for verbs with *-ing* endings.

 The future continuous tense often gives a friendlier and more conversational feeling than the simple future does. Change the following sentences to the future continuous.

> example: I'll see you.
>
> **I'll be seeing you.**

1. We'll see you later this evening.
2. Will you go to the party tomorrow night?
3. They'll arrive in town the day after tomorrow.
4. I'll call you soon.
5. He won't come home for dinner tonight.
6. When will we have our next exam?

 Complete the following in your own words, using the future continuous.

> example: Right now I am sitting in class. At this time tomorrow . . .
>
> **I'll be studying at the library.**

1. Right now I am living . . . (with my parents / in an apartment). A month from now . . .
2. This session I am going to . . . (name of school). Next session . . .
3. This session I am taking English. Next session . . .
4. Right now I am studying grammar. At this time tomorrow . . .
5. Today I'm wearing . . . Tomorrow . . .
6. Tonight I'm . . . Tomorrow night . . .

exercise 6 In pairs, take turns asking and answering the following questions.

> **example:** What will you be doing the day after tomorrow?
> **I will probably be studying for a test.**

1. What will you be doing at this time on Saturday?
2. What will you be studying a month from now?
3. Will you still be going to school six months from now?
4. Will you be working a year from now?
5. Where will you be living at that time?
6. Will you be using English then?

D. The Future Perfect and Future Perfect Continuous Tenses

These tenses refer to situations or actions that will have occurred *before* another event or time in the future. They appear in written English, but they are not used often in spoken English.

	examples	notes
Future Perfect	By the end of this trip, we **will have traveled** over ten thousand miles.	Time expressions used with these tenses include: *before, when, by the time . . . , by* + date or time.
Future Perfect Continuous	When you arrive, you **will have been flying** for more than twenty-two hours.	

Note: See page 52 for a list of verbs not normally used in the continuous tenses. See Appendix One for a list of irregular past participles and for spelling rules for the *-ed* and *-ing* endings.

exercise 7  Change the following sentences to the future perfect tense. Use *more* or *even more* (for emphasis) in your new sentences.

> **example:** The role of women has changed greatly.
> **By 2020, the role of women will have changed even more.**

1. Families have become smaller.
2. The cost of living has increased.
3. Raising children has gotten more expensive.
4. Many men have begun to do housework.
5. Many women have gone back to school.
6. Many women have started to work outside the home.

Using What You've Learned

 activity 1 In pairs or small groups, role-play the following scenes.

1. Imagine you are talking to your boyfriend or girlfriend.
  a. Make him or her an offer.
  b. Make him or her a promise.
  c. Make a prediction.
2. Imagine you are talking to your father or mother.
  a. Make him or her a promise.
  b. Make a request of him or her.
3. Imagine you are talking to your teenage son or daughter.
  a. Make a request of him or her.
  b. Make a prediction.

activity 2 What do you think life will be like in the twenty-first century? What do you hope you will be doing? Where will you be living? Will you have gotten married? Will you have children? Grandchildren? Will you still be in the same career?

In small groups, discuss your plans and dreams for jobs, marriage, and family. Also consider changes that will be occurring in the world around you—politically, economically, and technologically. After you have finished, choose one member of the group to give a brief summary of your discussion to the class.

TOPIC **four**
Past Verb Forms (2)

Setting the Context

previewing the passage The following passage is a childhood story from a great storyteller, Al Monom. As you go through it, think about your childhood. Was there a storyteller in your family? Was storytelling an important part of family gatherings? Is it an important part of your culture?

The Old Days

My Pa used to play the violin. Us children* would gather around the potbelly stove in the kitchen during those long, freezing-cold winter nights in Wisconsin, and we would be glued to the sounds of that old violin. My Pa made that violin sing.

---

us children   colloquial for "we children"

5　　That violin gave us our best entertainment because my Pa used to play for dances around the county. We would get so excited when he told us that we were going to go to a dance. About one Saturday night a month, he would hitch the horses, pack the entire family into the wagon, and take us off to the dance. Now that was real excitement!

10　　I still have that violin. It has got to be at least a hundred and fifty years old now. I've played it on and off through the years, and others have picked it from time to time. But nobody has made it sing the way Pa used to.

Al Monom, age 87, Middleton, Wisconsin

discussing ideas

Al Monom grew up a long time ago, and his childhood was very different from childhood today. Think about children growing up now. For a child, how is life different today from what it used to be fifty, sixty, or seventy years ago?

A. The Habitual Past: *would* and *used to*

Both *would* + simple form and *used to* + simple form are used to describe actions in the past that were repeated on a regular basis. For situations and continuous actions in the past, however, only *used to* is possible; *would* cannot be used. *Used to* can also refer to actions or situations in the past that no longer exist.

uses	examples
Repeated Actions in the Past	When I was a child, my family **would travel** in the West every summer. We **used to visit** the Teton Mountains every year.
Continuous Actions or Situations in the Past	My father **used to live** near the mountains. (not: *would live*) He **used to work** as a forest ranger. (not: *would work*)
Past Actions or Situations that No Longer Exist	Campsites **used to be** free; now you have to pay to camp. (not: *would be*)

Note: Do not confuse the constructions *used to* + simple form and *be used to* + gerund, which means "be accustomed to." Compare: *I used to get up early. (I don't anymore.) I am used to getting up early. (I frequently get up early and it doesn't bother me.)*

Underline all uses of *would* and *used to* in the passage "The Old Days" on pages 87 and 88. Then substitute simple past verbs in each case. Does the meaning change?

Using *would* in a sentence can give a nostalgic, almost poetic, feeling to the words. Add *would* to these sentences, making any necessary changes. Then discuss the differences in meaning between the original and the new sentences.

example: My grandfather often spent hours reading.

My grandfather would often spend hours reading.

1. On Sundays, my grandfather often sat in his old oak rocking chair.
2. He smoked his pipe.
3. He read for hours and hours.
4. Sometimes he stopped reading for a while.
5. He took out his old mandolin.
6. He played songs for us.
7. He sang lovely melodies to us.
8. He held us on his lap in the big old rocking chair.

Using *would* or *used to*, change the following sentences from the simple past tense to the habitual past. Note any cases where *would* cannot be used.

example: We lived in a small town.

We used to live in a small town. (Would cannot be used.)

1. Our family had a television, but we seldom watched it.
2. We always found other ways to pass the time.
3. All of the children in the neighborhood were friends.
4. In the summer, we always played games, rode our bicycles, and went swimming.
5. All of us liked to swim.
6. In autumn, we always made big piles of leaves to jump in.
7. In winter, we skated and skied all the time.
8. We built snow slides through the backyards and went down them on sleds every day after school.
9. Finally springtime came after months of winter.
10. We waited for summer to arrive again.

B. The Future in the Past: *was/were going to*

Was/were going to + verb is used to describe past intentions. In many cases, the action was not completed.

uses	examples
Past Intentions (Action Completed)	I said I **was going to get** an "A" in English, and I did. Last summer, our family **was going to visit** friends in Colorado. We did.
Past Intentions (Action Not Completed)	Last summer, we **were going to visit** friends in Colorado, but we didn't have enough time.

 In pairs, use the following cues to ask and answer questions.

example: clean your room

Have you cleaned your room yet?
I was going to clean it a while ago, but I didn't have time.
or **I said I was going to clean it a while ago, and I did.**

1. make your bed
2. sweep the floor
3. take the garbage out
4. pick your clothes up

5. do the laundry
6. iron your shirts
7. straighten your room up
8. do your homework

 Make sentences using *was/were going to*. Use the following cues and add ideas of your own.

example: Ann / make a cake / no sugar

Ann was going to make a cake, but she didn't have any sugar.

1. the man / use the pay phone / no coins
2. you / tell me a story / forget
3. her friends / visit her new apartment / get lost
4. the children / eat ice cream / melt
5. Bob / ride his bicycle / flat tire
6. Jose / play tennis / start raining
7. Dorothy / study in the library / too noisy
8. Craig and Gus / go swimming / too cold

Using What You've Learned

activity 1

Imagine these people's lives. All have experienced major life changes. In pairs or small groups, create stories about each. Make original sentences with *used to* and *would* to compare their lives in the past with their lives today.

example: a couple with a new baby

Before their baby arrived, John and Susan used to do lots of things. They used to go to the movies often, but now it's more difficult because they need to get a babysitter. And, they would often go out for dinner, but they don't have as much money as they used to, so they eat at home a lot. Above all, they used to be able to sleep all night. Now they wake up every three hours.

1. a person who suddenly becomes famous
2. newlyweds
3. a freshman at a university
4. a foreigner in a strange country
5. a newly elected president
6. a person beginning his or her first job
7. children of recently divorced parents
8. a person who wins the lottery

activity 2

Your childhood may have been very different from those of your classmates. In small groups, choose a certain period and take turns describing it in detail. You may want to tell about school vacations, or your first year in high school, or weekends when you were seven or eight. To get started, try to think of some of the funniest, most interesting, most awkward, or most memorable periods of your childhood. Then, after you have shared your story, write a short composition about it. As a class, you may want to put together a collection of childhood memories.

examples: **When we were children, our family used to go to the mountains for a month every summer. Our vacations were always in the mountains because my dad used to do a lot of climbing. On those vacations, we'd usually camp for most of the time. I'd share a tent with my two brothers. . . .**

When I was a freshman in high school, I started going to dances. Our school used to have dances every Saturday night. They were terrible! All the boys would stand along one side of the room and all the girls along the other side. For the first hour or so, no one would dance. The girls would giggle and the boys would push and shove each other. . . .

What did you learn about yourself in Activity 2 on page 81? Are you a procrastinator or not?

Use your list from Activity 2 or make a new list of the important things you wanted to do during the past month. Then note whether or not you did each. If you did not, give a sentence explaining why not. If you wish, make a chart like the one below.

PLANNED TO DO	DONE	STILL HAVEN'T DONE	WHY NOT
write my brother		X	I was going to write a long letter telling about my life, but I got too busy.
balance my checkbook			
organize my apartment			

TOPIC **five**
Past Verb Forms (3)

Setting the Context

previewing the passage

All over the world, people have been moving from rural areas into the cities. What effects has this migration had?

The Urbanization of America

*L*ike much of the world, the United States did not develop large urban centers until this century. Before World War I, the majority of Americans had lived in rural areas or in small towns. In 1900, for example, over 40 percent of the U.S. population lived or worked on farms.

5   World War I and the Depression of the 1930s changed American life dramatically. By 1930, for example, the farm population had dropped to 30.1 percent. During the Depression, over three-quarters of a million farmers lost their land. As individuals and entire families moved to cities in search of work, urban areas grew tremendously. Today, almost 80 percent of Americans live in
10 metropolitan areas.

    This migration from rural to urban areas has had a great impact on American society, just as it has in many parts of the world. In general, people in urban areas are more mobile and more independent, families are less stable, and friendships are often short-lived. Although cities may offer greater economic
15 opportunities, they also present many difficulties in maintaining "the ties that bind": close, long-term relationships with family and friends.

discussing ideas

Is this pattern of rural-to-urban migration true in your native country also? Why do people leave their rural homes? How does the move to a city affect them, their families, and their friends?

A. The Past Perfect Tense

The past perfect tense refers to an activity or situation completed *before* another event or time in the past. This tense may be used in a simple sentence, but it normally contrasts with the simple past in a compound or complex sentence.

	examples	notes
Simple Sentences	Until 1932, the O'Keefes **had lived** on a farm. By the end of 1932, they **had** already **lost** their farm and moved to the city.	Time expressions such as *already, barely, just, no sooner, rarely, recently, still, yet, ever, never,* or connecting words such as *after, before, by, by the time (that), until, when* are often used with the past perfect. Chapter Eight includes more information on uses of this tense with connecting words and complex sentences.
Complex Sentences	Before the Depression began, the O'Keefes **had been** prosperous farmers. The children **had** just **begun** school when their parents lost the farm.	

Note: See Appendix One for a list of irregular past participles and for spelling rules for the *-ed* ending.

The Simple Past Versus the Past Perfect Tense

Although the past perfect tense is often preferable in formal English, the simple past is frequently used instead of the past perfect in conversation. The meaning of the sentence must be clear, however. For example, in sentences with *when*, the time difference in the two tenses can change the meaning of the sentence. Compare:

	examples
Simple Past + Simple Past	It **began** to rain **when I went** out. (The rain began at that time.)
Past Perfect + Simple Past	It **had begun** to rain **when I went** out. (The rain had begun earlier.)

This exercise tells the story of an immigrant family in the United States. Using *by* and the past perfect tense, form complete sentences from the cues below.

example: 1848 / John and Mary O'Keefe / leave Ireland
By 1848, John and Mary O'Keefe had left Ireland.

1. 1850 / the O'Keefes / start a farm in Wisconsin
2. 1880s / the O'Keefes / raise a family of ten children
3. 1885 / their son John / marry Catherine
4. 1890 / Catherine / give birth to a daughter, Amanda
5. 1910 / Amanda / get married to Ed
6. 1920 / they / have a beautiful baby girl

Complete the following sentences by using either the simple past or the past perfect tense of the verbs in parentheses, as in the example.

example: Before changing lifestyles ____began____ (begin) to separate
modern families, several generations of the same family
had often lived (live / often) together.

1. Until the automobile, the Depression, and the world wars _____ (bring) changes in U.S. society, American lifestyles _____ (remain) constant for a century.

2. American society _____ (begin / already) to change when World War II _____ (break out).

3. After rural families _____ (move) to the cities in search of work, they _____ (create) new lives there instead of returning to their farms.

4. Women _____ (work / rarely) outside the home before World War II _____ (produce) a labor shortage.

5. After women _____ (experience) the world of work, many _____ (find) it difficult to return to their traditional roles.

6. By the time that World War II _____ (come) to an end, the American way of life _____ (change) tremendously.

The Past Perfect Continuous Tense

The past perfect continuous tense, like the past perfect tense, is used to contrast an earlier and a later time in the past. It may be used instead of the past perfect tense to emphasize the continuous nature of the earlier activity. The past perfect continuous tense is seldom used in conversation but does appear in written English.

	examples	notes
Simple Sentences	Before the Depression, the O'Keefes **had been making** a decent living. Until the Depression, they **had been planning** to buy a larger farm.	The following time expressions are commonly used with the past perfect continuous: *after, already, before, by, by the time (that), until,* and *for +* a period of time. Chapter Eight includes more information on this tense in complex sentences.
Complex Sentence	Before they lost their farm, the O'Keefes **had been making** a good living.	

Note: See page 52 for a list of verbs not normally used in the continuous tenses. See Appendix One for spelling rules for the *-ing* ending.

 **exercise 3** Using *by the time that* and *already*, combine the following pairs of sentences. Be sure to change verb tenses when necessary.

example: Women fought to get the vote for years.
The nineteenth Amendment was ratified in 1920.

Women had already been fighting to get the vote for years by the time that the Nineteenth Amendment was ratified in 1920.

1. Serious economic problems affected world trade for several years.
The stock market crashed in 1929.

2. Farmers struggled to maintain their farms for several years.
The drought of 1935–36 began.

3. Blacks and other minorities tried for years to receive equality under the law.
Congress passed the Civil Rights Act in 1964.

4. Martin Luther King worked for civil rights for more than a decade.
He received the Nobel Peace Prize in 1964.

5. The Soviet Union experimented with spacecraft for several years.
The United States began its space program.

6. Young Americans explored ways of working and helping abroad.
John F. Kennedy established the Peace Corps in 1961.

Review. Complete the following passage with appropriate past forms of the verbs in parentheses. In some cases, more than one choice may be possible. Be prepared to discuss your choices. The first two are done as examples.

IMMIGRANT FAMILIES AND THE GREAT DEPRESSION

It ___was___ 6:45 in the morning, and Katherine Nuss ___was going___

out into the gray morning light. She _____ around the corner to
                                        3 (walk)

the streetcar stop and _____ the journey to the great houses of High
                            4 (begin)

Street. The wages _____ low—$2 for a twelve- or thirteen-hour
                       5 (be)

day. Some nights it _____ nearly nine o'clock by the time she
                        6 (be)

_____ from the trolley to her own home at 1020 West Mulberry
    7 (trudge)

Street. Nevertheless, the work _____ money. While she _____
                                    8 (mean)   9 (scrub)

floors, _____ windows, _____ woodwork, and _____
            10 (wash)   11 (polish)   12 (cook)

meals for the rich families of Springfield, she _____ her children
                                                     13 (support)

and _____ the family together.
        14 (keep)

Immigrants arriving at Ellis Island.

In 1933, the economic situation _____ worse in her town, as
15 (get)

in the rest of the nation. At that time, America _____ close to the
16 (come)

bottom of the Great Depression. Her husband _____ disabled,
17 (be)

and they _____ many children to feed. So, Katherine Nuss
18 (have)

_____ back to work. Once again, she _____ houses,
19 (go)   20 (clean)

the same thing she _____ as a teenage immigrant fresh off the
21 (do)

boat from Europe. She _____ house for the wealthy families on
22 (clean)

the hill in order to keep her own family together.

Both she and her husband _____ the preciousness of family
23 (know)

because of their own hard experiences. Many years before, as children, both

_____ their own parents because of death or immigration to
24 (lose)

America. Both, as adults, _____ family next to God as the
25 (place)

highest values of life.

Katherine _____ a little girl in Austria-Hungary when her
26 (be)

mother _____. Her father _____ her with relatives
27 (die)   28 (leave)

and _____ for America. Like millions of other immigrants, he
29 (sail)

_____ for his future in the New World.
30 (look)

Katherine _____ fourteen years old when her father
31 (be)

_____ for her. She _____ at Ellis Island, New York, in
32 (send)   33 (arrive)

1910—alone, frightened, and unable to speak a word of English. All she

_____ _____ a slip of paper with her father's home
34 (have)   35 (be)

address in Cincinnati.

Review. Complete the passage with appropriate forms of the verbs in parentheses. Add adverbs when indicated. The first one is done as an example.

FAMILY RESPONSIBILITIES

Household chores ___are usually___ boring. All of us in the Peterson house-
1 (be / usually)

hold _____ busy schedules, so we _____ to share the
2 (have)   3 (try)

chores. Our plan _____ out though! For example, our sons, Dan and
4 (work / seldom)

Ed, _____ the dinner dishes, but tonight they _____ for
5 (do / usually)   6 (study)

exams. So guess who _____ the dishes tonight? Me! Our daughter,
7 (wash)

Sue, _____ care of the laundry, but she _____ friends out
8 (take / normally)   9 (visit)

of town. So guess who _____ the laundry this week? Me! My hus-
10 (do)

band and I _____ cooking, as a rule, but he _____ with
11 (alternate)   12 (meet)

one of his most important clients this evening. So guess who _____
13 (make)

dinner again? Me!

I _____ doing all these chores, and, in fact, I _____
14 (not mind)   15 (like / even)

housework. Time _____ my problem, however. I _____
16 (be / always)   17 (work)

thirty-five hours a week, and I _____ to stay late at my job. I
18 (have / often)

_____ that the family schedules _____ and that "some-
19 (understand)   20 (change)

one" _____ to keep up the house. But I _____ to be
21 (need)   22 (seem / almost always)

the "someone." It _____ easy to have two full-time jobs!
23 (not be)

Review. The opening passage of the chapter is repeated on pages 99 to 101. First, complete the passage with appropriate forms of the verbs in parentheses. Then, look back at page 66 and compare your choices with the original. The first one is done as an example.

FAMILIES PAST AND PRESENT

Exactly what _is_ a family? In the past, the traditional American family
1 (be)

_____ of a working husband, a wife at home, and children.
2 (consist)

Responsibilities _____ clearly divided: while the husband
3 (be)

_____ a living, the wife _____ for the home and
4 (earn)   5 (care)

_____ the children. Of course, there _____ exceptions,
6 (raise)   7 (be)

but this concept of the family _____ the general rule until the 1960s.
8 (be)

Since the 1960s, however, the family _____ more diverse,
9 (become)

fragile, and changeable. Americans _____ differing concepts of
10 (accept)

families, including single-parent, blended, two-paycheck, interracial, childless,

and commuter families.

Nowadays, when people _____ about their families, their de-
11 (talk)

scriptions _____ greatly. One teenager _____ her family
12 (vary)   13 (describe)

structure as "a dad, two moms, two sisters and a brother, and a baby on the

way, eighteen cousins, four-and-a-half grandmas and five grandpas, five

uncles, and eight aunts." (Her "half"-grandmother is a step-grandparent.)

Some critics _____ that the American family _____
14 (believe)   15 (suffer)

greatly because of all the changes in society. According to these critics, the

family _____ much stronger before it _____ to struggle
16 (be)   17 (begin)

with issues such as divorce, working wives and mothers, gay couples, femi-

nism, and unmarried relationships. Today's strongest critics _____
18 (feel)

that the traditional nuclear family _____ society's basic unit in the
19 (not be)

twenty-first century.

Nationwide, however, most Americans _____ that the
20 (believe)

family _____. In fact, almost all major surveys in recent years
21 (survive)

_____ that, in spite of what the critics say, the American family
22 (find)

_____ as strong as it _____. For most Americans, the
23 (be)   24 (be)

family _____ to provide their deepest source of satisfaction and of
       25 (continue)

meaning in life. Thus, although today's family _____ different from
                                               26 (be)

what it _____, it _____ to be thriving.
        27 (be)   28 (seem)

Using What You've Learned

The twentieth century has been a period of tremendous change worldwide: in work and careers, family life, education, medical care, transportation, eating habits, shopping, and entertainment, to name only a few areas. Choose one area of change as the topic for a short composition. First, describe the situation in your culture 25, 50, 75, or 100 years ago. Then, describe the situation today, making comparisons between the past and present. Finally, use your composition as the basis for a three-minute presentation to the class.

example: **Until the age of television, most Italian families had spent their evenings together. They would talk, read, sing, or tell stories. . . .**

Every culture has favorite folk stories. Many of these often teach us lessons about life. Can you remember a folk story that you particularly liked as a child? In small groups, share some stories from your cultures. Do you find similar stories in different cultures? You may want to write these stories and make a short collection of folktales from around the world.

focus on testing

Use of Verbs

Verb forms and tenses are frequently tested on standardized English proficiency exams. Review these commonly tested structures and check your understanding by completing the following sample items.

Remember that . . .

* All tenses should be formed correctly, and the tense should be appropriate for the time frame(s) of the sentence.
* Verbs of feeling, perception, and possession are not generally used in continuous tenses. Also, many of these verbs are linking verbs; adverbs cannot be used as complements after linking verbs.
* A singular verb is used with a singular subject, and plural verbs are used with plural subjects.

Part 1: Circle the correct completion for the following.

example: John _____ quite ill in the past few days.
    a. had became   **c.** has became
    b. had become   (**d.**) has become

1. Most major surveys in recent years _____ that Americans are satisfied with their family life.
    a. have find   **c.** has found
    b. find   **d.** have found

2. The Jacksons appear to be _____ with their decision to move.
    a. please   **c.** happily
    b. happy   **d.** pleasant

3. When Mary was younger, she _____ tennis much more than now.
    a. used to like   **c.** was liking
    b. would like   **d.** like

Part 2: Circle the letter below the word(s) containing an error.

example: An individual may feel frustratedly if she has difficulties in
     A   B   Ⓒ
speaking the language where she is living.
                    A

1. Long before the Prime Minister left for Canada, she had discussing
      A   B   C
the issue in depth with the entire cabinet.
        D

2. By the time that the report is finished, the committee will have
      A   B   C
spending over two months working on it.
   D

3. Since the Depression of the 1930s, the farm population in the
     A   B
United States have dropped from around 30 percent to less than
          C   D
4 percent.

CHAPTER **four**

Health

Introduction

In this chapter you will study the forms and functions of the modal auxiliaries, as well as some structures related to them in usage. This chapter emphasizes the present forms, active voice. In Chapter Five, you will study the passive forms. In Chapter Ten, you will review these and study the past forms in more detail.

The following passage introduces the chapter theme, Health, and raises some of the topics and issues you will cover in the chapter.

How Healthy Are You?

Good health is not something you are able to buy at the drugstore, and you can't depend on getting it back with a quick visit to the doctor when you're sick, either. Making your body last without major problems has to be your own responsibility. Mistreating your system by keeping bad habits, neglecting symp-
5   toms of illness, and ignoring common health rules can counteract the best medical care.

Nowadays, health specialists promote the idea of wellness for everybody. Wellness means achieving the best possible health within the limits of your body. One person may need many fewer calories than another, depending on
10 metabolism. Some people might prefer a lot of easier exercise to more strenuous exercise. While one person enjoys playing seventy-two holes of golf a week, another would rather play three sweaty, competitive games of tennis.

Understanding the needs of your own body is the key. Everyone runs the risk of accidents, and no one can be sure of avoiding chronic disease. Neverthe-
15 less, poor diet, stress, a bad working environment, and carelessness can ruin good health. By changing your habits or the conditions surrounding you, you can lower the risk or reduce the damage of disease.

discussing ideas Have you noticed any major differences in health care issues in North America and health care issues in your country? What is the general attitude toward medical care in your country or culture?

Modal Auxiliaries and Related Structures of Ability and Expectation

Setting the Context

What is *physical fitness*? Can you describe a physically fit person?

Are You Physically Fit?

- Physically fit people can go through a busy day and feel good the next morning.
- They are able to lift approximately one-half their body weight.
- They can bend and twist easily in all directions.

5

- Wearing the right clothing, a physically fit person should be able to walk a mile in fifteen minutes or less.
- Physically fit people should be able to stay the same weight.

How physically fit are you? Can you do all the above?

A. Introduction to Modal Auxiliaries

A modal has only one form for all persons of the verb, but it can have several meanings and time frames, depending on the context in which it is used. A complete list of the modals discussed in this chapter appears in Appendix Three; the list also includes related structures (structures often used in place of modal auxiliaries).

	examples	negative contractions*	
Statements	He **should get** more exercise.	can't	shouldn't
		couldn't	won't
Questions	**Would** you **like** to go jogging?	mustn't	wouldn't
Negatives	I **can't play** tennis today.		

*Note: Negative contractions vary in different parts of North America. These are the most commonly used.

B. Expressing Present and Past Ability

modals		examples	notes
PRESENT ABILITY			
can (cannot)	} + Simple	John **can** run five miles, but I **can't** (**cannot**).	Affirmative and negative statements and questions all give the meaning of ability. In rapid speech, *can* is weakly stressed (*kin*). *Can't* is stressed more strongly.
(not) be able to	Form	How many miles **are** you **able** to run?	
PAST ABILITY			
could (not)	} + Simple	He **couldn't** run as fast as she **could**.	
(not) be able to	Form	I **wasn't able to** run because of the rain.	

 It is often difficult to distinguish *can* and *can't* in rapid conversation. Of course, there is a tremendous difference in meaning! As your teacher rapidly reads the following sentences, circle *can* or *can't* according to what you hear. *Hint:* **Can** has little stress, and **can't** is more clearly pronounced.

1. I (can / can't) swim a mile.

2. John (can / can't), run a mile.

3. I (can / can't) walk a mile.

4. She (can / can't) ski very well.

5. He (can / can't) jog ten miles.

6. They (can / can't) skate very well.

7. I (can / can't) ride a bike.

8. I (can / can't) hear the difference between the two words!

 **exercise 2**   Work in pairs and take turns making statements. Choose one sentence in each pair, but don't tell which sentence you are choosing. Your partner should tell you which one she or he heard.

1. **a.** I can swim.
   b. I can't swim.

2. **a.** I can roller-skate.
   b. I can't roller-skate.

3. **a.** I can play the guitar.
   b. I can't play the guitar.

4. **a.** I can speak Japanese.
   b. I can't speak Japanese.

5. **a.** He can ride a bike.
   b. He can't ride a bike.

6. **a.** She can touch her toes.
   b. She can't touch her toes.

7. **a.** He can do a cartwheel.
   b. He can't do a cartwheel.

8. **a.** She can work tonight.
   b. She can't work tonight.

 **exercise 3**   Which of the following activities can you do well? Which can't you do? For each of the twelve items in the following chart, check the appropriate boxes. Then, work with a partner and take turns making statements and asking questions about the chart.

example: A: **I can swim fairly well. Can you?**
              B: **I can't swim very well, but I can roller-skate well. Can you?**

	CAN DO WELL	CAN DO FAIRLY WELL	CAN'T DO VERY WELL	CAN'T DO AT ALL
1. swim	☐	☐	☐	☐
2. roller-skate	☐	☐	☐	☐
3. roller-blade	☐	☐	☐	☐
4. ice-skate	☐	☐	☐	☐
5. cook	☐	☐	☐	☐
6. play squash	☐	☐	☐	☐
7. dance to country western music	☐	☐	☐	☐
8. dance to Latin music	☐	☐	☐	☐

	CAN DO WELL	CAN DO FAIRLY WELL	CAN'T DO VERY WELL	CAN'T DO AT ALL
9. speak Chinese	☐	☐	☐	☐
10. play the piano	☐	☐	☐	☐
11. whistle	☐	☐	☐	☐
12. use a word processor	☐	☐	☐	☐

 **exercise 4** The chart that follows gives you the approximate calories you burn in sports and other activities. Use the information to form at least six sentences with *can*. Note that you must use the *-ing* form of a verb after *by*.

> example: **You (A person) can burn over 300 calories by walking briskly for an hour.**

How Many Calories Can You Burn?

Food produces energy. One ounce of fat gives 267 calories of energy. A pound of fat is equivalent to 4,272 calories.

CALORIES BURNED PER HOUR	ACTIVITY
72–84	sitting and talking
120–150	walking at a slow pace
240–300	doing housework (cleaning, mopping, scrubbing)
300–360	walking briskly; playing doubles tennis; playing Ping-Pong (table tennis)
350–420	bicycling; ice- or roller-skating
420–480	playing singles tennis
480–600	downhill skiing; jogging
600–650	running (5.5 mph); bicycling (13 mph)
over 660	running (6 or more mph); handball; squash; swimming (depends on stroke and style —excellent overall conditioner)

 **exercise 5** Look at the various activities listed in Exercise 4. Which can you do now? Which could you do when you were younger? Make at least six original sentences following these patterns:

> *When I was younger, I could (couldn't) . . .*
> *Now that I'm older, I can . . .*
> > *I still can't . . .*
> > *I can't . . . anymore.*

   example: **When I was younger, I couldn't ski, and I still can't!**

 # C. Expressing Expectation

Should and *ought to* have two different meanings. One meaning is *will probably*. The other meaning of advice is covered later in this chapter. With both meanings, *should* is more commonly used.

modals		examples	notes
should (not)	+ **Simple Form**	He **should arrive** very soon. **Shouldn't** she **arrive** soon? This **shouldn't take** long to do.	Negative questions with *should* are often used for emphasis. In rapid speech, *ought to* sounds like /otta/.
ought (not) to	+ **Simple Form**	We **ought to be** finished soon.	

 **exercise 6**

 Work in groups of three. Take turns reading the following statements and creating new statements. The first student reads the statement from the text. The second student forms a sentence with *should,* and the third student uses *ought to* for the same sentence. As an alternative, write your new versions of the original statement, one with *should* and one with *ought to.*

   example: We expect the doctor to arrive at any minute.

   A: We expect the doctor to arrive at any minute.
   B: **The doctor should arrive at any minute.**
   C: **The doctor ought to arrive at any minute.**

   1. The doctor expects the exam to take only a few minutes.
   2. She doesn't expect there to be any problems.
   3. She expects to have plenty of time to answer questions.
   4. The doctor expects your exam to be normal.
   5. She doesn't expect you to need another checkup for at least a year.
   6. You can expect your bill to arrive within a week.
   7. We expect the insurance to cover most of your bill.
   8. We don't expect to have any problems with your coverage.
   9. The company doesn't expect insurance premiums to go up until next year.
   10. The company expects premiums to increase within eighteen months.

exercise 7 Complete the following items, using *be able to, can, could,* or *should.* Use each form at least once. The first one is done as an example.

Before

1. Before I began exercising at Ernie's Exercise

    Emporium, I ___wasn't able to lose___ weight,
    1 (not lose)
    and I _____ any clothes that fit me
    2 (not find)
    well.

After

2. Now that my muscles are so big, I

    _____ anything. Well, my
    1 (not find)
    instructor said that I _____
    2 (be)
    able to find some clothes at "Miki's

    Muscle Shop for High Powered Females."

    They _____ something that
    3 (have)
    fits me!

Before

3. Before I began exercising at Ernie's Exercise

    Emporium, I _____, I
    1 (not run)
    _____, I _____, I
    2 (not jog)   3 (not walk)
    _____ without getting tired.
    4 (not sit / even)
    I _____ anything!
    5 (not do)

After

4. Now I _____ anything!
    1 (not do / still)
    But the doctor says that I _____
    2 (be)
    able to leave the hospital soon.

Using What You've Learned

activity **1**

In recent years, Americans have become more concerned about their health. In fact, for many people, fitness has become almost an obsession. In large cities and small towns alike, people jog regularly, join sports teams, and go to health clubs to work out.

What is the attitude toward fitness in your culture(s)? Have attitudes changed in recent years? Are there differences for males and females? In small groups, discuss the following questions and then give a brief report to your class. As an alternative, you can write a brief composition giving your own experiences and opinions, or you can interview another person.

Note that for this activity, you may want to separate into groups of all males and all females. Or, you may want to separate by language or cultural groups.

- In your culture, what was the attitude toward fitness twenty–twenty-five years ago? Were there differences for males and females?
- Has this attitude changed in recent years? If so, why?
- What is the general attitude toward health and fitness today? Are there differences for males and females?

activity **2**

Make a list of at least five things you can do now that you couldn't do ten or fifteen years ago. Then make another list of at least five things you could do before but that you can't do now. From your lists, choose the one thing that is most important to you—the one you are proudest of or the one you are saddest about, for example. Write a brief composition about it, explaining your change in abilities and why this is important to you.

example: When I look back to ten years ago, I realize that I could do many, many things. I could go where I wanted and I could do what I wanted. This is because I didn't have many responsibilities. I didn't have a family. With a family, the biggest change for me has been in the loss of freedom. It's a happy change, but it's also a difficult change. Now I can . . .

Modal Auxiliaries of Request, Permission, and Preference

Setting the Context

A trip to the dentist is often a feared event, and many people frequently wait until "it's too late." Is this true for you?

Office Visits

RECEPTIONIST: May I help you?

PATIENT: Could I see a dentist, fast?!

What experiences have you had with dentists in North America?

A. Requesting Action

One form of request involves asking someone to do something. The following modal auxiliaries are often used in these requests.

modals	examples	notes
Would you mind . . . ? + *Gerund* (*Verb* + ing)	**Would** you **mind** calling a doctor? **Would** you **mind** not talking so loudly?	*Would you mind . . .* is always followed by a gerund. A negative response means "I will." Informal answers are often affirmative, however.
Would you . . . ? **Could you . . . ?** **+ *Simple*** **Can you . . . ?** ***Form*** **Will you . . . ?**	**Would** you call a doctor, please? **Could** you call Dr. Fox? **Can** you please come soon? **Will** you come immediately?	*Please* is often added to any request. *Could* and *would* are appropriate in most circumstances. *Can* is informal, and it is used among friends. *Will* is somewhat rude in tone. It is used in urgent situations or among friends.

Pronunciation Note

In rapid speech, *can, could, will,* and *would* are seldom pronounced clearly. Listen carefully as your teacher reads the following words:

NORMAL SPEECH	RAPID SPEECH	NORMAL SPEECH	RAPID SPEECH
Can you . . . ?	/kenya/	Will you . . . ?	/willya/
Can he . . . ?	/keni/	Will he . . . ?	/willi/
Could you . . . ?	/kudja/	Would you . . . ?	/wudja/
Could he . . . ?	/kuddi/	Would he . . . ?	/wuddi/

 Your teacher will read the following requests, but *not* in the order listed. Listen carefully and write down the form that you hear.

1. Could you help?
2. Could he help?
3. Would you help?
4. Wouldn't he help?

5. Can't you help?
6. Couldn't you help?
7. Can you help?
8. Wouldn't you help?

 **exercise 2**   In an emergency, being polite is not as important as taking care of the situation. In emergencies, people often use commands. In most other circumstances, abrupt commands are considered rude.

Imagine that you are in a first aid class (not in an emergency situation). In pairs, take turns making and responding to requests. Change the following commands to polite requests for action by using *could, would,* or *would you mind.*

example: Quick! Call the doctor!

Would you please call the doctor?
Certainly. Which doctor would you like me to call?

1. Hurry! Get me some bandages!
2. Find some clean towels!
3. Open all the windows!
4. Don't touch that!

5. Help me move this!
6. Wash your hands!
7. Get a blanket!
8. Hold this!

 # B. Requesting Permission

Another form of request involves asking permission from someone so that you can do something. The following modal auxiliaries are often used in these requests.

modals	examples	notes
Would you mind if I . . . ? + *Past Form*	**Would** you **mind** if I came late for my appointment?	*Would you mind if I . . .* is always followed by the past tense of a second verb. It is polite and very formal. A negative response means "It's all right."
May I . . . ? **Could I . . . ?** **Can I . . . ?** + *Simple Form*	**May** I help you? **Could** I talk with the doctor? **Can** I see the nurse?	*May* is formal. It is most often used in service situations. *May* and *could* are preferred in polite speech. *Can* is very informal, but it is often used in conversation.

In pairs, take turns making and responding to requests for permission. Complete the following conversations by using *may, could,* or *can.* (Remember that *can* is informal and may not be appropriate for all situations.)

> **example:** (see the nurse)
> I'm sorry, but . . .
>
> A: **May (Could) I see the nurse?**
> B: **I'm sorry, but she's not available at the moment.**

1. (make an appointment now)
Yes, of course . . .

2. (speak with Dr. Fox)
I'm sorry, but . . .

3. (get this prescription filled)
Certainly, . . .

4. (pay by check)
Yes, if . . .

5. (borrow your pen)
Sure . . .

6. (use the telephone)
Sorry, but . . .

In pairs, complete the following conversations asking for permission or for action. Use *can, could, may, would, would you mind . . . ,* or *would you mind if . . .* in your requests. Use each form at least once.

> **example:** A: Would you mind helping me for a little while?
> B: No, I wouldn't. I'd be happy to help you.

1. A: _____
B: Of course. When would you like to see the doctor?

2. A: _____
B: No problem! I can stop by the pharmacy for you.

3. A: _____
B: Sure, I could. Where do you want to go?

4. A: _____
B: Of course I wouldn't mind. What would you like me to do?

5. A: _____
B: No, not at all. Open as many windows as you'd like.

6. A: _____
B: Sure. I don't need that book for several days.

7. A: _____
B: No, I wouldn't. I'd be happy if you joined me.

8. A: _____
B: Thank you, but I'm just looking.

Make a chain around the class. Turn to your neighbor and make a request. Before you make your request, tell the class "who" you are addressing. Then make you request, and your neighbor will respond. Your neighbor then asks his or her neighbor, and so on, continuing the chain. After each, the class should decide if the form of the request was appropriate or not (for example, was the request polite enough? too polite?). Add other situations if necessary.

example: A: (*to my grandfather*) **Grandpa, would you please let me use your car?**

B: **Why of course! Would you like the Rolls Royce or the Mercedes?**

B: (*to a stranger*) **Excuse me, sir. Could I . . .?**

1. You would like to borrow your sister's (brother's, roommate's, father's, aunt's, grandfather's) car.
2. You need to use a telephone. Ask a stranger (your teacher, your friend, the school administrator, your roommate) for change for the pay phone.
3. You would like to use your sister's (brother's, roommate's, cousin's) favorite sweater (jacket, coat) for a special night out. Ask to borrow it from him or her.
4. You would like your roommate (brother, sister, friend, cousin) to lend you a bicycle. Ask him or her to lend it to you for a couple of days.
5. You need to talk with your advisor. Ask the secretary for an appointment.
6. You need to make a dentist appointment. Ask the secretary for an appointment.
7. You need to get a prescription filled in a drug store. Ask the pharmacist (the cashier) to help you.
8. You don't have enough money for the rent and you desperately need to borrow $100. Ask your mother (father, roommate, best friend, boyfriend, girlfriend, classmate) to lend (or give) you the money.

 # C. Expressing Preference

modals		examples	notes
I would (not) like . . . Would you like . . . ? Wouldn't you like . . . ?	+ *Infinitive Or Noun*	I **would like** an appointment. No, I **would like** (**prefer**) to see Dr. Fox. **Would** you **like** to see Dr. Jones? **Wouldn't** you **like** (**prefer**) to see the doctor sooner?	Affirmative and negative statements and questions with *would like (prefer)* may express desires or preferences. *Would like (prefer)* is followed by either a noun or an infinitive.

modals	examples	notes
I would rather (not) . . . **Would you rather (not) . . . ?** **Wouldn't you rather . . . ?** } + **Simple Form**	**I'd rather not** come in the afternoon. **Would** you **rather** come in the morning or the afternoon? **Wouldn't** you **rather** come in the morning?	Affirmative and negative statements and questions with *would rather* express preferences or choices. The contracted form (*I'd,* etc.) is almost always used in conversational English.

 **exercise 6**

Imagine that you have unlimited time and money. What would you like to do? Choose from the following list and add your own ideas. *Note:* for emphasis, you can say *I would really like to . . .* or *I would love to . . .* Make at least eight sentences.

>   **example:**   travel around the world
>
>   **I would like (love) to travel around the world.**

1. spend a month at a health spa
2. hire my own private chef
3. move to Paris
4. run a marathon
5. get a Ph.D.
6. compete in the Olympics
7. buy a yacht
8. become a vegetarian
9. learn yoga
10. take the TOEFL five times
11. play a musical instrument well
12. study a lot more English grammar

 **exercise 7**

Look at the list in Exercise 6. Choose five things you wouldn't like to do. Then give an alternative for each.

>   **example:**   travel around the world
>
>   **I wouldn't like to travel around the world. I'd rather stay here and study grammar.**
>
> *or*
>
>   **I'd rather not travel around the world. I'd much rather stay here and study grammar.**

Review. Add appropriate words or phrases to complete the following conversation. The first two are done as examples.

RECEPTIONIST: Good afternoon. Doctor's office. ___Would___ you ___mind___
holding for a minute? *(click)* Hello. Thank you for holding.
_____ _____ help you?

ESTELA: Hello. This is Estela Ortiz. I _____ _____ to
make an appointment to see Dr. Fox soon for a checkup.

RECEPTIONIST: Dr. Fox will be on vacation for the next three weeks. _____
_____ like _____ see one of the other doctors?

ESTELA: No, I'd _____ wait to see Dr. Fox. When is the earliest
that I _____ schedule an appointment?

RECEPTIONIST: He has openings during the week of September 12. Would
_____ _____ come in the morning or in the
afternoon?

ESTELA: I _____ _____ not come in the morning.
_____ _____ give me an appointment after
4:00 P.M. on either Tuesday or Thursday?

RECEPTIONIST: I _____ schedule you for 4:15, Tuesday afternoon.

ESTELA: Thanks. That'll be fine.

Using What You've Learned

 activity **1**

Have you been to the doctor or dentist recently? Will you see one soon? In pairs, practice making telephone calls to arrange appointments. Role-play making appointments, by phone for:

1. a routine medical checkup
2. getting your teeth cleaned
3. an emergency dental or doctor's appointment

 activity **2**

Work in pairs and role-play the following situations. Make the characters male or female, depending on each pair. As you role-play, think about how polite you should be when you make your requests.

1. You are in a movie theater watching an excellent new movie. The person next to you is an older man (or woman) around sixty. He (She) keeps on talking during the film. Ask him (or her) to be quiet.
2. You are at a basketball game. The person in front of you is about 20 years old and is wearing a fairly large hat. Ask him or her to take off the hat.
3. This is your first time in a small neighborhood restaurant and bar where people seem friendly and most know each other. Someone nearby is smoking. Ask the person not to smoke.
4. You are at home and it is 1:30 A.M. Your neighbors are young, and many are college students. They often make noise, and tonight they are making a lot of noise. You have an important exam tomorrow and you want to be able to sleep. Ask them to be quiet.

 activity **3**

Work with a partner, and make suggestions and responses. Imagine that you have a friend visiting from out of town. Your friend is a good friend but very hard to please. He or she is very particular about what to do. Make at least five good suggestions of things to do. They may include suggestions on movies, restaurants, trips, classes, concerts, and so forth. Your "finicky" friend will respond.

example: A: **Let's go out and see New York at night. Would you like to hear some jazz in Greenwich Village?**
B: **Jazz is boring. I'd rather stay here and do crossword puzzles.**
A: **Well, would you like to . . .?**

Modal Auxiliaries and Related Structures of Need and Advice

Setting the Context

previewing the passage

What is the Red Cross? Have you ever visited or needed the Red Cross?

Medical Emergencies

*E*veryone ought to know the basic steps to follow in case of a medical emergency. If you don't, you should contact your local Red Cross. The Red Cross gives guidelines and offers short courses on what to do in emergency situations.

discussing ideas

Do you know what to do in a medical emergency? What are some of the basic steps to follow? If you don't know, the following pages will give you at least the basic information.

A. Expressing Present Need or Lack of Need

modals and related structures	examples	notes
PRESENT NEED **must (not)** **have to** } + **Simple Form**	You **must** practice every day if you want to improve. John **has to** study, so he can't play today. You **must not** let tennis interfere with your work.	In affirmative statements and questions, *must* and *have to* have similar meanings. Both mean "need to." In rapid speech, *have to* and *has to* sound like *hafta* and *hasta.* *Must not* expresses a strong need *not* to do something.
PRESENT LACK OF NEED **don't (doesn't)** **have to** } + **Simple Form**	I **don't have** to study, so I can play tennis.	In negative statements, *do/does not have to* refers to something that is *not* necessary to do. Its meaning is very different from *must not.*

 **exercise 1**   Change commands using *must/must not.*

> **example:**   Don't use electrical appliances in the water!
>   You must not use electrical appliances in the water!

1. Call a doctor right away!
2. Get an ambulance immediately!
3. Don't move!
4. Don't touch that!
5. Turn off the electricity!
6. Find someone to help!
7. Don't drink that!
8. Give me some bandages!

The American Red Cross gives these guidelines to follow in emergency situations.

1. If necessary, rescue the victim as quickly and carefully as possible.
2. Call for medical help immediately.*
3. Check to see if the victim is breathing, and give him or her artificial respiration if necessary.
4. Control severe bleeding.
5. If you suspect poisoning, immediately give a conscious victim water or milk to dilute† the poison. If you suspect a chemical poison, don't let the victim vomit. If the victim is unconscious or having convulsions,‡ however, do not give any fluids.
6. In an accident, do **not** move the victim unless absolutely necessary.
7. Always check for injuries **before** moving the victim, if possible.

---

*In most areas in the United States, dial 911.
†*dilute*   make thinner or weaker
‡*convulsions*   violent muscle contractions

---

example: If the victim has a neck injury, you _must not_ move him or her.

1. If you _____ make an emergency rescue, do not move the victim.

2. You _____ move a person with a neck or back injury unless absolutely necessary.

3. If your victim has swallowed a poison and is unconscious, you _____ give him or her anything.

4. If your victim has swallowed a chemical poison, you _____ try to make her vomit.

5. You _____ try different remedies with a poison victim if you are not sure of the poison.

6. You _____ study first aid, but it may be helpful someday.

7. A person who knows first aid _____ call a doctor about every small accident.

8. In a true emergency, you _____ wait. Call a doctor immediately.

Read the following medicine label. Then rephrase the instructions to tell what the user *must* or *must not* do. Make at least five statements.

example: You must not use this medicine if the printed seal is not intact.

USE ONLY IF PRINTED SEAL UNDER CAP IS INTACT.

Adult Dose: Use only as directed by your physician.

WARNINGS: Do not give this medicine to children under age 12. Keep this and all drugs out of the reach of children. In case of an overdose, contact a physician or a poison control center immediately. Do not use this product if you are pregnant or nursing a baby. Do not use this product while operating a vehicle or machinery. Consult your physician before using this product if you have any of the following conditions: heart problems, high blood pressure, asthma.

An important part of first aid is knowing what is serious and what is not—what we must do versus what we don't have to do immediately. Use *must, must not,* or *don't/doesn't have to* to complete each set of sentences.

example: **a.** This is very serious. We _____must_____ hurry!

b. This is not very serious. We _don't have to_ rush.

c. This is very serious. We ____must not____ wait any longer.

1. a. I _____ see a doctor because I'm feeling much better.

   b. I really _____ see a doctor because I've been feeling worse every day.

   c. I _____ wait any longer. I need to see a doctor because I'm very sick.

2. a. This accident is not very serious. We _____ call for an ambulance.

   b. This accident has caused serious injuries. We _____ call for an ambulance.

   c. This accident is serious. We _____ wait a moment longer.

3. a. There is no emergency. We _____ hurry with the victim.

   b. There is an emergency. We _____ delay!

   c. There is an emergency. We _____ get help for the victim immediately.

4. a. That car is going to explode. We _____ move the victim right away.

b. That car is about to explode. We _____ wait. We need to rescue the victim.

c. That car is not in danger. We _____ rescue the victim immediately.

5. a. The situation is under control and everything will be OK. We _____ worry.

b. The situation is serious, and everyone is nervous, but we _____ panic.

c. This situation is very serious, but we all _____ remain calm.

B. Expressing Past Need or Lack of Need

Had to and *didn't have to* are used to talk about past needs. Note that *must* does not have this meaning in the past.

modals	examples	notes
PAST NEED **had to +** *Simple Form*	I **had to** make reservations for a tennis court. **Did** you **have to** give them a deposit?	In affirmative statements and questions, *had to* implies that the action was completed.

modals	examples	notes
PAST LACK OF NEED **didn't have to +** *Simple Form*	I **didn't have to** give a deposit. We **didn't have to** pay in advance.	In negative statements, *did not have to* refers to something that was *not* necessary to do.

 **exercise 5** Imagine that you took a first aid class and practiced what to do in an emergency— a fire in an apartment. Tell what you *had to do* and *didn't have to do* by changing these commands to past tense statements.

example: Rescue the victims quickly and carefully.

We had to rescue the victims.

1. Call the fire department fast!
2. Get a doctor!
3. Check the victims carefully!
4. Don't worry about the cat! It already jumped out the window.
5. Give the child artificial respiration!
6. Don't worry about the dog! It wasn't inside.
7. Check the man for injuries!
8. Control the man's bleeding!

C. Expressing Advice About the Present

modals and related structures		examples	notes
had better (not) should (not) ought (not) to	+ *Simple Form*	He **had better** lose some weight. He **had better not** gain more weight. You **should** get more exercise. **Should** I start an exercise program? You **ought to** start tomorrow.	In affirmative and negative statements and questions, *had better, should,* and *ought to* all express advice. *Had better* and *ought to* are seldom used in questions, however. In rapid speech, *had* is not always pro-nounced in *had better. You'd better* often sounds like /*ya bedder*/. *Ought to* sounds like /*otta*/.

In pairs, take turns making the following statements and responding to them. Make suggestions from the phrases in parentheses or invent your own suggestions. Use *had better, ought to,* and *should.*

> **example:** A: My knee has been swollen and sore since I played tennis.
> (go to an orthopedist)
> B: **You'd better go to an orthopedist.**

1. I've had a headache for several days. (call the doctor)
2. I've had a toothache since last week. (see a dentist)
3. I can't see well at night anymore. (have your eyes checked)
4. I can't get rid of this cold. (stay in bed for a few days)
5. None of my clothes fit anymore. (go on a diet)
6. I'm not doing well in my classes. (study more)
7. I don't understand the next assignment. (talk to the teacher about it)
8. I have a problem with my visa. (check on it right away)

Test your understanding and your memory! Without looking back, write T (true) or F (false) next to the following statements. After you have finished, look back at Exercise 2 on page 122 and check your answers.

1. _____ You should always rescue an accident victim immediately.

2. _____ You should check to make sure the victim is breathing.

3. _____ If the victim is breathing, you ought to try artificial respiration.

4. _____ If you believe that the victim has swallowed a poison, you should give the person water or milk to dilute it.

5. _____ You shouldn't try to give liquids to someone who is unconscious.

6. _____ You should always check for injuries before you try to move a victim.

7. _____ The last thing you ought to do is call for medical help.

8. _____ In most parts of the United States, you should dial 911 for emergency help.

Change the following from commands to affirmative or negative statements by using *should, ought to, had better, have to,* or *must.*

example: If someone feels faint:

- Have the person lie flat with his head low.
  or
- Make the person lower his head between his knees and breathe deeply.

If someone feels faint, you should have him lie flat. You must keep his head low. You should make him breathe deeply.

1. If someone gets cut seriously:
- Try to stop the bleeding at once.
- Use a clean bandage to cover the wound.
- Do not remove the bandage when the bleeding stops.
- Try to raise the wound up high.

2. If you suspect a broken bone:
- Don't let the victim bend the surrounding joints (knee, ankle, elbow, and so on).
- Give first aid for shock.
- Don't touch an open wound.
- Cover the wound gently.

3. If you suspect a head injury:
- Keep the person quiet.
- If possible, do not move him.
- Loosen the clothing around his neck.
- Do not give the person any stimulants (coffee, and so on).

4. If someone is choking:
- Hit the person's back, between the shoulder blades, with the heel of your hand as quickly and forcefully as possible.
  or
- Press against the upper stomach or lower chest several times quickly (the Heimlich maneuver).

5. If someone gets burned (first- or second-degree burns):
- Apply cold water until the pain goes away.
- Dry the burned area very gently.
- Cover the burn with a bandage to protect it, if necessary.
- Do not break any blisters or remove any skin.

D. Expressing Advice About the Past (Not Taken)

modals		examples	notes
should (not) have **ought (not) to have** } + *Past Participle*		You **should have** spent more time practicing. **Should I have** practiced every day? We **ought to have** played much better than we did.	In affirmative and negative statements and questions, *should have* and *ought to have* give advice on past actions or situations. *Ought to have* is seldom used in questions, however. Both imply that the subject did not complete the action or take the advice. In rapid speech, these sound like */shudda/* and */ottuv/*.

In rapid conversation, it is often difficult to distinguish present and perfect modals. As your teacher reads the following sentences, circle the modal form (present or perfect) that you hear.

1. They (should come / should have come).
2. He (ought to set / ought to have set) a specific time.
3. She (should become / should have become) a doctor.
4. She (ought to quit / ought to have quit) her job.
5. It (should cost / should have cost) less.
6. We (shouldn't let / shouldn't have let) that happen.
7. He (ought to run / ought to have run) more often.
8. We (shouldn't shut / shouldn't have shut) all the windows.
9. That (shouldn't hurt / shouldn't have hurt) very much.
10. I (should bet / should have bet) on that horse!

In pairs, respond to the following sentences with a statement using either *should have* or *ought to have*.

example: Jack studied first aid last semester.
I should have studied it too, but I didn't.

1. Veronica went to the dentist last week.
2. Centa ran six miles this morning.

3. Midori took an exercise class last quarter.
4. Ted swam for two hours this morning.
5. Futoshi had a checkup yesterday.
6. Nancy rode her bicycle to school today.
7. Carlos spent several hours in the language lab.
8. Ali studied a lot for the TOEFL.

Veronica was the first to arrive at a car accident. She tried to help, but she panicked and did everything wrong. Use the information from Exercise 8, page 127, to help you tell what she *should (not) / ought (not) to have done.*

> **example:** A young girl had a burn from an accident. Veronica washed the burn with hot water.
>
> **Veronica shouldn't have washed the burn with hot water. She should have applied cold water until the pain stopped.**

1. One man started to faint. Veronica made him stand up quickly.
2. A woman had a head injury. Veronica had the woman walk around and drink several cups of coffee.
3. A boy had serious cuts. Veronica let the boy bleed for a few minutes. Then she covered the wound with a newspaper.
4. Another man had a broken arm. Veronica moved his elbow and shoulder to check them.

Using What You've Learned

Think about the information on first aid that is given in this section. Then work in pairs or small groups and try to give "common sense" answers to the following questions.

> **example:** If someone feels faint, why should you make the person lower his head and breathe deeply?
>
> **The person needs more oxygen going to his brain. Lowering his head will send more blood to the brain.**

1. Should you try to move anyone who has had an accident? Why or why not?
2. Why should you check for injuries before moving a victim?
3. When should you move a victim? Try to give an example.
4. If someone has a serious cut, why should you raise the wound up high?
5. If someone is choking, where and why should you hit the person?
6. If someone has swallowed a chemical poison such as a cleaning fluid, why shouldn't you make the person try to vomit?

activity 2

Around the world, many remedies exist for common problems and ailments. In small groups, share some of your own remedies for the following. Try to use *ought to, should,* and *have to* when possible as you discuss your cures.

1. indigestion	**5.** insomnia	**9.** heartburn
2. hiccups	**6.** a cold	**10.** a cramp in your leg
3. a rash	**7.** a toothache	**11.** stress
4. a headache	**8.** a stomachache	**12.** carsickness or airsickness

activity 3

What did you have to do in order to live and study where you do now? What did your classmates have to do? First, complete the following chart. Try to add two items of your own. Then ask two classmates about their experiences. Finally, take a survey of the classroom. Is there something no one had to do? Are there things everyone had to do?

THINGS TO DO	YOUR NAME: HAD TO	YOUR NAME: DIDN'T HAVE TO	CLASSMATE'S NAME: HAD TO	CLASSMATE'S NAME: DIDN'T HAVE TO	CLASSMATE'S NAME: HAD TO	CLASSMATE'S NAME: DIDN'T HAVE TO
1. apply to many schools	☐	☐	☐	☐	☐	☐
2. pay an application fee	☐	☐	☐	☐	☐	☐
3. take the TOEFL or other tests	☐	☐	☐	☐	☐	☐
4. have an admissions interview	☐	☐	☐	☐	☐	☐
5. obtain a financial statement from your bank	☐	☐	☐	☐	☐	☐
6. get a passport	☐	☐	☐	☐	☐	☐
7. pay a lot of money for a passport	☐	☐	☐	☐	☐	☐
8. get a visa	☐	☐	☐	☐	☐	☐
9. have a medical exam	☐	☐	☐	☐	☐	☐
10. buy medical insurance	☐	☐	☐	☐	☐	☐
11. get a credit card	☐	☐	☐	☐	☐	☐
12. find a place to live	☐	☐	☐	☐	☐	☐
13. buy books	☐	☐	☐	☐	☐	☐
14.	☐	☐	☐	☐	☐	☐
15.	☐	☐	☐	☐	☐	☐

Modal Auxiliaries of Possibility and Probability

Setting the Context

What are *symptoms*?

Test Your Knowledge of Symptoms

You are at the scene of an accident. The victim is weak, pale, and dizzy. His pulse is fast, the pupils of his eyes are different sizes, and his arm is swollen and painful. What are the possibilities? (The answer is at the bottom of the page.)

1. The victim may be in shock.

5

2. The victim might have a head injury.
3. The victim may have broken his arm.
4. All of the above.

Can you give some of the symptoms for these common ailments: a cold, the flu, a sprained ankle?

Answer: 4. All of the above.

A. Expressing Present and Past Possibility

modals	examples	notes
PRESENT POSSIBILITY **may (not)** **might (not)** $\Big\}$ + *Simple Form* **could (not)**	He **may** have a bad case of the flu. He **might** have a bad cold. He **might not** come to school tomorrow. **Could** he have pneumonia?	In affirmative and negative statements, *may (have), might (have),* and *could (have)* all express possibility. All mean "possibly" or "perhaps." *May* is not used with questions with this meaning. In rapid speech, *may have* is pronounced /mayuv/, *might have* is pronounced /mituv/, and *could have* is pronounced /cudduv/.
PAST POSSIBILITY **may (not) have** **might (not) have** $\Big\}$ + *Past Participle* **could (not) have**	She **may have** hurt her leg. She **might have** broken her leg. She **couldn't have** broken it.	

 **exercise 1**   The modals *may, might,* and *could* are often used to suggest possibilities. Negative questions beginning *Why don't you* or *Why don't we* are also used to make suggestions. In threes, practice negative questions and modals of possibility by making short conversations from the following cues. Use the example as a model.

example: have problems with my eyes
see an eye doctor
need glasses

A: **I've been having problems with my eyes.**
B: **Why don't you see an eye doctor?**
C: **You might need glasses.**

1. have a problem with my teeth
see a dentist
have a cavity

2. get earaches lately
go to an ear doctor
have an infection

3. worry a lot lately
take a short trip
need some rest

4. gain weight
get more exercise
go on a diet

5. not do well in my math class
check at the Student Association
be able to get a tutor

6. run out of money each month
talk to someone at the International Students' Office
help you make a budget

7. not get along with my roommate
talk things over
have just a simple misunderstanding

8. feel homesick a lot lately
come to a movie with us
cheer up a little

 Rephrase the following statements to use *may, might,* or *could have.*

example: Mary thinks that she sprained her wrist when she fell down.

Mary may (might) have sprained her wrist when she fell down.

1. Alex fell while skiing, and I think he hurt his leg badly.
2. The nurse thinks that he broke his leg.
3. He's a good skier, but he thinks that he slipped on some ice.
4. Camila thinks she hurt her arm playing tennis.
5. Camila thinks that she sprained her elbow while she was serving.
6. She thinks she tried to serve the ball too hard.
7. She thinks that she twisted her arm while she was serving.
8. Martin thinks he damaged his back while moving.
9. I think he tried to lift too many boxes at once.
10. He thinks he pulled a muscle.

exercise 3 In medicine, the clues used in making "educated guesses" are called *symptoms*. Use the information in the following chart or your own knowledge to diagnose the symptoms below. Use *may, might,* or *could (have)* to make your diagnoses.

SYMPTOMS	POSSIBLE INJURY OR ILLNESS
If the victim is weak, pale, thirsty, cool, nauseated, or sweaty— If the pulse is fast but weak—	the person may be in shock.
If the victim is dizzy or bleeding from the nose, ears, or mouth— If the pulse is slow and strong *or* fast and weak— If the victim cannot move an arm or leg— If the pupils* of the eyes are different sizes—	the person may have a head injury.
If the victim's knee, wrist, ankle, and so on is swollen, tender, bruised, or painful when moved— If the victim's arm, leg, hip, and so on is swollen, tender to the touch, bruised, very painful when moved, or deformed in shape—	the person may have sprained a joint (knee, wrist, ankle, and so on). the person may have broken a bone (arm, leg, hip, and so on).
If the victim is coughing, nauseated, or dizzy— If the victim has pain in the chest, trouble breathing, or a bluish color in the lips and around the fingernails—	the person may have had a heart attack.

*pupil   center point in the eye

example: The victim is weak and pale.

The victim could be in shock.

1. The victim's pulse is fast.
2. The victim is dizzy.
3. The victim's knee is swollen.
4. The victim is very thirsty.
5. The victim's pupils are different sizes.
6. The victim feels great pain when his arm is moved.

7. The victim suddenly felt sharp pains in his chest. He is breathing with great difficulty.
8. The victim fell while roller-skating. Her wrist is swollen and tender. She cannot move it without a great deal of pain.
9. The victim was in a car accident. She is dizzy and cannot move her arm.
10. The victim was jogging. His ankle and the back of his leg are very sore.

B. Expressing Present and Past Probability

modals	examples	notes
PRESENT PROBABILITY **must (not) +** *Simple Form*	You **must** be in shock from the accident. Your head **must** hurt a lot! You **must not** feel good.	In affirmative and negative statements, *must* and *must have* express probability. Both mean "probably." *Must* is not used in questions with this meaning. In rapid speech, *must have* is pronounced /mustuv/.
PAST PROBABILITY **must (not) have +** *Past Participle*	You **must have** been in shock after the accident. Your head **must have** hurt terribly. You **must not have** felt good.	

 **exercise 4**   In pairs, take turns making statements and responses. Use *must* with the cues in parentheses to form your responses.

example: I didn't sleep very well last night. (be tired)
You must be tired.

1. The food at lunch today was very salty. (be thirsty)
2. The food at the other cafeteria is good today. (have a new cook)
3. Every time I eat carrots, I get a rash. (be allergic to them)
4. I burned my hand on the stove last night. (hurt)
5. I can't read signs when I'm driving. (need glasses)
6. My friend sprained her knee playing tennis. (not be able to walk very well)
7. Every time I'm near a cat, I sneeze. (have an allergy to them)
8. My roommate stayed up all night studying. (feel exhausted)

We use statements with *must have* + past participle to empathize with another person's problems or pain. In pairs, use the cues and take turns making statements and responses with *must have*. Use the example as a model.

> **example:** break / leg
> walk
>
> > A: **I broke my leg last year (last month, last week).**
> > B: **It must have been difficult for you to walk.**

1. break / jaw
   eat

2. sprain / wrist
   write

3. have / ear infection
   hear

4. drink / coffee constantly
   sleep

5. have / noisy roommates
   study

6. lose / my glasses
   read

Use *must have felt* + adjective in responses showing empathy. In pairs, take turns making the following statements and responding.

> **example:** Before I came here, I applied for a scholarship and I got it.
>
> > A: **Before I came here, I applied for a scholarship and I got it.**
> > B: **You must have felt happy (thrilled, excited).**

1. I had to have all my wisdom teeth pulled last month.
2. I went to a lecture last week that was so long and complicated I couldn't understand a word.
3. Last weekend, I tried skydiving for the first time.
4. Someone tried to break into my apartment last week.
5. I won a contest for a poem I wrote.
6. I ran in the marathon this past weekend.

Review. Make statements about the following. Use the different types of modals indicated.

> **example:** The Nelsons are coming here for dinner around 6:00. It's 5:00.
>
> Expectation: They should arrive in about an hour.

1. I haven't put the roast in the oven yet.

   Advice: _____

2. The house is a mess.

   Advice: _____

   Past advice: _____

3. I don't have enough time to get everything ready by 6:00.

Past advice: _____

Possibility: _____

4. I'm going to call the Nelsons to ask them to come at 6:30.

Request (to the Nelsons): _____

5. It's 6:45, and the Nelsons are not here yet.

Possibility: _____

Possibility: _____

6. It's 6:50, and the phone is ringing.

Probability: _____

7. The Nelsons are at the hospital.

Present or past probability: _____

Request (to the Nelsons): _____

8. Present probability: _____

exercise 8   Reread the opening passage "How Healthy Are You?" on page 104. Then do the following:

1. Underline all the modal auxiliaries in the passage. What form of the verb follows each modal?
2. Find the verb in line 1. What form follows the expression *are able*? Can you substitute a modal auxiliary and keep the same basic meaning? Do you need to make any changes?
3. Find the verb in line 3. What form follows the verb *has*? Can you substitute a modal auxiliary and keep the same basic meaning? Do you need to make any changes?
4. Look at these pairs of sentences. Can you explain any differences in meaning?

   a. That person may need fewer calories per day.   That person needs fewer calories per day.

   b. Some people might prefer strenuous exercise.   Some people prefer strenuous exercise.

   c. Another person would rather play golf.   Another person plays golf.

   d. You can lower the risk by exercising.   You lower the risk by exercising.

Using What You've Learned

activity

Is anyone absent from your class today? Does anyone look particularly excited or happy? Does anyone look worried? Try to guess why.

example: Jorge's not here.

He may be sick.
He might have gone away for a long weekend.
He must not have done his homework!

activity 2

In emotional situations, we often use *must feel* + adjective in a response to empathize with someone—to show that we understand. In pairs or small groups, take turns making statements and responding. Choose appropriate adjectives for your responses. Use these words and statements, or create your own.

POSITIVE EMOTIONS	NEGATIVE EMOTIONS
ecstatic	angry
excited	awful
happy	bored
pleased	depressed
proud	exhausted
thrilled	frightened
	frustrated
	nervous
	sad
	scared
	stressed
	terrible
	upset

example: A: I just won $500 in a contest!
          B: **You must feel ecstatic!**

1. I just went to the dentist, and I have a lot of cavities.
2. I just got a bill from the doctor for $700!
3. I stayed up all night studying.
4. I just got some very bad news from home.
5. I have an interview this afternoon for admission to the university.
6. I'm taking the GMAT* on Saturday
7. I just got my TOEFL† scores back. I got 680!
8. I just got my TOEFL scores back. I got 380.

GMAT   Graduate Management Admission Test
†*TOEFL*   Test of English as a Foreign Language

Use of Modal Auxiliaries

Modal auxiliaries are frequently tested on standardized English proficiency exams. Review these commonly tested structures and check your understanding by completing the sample items below.

Remember that . . .

- Modal auxiliaries are followed by the simple form of a verb.
- Perfect modal auxiliaries used modal + *have* + past participle.

Part 1: Circle the correct completion for the following sentences.

example: John _____ sick; he didn't go to class yesterday.
    a. may   **c.** must
    b. may have being   (**d.**) must have been

1. A person who is physically fit _____ the same weight.
    a. should be able stay   **c.** should being able to stay
    b. should to be able stay   **d.** should be able to stay

2. Syrup of ipecac _____ the best known antidote to most poisons.
    a. maybe   **c.** may be
    b. may to be   **d.** may being

3. If an accident victim is dizzy and cannot move an arm or leg, she _____ a head injury.
    a. could be have   **c.** could be had
    b. could have   **d.** could had had

Part 2: Circle the letter below the underlined word(s) containing an error.

example: An individual may to feel frustrated if she has difficulties in
                 Ⓐ   B
    speaking the language of the country where she is living.
      C   D

1. She would much rather to exercise moderately than strenuously.
           A   B   C   D

2. A person may had had a heart attack if he or she has chest pain
              A   B   C
    and breathing difficulties.
        D

3. Most people who eat a healthy diet should be able get all the
              A   B
    calcium they need from their normal food intake.
        C   D

Review: Chapters One to Four

exercise **1** **Review.**   The following story is about a serious accident. First read the passage to become familiar with the story; don't focus on the verbs. Then go back and choose the correct form from each pair in parentheses. Finally read the story a third time, aloud or to yourself, using each correct verb form.

AN UNFORGETTABLE EMERGENCY

This experience (happened / was happening) several years ago, but I
1
(still have not forgotten / still am not forgetting) any of it. It (is / was) a
2   3
beautiful afternoon in November, and the sun (was setting / is setting). I
4
(was driving / drove) up the California coast just north of Shell Beach when I
5
(was coming / came) upon an accident. A car and a truck (had crashed / were
6   7
crashing) a few moments before I (got / get) there, and I (can see / could see)
8   9
injured people in both. Smoke (had already started / had started already) to
10
come out of the car, and I (am / was) afraid that it (started / was going to start)
11   12
burning in a minute. I (stopped / was stopping) my car and (jumped / was
13   14
jumping) out. Then I (froze / had frozen). For a moment, I (shouldn't
15
remember / couldn't remember) any first aid. What (should / may) I (do / to do)
16   17   18
first? I (was shaking / had shaken) like crazy. It (was seeming / seemed) like
19   20

hours (pass / had passed), but it (must have been / must be) only about ten seconds. Then I (say / said) to myself, "Get control! You (have to / don't have to)
help these people!" Finally, I (was able to / am able to) move. I (run / ran) to
the car. The man in the car (was / were) unconscious, and he (was bleeding /
were bleeding) badly. I (had / should) to move him because of the fire. He
(be / was) very heavy, but I (was able / could) to pull him out and drag him
far enough away. Then I (helped / was helping) the man out of the truck. His
legs (was / were) broken, so I (had to be / must have been) very careful. I
(should make / should have made) a splint, but there (wasn't / weren't)
enough time. Just after I (had rescued / have rescued) both men, the car (had
exploded / exploded). Both men (survived / were surviving), thank goodness.

exercise 2

Review.   Complete the following passage with appropriate forms of the verbs in
parentheses. In some cases, more than one tense is possible. Explain any differences in meaning in these cases. The first one is done as an example.

AMERICAN EATING HABITS

In recent years, many changes <u>have taken (have been taking)</u> place in the

                                        1 (take)

American diet. Traditional meals _____ less common. Today, Amer-

                                        2 (become)

icans _____ meals "from scratch" as often as they _____

            3 (not make)   4 (do)

in the past. More and more Americans _____ microwavable and

                                                        5 (buy)

other fast foods to heat at home.

Eating at home _____ less common, and restaurants _____

                            6 (become / also)   7 (become)

_____ a major part of Americans lives. Today, Americans _____

                                                                        8 (spend)

43 cents of every food dollar on meals that they _____ away from

                                                        9 (eat)

home. In 1980, Americans _____ 36 cents on meals away from

                            10 (spend)

home. In 1955, the amount _____ only 25 cents.

                                        11 (be)

Over the years, these changes in eating habits _____ jobs

                                                        12 (affect)

nationwide. Since the 1970s, the restaurant industry _____ tre-

                                                        13 (grow)

mendously in the United States. Today, approximately 9 million people

_____ in food service industries.

        14 (work)

exercise 3   **Review.**   In the following sentences, add the words in parentheses to each sentence.

> **example:**   Americans don't have healthy diets.
> (very, many)
>
> **Many Americans don't have very healthy diets.**

1. Scientists say that many habits may be dangerous to health.
   (eating, very, American, our)

2. American rates are among the highest.
   (of heart disease, in the world, and, of cancer)

3. Studies have been done on diet and health.
   (between, in the last twenty years, numerous, the connection)

4. Today, Americans are worried about diets.
   (their, many)

5. Half don't eat fruit.
   (daily, any, of all Americans)

6. Researchers believe that fruit and vegetables protect against cancer.
   (us, many, actively)

7. Fruit and vegetables protect against disease.
   (also, heart, may)

8. Vegetables are rich in vitamins and minerals.
   (such as broccoli, important, green, dark)

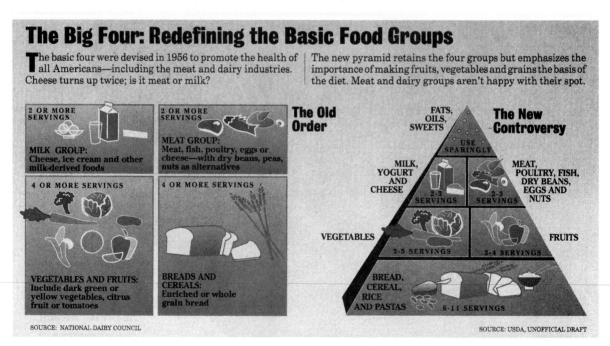

The Big Four: Redefining the Basic Food Groups

The basic four were devised in 1956 to promote the health of all Americans—including the meat and dairy industries. Cheese turns up twice; is it meat or milk?

The new pyramid retains the four groups but emphasizes the importance of making fruits, vegetables and grains the basis of the diet. Meat and dairy groups aren't happy with their spot.

The Old Order

2 OR MORE SERVINGS

MILK GROUP:
Cheese, ice cream and other milk-derived foods

2 OR MORE SERVINGS

MEAT GROUP:
Meat, fish, poultry, eggs or cheese—with dry beans, peas, nuts as alternatives

4 OR MORE SERVINGS

VEGETABLES AND FRUITS:
Include dark green or yellow vegetables, citrus fruit or tomatoes

4 OR MORE SERVINGS

BREADS AND CEREALS:
Enriched or whole grain bread

SOURCE: NATIONAL DAIRY COUNCIL

The New Controversy

FATS, OILS, SWEETS   USE SPARINGLY

MILK, YOGURT AND CHEESE   2-3 SERVINGS

MEAT, POULTRY, FISH, DRY BEANS, EGGS AND NUTS   2-3 SERVINGS

VEGETABLES   3-5 SERVINGS

FRUITS   2-4 SERVINGS

BREAD, CEREAL, RICE AND PASTAS   6-11 SERVINGS

SOURCE: USDA, UNOFFICIAL DRAFT

 Work in pairs, asking and answering questions in order to complete the charts below and on page 144. One student should look at Chart 1, and the other should look at Chart 2. Here are some sample questions. Try to add your own questions, too.

Which foods give us Vitamin _____ ?
Where can we get Vitamin _____ ?

What are the benefits of Vitamin _____ ?
How does Vitamin _____ help us?

What are the possible benefits of _____ ?
How might _____ help us?

Vitamins—Chart 1					
A / BETA CAROTENE	B	C	D	E	K
A: liver, egg yolks, whole milk, butter Beta Carotene: dark green leafy vegetables, yellow and orange vegetables and fruits			Liver, butter fatty fish, egg yolks, fortified milk. Also produced when your skin is exposed to sunlight		Leafy vegetables, corn and soybean oils, liver, cereals, dairy products, meat, fruit
	Helps prevent anemia and nerve damage			Helps prevent anemia	
		May help reduce the risk of cancer, heart disease, and blindness in the elderly	May help prevent bone and kidney disease	May reduce the risk of heart attacks	Possible role in cancer prevention

Vitamins—Chart 2					
A / BETA CAROTENE	**B**	**C**	**D**	**E**	**K**
	Meat, poultry, fish, fruit, nuts, vegetables	Citrus fruit, green peppers, strawberries, raw cabbage, green leafy vegetables		Nuts, seeds, whole grains, vegetables, and fish-liver oils.	
Prevents night blindness		Prevents loose teeth; fights hemorrhage	Prevents the malformation of bones		Helps prevent hemorrhage
May reduce the risk of cancer, heart disease, and blindness in the elderly	May protect against nerve damage in unborn babies				

focus on testing

Review of Problem Areas: Chapters One to Four

A variety of problem areas are included in this test. Check your under-standing by completing the sample items below.

Part 1: Circle the correct completion for the following.

example: John seems _____ with his work.

    a. happily   **c.** contentment

    (b.) happy   **d.** contentedly

  1. The new research park being developed here _____ to a consortium of investors.

    a. is belonging   **c.** is belong

    b. belonging   **d.** belongs

  2. Would they mind _____ late?

    a. if I come   **c.** if I came

    b. to come   **d.** to coming

3. Dust devils spins like tornados but _____ more than two or three hundred feet in the air.
- **a.** rarely reaches
- **b.** reaches rarely
- **c.** reach rarely
- **d.** rarely reach

4. Vitamins C and E _____ help to deter cataracts from developing.
- **a.** may
- **b.** may be
- **c.** must be
- **d.** must

5. Using a different order of words can _____ of a sentence.
- **a.** change often the meaning
- **b.** change the meaning often
- **c.** to change often the meaning
- **d.** often change the meaning

Part 2: Circle the letter below the underlined word(s) containing an error.

example: An individual may feel frustrated if she <u>have</u> <u>difficulties</u> in
           (A)   B
           <u>speaking</u> the language of the country <u>where she is living.</u>
           C   D

1. <u>Physically fit</u> people <u>should</u> be able <u>stay</u> the <u>same weight</u> over a
       A   B   C   D
period of several years.

2. Before the Second World War <u>had ended</u>, the number of people in
       A   B
the United States <u>working</u> in agriculture <u>had dropped</u> substantially.
                  C   D

3. Doctors <u>has discovered</u> that <u>chronic pain</u> <u>can have</u> a <u>strong</u>
               A   B   C   D
psychological component.

4. Coal and oil were formed <u>when</u> plants <u>become</u> buried <u>in marshes</u>
                               A   B   C
or swamps and then <u>decayed.</u>
                   D

5. Although <u>traveling</u> in a foreign country is <u>usually</u> very interesting
                A   B
and exciting, it <u>can often be</u> tiring <u>extremely.</u>
                 C   D

CHAPTER five

High Tech, Low Tech

in this chapter

Introduction

In this chapter you will study the forms and uses of verbs in the passive voice. You will notice that the time frame of a passive verb may be the same as that of an active verb, but the focus of the passive sentence is quite different. As you study the chapter, pay careful attention to the focus of the passive constructions.

The following passage introduces the chapter theme, High Tech, Low Tech, and raises some of the topics and issues you will cover in the chapter.

Old and New Technology

Old inventions are not necessarily eliminated by new ones. After all, people did not stop riding bicycles after the car was invented. Thus, older inventions may be replaced, but they seldom disappear because new roles are created for them. Some of the best examples of this are from the field of long-distance
5 communication.

Until the nineteenth century, communication had been limited by distance and time. Then came a series of amazing inventions that extended the range of human communication. Each of these inventions was expected to replace existing technology. For example, when the telephone was invented in 1876, it was
10 feared that letters would become obsolete. When television was introduced in the 1940s, many people predicted the "death" of radio. And as television became more popular, people worried that it would lead to the "death" of books and reading.

But it is clear that these predictions were wrong. The older technologies—
15 letters, books, and the radio—have not disappeared. Instead, their roles have been changed by the appearance of new technology. Television, together with the automobile, has provided a new role for the radio. Both television and the radio have created new roles for the newspaper. And all of these have affected the book.

20 We can only imagine what means of communication may be invented in the twenty-first century. But one thing is certain: Older inventions—like the book, the newspaper, the telephone, or the television—will not be eliminated, although their roles may be changed greatly.

discussing ideas

Something becomes obsolete when it no longer has any useful purpose. In today's world of high technology, new developments may seem to make old inventions obsolete almost overnight. Yet is this true? Are any of these old inventions really obsolete?

The Simple Tenses

Setting the Context

What do you know about early forms of long-distance communication? How did people communicate with each other from far away?

The Telephone: Past, Present, and Future

During most of human history, even the most important news was difficult to deliver. Then, in the 1800s, the telephone was invented. At first people were suspicious of the new technology, but today millions of phone calls are made daily by people all over the world. Some offices already have "videophones"— telephones connected to video screens that allow callers to see one another as they speak. In the future, videophones will be installed in every home and office, just as ordinary telephones are today.

5

What would your life be like today without telephones? What will your life be like in a world of "videophones"?

A. Introduction to the Passive Voice

Most transitive verbs (verbs that take an object) can be used in both the active voice and the passive voice. A form of the verb *be* is always used in passive sentences. It is singular or plural to agree with the subject, and it also tells the tense of the passive construction. You will notice that the time frame of a passive verb may be the same as that of an active verb, but the focus of the sentence is different.

	examples	focus
Active	subject verb direct object Alexander Graham Bell **invented** the telephone.	Alexander Graham Bell
Passive	agent The telephone **was invented** by Alexander Graham Bell.	the telephone
Active	subject verb direct object Millions of people **use** telephones every day.	millions of people
Passive	agent Telephones **are used** by millions of people every day.	telephones

exercise 1 Which of the following sentences are in the active voice and which are in the passive voice? Label each. Then label the subject (S), verb (V), object (O), and/or agent (A) in each sentence. Finally, tell the primary focus of each sentence.

example:

                                  S   V   A

    <u>Passive</u> The first fax machine was manufactured by Muirhead, Ltd., of England. Focus: the first fax machine

                                    S   V

    <u>Active</u> Muirhead, Ltd., of England manufactured the first fax

                    O

    machine. Focus: Muirhead, Ltd.

1. _____ The telephone was invented by Alexander Graham Bell in 1876.

2. _____ Intel Corporation created the first microprocessor for computers in 1971.

3. _____ The Walkman was developed by Sony Corporation in 1979.

4. _____ Bank credit cards were first introduced by Bank of America in 1958.

5. _____ Willis Carrier of the United States invented air conditioning in 1911.

6. _____ Mattel Toy Co. created the Barbie doll in 1958.

7. _____ Penicillin was discovered by Sir Alexander Fleming in 1928.

8. _____ Warner Brothers introduced movies with sound in 1927.

9. _____ The phonograph was invented by Thomas Edison in 1877.

10. _____ Coca-Cola was formulated by Dr. John Pemberton in 1886.

11. _____ Chocolate in the form that we eat today was first produced by Rodophe Lindt of Switzerland in 1880.

12. _____ The American Express Company invented travelers' checks in 1891.

 # B. The Passive Voice with Simple Tenses

The passive voice of verbs in simple tenses is formed in this way: *(will) be (am, is, are, was, were)* + past participle *(+ by + agent)*. Adverbs of frequency usually come after the first auxiliary verb. The passive forms have the same general meanings and time frames as verbs in the active voice.

		examples	**focus**
Simple Past	**Active**	The phone company **installed** a new phone system in our office.	the phone company
	Passive	A new phone system **was installed** in our office (by the phone company).	a new phone system
Simple Present	**Active**	The phone company **installs** many new phone systems every day.	the phone company
	Passive	Many new phone systems **are installed** (by the phone company) every day.	many new phone systems
Simple Future	**Active**	The phone company **will install** a new system next week.	the phone company
	Passive	A new phone system **will be installed** (by the phone company) next week.	a new phone system

exercise 2 Underline all uses of the passive voice in the passage "The Telephone: Past, Present, and Future" on page 149. Give the tense and time frame of each.

exercise 3 Complete the following by using the past, present, or future tense of the verbs in parentheses. Use the passive voice.

example: Until 1876, most day-to-day information <u>was communicated</u> (communicate) by letter, newspapers, or conversation.

1876

1. The telephone _____ (invent) in 1876.

2. Today the telephone _____ (take) for granted by much of the world.

3. Between 1950 and 1975, over 2.3 *trillion* (2,300,000,000,000) telephone calls _____ (make) by Bell Telephone customers in the United States.

1886

4. Over 400 million telephones _____ (use) daily by people throughout the world.

5. Today, almost the entire world _____ (connect) by telephone.

6. In many offices, the phone _____ (connect) to other "high-tech" communication devices.

1927

7. Messages _____ (record) on answering machines.

8. Written documents _____ (transmit) by fax machine millions of times each day.

9. In the future, new ways of conveying information _____ (invent).

1990

10. All of our lives _____ (affect) by these new means of communication.

C. The Passive Voice in Sentences with Indirect Objects

In active-voice sentences with both a direct and an indirect object, either object may become the subject of the corresponding passive sentence.

	Active	Passive
Direct Object	The United States gave **the patent** for the telephone to Bell.	**The patent** for the telephone was given to Bell by the United States.
Indirect Object	The United States gave **Bell** the patent for the telephone.	**Bell** was given the patent for the telephone by the United States.

Sit in groups of three students. Student A should read the active-voice sentences below. Students B and C should change them to the passive voice. Follow the example.

example: A: The school secretary gave Sam an important message.
B: **Sam was given an important message by the school secretary.**
C: **An important message was given to Sam by the school secretary.**

1. The phone company sent me information about new types of phone service.
2. Mrs. Jones will give the results of the test to the students within the next week.
3. The salesman showed Mr. Sanchez some computer software.
4. Every year, a rich businesswoman gives our town $100,000 to spend on the schools.
5. The judges awarded Joseph first prize in the essay contest.
6. My father lent me that beautiful sports car.

The sentences on the next page are in the active voice. Some of the sentences have objects, but others, with linking verbs, do not. Decide which sentences can be changed to the passive voice. Label the subject (S), verb (V), and object (O) in each sentence. Then change the sentence to the passive voice. In sentences with a direct and an indirect object, give both possibilities.

example: Philipp Reis was a German inventor.   *cannot be changed*
              S   V

              S   V   O
             Reis designed an early telephone around 1861.   *can be changed*
             An early telephone was designed by Reis around 1861.

1. We learn in school that Alexander Graham Bell invented the telephone.

2. The true story is more dramatic, however.

3. In 1876, two inventors completed patent applications on the same day.

4. One was a schoolteacher named Alexander Graham Bell.

5. The other was a professional inventor named Elisha Gray.

6. Gray and Bell did not work together.

7. The two inventors developed very similar telephones.

8. Gray finished first.

9. However, the U.S. patent office received Bell's application two hours before Gray's.

10. Thus, the Patent Office gave the official patent to Alexander Graham Bell.

11. Elisha Gray took Bell to court.

12. Gray sued Bell for the rights to the talking machine.

13. Bell won in court.

14. To this day, the whole world gives credit to Bell for inventing the telephone.

 **exercise 6** Marc, Sharon, and Annette McLean are planning a surprise party for their parents' anniversary Friday evening. Today is Thursday. The list below shows which tasks the children completed before today. (These tasks are indicated by a √). Other tasks will be done as indicated. Use the information in the list to write ten additional passive sentences in the past and future tenses.

example: The invitations were ordered by Marc two months ago.
The turkey will be cooked by Annette on Friday afternoon.

MARC	SHARON	ANNETTE
√ order invitations— 2 months ago	√ pick up invitations from printer—1 month ago	√ address and mail invitations—3 weeks ago
buy flowers—Friday afternoon	bake the cake— Wednesday night	cook the turkey— Friday afternoon
set the table—Friday afternoon	√ buy champagne— Tuesday	√ buy decorations—last week
clean the house— Friday morning	clean the house— Friday morning	put up the decorations—Friday afternoon

D. *by + Agent*

By + noun (or pronoun) can be used in passive sentences to tell who or what performed the action of the verb. However, most passive sentences in English do *not* contain these phrases. Use *by* + agent only if the phrase gives the following information.

	examples	notes
Information Necessary to the Meaning of the Sentence	The majority of overseas phone calls are transmitted **by satellite.**	*By* + agent must be used if the sentence is meaningless without it.
A Name or Idea that Is Important in the Context	The telephone was invented by **Alexander Graham Bell.** Telephones are made ~~by people~~ in factories.	Proper names are often included because they give specific information. Other nouns and pronouns are often omitted.
New or Unusual Information	Today most overseas calls are transmitted **by satellite.**	*By* + agent is generally included if the phrase introduces new or unusual information.
	The calls are beamed ~~by satellite~~ from one country to another.	After the agent is understood, the phrase is usually omitted to avoid repetition.

 In a "team" or "group" effort, the final result or product is more important than the effort of each individual. In speaking and in writing, passive sentences are often used to focus on the product or result. Passive sentences without *by* + agent give even more emphasis to *what was done,* not *who did it.*

Look at your sentences from Exercise 6 again. Rewrite each sentence, but this time, omit *by* + agent. Compare each set of sentences, and notice the difference in emphasis.

example: order invitations—two months ago

The invitations were ordered by Marc two months ago.
The invitations were ordered two months ago.

(The second sentence puts more emphasis on the action.)

Read the passive-voice sentences below and underline the phrase with *by* in each sentence. Then decide whether each *by* + agent is necessary to the meaning of the sentence. Tell which phrases you would omit and why.

examples: SENTENCE 1 **Do not omit the phrase because it tells *who* started the company.**

SENTENCE 2 **The phrase can be omitted. It is obvious that the companies were created by people.**

1. Federal Express, the first overnight package delivery company, was started by Frederick Smith in 1973.
2. Similar companies were created by people in the years that followed.
3. Before Federal Express was created by Smith, packages were always shipped by air freight companies on regular commercial airlines.
4. In those days, fast delivery of packages was never guaranteed by anybody.
5. Commercial airline flights were often delayed by bad weather or equipment problems.
6. Packages were sometimes lost by the airlines.
7. Sometimes packages were delivered by the air freight companies weeks after the mailing date.
8. At Federal Express, overnight delivery is guaranteed by the company.*
9. Federal Express planes and trucks are used by the company in order to guarantee service.
10. Currently, over 2 million packages are delivered worldwide by Federal Express each day.

One very common use of the passive voice is in the description of processes. The paragraph below describes a process. Rewrite it, changing sentences from the active voice to the passive whenever possible. Use *by* + agent only if it is important to the meaning of the passive sentence.

THE WORK OF AN URBAN BOMB SQUAD

Bomb squads are an unfortunate necessity in many cities these days. These squads are special police units. Their function is to respond to bomb threats, locate a bomb if there is one, and remove it safely from the premises. As soon as the bomb squad arrives at the scene of a bomb threat, several things happen. First, the bomb squad evacuates the building. Then, the bomb squad searches the building. If the members of the squad find a bomb, they remove it from the building. They take the bomb outside, and they place it inside a specially designed van. Once the bomb is inside the van, the bomb squad explodes it. The

---

*The slogan of Federal Express is "absolutely positively overnight."

bomb squad allows the occupants of the building to go back inside only after the squad has determined that it is safe.

 exercise 10   Working in pairs, take turns asking and answering questions using the cues below. Add words as needed to form correct sentences. Use the passive voice in your answers whenever possible.

> **example:**   car / steal
>> A: **What happened to your car?**
>> B: **It was stolen.**

1. goldfish / die
2. brother / transfer to New York
3. photocopier in your office / break down
4. house / paint
5. cat / disappear two weeks ago
6. children / go inside to eat lunch
7. grandmother's house / destroy in a fire
8. newspaper / not deliver today
9. the receptionist / promote to office manager
10. baseball game / cancel

E. Verbs Commonly Used in the Passive Voice

These verbs are frequently used in the passive voice. A variety of prepositions can follow them; *by* is also used, depending on the context.

verbs		examples
be based on	be located in (at, on)	The movie **was based on** the novel.
be connected to	be made of (from)	Wash your hands! You **are covered with** dirt!
be covered with	be made up of	
be filled with (by)	be related to	He **was known for** his honesty.
be formed of (from, by)	be used for (as, with)	He **was known as** a very honest person.
be known for (as)	be used to + *verb*	
be known to + *verb*		The class **is made up of** students from many places.
be involved in (with)		She **is related to** the president of the firm.

Note: See Chapter Seven for information on verbs of emotion in passive constructions (*He's interested in sports. I'm bored with this book*).

Complete the following sentences by adding appropriate forms of the verbs in parentheses. Use past, present, or future tenses. Then add appropriate prepositions in the spaces provided. Include adverbs when indicated.

> **example:** Today, magazines and newspapers ___are filled___ (fill) _with_ stories about the Internet.

1. Electronic mail, which _____ (know / commonly) _____ e-mail, is the fastest growing means of communication in the world.

2. Today, over 30 million people from all seven continents _____ (connect) _____ each other through the Internet.

3. Today's Internet _____ (base) _____ a network for researchers in the United States during the 1970s.

4. The original network of the 1970s _____ (use) _____ communicating about research projects at different universities.

5. At that time, most of the research projects _____ (relate) _____ the defense industry.

6. Today, the Internet _____ (make / actually) _____ _____ hundreds of regional computer networks.

7. Today, networks _____ (locate) _____ in over sixty countries.

F. Anticipatory *it* and the Passive Voice

The passive voice is often used with *it* to avoid mentioning the agent or source. *By* + agent is rarely used with these constructions. *It* is often used with the passive form of verbs such as *believe, confirm, deny, estimate, fear, hope, mention, report, say,* and *think*.

	examples	notes
Active	**People said,** "The earth is flat."	Past expressions like *it was believed* indicate that these ideas often have changed. *That* is added when a direct quote is changed to reported speech. In reported speech, verbs often shift to past tenses. See Chapter Twelve for more information on reported speech.
Passive	**It was said,** "The earth is flat."	
	It was said that the earth **was** flat.	

As we learn more about our world, many of our beliefs change. Expressions such as *it was believed, felt, thought,* or *said that . . .* are used to indicate past beliefs that have changed. In these cases, *would* and *was/were going to* express "the future in the past."

Rephrase the following quotations to include these expressions:

- It was believed that . . .
- It was said that . . .
- It was felt that . . .
- It was feared that . . .
- It was thought that . . .
- It was hoped that . . .

Note: remember to use past forms in the *that* clause.

examples: "The telephone is going to change people's lives."

It was feared that the telephone was going to change people's lives.

"People won't write letters anymore."

It was believed that people wouldn't write letters anymore.

1. "People will forget how to read."
2. "Parents will not be able to supervise their children's conversations."
3. "Telephones are going to eliminate the postal service."
4. "Paper companies will go out of business."
5. "People are going to gossip more."
6. "People are not going to have any privacy."
7. "People won't send telegraphs anymore."
8. "Letters will become obsolete."

 exercise **13**

First read the passage here and on the next page for meaning. Then complete the passage with either active or passive forms (simple present or past tenses) of the verbs in parentheses. The first two are done as examples.

THE IMPACT OF THE TELEPHONE

Many new inventions ___*are used*___ every day, but the telephone
                        1 (use)

___*became*___ an everyday item faster than almost any other invention in
  2 (become)

history. In May 1877, 6 telephones _____ in commercial use. In
                                          3 (be)

November 1877, there _____ 3,000, and by 1881, 133,000.
                            4 (be)

Today, people everywhere _____ by the telephone,
                                5 (affect)

although most of us _____ it without really thinking about it. In
                          6 (use)

the beginning, however, many people _____ the telephone. It
                                          7 (fear)

_____ by some that the telephone _____ evil, and laws
  8 (believe)   9 (be)

_____ by a few to prohibit telephones in bedrooms in order to
  10 (suggest)

prevent secret conversations. (Telephones would allow private romantic conversations, and this would corrupt people, especially young girls!) But, these ideas and fears _____ as the demand for telephones grew.

<u>11 (overcome)</u>

At first in the United States, young boys _____ to operate the

<u>12 (employ)</u>

telephone switchboards, but because of their bad language and tricks many of them _____ their jobs. Soon, in September 1878, Emma M. Nutt

<u>13 (lose)</u>

_____ as the first woman telephone operator. In France, women

<u>14 (hire)</u>

_____ from the beginning. This was in part because all boys and

<u>15 (employ)</u>

young men _____ to serve in the army. More important, the

<u>16 (require)</u>

female voice _____ much clearer over early telephone lines.

<u>17 (sound)</u>

In the late 1800s, the telephone, together with the typewriter,

_____ thousands of women to work in offices. New fashions

<u>18 (bring)</u>

_____ to suit the needs of female workers, and "appropriate"

<u>19 (create)</u>

clothing for work _____. The shirtwaist dress and the blouse

<u>20 (introduce / soon)</u>

_____ for women "going to business." The telephone, obviously,

<u>21 (design)</u>

_____ begin the social revolution that _____ today.

<u>22 (help)</u>   <u>23 (continue)</u>

Today, the telephone _____ so much a part of our lives that we
24 (be)

_____ it unless it _____ out of order. In fact, with over
25 (not notice)   26 (be)

300 million telephones worldwide, no other invention _____ so
27 (use)

much.

Using What You've Learned

activity

Have you ever played quiz games like $10,000 Pyramid or Trivial Pursuit? These
are question-and-answer games based on categories of information. To play a
classroom version, first choose several (five or six) categories: music, art, inventions, buildings, discoveries, and so forth. Then separate into two teams, and make
at least five questions for each category. For example, "Who invented the sewing
machine?" or "Name the composer(s) of 'Hey Jude.'" Don't let the other group
hear you; they will be asked these questions. After you have completed your questions, give them to your teacher.

Play the game by choosing categories and questions. Your teacher will ask
each team the questions; a different member must answer each time. You may play
until you reach a certain score or until all the questions have been asked. You may
also add special rules such as, "An answer must be grammatically correct to score
points," or "Five bonus points are given for a correct answer using the passive
voice."

TOPIC **two**
The Perfect Tenses

Setting the Context

*previewing
the
passage*

What are *gadgets*? Can you give any synonyms—words that have the same
meaning?

Gadgets, Gadgets, and More Gadgets!

In the past 50 years, our way of life has been revolutionized by gadgets of all
types: television sets and VCRs, microwave ovens and garage door openers,
cordless phones and laptop computers, just to name a few. Until the 1940s or
1950s, however, most of these common household items had not even been
5   dreamed of!

COMMITTED By Michael Fry

Can you name other common gadgets that did not exist fifteen or twenty years ago? What new gadgets do you think will be created soon?

The Passive Voice with Perfect Tenses

The passive voice of verbs in perfect tenses is formed in this way: *have (has, have, had)* + *been* + past participle (+ *by* + agent). Adverbs of frequency usually come after the auxiliary *have*.

		examples	focus
Present Perfect	**Active**	New technology **has revolutionized** the communications industry.	new technology
	Passive	The communications industry **has been revolutionized** by new technology.	the communications industry

		examples	focus
Past Perfect	**Active**	Before the 1950s, researchers **had not yet developed** high-quality audio and video equipment.	researchers
	Passive	Before the 1950s, high-quality audio and video equipment **had not yet been developed.**	high-quality audio and video equipment

 The list below shows "old" inventions and the newer inventions that have replaced them. Form sentences using the present perfect tense, passive voice. If possible, add information to make the sentences interesting.

> **example:** typewriters / word processors
>
> **In many offices and homes, typewriters have been replaced by word processors.**

1. shoelaces and zippers / Velcro
2. LPs and turntables / CDs and CD players
3. brooms / vacuum cleaners
4. electric fans / central air conditioners
5. conventional ovens / microwave ovens
6. telephone operators / voice-mail systems
7. eyeglasses / contact lenses
8. orchestras / music synthesizers
9. home-movie cameras / camcorders*
10. letters / e-mail

 Imagine that you work in a recording studio, and you are going to videotape a TV commercial. In pairs, go over your final checklist before you begin recording. Ask questions using the present perfect tense of the passive voice. Give short answers using the past participle, as in the example.

> **example:** call the actors
>
> A: **Have the actors been called?**
> B: **Called!**

1. test the microphones
2. check the lights
3. clean the camera lenses
4. focus the camera
5. test the loudspeakers
6. adjust the sound
7. load the film
8. close the doors

---

camcorders video camera-recorder combinations

First underline the object in each sentence. Then change the sentences from the active to the passive voice. Omit the agent unless it is important to the meaning of the sentence.

example: In just forty years, companies have introduced <u>an amazing selection of audio and video equipment</u>: color television, transistor radios, cassette players, video recorders, and compact discs.

In just forty years, an amazing selection of audio and video equipment has been introduced: color television, transistor radios, cassette players, video recorders, and compact discs.

1. In the past forty years, researchers have revolutionized audio and video technology.

2. By the mid-1950s, Ampex Corporation had introduced the first modern video recorder.

3. The television industry has used the Ampex system since that time.

4. By the late 1950s, companies had introduced the first stereo record.

5. Since 1960, researchers have developed high quality sound systems.

6. By the late 1980s, scientists had developed compact discs and lightweight camcorders.

7. In recent years, MCA, RCA, and several European companies have designed and produced videodisc systems.

8. Apple Computer has created a computer program that will program your VCR for you, if you don't know how!

Use simple or perfect forms of the verbs in parentheses to complete the following passage. Choose between active and passive forms. The first one is done as an example.

THOSE AMAZING MACHINES!
(ALSO KNOWN AS MICROELECTRONIC DEVICES*)

In recent years, we ___*have grown*___ very dependent on machines of
1 (grow)
all kinds—in business, in industry, and in our own homes. Nowadays the

average person _____ every day by hundreds of devices that
2 (surround)

---

*Microelectronics deals with electric currents in small components such as transistors and microchips.
 Microelectronic devices are found everywhere today.

_____ microelectronic technology. For example, this technology
3 (use)

_____ in microwave ovens and digital clocks.
4 (employ)

In just half a century, microelectronic technology _____ it pos-
5 (make)

sible to produce practical devices for everyday life. High-speed cameras with

automatic focusing _____. Compact disc players _____.
6 (create)   7 (develop)

Remote control devices _____ for televisions and video recorders
8 (produce)

and for telephone answering machines. Fifty years ago, none of these devices

_____ because microelectronic technology _____.
9 (exist)   10 (not invent / yet)

All microelectronic devices _____ with similar types of compo-
11 (construct)

nents, which are smaller, cheaper, and more reliable than components of the

past. This explains why some devices, such as VCRs, answering machines,

and especially home computers, _____ much less now than they
12 (cost)

did when they first _____ on the market. It also explains why the
13 (appear)

average home today _____ more than thirty machines and elec-
14 (contain)

tronic devices!

Using What You've Learned

Make a list of all the gadgets that are mentioned in this section. Put a check mark next to each device that you own (either here or in your native country) and count the number of check marks. Then talk with your classmates to see which student has the largest number of these gadgets.

Next, make a list of gadgets that you have in your home but that were not mentioned in these exercises. Again, compare with your classmates to see who has the largest number of gadgets.

Finally, choose *one* gadget that you absolutely could not live without and prepare a short presentation about it. Include the following:

- When was the item invented?
- By whom was it invented?
- How is it made?
- How is it used today?
- How as it used in the past or what was used instead of it?
- How has this item been modified or changed in recent years?

TOPIC three
The Continuous Tenses

Setting the Context

previewing the passage

When were the first cars developed? Since then, what other major breakthroughs in transportation have occurred?

The Future of Transportation

Amazing changes are taking place in all the methods of transportation that we use every day. It was only about 100 years ago that gasoline-powered cars were being developed. Today, prototypes of electric cars are being tested by large automakers such as Ford and Honda. Planes are being designed that will travel from New York to Tokyo in 2½ hours. And trains that travel as fast as 300 miles per hour are being built in several countries.

5

discussing ideas

Name all the types of transportation that you have used in your lifetime. Can you give the normal speed for each of these today? Does your list include any high-speed transportation? Which? How fast could you travel on this?

The Passive Voice with Continuous Tenses

The passive voice of verbs in the present and past continuous tenses is formed in this way: *be (am, is, are, was, were) + being* + past participle (+ *by* + agent). Adverbs of frequency generally come after the first auxiliary verb.

		examples	focus
Present Continuous	**Active**	Many cities **are using** computers to help regulate traffic.	many cities
	Passive	Computers **are being used** in many cities to help regulate traffic.	computers

		examples	focus
Past Continuous	**Active**	Ten years ago, cities **were using** traffic officers to regulate traffic.	cities
	Passive	Ten years ago, traffic **was being regulated** by traffic officers.	traffic

Note: The future continuous tense (*will be* + verb + *ing*) and the present and past perfect continuous tense (*have, has,* or *had been* + verb + *ing*) are not used in the passive voice.

 Working in pairs, take turns asking questions and forming answers using the present continuous tense, passive voice. Make up some other examples.

> **example:** A: Why are you wearing your black suit?
> B: (brown suit / cleaned) **My brown suit is being cleaned.**

A	B
1. Why is the traffic so slow today?	Main Street / repaired
2. Why don't you practice piano today?	piano / tuned
3. Why is your office closed?	new computer system / installed
4. Why can't we go into the cafeteria?	floor / washed
5. Why are they staying in a hotel?	their house / painted
6. What is happening to that bus?	it / towed away

 With the same partner or a new partner, repeat Exercise 1. This time, change the questions and answers to past time.

> **example:** A: **Why was the traffic so slow today?**
> B: **Main Street was being repaired.**

exercise 3 In pairs, change the following sentences from the present continuous, active voice to the past continuous, passive voice.

> **example:** A: Today computers are typing letters. (secretaries)
> B: **Twenty-five years ago, letters were (still) being typed by secretaries.**

1. Today computers and pilots are navigating planes. (only human pilots)
2. Today private package delivery services are delivering packages. (only the U.S. Postal Service)
3. Today computers are controlling traffic signals. (traffic officers)
4. Computers are running automobile assembly lines. (assembly line foremen)
5. Today computers are controlling switches in train tracks. (human switch operators)
6. Today Japan is making most of the world's motorcycles. (the United States)
7. Today several countries are operating high-speed trains. (only Japan)
8. Today many countries are exporting cars. (only a few countries)

 **exercise 4**　The following sentences give some information about the history of the automobile. Change the sentences to the passive voice. Omit *by* + agent if it is not necessary to the meaning of the sentence.

> **example:**　Already in 1890, people were driving gasoline-powered cars in France.
>
> **Already in 1890, gasoline-powered cars were being driven in France.**

1. By 1929, American automakers were producing approximately 5 million cars a year.
2. In 1950 the United States was manufacturing two-thirds of the world's motor vehicles.
3. By 1960, manufacturers were introducing compact cars because of competition from Europe.
4. By the 1970s, competition from Japan was threatening the U.S. auto industry.
5. By 1980, the United States was producing only one-fifth of the world's cars.
6. Today, foreign manufacturers are actually making many so-called "American" cars.
7. These days, automakers are finding ways to make automobile engines more fuel-efficient.
8. Several big automakers are building and testing electric cars.
9. They are testing alternative fuels such as methanol.
10. People are also building new mass-transport systems.

 **exercise 5**　Complete the following passage with either active or passive forms (simple, perfect, or continuous tenses) of the verbs in parentheses. Include adverbs when indicated. In some cases there may be more than one correct answer. The first one is done as an example.

DEVELOPMENTS IN TRANSPORTATION

Amazing developments _are currently taking_ place in transportation
1 (take / currently)

technology. Some technological changes _____ and others
2 (implement / already)

_____. In the twenty-first century, the major forms of trans-
3 (implement / soon)

portation that _____ today—cars, trains, and planes—will still
4 (use)

be popular, but they _____ in significant ways. Here are three
5 (modify)

examples of work that _____ now to improve our familiar methods
6 (do)

of transportation:

Electric Cars.　Air pollution is a serious problem in many large cities, and

most of this pollution _____ by exhaust from automobiles. In
7 (cause)

California, a law _____ stating that by 1998, 2 percent of the cars
8 (pass / already)
sold there must be electric. This percentage must go up to 5 percent by 2001

and 10 percent by 2003.

Consequently, big automakers in the United States and other countries

_____ hard to create a cheap, efficient, and attractive electric car.
9 (work)
Their biggest challenge is to invent an electric battery that can equal the power

and range of gasoline-powered engines. Existing batteries _____ a
10 (have)
range of only 80 to 100 miles, and they _____ up to five hours to
11 (require)
recharge.

Trains. The Maglev (Magnetic Levi-

tation System) is a futuristic-looking,

high-speed magnetic train that

_____ in Japan. The train
12 (develop / currently)
will be capable of covering the 340 miles

from Tokyo to Osaka in one hour. A

special track _____ to test the
13 (build)
Maglev. It _____ that the
14 (project)
train will be ready for service by 2001.

In the United States, the first high-

speed rail transportation system

_____ to start service be-
15 (expect)
tween Dallas and Houston in July 1998. The electrically powered train

Test run of Maglev train

_____ at speeds of up to 200 miles an hour.
16 (travel)

Airplanes. Researchers _____ on a plane that would be able to
17 (work / now)
travel from New York to Tokyo in 2½ hours. It would do this by flying above

the earth's atmosphere. It _____ that the first models of such planes
18 (predict)
will be ready around the year 2015.

Using What You've Learned

activity **1**

The time is the year 2015. The place is an airport in New York, where, in about one hour, the new "hyperspace" plane described above will be taking off on its first regularly scheduled flight to Tokyo.

Imagine that you are a radio news reporter at the scene on this history-making day. Your assignment is to describe to your listeners the activities that are taking place during these last moments before takeoff. Try to provide as many details as possible concerning the activities of the following:

- the passengers
- the plane
- the flight crew
- the ground crew
- the luggage and cargo

Write your description. Use the present continuous tense, active or passive voice. Then role-play your description for the class.

activity **2**

Write a brief composition about changes that are occurring in your work or field of study. Try to include information on research that is currently being done, new technology that is being introduced, and other changes that are being implemented.

Use your composition as the basis for a presentation for the entire class or for a small group discussion. If you work in groups, you may want to separate according to general areas of interest—for example, those who are interested in business, those who are involved in the sciences, and so on. If you prepare a presentation, you might include drawings, diagrams, or other visual aids to help in explaining.

TOPIC **four**
Modal Auxiliaries

Setting the Context

previewing the passage

What do you know about the first computers? When were they built? What were they used for?

Computers in Our Lives

It was only about fifty years ago that the first computer, Mark I, was developed for military use. Since then computers have come to play a vital role in almost every aspect of our lives. Today, phone calls can be directed by computers, cars can be assembled by computerized robots, messages and files can be sent over the Internet, children may be taught with the help of computers, and much more. Computers can even be used to arrange people's romantic relationships!

5

BIZARRO   By DAN PIRARO

I'M MARRIED TO A WOMAN I MET THROUGH THE COMPUTER ON THE INTERNET.

HOW INTERESTING! I'D LOVE TO MEET HER!

SO WOULD I — WE'RE TRYING TO ARRANGE SOMETHING NOW.

discussing ideas   What other current uses of computers can you think of? What possible future uses of computers can you suggest?

The Passive Voice with Modal Auxiliaries

The passive voice of modal auxiliaries is formed in this way: modal *(can, could, may, might, must, ought to, shall, should, will, would)* + *be* + past participle (+ *by* + agent).

	examples	focus
Active	Today we **can use** personal computer to write letters.	we
Passive	Today computers **can be used** to write personal letters.	computers
Active	Writers **may use** computers to help them do research.	writers
Passive	Computers **may be used** by writers to help them do research.	computers
Active	A doctor **might use** a computer to get the latest information about a drug.	a doctor
Passive	A computer **might be used** by a doctor to get the latest information about a drug.	a computer

In the following sentences, change the verbs from the active voice to the passive voice whenever possible. Omit the agent unless it is important to the meaning of the sentence.

Industrial robot assembling electronic circuit boards

example: Nowadays we may find robots in hundreds of different industries.

Nowadays robots may be found in hundreds of different industries.

1. We can define a robot as an "intelligent" machine.
2. Robots can copy the functioning of a human being in one way or another.
3. One early robot, "Planobot," was simply a mechanical arm that people could tilt or rotate.
4. Nowadays, people can design robots to do many jobs that would be dangerous or boring for humans.
5. For example, robots might replace human workers in dangerous areas such as nuclear power plants or coal mines.
6. In hospitals, people can program "nursing" robots to lift patients, wash them, and put them back in bed.
7. In the future, we might use robots for such complex tasks as making beds and preparing a steak dinner.
8. Though some robots are able to "say" a limited number of words, people cannot yet program robots to think like people.
9. In the future, however, people will use artificial intelligence to create robots that are more humanlike.
10. Wouldn't it be wonderful if people could design computers to perform all kinds of unpleasant tasks—such as homework?

exercise 2 Complete the following with the active or passive forms of the modals and verbs in parentheses. The first one is done as an example.

HERO

How would you like to have your own personal robot "servant"?

Although not quite as advanced as the robots portrayed in Hollywood movies,

some household robots are now available. One of them, named HERO,

<u>can be programmed</u> to perform a number of useful tasks around the house.
  1 (can / program)

HERO _____ lights on and off. He _____ packages.
       2 (can / turn)   3 (also / can / carry)

Amazingly, he _____ to teach languages!
                 4 (can / even / use)

Personal robots of the future will be more sophisticated. They

_____ as complete entertainment centers, with the ability to sing,
   5 (will / design)

dance, even tell jokes! Moreover, all the electronic equipment in the house—

television, radio, phone, computer, and so on— _____ by these
                                                  6 (will / regulate)

robots. Imagine: Someday, our dinners _____, our dishes
                                          7 (may / cook)

_____, our laundry _____, and our cars _____
   8 (may / wash)   9 (may / fold)   10 (may / repair)

— all by our own personal robots! For the time being, however, all of those

chores _____ by humans.
         11 (must / still / perform)

exercise 3 The following passage is written entirely in the active voice. It contains sentences that could be improved by using the passive voice. Rewrite the selection, using sentences in the passive voice when appropriate. Omit the agent if it is not necessary to the meaning of the sentence.

COMPUTERIZED ROBOTS

Never temperamental, always on time, always efficient, Epistle reads the mail each morning, chooses the most important letters, and marks the most important parts long before the boss arrives. Epistle is not an ordinary secretary. Epistle is a robot.

IBM developed Epistle several years ago. Today people are designing computerized robots that are even more sophisticated than Epistle to think and reason like the human brain. These machines will use artificial intelligence to perform their functions.

Artificial intelligence has already begun to affect the lives of millions. People are building both robots and computers that can do amazingly human-like work. For example, in many U.S. hospitals, computers can diagnose diseases with at least 85 percent accuracy. In England, scientists have developed a "bionic nose" that can distinguish subtle differences in smell. They can use the nose in the food and wine industries to check freshness and quality.

Until recently, we could program robots to perform only routine tasks. In the near future, computers utilizing artificial intelligence may give robots full mobility, vision, hearing, speech, and the "sense" to make logical decisions.

 **exercise 4**

Review. Complete the following passage by using either the active or passive voice of the verbs in parentheses. Use any of the tenses and modals covered in this chapter. The first one is done as an example.

THE HISTORY OF COMPUTERS

In 1944, the first general-purpose computer, Mark I, _____was put_____ into
                                                         1 (put)
operation. It was very slow and very large. In fact, all the early computers

were extremely large, and several floors of a building _____ to
                                                             2 (need)
house them.

By the end of the 1950s, computers _____ to use transistors.
                                          3 (develop)
Transistors _____ computers smaller, less expensive, more power-
              4 (make)
ful, and more reliable. Today these _____ as second-generation
                                         5 (know)
computers.

Third-generation computers, which _____ in the 1960s,
                                        6 (develop)
_____ chips to store the memory of the computer. These computers
    7 (use)
were still very large, however. But by the 1970s, when the silicon chip

_____, computers _____ truly small and affordable.
    8 (develop)   9 (become)
Computers with these silicon chips _____ fourth-generation com-
                                         10 (call)
puters. There are more than 30 million fourth-generation computers in U.S.

homes today—roughly 1 computer for every 4 Americans.

Review. Complete the following passage by using either the active or passive voice of the verbs and modals in parentheses. Use any of the tenses and modals covered in this chapter. The first one is done as an example.

DEVELOPMENTS IN TELECOMMUNICATIONS

During most of human history, communication ___was limited___ by time

1 (limit)

and distance. In the past 200 years, however, revolutionary changes in

communication _____. In the nineteenth century, the telegraph

2 (occur)

and telephone _____. Radio, television, and computers

3 (invent)

_____ in the early and mid-twentieth century. Since then, these

4 (develop)

inventions _____ the way people live and work.

5 (change / completely)

Today all these communications devices _____ together.

6 (can / link)

This new wave of technology _____ "telecommunications"—the

7 (call)

use of television, radio, telephones, and computers to communicate across

distance and time. In the 1990s, telephones, computers, and video screens

_____, allowing some offices to have "videoconferences" in which

8 (may / connect)

participants can see and talk to each other and in which computer files

_____. Some home computers _____ to news publishing

9 (can / share)   10 (tie / now)

services so that people can receive information at home instead of going to a

library. Because of satellite technology, people living in one part of the world

_____ almost instantly about events occurring thousands of miles

11 (can / inform)

away.

According to *U.S. News and World Report* (May 2, 1994), the 1990s

_____ "as a period when American businesses, large and small,

12 (someday / view)

_____ fundamentally. The widespread adoption of information

13 (transform)

technologies will be a major reason." In the not-too-distant future, *everyone,*

not just Americans, _____ by developments in telecommunications.

14 (affect)

Review.   Reread the opening passage "Old and New Technology" on page 148. Then, individually or in pairs, do the following:

1. Underline the subject and verb of the first sentence. Is the verb in the active or passive voice? Can you rephrase the sentence to begin with *new inventions*?
2. Underline the subjects and verbs in the second sentence. Unlike the first sentence, the second sentence does not have a phrase with *by*. Can you add one? Why do you think the phrase with *by* was not used?
3. Underline all the other passive-voice verbs in the passage. Tell whether they refer to past, present, or future time. Then tell the agent for each. If the agent is not included in the passive construction, tell who or what you think the agent is.

Using What You've Learned

Think of the tremendous changes that computers have brought during our lifetimes. For example, look at the tasks below. All of these can now be done electronically. In the past, however, they had to be done manually.

In pairs or small groups, discuss the changes in these tasks and add others that you can think of. Then choose one or two that you are particularly familiar with. Prepare a brief report for your classmates, telling how the process was done in the past and how it is done today. If possible, include changes that may occur in the near future too. Use the passive voice whenever possible in your report.

example: Until the last twenty years or so, letters could be only hand-written or typed. And, they could only be sent by regular mail or by someone who was traveling to a certain place. Today they can be mailed, faxed, or sent through a computer network. They can be sent by express mail and delivered overnight to almost any part of the globe.

compose music
design cars
diagnose illnesses
draw three-dimensional objects
figure taxes
keep household records (balance checkbooks, pay bills, and so on)
mix paint
obtain information from libraries
purchase tickets (for airlines, concerts, sports events, and so on)
sort mail
teach children
write and send letters

Use of the Passive Voice

Verbs in the passive voice are frequently tested on standardized English proficiency exams. Review these commonly tested structures and check your understanding by completing the sample items below.

Remember that . . .

- The passive is formed in this way: (modal auxiliary) + *be* + past participle.
- The verb *be* is singular or plural depending on the subject of the passive sentence.
- The verb *be* gives the appropriate tense and time frame for the sentence.

Part 1: Circle the correct completion for the following.

example: John _____ never complaining with his work.
    a. be known for
    b. is know for
    c. is known for
    d. was known for

1. Nowadays the majority of overseas telephone calls _____ by satellite.
    a. transmit
    b. transmitting
    c. are transmitted
    d. are transmitting

2. Their house _____ three times since they bought it twenty years ago.
    a. has been redecorated
    b. had been redecorated
    c. has been redecorating
    d. has redecorated

3. Before turning on the switch, make sure the machine _____.
    a. plugs in
    b. is plugged in
    c. has plugged in
    d. be plugged in

Part 2: Circle the letter below the underlined word(s) containing an error.

example: Difficulties with <u>culture</u> shock <u>are</u> often <u>relate</u> to an individual's
                                  A   B   ⓒ

        ability to speak the language of the country <u>where she is living</u>.
                                                                            D

1. The top floor of the parking structure <u>collapsed</u> during the earth-
                                               A

   quake and <u>could not</u> used <u>for</u> the next <u>six months</u>.
                 B   C   D

2. A plane is currently <u>been</u> designed <u>that</u> will <u>allow for</u> travel be-
                       A   B   C

   tween New York and Tokyo in approximately <u>two-and-a-half</u> hours.
                                                       D

3. Everyone <u>was relieved</u> to hear that the child who <u>had been missing</u>
                 A   B

   for three days <u>were found</u> <u>unharmed</u>.
                    C   D

Money Matters

in this chapter

Introduction

In this chapter, you will study many uses of nouns, pronouns, articles, and adjectives. As you study, try to understand the differences between types of nouns in English. This will help you with singular and plural forms as well as the various words and expressions used with nouns.

The following passage introduces the chapter theme, Money Matters, and raises some of the topics and issues you will cover in the chapter.

The Global Economy

Of all the sciences, only two are subjects that have a direct and noticeable effect on our lives every day. One is meteorology, the study of weather. Heat, cold, sun, and rain affect us in many ways—in the kind of clothing we wear, for example, and the types of activities we do outdoors. Economics is the other science that affects the daily life of all of us. Each time we spend money, or it is spent on us, we are contributing to the economic life of our country, and in fact, of the world.

Most people have a basic understanding of the weather, but how many people feel comfortable with the subject of economics? Often, economics seems to be a mysterious subject. Newspapers and television use terminology that can resemble a foreign language. They speak of *the gross national product, the balance of payments, the cost of living, interest, productivity,* and so forth.

In some ways, economics is like an enormous jigsaw puzzle. Each piece is basic, but the pieces interconnect, one to another, in a large picture. To look at the whole picture, you must begin piece by piece. Knowledge of the individual pieces and their interconnection will help you understand the global picture.

discussing ideas According to the passage, which sciences affect us every day? Why? Can you give some examples of economic activities in your daily life? What are other economic terms you have heard recently? Can you explain them?

Count Versus Noncount Nouns

Setting the Context

What does *wealth* mean? Can you give some examples?

What Is Wealth to You?

- To some people, wealth may mean ownership of businesses, houses, cars, stereos, and jewels.
- To others, wealth may mean control of resources, such as oil, gold, silver, or natural gas.

5

- To the philosophical, wealth may be intangible. It can be found in honesty, love, courage, and trust.
- To much of the world, however, wealth is having enough food: bread, rice, fish, meat, and fruit.

How would you describe a *wealthy* person?

A. Introduction to Count and Noncount Nouns

A noun can name a person, a place, an object, an activity, an idea or emotion, or a quantity. A noun may be concrete (physical or tangible) or abstract (non-physical or intangible). Both abstract and concrete nouns can be classified into two types: count nouns and noncount nouns.

Count Nouns

	examples	notes
Singular	I have a **friend.** My **friend** owns a **car.**	Count nouns are nouns that can be counted (*apples, oranges,* and so on). They have both singular and plural forms. Most count nouns are concrete, but some can be abstract.
Plural	**Friends** are very important. New **cars** are expensive.	

Noncount Nouns

	examples	notes
Concrete Mass Nouns	**Air** and **water** are necessary for life. We need to buy **coffee, rice,** and **sugar.**	Noncount nouns are usually mass concrete nouns (*food, water,* and so on) or abstract nouns (*wealth, happiness,* and so on) that we don't count. Noncount nouns are singular, even though some end in *-s* (*economics, news*).
Abstract Nouns	**Honesty** is the best policy. We need more **information.** We're concerned about your **health.** Have you studied **economics** or **physics?**	

 **exercise 1**   Quickly reread "What Is Wealth to You?" on page 181 and then do the following:

1. Underline all the nouns.
2. Group the nouns in the chart on the next page.
3. Make a list of any nouns that are confusing to you and discuss these as a class. For example, are there nouns that can go in more than one category?

Count Nouns		Noncount Nouns	
SINGULAR	PLURAL	CONCRETE (TANGIBLE)	ABSTRACT (INTANGIBLE)
	people		

B. Groups of Count and Noncount Nouns

Certain patterns exist with count and noncount nouns. For example, noncount nouns often refer to categories or groups, while specific items in these groups are often count nouns. Some groups of words are usually noncount, such as food items and weather terms. Other nouns may be count or noncount, depending on the meaning. Compare:

noncount	count	noncount	count
advice	hints ideas suggestions	information, news	articles magazines newspapers
equipment	machines supplies tools	money	cents dollars quarters
friendship, love	feelings friends relatives	nature	animals forests mountains oceans
furniture	chairs lamps tables	time	days hours minutes
homework	assignments essays pages	traffic, transportation	buses cars trains

	common noncount food items			common noncount weather items	
	bread	fruit	rice	air	water
	butter	meat	sugar	rain	weather
	coffee	milk	tea	snow	wind

Nouns That Can Be Both Count and Noncount

Noncount	I studied **business** in college.	business = an idea or activity
Count	We have a **business** in Florida.	a business = a store or firm
Noncount	We had **chicken** for dinner.	chicken = a type of food
Count	My uncle has a **chicken**.	a chicken = a bird
Noncount	I have **time** to go there now.	time = an unspecified period of minutes, hours, and so on.
Count	I have gone there many **times**.	times = occasions
Noncount	That window needs new **glass**.	glass = a transparent material
Count	Would you like **a glass** of water?	a glass = a container to drink from
	I need new **glasses**.	glasses = a device to help people see better

exercise 2 In each pair of sentences, the same noun acts as a count and a noncount noun. Identify count (C) and noncount (N) nouns.

example: _N_ We're having fish for dinner tonight.

   _C_ My uncle caught three fish this morning.

1. _____ What time is it?

_____ We had a wonderful time on Saturday.

2. _____ Is a tomato a fruit or a vegetable?

_____ Fruit is good for you.

3. _____ My friend eats salad every day.

_____ Would you like a salad?

4. _____ My brother is majoring in business.

_____ We hope to start a small flower business.

5. _____ Lucy bought some new wine glasses.

   _____ Glass can be recycled fairly easily.

6. _____ We're having turkey on Thanksgiving.

   _____ He's never seen a live turkey.

7. _____ Jane bought some Colombian coffee.

   _____ Could we have two coffees, please?

8. _____ Living abroad can be a wonderful experience.

   _____ How much work experience do you have?

 **Error Analysis.** Many of the following sentences have errors in their use of singular and plural with nouns. Find and correct the errors.

example: Do you know where my (glass) are? I can't see without them.
glasses

1. How many time have you been to New York?

2. We need more informations about that.

3. Do you have any advice for me?

4. The office manager recently purchased some new equipments.

5. We have a lot of homeworks to do for Monday.

6. There are several new student here from Taiwan.

7. I brought ten dollar with me.

8. He has some very nice furniture in his new apartment.

9. I have three assignment for tomorrow.

10. Traffic is very heavy today.

 Working in pairs, separate these nouns into groups. Make a chart like the one on the next page to help you. *Note:* Many of the terms below appear throughout the chapter; check their meanings if you do not know them.

√ advice	employment	market	salary
√ automobile	gasoline	money	series
√ belief	gold	news	supply
√ business	honesty	oil	time
capitalism	inflation	price	traffic
company	interest	product	wealth
consumer	investment	productivity	weather
economics	machine	profit	work
employee	machinery	resource	

	COUNT		NONCOUNT*	MEANING OF NOUNS THAT ARE BOTH COUNT AND NONCOUNT
SINGULAR	**PLURAL**			
automobile	automobiles		advice (abstract)	business—C = store or company
belief	beliefs		business	business—N = activity or idea
business	businesses		(abstract)	

C. Singular and Plural Forms: Subject/Verb Agreement

Plural subjects take plural verbs, and a singular subject takes a singular verb. When the subject is a noncount noun, it always uses a singular verb. Some count nouns can be collective; they refer to a group as *one* unit. Collective nouns can be singular or plural, but in American English, they are generally singular. Other nouns are always plural; they have no singular form. For all nouns, words or phrases that come between the subject and verb do not usually affect the use of singular or plural.

	singular	plural
Count Nouns	A **friend is** someone who cares about you.	**Friends are** people who care about you.
Noncount Nouns	**Friendship is** very important to me.	

*You might try to separate your list of noncount nouns into abstract and mass nouns.

nouns			examples
Common Collective Nouns *(generally singular)*	army assembly audience class committee congregation congress couple crew	faculty family government group public senate staff team	**The staff was** in agreement about the changes. **The audience was** eager for the show to begin. **The public** is upset about the issue.
Nouns with No Singular Form *(always plural)*	binoculars clothes glasses pajamas pants pliers police	premises shears shorts slacks scissors tongs tweezers	**The scissors are** in that drawer. **Your pants are** in the laundry. Where **are the tweezers?**

exercise 5   In these sentences, choose the correct form (singular or plural) of the verb in parentheses.

> **example:**   News from home ((is)/ are) very important to me.

1. Finance (is / are) one of five major area studies in business.
2. The class (is / are) preparing a report on international finance.
3. Economics (is / are) a difficult subject for many people.
4. Economists often (helps / help) shape government policies.
5. The economic theories of John Maynard Keynes (has / have) shaped the policies of many governments.
6. The government (has / have) changed economic policies several times.
7. The advice from the accountants (was / were) very valuable.
8. Congress (has / have) voted not to raise taxes.
9. The staff (has / have) written a full report on the issue.
10. The police (is / are) on the way here.
11. The information that we were given about the new machines (was / were) useful.
12. The new equipment (has / have) worked very well.

D. Indefinite Articles: *a* and *an*

A or *an* is used before a singular count noun. The indefinite article may mean *one*, or it may mean an unspecified person or thing.

	examples	notes
a	I bought **a** banana. I bought **a** house. **A** European man lives next door.	*A* is used before a singular count noun that begins with a consonant sound.
an	I wasted **an** egg. I wasted **an** hour.	*An* is used before a singular count noun that begins with a vowel sound.

Note: A or *an* is never used with a noun that functions as a noncount noun.

 **exercise 6**

Rapid Oral Practice.   The following nouns are all singular. Some are count and some are noncount. Form complete sentences by using *We have* or *We don't have.* Use *a* or *an* with count nouns and nothing with noncount nouns.

examples: imported car
We have an imported car.

delicious food in . . .
We have delicious food in Italy.

1. computer
2. heavy traffic in . . .
3. problem with traffic in . . .
4. income tax in . . .
5. high inflation in . . .
6. high inflation rate in . . .
7. information for you
8. time for . . .
9. news for you
10. hot (cold) weather during . . .
11. suggestion for you
12. advice for you

E. Unspecified or Unidentified Count and Noncount Nouns

Both count and noncount nouns may be used to refer to unspecified or unidentified people, things, and so forth. In this case, a singular count noun is preceded by *a* or *an,* but plural count nouns and noncount nouns are used without articles.

	examples	notes
Count Nouns	**SINGULAR** **A house** can be expensive.	*a house* = one house or any house in general *Remember:* Either an article or an adjective *must* be used with a singular count noun.
	PLURAL **Houses** are getting more expensive.	*houses* = all houses in general *Remember:* Articles are not used with unspecified or unidentified plural count nouns.
Noncount Nouns	**Love** is wonderful. **Time** is **money**. **Health** is better than **wealth**.	*Remember:* Articles are not used with unspecified noncount nouns. Noncount nouns always take singular verbs.

exercise 7

What does wealth mean to you? What do you value and why? From the list below, choose six items that are important to you. Put them in order (first, second, and so on). Make count nouns plural and use *are*.

example: I think . . . is / are (very) important because . . .

First, I think good health is important because without health, we have nothing. Second, I think . . .

accurate information	homework
clean air	honesty
courage	jewelry
elegant clothes	large family
expensive car	love
free time	money in the bank
good advice from family	peace in the world
and friends	reliable transportation
good health	respect
good neighbor	safe housing

exercise 8 The following statements include noncount nouns and singular and plural count nouns. Complete each statement by using *a* or *an,* or use *X* to indicate that no article is necessary.

    examples: I've always been interested in __X__ economics.

                    I've never taken __an__ economics class.

    1. _____ economics is concerned with two basic groups: _____ consumers and _____ suppliers.

    2. _____ economists study the interrelationship between the two groups.

    3. For example, _____ economist might study the way _____ supplier creates _____ market for _____ new product.

    4. _____ economics also deals with the interrelationship between _____ larger groups, including _____ regions and _____ countries.

    5. As we all know, _____ change in the economy of _____ country such as Japan can affect _____ people all over the world.

    6. Economists study how events in _____ region can affect _____ markets and _____ prices in other regions.

    7. For example, _____ weather in California can affect the price of _____ fruit in Boston.

exercise 9 The following definitions of economic terms include both count and noncount nouns. Complete the definitions by using *a* or *an,* or use *X* to indicate that no article is necessary.

    example: The *balance of* __X__ *payments* is the difference between the amount of __X__ money that leaves __a__ country and the amount that comes in through __X__ imports, __X__ exports, __X__ investments, and so on.

    1. _____ *black market* is the illegal sale of _____ products.

    2. *Capital* is _____ money or _____ assets such as _____ gold or _____ buildings that can be used to make _____ investments.

    3. _____ *depression* is _____ very severe drop in economic activity. _____ high unemployment and _____ low production usually occur during _____ depression.

4. The *gross national product (GNP)* is the total value of _____ goods and _____ services produced in _____ country during _____ specified period of _____ time (usually a year).

5. The *money supply* is the total amount of _____ money in circulation.

6. _____ *productivity* is the total national output of _____ goods and _____ services divided by the number of _____ workers.

 **exercise 10**

The following sentences make generalizations about large companies. Change the nouns or noun phrases in italics from plural to singular or from singular to plural. Add or omit *a* or *an* and make other changes in verbs and pronouns. (Note that in this exercise, *multinational* and *multinational corporation* have the same meaning.)

example: *Multinational corporations* are *companies* that operate in more than one country.

A multinational corporation is a company that operates in more than one country.

1. *Multinationals,* such as IBM or Pepsi, may operate in over 100 countries.
2. Because of their size, *multinational corporations* can often make *products* at *lower costs* than *local industries* can.
3. *Multinationals* can also make *countries* dependent on them.
4. *A multinational corporation* may import *a raw material* from *a foreign country.*
5. *A multinational* may make *a product* in one country and export it to another country.
6. Today *a country* may require *a company* to build *an assembly plant* in *an area* where *a product* will be sold.
7. Building *a factory* in *a foreign country* can still benefit *a multinational.*
8. It eliminates *a major expense* in transportation.

Using What You've Learned

 **activity 1**

A *generalization* is a general statement that expresses an idea or an opinion about people, things, ideas, and so on. It often gives a general rule or conclusion based on limited or insufficient information. For example, consider these statements. Are they always true?

1. French people drink wine.
2. Japanese people always have dark hair.
3. American men are tall.
4. Latin Americans are fantastic dancers.

Note that these generalizations use nouns without articles. This is one of the most common ways to make generalizations. As a class or in small groups, share some of the generalizations that are common in your culture. Include both generalizations that people in your culture make and generalizations that others make about people in your culture.

activity 2

Form teams of two or more students each. Take turns giving nouncount noun categories for each of the following groups of count nouns. The team with the highest number of correct answers wins. Your teacher or a classmate can be the judge of correct answers. A classmate can also be the timekeeper. Set a ten- or fifteen-second limit for answering. Then try to add new items of your own.

example: movies and plays

entertainment

1. taxis and subways
2. dimes and nickels
3. beds and dressers
4. newspapers and magazines
5. compositions and reading assignments
6. snowstorms and thunderstorms
7. minutes and seconds
8. paintings and sculptures
9. records, tapes, and CDs
10. earrings and necklaces

activity 3

Proverbs are wise sayings that have endured over time. These proverbs deal in part with how we manage our financial matters—are we wise or foolish with our resources?

In groups, read the proverbs and compare them to proverbs in your own languages and cultures. Can you explain the meaning of each?

1. A penny saved is a penny earned.
2. An ounce of prevention is worth a pound of cure.
3. A fool and his money are soon parted.
4. A bird in the hand is worth two in the bush.

TOPIC **two**
Indefinite Adjectives and Pronouns

Setting the Context

previewing the passage

Is economics a mystery to you? The following observation gives you one man's explanation of economics in very simple terms.

Economics in My Life

For many people, economics is a mystery, but I deal with it every day. Economics is just a complicated way of explaining why I make only a little money and why another guy makes a lot of money.

discussing ideas

Can you give your own very simple definition of economics?

A. Indefinite Adjectives and Pronouns with Both Count and Noncount Nouns

Indefinite adjectives such as *some, many,* and *little* are used with nouns instead of giving specific amounts. Indefinite pronouns such as *some, someone, any, anyone* replace nouns. Certain expressions work with both count and noncount nouns: *any, some, a lot (of), lots (of), plenty (of), no,* and *none.* Compare:

	indefinite adjectives	indefinite pronouns
Count Nouns	Do you have **any** dollar bills?	I don't have **any**.
	Jack has **some** dollar bills.	Jack has **some**.
	Harry has **a lot of** dollar bills.	Harry has **a lot**.
	I have **no** dollar bills.	I have **none**.
Noncount Nouns	Do you have **any** money?	Do you have **any**?
	Jack has **some** money.	Jack has **some**.
	Harry has **a lot of** money.	Harry has **a lot**.
	I have **no** money.	I have **none**.

Note: In formal English, *none* is always followed by a singular verb: *None of the people has arrived.* (formal) *None of the people have arrived.* (informal)

 **Rapid Oral Practice.** In pairs, ask and answer questions using these cues and words such as *some, any,* and *a lot (of).*

examples: homework tonight

A: **Do you have any homework tonight?**
B: **Yes, I have some homework.**

money

A: **Do you have some money?**
B: **No, I don't have any.**

1. extra cash
2. $5 bills
3. credit cards
4. interesting news (about . . .)
5. information about good dentists (doctors, therapists, and so on)
6. assignments tonight
7. free time today
8. advice (about . . .)
9. change
10. quarters

 B. *(a) few* and *(not) many* with Count Nouns

examples	meanings	notes
How **many** (dollars) do you have? I have **a few** (dollars).	I have some dollars, but not a lot.	*Few, a few, many,* and *not many* are used with count nouns. *Many* can be used in affirmative statements, but it is more common in questions with *how* and in negative statements.
I **don't** have **many** dollar bills.	I have only a small number of dollars, probably not enough.	
I have **few** dollar bills.	I probably don't have enough.	

C. (a) little and (not) much with Noncount Nouns

examples	meanings	notes
How **much** (money) do you have?		
I have **a little** (money).	I have some money, but not a lot.	*A little, little, much,* and *not much* are used with noncount nouns. *Much* can be used in affirmative statements, but it is more common in questions with *how* and in negative statements.
I **don't have much** money.	I have only a small amount of money, probably not enough.	
I have **little** money.	I probably don't have enough.	

Note: Other expressions such as *numerous, several, a number of,* and *a couple (of)* can be used with plural count nouns. Expressions such as *a good deal of, a great deal of,* and *a large (small) amount of* can be used with noncount nouns.

 **exercise 2**   *Few* and *little* mean "not many (much)," but *a few* and *a little* mean "some." Indicate the differences in meaning in the following sentences by using + ("some") or – ("not many or much").

examples: __+__ There are a few good restaurants in town.

__–__ There are few good restaurants in town.

1. _____ We have little homework for the weekend.

2. _____ We have a little homework for the weekend.

3. _____ I have a little advice for you.

4. _____ I have a few ideas for you.

5. _____ He has little information on that.

6. _____ There is little traffic today.

7. _____ Do you have a little time?

8. _____ We have a few pages to read for tomorrow.

9. _____ She has a few friends here.

10. _____ She has few friends here.

11. _____ I've got a little money with me.

12. _____ I've got a few dollars with me.

exercise 3 **Rapid Oral Practice.** Take turns making statements and responses following the examples below. Make count nouns plural and use *a little, little, not much, a few, few,* or *not many.*

examples: money with me

A: **I have a little money with me. How about you?**
B: **I don't have much money this week.**

dollar with me

A: **I have a few dollars with me. How about you?**
B: **I have a few dollars too.**

1. free time today
2. furniture in my house (apartment)
3. friend from . . .
4. problem with . . .
5. extra energy
6. homework tonight
7. news from home
8. assignment this week
9. change
10. food at home

D. Modifiers with *a lot of, a little, a few, little,* and *few*

A lot of, a little, a few, little, and *few* occur frequently in conversation. They are often used with other modifiers. The most common are *quite, just, only, very,* and *too.*

quite with *a lot (of)* and *a few*

count nouns	noncount nouns	meaning
She has **quite a few** assignments.	She has **quite a lot of** homework.	a large number or amount

just and *only* with *a few* and *a little*

count nouns	noncount nouns	meaning
She has **just a few** assignments.	She has **just a little** homework.	a moderate number or amount
She has **only a few** assignments.	She has **only a little** homework.	a small number or amount

very and too with few and little

count nouns	noncount nouns	meaning
She has **very few** assignments.	She has **very little** homework.	a very small number or amount
She has **too few** assignments.	She has **too little** homework.	not enough

Note: *Too* can also be used with *many* and *much* to mean "more than enough." Compare the following:
  That teacher gives *too many* assignments.
  That teacher gives *too much* homework.

exercise  Choose the correct form of the word(s) in parentheses.

> **example:** Changes are occurring in the economies of (many / much) countries around the world.

1. Since the end of the 1980s, tremendous changes have occurred in (many / much) parts of the world.

2. (Few / Little) countries have escaped the major political changes that began in the 1980s.

3. When countries change their political systems, (many / much) other changes also occur.

4. Major economic changes have occurred in more than (a few / a little) countries in the world.

5. With economic changes have come (a number of / a great deal of) social dilemmas.

6. Countries that used to have (very few / very little) difficulty with unemployment and crime are now dealing with serious problems.

7. In controlled economies, often there wasn't (many / much) unemployment or (many / much) crime.

8. In free market economies, there can be (quite a few / quite a little) social problems that hadn't existed before.

 **exercise 5** In pairs, ask and answer questions about your hometown or home country. Use the examples and the following cues, changing any count nouns to plural.

Give your own opinions and offer any additional information you know about the subject. If your country has experienced major changes in recent years, talk about both the past and the present.

QUESTIONS: Is there much (any) . . . ?
Are there many (any) . . . ?

ANSWERS: There is quite a lot (some, just a little, and so on) . . .
There are quite a few (only a few, too few, and so on) . . .

examples: oil

A: **Is there much oil in your country?**
B: **Unfortunately, there isn't much oil in my country.**

taxi

A: **Are there many taxis in Buenos Aires?**
B: **There are quite a few—maybe thousands!**

1. tax in . . .
2. poverty in . . .
3. crime
4. discrimination
5. air and water pollution
6. high-tech industries

7. farm
8. factory
9. unemployment
10. news from . . . in U.S. news-papers or on U.S. television

 # E. More Indefinite Pronouns

pronouns		examples	notes
everyone everybody everything	someone somebody something	FORMAL **Everyone has his or her** own problems from time to time. **Everyone has his** own problems at times.	Indefinite pronouns are singular. They are always used with singular verbs. In formal English, singular pronouns are used to refer to them.
anyone anybody anything	no one nobody nothing	INFORMAL **Everyone has their** own problems at times.	In informal English, plural pronouns are often used.

Note: Each + noun is always singular. *All* is always plural. *None* generally uses a singular verb in formal English, but a plural verb is sometimes considered correct.

Choose the form of the word(s) in parentheses that is correct in formal, written English.

> **example:** No one (want / (wants)) to be in a bad economic situation.

1. In today's changing economies, anyone with a good job (is / are) very fortunate.
2. Everyone (worry / worries) about losing (her / their) money.
3. In some parts of the world, you can only get a good job if you know people who (is / are) in a position of power.
4. Every company (has / have) (its / their) own employment policies.
5. Some companies allow everyone to give (his or her / their) ideas.
6. In some companies, all workers can contribute (his or her / their) ideas.
7. Nobody (is / are) surprised when people complain.
8. Anybody can bring (his or her / their) complaints to meetings.
9. None of the workers (was / were) at the meeting last night.
10. No one (was / were) available to give (his / their) opinion.

 **exercise 7**

Reread the sentences in Exercise 6. Indicate any sentences that have an informal, conversational alternative.

> **example:** Everyone (worry / worries) about losing (her / their) money.
> **Everyone worries about losing their money.**   Informal

F. one, another, the other, others, the others

These pronouns and adjectives are often used to list more than one item. The choice depends on how many items are in the group and whether the speaker is referring to the entire group. Compare:

> We have *two* problems. *One* is lack of money. *The other* is lack of time.

> We have *several* problems. One is lack of money. *Others* are lack of time and transportation.

> We have *four* problems. *One* is lack of money. *Another* is lack of time. *The others* are lack of transportation and equipment.

	adjective	pronoun	meaning
Singular	one problem another problem the other problem	one another the other	 an additional problem the second of two or the last of a group
Plural	some problems other problems the other problems	some others the others	 additional problems the last of a group

Complete the following sentences by using a form of *other (another, other, others, the other, the others).* The first one is done as an example.

1. There are five major areas of business. One is accounting, and

   _____another_____ is data processing. _____ are finance,

   management, and marketing.

2. Accounting is sometimes divided into two branches. One is public account-

   ing and _____ is private accounting.

3. Marketing experts are responsible for promoting and selling a product.

   This involves many things, beginning with product design and develop-

   ment. _____ aspects of marketing include packaging, pricing,

   and advertising.

4. Financial experts can be divided into three major groups. Financial analysts

   form one group. _____ groups are bankers and stockbrokers.

5. Although they may make different products, most factories are organized

   in a similar way. Two areas of factory organization are purchasing and in-

   ventory control. _____ areas include control of production and

   of distribution.

Review. Choose the form of the word(s) in parentheses that is correct in formal, written English. The first two are done as examples.

In (all)/ any) economic systems today, most businesses plan their organization carefully. (Another / (One)) common organizational system is the division of labor.

Division of labor means all of the workers (is / are) specialized. Each worker has (his or her / their) own particular duties to perform. Each duty (is / are) one part of the whole operation. A good example of the division of labor is an assembly line in an automobile factory. (One / Other) worker may install a door while (another / others) is installing the hood. (The other / The others) add lights, windshield wipers, and so on. Normally, the workers don't move. Everyone (stay / stays) in one place, and a conveyor belt moves the product to (him or her / them).

The division of labor permits mass production, but it does have (any / some) disadvantages. For one thing, (few / little) people know or understand all (aspect / aspects) of an operation. In addition, mass production may be efficient, but (many / much) workers complain that they get (few / little) job satisfaction from working on one small duty, day after day. To them, there is (many / much) more satisfaction in doing a job from start to finish.

 **Error Analysis.**   Many of the following sentences have errors in indefinite pronouns and adjectives. Find and correct the mistakes. Use formal, written English.

example: Motor City is a town with many automobile factories. *Correct*

many
How ~~much~~ factories are there in Motor City?

1. I've worked at Mass Production Motors for a few years.

2. We have a lot problems in this factory.

3. The workers are paid very few money.

4. We don't get no job satisfaction here.

5. There are too much unhappy workers in this factory.

6. Only a little people are happy with their jobs.

7. Last year there weren't much strikes, but this year we're going to have plenty of.

8. So far we haven't had much success in changing things.

9. The management has tried to make some changes, but it's had very little success.

10. Many of workers are against the changes.

11. Everyone has his own opinion about the situation.

12. One person thinks things are getting better, but other person thinks they're getting worse.

Using What You've Learned

This cartoon was published on April 14, one day before "tax day" in the United States. On April 15, Americans must file their income tax returns. In the United States, as everywhere perhaps, people try hard to find ways of reducing the amount of taxes they must pay. These ways of reducing taxes are called *loopholes*.

After you have read the cartoon, work in pairs and rewrite the dialogue. Make complete questions for the first two frames. For the second two frames, try to put the ideas in your own words. Then compare your new dialogue with those of your classmates.

cathy®   by Cathy Guisewite

Think about the ideas that you discussed in Exercise 5, page 198. Write a short composition about an important economic or social issue in your country today. It may be poverty, air pollution, or crime, for example. In your first draft, explain the issue as you see it in more general terms. Later you might want to revise your composition to include specific examples. If your country has experienced significant changes in recent years, you can write a general comparison of the past and present.

Use of Singular and Plural Forms

Singular and plural forms of nouns and verbs are frequently tested on standardized English proficiency exams. Review these commonly tested structures and check your understanding by completing the sample items below.

Remember that . . .

- A singular subject uses a singular verb. Plural subjects use plural verbs. Generally, words that come between the subject and verb do not affect the use of singular or plural forms.
- A noncount noun always takes a singular verb.
- A collective noun (*committee, staff,* and so on) generally takes a singular verb. Many indefinite pronouns and adjectives are singular.

Part 1: Circle the correct completion for the following.

example: John _____ happy with his classes.
    a. seem
    b. is seem
    c. seeming
    (d.) seems

1. Physics _____ the study of matter, energy, force, and motion.
    a. is being
    b. are
    c. is
    d. have been

2. The economic theorist who has perhaps most influenced government policy making in the last sixty years _____ John Maynard Keynes.
    a. is
    b. are
    c. have been
    d. has being

3. Homesickness _____ a problem for students studying far from their homes.
    a. have often been
    b. has often been
    c. has been often
    d. has often being

Part 2: Circle the letter below the underlined word(s) containing an error.

example: Anyone can <u>feel frustrated</u> if <u>they have</u> <u>difficulties</u> in speaking
                             A   Ⓑ   C

a <u>foreign</u> language.
   D

1. The committee <u>has been discussing</u> the issue of how each <u>member</u>
                   A   B
should <u>officially</u> register <u>their opinion</u> on a particular matter.
         C   D

2. In <u>recent years</u>, unemployment <u>have grown</u> <u>considerably</u> among
        A   B   C
certain segments of the population, <u>especially those</u> in urban areas.
                                       D

3. <u>Almost</u> everyone <u>who live</u> on earth is in one way or <u>another</u>
   A   B   C
<u>affected by</u> global economics.
   D

TOPIC **three**

The Definite Article

Setting the Context

previewing the passage

What are *natural resources*? Give some examples of resources you are familiar with.

World Resources: Where Are They?

Some of the world's most important resources are coal, iron ore, petroleum, copper, gold, silver, and diamonds. Many deposits are concentrated in small areas, such as the petroleum deposits off the coast of Venezuela and in the deserts around the Persian Gulf.

discussing ideas What are the most important natural resources in your native country? Where are they located?

A. Introduction to the Definite Article

The definite article—*the*—can be used with both count and noncount nouns when the noun is specifically identified or its identity is already clearly understood. Many times, the particular context determines if *the* should be used or not, but in certain cases, such as with place names and locations, specific rules exist about when to use and not to use *the*.

B. *the* with Count Nouns

	examples	notes
Nonspecific (Without the)	SINGULAR Today **a company** may earn over $1 billion annually. PLURAL Today **companies** may earn over $1 billion annually.	
Specific (With the)	Today, **the companies** that earn over $1 billion annually are primarily oil companies.	*The* is used before a singular or plural count noun when that noun is specifically identified or its identity is already understood.
Unique Nouns	Many of the largest companies **in the world** are oil companies. Oil companies control most of **the earth's** known oil reserves.	*The* is used with names of people, places, and so on that are considered to be one of a kind. These include *the earth, the world, the moon, the sun, the universe, the president,* and *the pope*. Exception: *on earth*

	examples	notes
Repeated Nouns	He works for **an oil company.** **The company** has sent him to work in many different parts of the country. He enjoys working for **the company,** but he is tired of traveling.	After a noun has been mentioned, once, *the* is used with later references to that noun.
Identifying Phrases	**The majority of companies** with billion dollar incomes are oil companies.	Phrases that come immediately after a noun often identify it, so *the* is used. *the* + noun + *of* is a frequent combination.
Identifying Clauses	Today, **the companies that earn over $1 billion** are primarily oil companies.	Like phrases, clauses may identify or specify *which* person, place, or thing.
Superlatives and Ordinal Numbers	The company with **the highest income** is Exxon.	*the* is normally used with superlatives (*the most, the least*) and ordinal numbers (*the first*).

**exercise** The following sentences include both specific and nonspecific count nouns. Complete them by using *the,* or use *X* to indicate that no article is necessary.

example: __X__ natural resources are important to all countries.

1. _____ most important resources in England are tin and iron ore.

2. _____ raw materials are used to make _____ products.

3. _____ raw materials that are used to make _____ cars include iron ore, rubber, and petroleum.

4. _____ petroleum deposits are located in many parts of the world.

5. _____ petroleum deposits in the Amazon will be difficult to extract.

6. _____ mines can be _____ very dangerous places to work.

7. _____ mines near Bogotá, Colombia, produce large quantities of salt.

8. _____ coal mines in West Virginia have caused many deaths.

C. *the* with Noncount Nouns

Articles are not generally used with noncount nouns. However, noncount nouns, like count nouns, may be preceded by *the* when the noun is *specifically identified.*

	examples	notes
Nonspecific (**Without** the)	**Gold** is a precious metal.	No articles are used with unspecified nouns.
Specific (**With** the)	**The gold in jewelry** is mixed with other metals. **The gold that is used in jewelry** is mixed with other metals.	*the* is used with a noncount noun when the noun is identified by a phrase or clause.
	South Africa produces **the most gold** in the world.	*the* is usually used with superlatives.

 **exercise 2**   The following sentences include both specific and nonspecific noncount nouns. Complete them by using *the,* or use *X* to indicate that no article is necessary.

   example: ___X___ silver is valuable.

1. Most of _____ silver in the United States is used to make photographic and X-ray film.

2. _____ iron ore is used to make _____ steel.

3. _____ iron ore from eastern Canada is high in quality.

4. Japan produces some of _____ best steel in the world today.

5. _____ oil from Saudia Arabia is lighter in weight than _____ oil from Venezuela.

6. _____ oil is the most important single factor in the world's economy.

7. _____ gold is perhaps _____ most highly treasured metal.

8. Since 1910, one-third of _____ gold in the world has been mined in South Africa.

D. *the* with Proper Nouns

The has specific uses with proper nouns, especially with geographical locations. Because proper nouns identify specific places, *the* is often used. There are few exceptions to the rules. Study the information in Appendix Four and use it for reference.

exercise 3 Use *the* or *X* with the following phrases.

examples: the Hawaiian Islands

   X Hawaii

1. _____ Great Lakes
2. _____ Lake Superior
3. _____ America
4. _____ United States
5. _____ Golden Gate Bridge
6. _____ equator
7. _____ Saudi Arabia
8. _____ 1995
9. _____ 1990s
10. _____ Philippine Islands

11. _____ Museum of Modern Art
12. _____ Rocky Mountains
13. _____ earth
14. _____ Canada
15. _____ president
16. _____ President Kennedy
17. _____ University of California
18. _____ Harvard University
19. _____ eighteenth of March
20. _____ Japanese (people)

exercise 4 Complete the following sentences by using *the,* or use *X* to indicate that no article is necessary. The first one is done as an example.

1. The world's major source of diamonds is __X__ southern Africa. _____ Star of _____ Africa, the world's largest cut diamond, was found there. Today _____ Star of _____ Africa is one of _____ British crown jewels kept in _____ Tower of _____ London.

2. The world's finest emeralds are mined in _____ Andes Mountains in _____ Colombia, _____ South America. The most important mine is located near _____ town of _____ Muzo on _____ Minero River.

3. The world's largest rock crystal, 1,000 pounds, was found in _____ Burma. A piece of this rock crystal is displayed at _____ National Museum in _____ Washington, D.C.

4. The largest known pearl was found in _____ Philippine Islands in _____ 1930s. It weighed 14 pounds, 1 ounce. The largest known black pearl was found near _____ Fiji in _____ 1984.

5. _____ world's largest gold mine is in _____ South Africa. _____ South Africa supplies 60 percent to 70 percent of _____ gold in _____ world. _____ largest uranium field in _____ world is also located in _____ South Africa.

 Make complete sentences from the following cues. Add *of, from,* and *in* and be sure to include *the* when necessary.

> example: large gold deposits / exist / Andes Mountains / South America
> **Large gold deposits exist in the Andes Mountains in South America.**

1. oil / be a valuable resource
2. oil / Sauda Arabia / be lightweight and high in quality
3. copper / South America / be easy to mine
4. copper / be important for the communications industry
5. silver / United States / be primarily found / Rocky Mountains
6. silver / be used to make photographic film
7. 40 percent / silver / United States / be used for photography
8. diamonds / be / precious gems
9. large diamond mines / exist / Ural Mountains / Russia
10. 25 percent / diamonds / world / be found / West Africa

 Complete the passage here and on the next page by using *the* or *X* (to indicate that no article is necessary). The first one is done as an example.

MINERAL RESOURCES

_____X____ minerals are abundant in _____ nature. _____ earth is made up of
  1
_____ minerals, and even _____ most valuable minerals are found in _____
  4   5   6
common rocks everywhere. Nevertheless, many of _____ minerals near _____
                                                      7   8
earth's surface exist in _____ small amounts. As a result, they cannot be mined
                     9
economically. Only _____ big deposits can be mined at a reasonable cost.
                10
_____ biggest deposits of _____ minerals are distributed unequally around
  11   12
_____ world. Some minerals, like _____ iron in _____ Mesabi Mountains in
  13   14   15
_____ Michigan, are almost gone. Others, like _____ copper, cobalt, and
  16   17
_____ petroleum, are located under _____ Atlantic and _____ Pacific Oceans
  18   19   20
and _____ Persian Gulf.
     21

We have already taken many of ____ mineral deposits that were easy to
mine. Today ____ companies have to look harder and deeper to find ____
minerals, and ____ cost of ____ minerals reflects this. Unless ____ explo-
ration and ____ technology keep up with our use of ____ resources, ____
cost of ____ minerals will increase dramatically.

exercise 7 Complete the following by adding *the* or *X* (to indicate that no article is
necessary).

WHERE MINERALS ARE LOCATED

Some of ____ earth's most valuable resources are found in only a few
countries. For example, ____ South Africa and countries in ____ former
Soviet Union produce one-third to one-half of many vital resources. They are
____ world's largest producers of ____ manganese, ____ chrome, ____
platinum, and ____ gold. ____ Australia is another country that contains
major resources. It has large deposits of ____ oil, ____ gas, ____ iron ore,
and ____ coal. In fact, ____ Japan gets almost one-half of its iron ore (which
is used to make ____ steel) and ____ large quantities of ____ coal from
____ Australia. ____ Canada, too, has ____ large mineral deposits. ____ oil
and ____ natural gas deposits in ____ Canada are some of ____ biggest in
the world.

exercise 8 Reread the opening passage "The Global Economy" on page 180. Then do the
following:

1. Look at the last paragraph of the passage, and underline the nouns. Which
   are singular and which are plural? Which are count nouns and which are
   noncount?
2. Look at the word(s) that come before each noun. Which nouns are
   preceded by articles (*a, an,* or *the*)? Which are preceded by adjectives?
   Which nouns stand alone?
3. Look at the second and third sentences in the last paragraph. Can you
   explain why *a* is used with *picture* in the second sentence, but *the* is used
   in the third sentence?
4. Look at the phrase *the study of weather* in the first paragraph. The pattern
   the + noun + *of* + noun is common in English. Underline all other examples
   of this pattern in the passage.
5. Does *economics* take a singular or a plural verb? Can you think of other
   examples of singular nouns that end in -*s*?

Using What You've Learned

activity

Are you interested in knowing more about gold? petroleum? diamonds? a certain kind of wood—mahogany, teak, ebony? a certain kind of rock—marble, slate, granite? As a group, pair, or individual project, choose one resource that you would like to learn more about and briefly research it at a library. Gather information on where this resource is found today, how it is extracted, and how it is used. Use your research as the basis for a short composition. Finally, share your information with the rest of the class in a three- to five-minute presentation.

TOPIC four

Units of Measurement

Setting the Context

previewing the passage

What is the typical diet of people in your culture? Does religion or tradition play an important part in deciding what people eat or don't eat?

Family in the 1950s having dinner

Family in the 1990s eating dinner in a fast-food restaurant

Diet and the Demand for Food

The demand for different food products depends on three factors: the number of people in the area, their standard of living, and their cultural attitudes. The first two factors are obvious. The third, cultural attitudes, often depends on diet habits and religion. Take attitudes toward diet in the United States, for example.

Changes in preferences and prices have had an interesting effect on consumption in America. In 1940, Americans consumed 19.4 pounds of butter and margarine per person, and most of it was butter. Now they eat less than 16 pounds, most of it margarine. Fruit consumption per person has dropped from 158 pounds to 100 pounds per year. Before World War II, Americans averaged 155

pounds of wheat flour a year; now they average about 120. On the other hand, Americans are eating more chicken, turkey, and vegetables.

discussing ideas

According to the passage, how are American eating habits changing? Have the diets and eating habits in your country or culture changed much in the last forty to fifty years?

Units of Measurement

Units of measurement are commonly used in this pattern: number or percent + unit + *of* + name of item. Note that *of* is not used with *dozen* or *half dozen*, however.

units of measurement	items
bar	hand soap, candy
bottle	liquids such as beer, soda pop, and wine
box	solids such as cereal and crackers
bunch	items that grow together—such as bananas, celery, or grapes—and items that are tied together, such as flowers. In informal English, *a bunch* is often used to mean "a lot."
can	liquids and solids such as soda pop, beer, and vegetables
carton	eggs; milk, ice cream, and other dairy products; cigarettes
dozen, half dozen	eggs; cookies, rolls, and other items bought in quantities of six or twelve
gallon, quart, pint, ounce	most liquids and ice cream
head	lettuce, cabbage, cauliflower
jar	jam, mayonnaise, and other items that are spread with a knife
loaf	bread
piece, slice	most solids, such as bread, cake, cheese, and meat
pound, ounce	cheese, butter, fruit, meat, poultry, and other solids
roll	paper towels, toilet paper
six-(twelve-) pack	soda pop and beer
tube	toothpaste, creams, and ointment

exercise 1

Complete the following grocery lists by adding appropriate units of measurement. Be sure to use *of* when necessary. The first one is done as an example.

2 _____pounds of_____ ground beef   1 _____ grapes

1 _____ butter   2 _____ crackers

1 _____ milk   1 _____ mayonnaise

1 _____ lettuce   1 _____ toothpaste

3 _____ cereal   1 _____ wine

2 _____ paper towels   1 _____ ice cream

1 _____ jam   3 _____ bread

1 _____ eggs   1 _____ celery

1 _____ soda pop   2 _____ cheese

exercise 2

Using the following list of equivalents, convert the amounts from metric to British units. You may give approximate (rounded-off) equivalents.

METRIC AND BRITISH UNITS

Length   Meter: about 1.1 yards (3 feet = 1 yard)
Centimeter: .01 meter: about .4 inch
Kilometer: 1,000 meters: about .6 mile

Volume   Liter: about 1.06 quarts
Milliliter: 0.001 liter: five make a teaspoon

Weight   Gram: 30 = 1.1 ounces
Kilogram: 1,000 grams: about 2.2 pounds

Temperature   Celsius: 0°C = 32°F

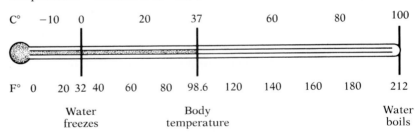

| C° | −10 | 0 | | 20 | 37 | | 60 | | 80 | | 100 |

| F° | 0 | 20 | 32 | 40 | 60 | 80 | 98.6 | 120 | 140 | 160 | 180 | 212 |

Water freezes   Body temperature   Water boils

example: four liters of milk

Four liters of milk are approximately equal to one gallon of milk.

1. one liter of milk   5. three kilograms of cheese
2. three meters of fabric   6. a meter of rope
3. thirty-two liters of gas   7. ten milliliters of sugar
4. ten centimeters of tape   8. twenty degrees Celsius

Use the list of equivalents on page 213 again. This time convert the following amounts from British to metric units. You may give approximate (rounded-off) equivalents.

example: four gallons of gas

Four gallons of gas is approximately equal to sixteen liters of gas.

1. two pounds of cheese
2. one quart of milk
3. five pounds of chicken
4. two yards of fabric
5. one teaspoon of salt
6. ten feet of rope
7. three inches of string
8. three teaspoons of sugar

Review. Complete the next passage by using *a, an* or *the,* or by using *X* to indicate that no article is necessary. Explain any cases where you feel more than one choice may be appropriate. The first two have been done as examples.

THE GREEN REVOLUTION

In 1910, __X__ farmers represented 33 percent of __the__ U.S. work force,
         1   2
and it took more than _____ hour of _____ work to produce _____ bushel of
                        3   4   5
_____ corn. By 1980, two minutes of _____ work produced _____ same
  6   7   8
amount, and _____ farm employment had fallen to about 3 percent.
             9

In 1950, _____ very good dairy cow could produce 1,200 gallons of _____
          10   11
milk per year. By 1987, _____ dairy cows were averaging 2,400 gallons _____
                         12   13
year, and some prize cows had even reached 6,000 gallons. During _____
                                                                  14
1990s, _____ milk production is expected to increase by at least 15 to 20
        15
percent.

These are only two examples of _____ dramatic changes that have occurred
                                16
in _____ agriculture. Through _____ advances in _____ science and _____ tech-
   17   18   19   20
nology, _____ modern agriculture has become one of _____ greatest success
         21   22
stories of this century.

Yet despite the "green revolution," _____ hunger plagues _____ earth.

23   24

According to _____ World Bank, at least 730 million people are malnour-

25

ished—so poorly fed that they are unable to lead _____ normal, active lives—

26

and, unfortunately, _____ number of _____ malnourished people will continue

27   28

to rise as _____ 85 million babies are born each year. We need _____ annual

29   30

food increase equal to _____ Canada's total yearly grain harvest just to keep up

31

with _____ growth in _____ population worldwide.

32   33

 **exercise 5**

Review. Complete the following passage by using *a, an, the,* or *X* (to indicate that no article is necessary). Explain any cases where you feel more than one choice may be appropriate.

CHANGING EATING HABITS

_____ population growth is not _____ only problem that we face in terms of

1   2

_____ world food supply. _____ changes in _____ eating habits are also causing

3   4   5

_____ problems.

6

As _____ countries become richer, they consume more meat. _____ meat

7   8

production normally uses more resources in _____ land, _____ water, and

9   10

_____ work. When _____ farmland is poor, raising _____ cows is efficient, but

11   12   13

when _____ farmland is rich, raising _____ crops gives much more food.

14   15

_____ wheat, _____ rice, or _____ other crops grown for _____ direct human

16   17   18   19

consumption produce much more human food per acre. _____ reason for this is

20

that _____ cow uses up to 90 percent of _____ energy from grain to convert it

21   22

to meat.

Today, about one-third of _____ world's grain production is fed to _____

23   24

livestock (cows, pigs, and so on). This amount of grain is enough to supply

_____ human energy needs of _____ China and _____ India.

25   26   27

Using What You've Learned

How well do you know grocery prices? Check your budgeting ability. First, make a list of at least ten items that you need to buy. Your list should include food and household items. Use specific units of measurement in your list, and write down what you believe each item costs. Then work with a partner. Do not let your partner see your estimated prices. Your partner should write down estimates for your list, while you write down estimates for your partner's list. Finally, during the next two or three days, go to a grocery store and check the prices. Report back to the class on how accurate you were. You can use the following chart to help you.

ITEM	ESTIMATED COST 1 NAME:	ESTIMATED COST 2 NAME:	STORE PRICE NAME:

In small groups, discuss household staples and daily necessities in your countries or cultures, including common household items as well as food. Compare changes that have occurred in recent years, including changes in diet or use and in price. Use a chart such as the one below to help you.

You may separate into groups from the same region, country, or culture. Then, as a class, compare the differences from group to group. Or, if possible, include representatives of various countries and cultures in each group. Compare the differences within each group.

COUNTRY OR CULTURE	ITEM	COMMENTS
Colombia	bread vs. arepas	Arepas made of corn produced in Colombia used to be a staple food, and a family would consume dozens of them a day. This has changed a lot. Now Colombians buy loaves of bread made of flour that has been imported.

CHAPTER seven
Leisure Time

in this chapter

Gerunds, Infinitives, and Other Verb Forms

Introduction

In this chapter, you will study the use of gerunds and infinitives, including how they can function as nouns, which verbs they often follow, and how the use of one or the other can change the meaning of a sentence. You will also look at a few uses of other verb forms: simple, present participle, and past participle forms.

The following passage introduces the chapter theme, Leisure Time, and raises some of the topics and issues you will cover in the chapter.

How Important Is Leisure Time?

How important is leisure time? How important is time to relax and to collect yourself? Many doctors believe that learning to relax in order to relieve day-to-day tension could one day save your life.

5 In our fast-paced world, it is almost impossible to avoid building up tension from stress. All of us confront stress daily; anything that places an extra demand on us causes stress. We encounter stress on the job, and we face it at home.

The body responds to stress by "mobilizing its defenses." Blood pressure rises and muscles get ready to act. If our tension is not relieved, it can start numerous reactions, both physical and psychological. Yet, we can learn to cope
10 with stress effectively and to avoid its consequences. How? By relaxing in the face of stress. According to researcher Hans Selye of the University of Montreal, the effects of stress depend not on what happens to us, but on the way we react. In times of stress, taking a few moments to sit quietly and relax can make anyone feel better.

discussing ideas According to the passage, what causes stress? How does the body react physically to it? What is the best way to cope with stress?

TOPIC one

Introduction to Gerunds and Infinitives

Setting the Context

previewing the passage What does *to each his own* mean?

To Each His Own

For some people, listening to classical music is fun, but it's really difficult for me to sit through a whole concert. Now rock music—that's another story!

discussing ideas

What is your favorite pastime? What about your classmates? Do you like similar pastimes? Or different ones?

A. Forms and Functions of Gerunds

	examples	notes
Noun Object of a Verb	I enjoy **the ocean**.	Gerunds have the same forms as present participles (simple form + *ing*), but they are used as nouns.
Gerund Object of a Verb	I enjoy **swimming**.	
Gerund Subject	**Swimming** is my favorite sport.	
Gerund Complement	My favorite sport is **swimming**.	See Appendix One for spelling rules for the *-ing* ending.
Gerund Object of a Preposition	By **swimming** a lot, I stay in shape.	

active	passive	notes
Losing a job is difficult. **Not having** a job can be very stressful. Everyone was worried about **John's finding** a new job. Everyone was worried about **his finding** a new job.	**Being fired** is a difficult experience. **Not being rehired** is almost like being fired. Everyone was concerned about **Miki's being fired**. Everyone was concerned about **her being fired**.	Passive gerunds are formed by using *being* + past participle. *Not* comes before the gerund. Possessive nouns or pronouns may also be used before gerunds.

Note: In informal English, object pronouns are often used before gerunds. Compare: *Everyone was worried about his finding a new job.* (more formal) *Everyone was worried about him finding a new job.* (informal)

 **exercise 1** Make six sentences with active gerunds after the verb *like* or *enjoy*. Use these ideas and add some of your own.

example: **I like (don't like) getting up early.**

cook	play tennis
drink coffee	roller-blade
√ get up early	read science fiction
jog	sleep late
listen to classical music	study English grammar

 **exercise 2** Make complete sentences from the following. Begin your sentences with *We appreciate. . . .* Use the example as a model.

example: you / help us

We appreciate your helping us.

1. you / call us
2. he / help us
3. John / send us a letter
4. Mary / tell us about that
5. they / write us
6. Mark / come to the party

 **exercise 3** Complete the second sentence in each pair with a passive gerund. Use the example as a model.

example: We like telling jokes to our children. Our children like

____being told____ jokes.

1. We like playing with our children. Our children like _____

_____ with.

2. We enjoy singing to our children. Our children enjoy _____

_____ to.

3. We enjoy telling stories to our children. Our children enjoy

_____ stories.

4. We like reading to our children. Our children like _____

to.

5. We like holding our children. Our children like _____ .

6. We enjoy including our children in many activities. Our children enjoy

_____ in many activities.

exercise 4 Complete the following sentences with active or passive gerunds formed from the verbs in parentheses. Include negatives and possessives when indicated.

example: ___Laughing___ (laugh) is one of the healthiest ways of

___relaxing___ (relax).

1. _____ (laugh) can keep you from _____ (worry)

about a problem.

2. Some humor is universal, but other humor depends on _____

(you / understand) certain types of jokes.

3. _____ (not understand) American humor is a problem

for many foreigners.

4. People everywhere enjoy _____ (listen) to jokes. In fact, some

people don't even mind _____ (tell) the same joke several times.

5. _____ (make) people laugh can be a full-time job. For example,

comedians and circus clowns earn their living by _____

(laugh) at.

B. Gerunds Following Prepositions

	examples	notes
Noun Object of a Preposition	Thanks **for the phone call.** Thanks **for the invitation.**	Only the gerund form of verbs may be used to replace nouns as the objects of prepositions. Infinitives may *not* be used.
Gerund Object of a Preposition	Thanks **for calling.** Thanks **for inviting us.**	

Common Expressions with Prepositions That Are Often Followed by Gerunds

be accused of	be sick of	plan on
be afraid of	be tired of	put off
be famous for	approve of (disapprove of)	talk about (talk over)
be fed up with	blame (praise) someone for	think about
be good at	complain about	worry about
be interested in	excuse someone for	How about . . . ?
be satisfied with (dissatisfied with)	get through	

Expressions with *to* That Are Often Followed by Gerunds

In the following idiomatic expressions, *to* is a preposition, and the gerund form follows it if a verb form is used. Do not confuse the preposition *to* with the *to* used in infinitives (*to* + verb).

	examples	expressions
Noun Object of to	I am looking forward **to the party**.	be accustomed to
		be opposed to
		be subjected to
Gerund Object of to	I am looking forward **to seeing you**. (*Not* I am looking forward to see you.)	be used to
		look forward to
		object to
		plead guilty (innocent) to

 **exercise 5** Complete the following three conversations by adding prepositions and forming gerunds from the verbs below. Use each verb and each preposition at least once. The first two are done as examples.

be	hear	√ watch	in
become	√ listen	write	of
get	lose	about	on
go	see	at	to
have	take	for	with

1. JOHN: I'm tired _of_ _watching_ television. Let's find some-

thing else to do.

SUSAN: Well, the news will be on the radio in a minute. Are you interested __in__ ____listening____ to it?

JOHN: No, I'm not. I'm fed up _____ _____ only bad news.

SUSAN: If you want to change things, how _____ _____ a news reporter? You're good _____ _____ stories. Then you could tell about good news!

2. NANCY: You look upset. What's the matter?

SANDY: Jim is afraid _____ _____ his job. He's worried _____ _____ fired.

NANCY: You both need some rest and relaxation. Why don't you think _____ _____ a short trip this weekend? I know a place that is famous _____ _____ very relaxing.

3. FRED: Aren't you looking forward _____ _____ to the movies tonight?

MARGARET: I like movies, but the movie you are planning _____ _____ is very violent.

FRED: Well, would you object _____ _____ dinner at a restaurant instead? How about _____ to the Club for their fabulous fish fry!?

 **exercise 6** Do you have a hobby, sport, or some other activity that you enjoy? Use this exercise to tell your classmates about it.

Complete the following sentences by using gerunds after the prepositions and by adding any other necessary information. You may want to use the verbs *do, watch, listen (to), try, study,* and *buy.*

example: Some people can learn . . . by . . .

Some people can learn photography by studying it.

1. Some people learn best by . . .
2. Other people learn from . . .
3. Here are my recommendations for . . .
4. You should start by . . .

5. Before . . . , you should . . .
6. While . . . , you should . . .
7. Instead of . . . , you should . . .
8. After . . . , you . . .

C. Forms and Functions of Infinitives

	examples	notes
Noun Object of a Verb	I would like **dinner**.	The infinitive is *to* + simple form. Like the gerund, it is a verb form that can replace a noun. It can also be used with or without *in order* to show purpose. It may *not* be the object of a preposition.
Infinitive Object of a Verb	I would like **to eat**.	
Infinitive Subject	**To eat** at Maxim's is his goal.	
Infinitive Complement	His goal is **to eat** at Maxim's.	
Infinitive of Purpose	**To pay** the bill, he'll save for a month. He'll save for a month **(in order) to pay** the bill.	

active	passive	notes
We wanted **to tell** John about the plans. Mary said **not to tell** him. It's important **for John to know** about this. It's important **for him to know** about this.	John has **to be told** about the plans. There is no reason for him **not to be told**. It's important **for John to be told**. It's important **for him to be told**.	Passive infinitives are formed by using *to be* + the past participle. *Not* comes before the infinitive. *For* + a noun or pronoun may also be used as the subject of an infinitive.

Note: When two or more infinitives appear in a series, it is not necessary to repeat *to*. Compare: *He loves to eat, to drink, and to be merry.* Or *He loves to eat, drink, and be merry.* In any series, it is important to use parallel structure: Do *not* mix infinitives and gerunds, if possible. INCORRECT: *He loves to eat, drinking, and to be merry.*

exercise  Make six statements with active infinitives after the verb *like*. Use these ideas and add some of your own.

example: **I like (don't like) to get up early.**

clean   play basketball
drink tea   read novels
get up early   sew
ice skate   swim
listen to country western music   watch TV

Make complete sentences from the following. Begin your sentences with *It's important. . . .* Use the example as a model.

example: you / help us
It's important for you to help us.

1. you / call us
2. he / help us
3. John / send us a letter
4. Mary / tell us about that
5. they / write us
6. Mark / come to the party

Gerunds are used more often than infinitives as subjects of sentences. However, infinitives are frequently used with anticipatory *it* as a subject. Change the following sentences to begin with *it*.

example: Listening to music is relaxing.
It's relaxing to listen to music.

1. For many people, hearing classical music is enjoyable.
2. For other people, going to a rock concert is more exciting.
3. Playing classical music well can be difficult.
4. Learning a piece of music can take several weeks.
5. Appreciating classical music was never easy for me.
6. For me, listening to country western music is more fun.

exercise 10 Complete the second sentence in each pair with a passive infinitive.

example: We like to tell jokes to our children. Our children like

_____*to be told*_____ jokes.

1. We like to play with our children. Our children like _____

_____ with.

2. We like to sing to our children. Our children like _____

to.

3. We like to tell stories to our children. Our children like _____

_____ stories.

4. We like to read to our children. Our children like _____

to.

5. We like to hold our children. Our children like _____.

6. We like to include our children in many activities. Our children like

_____ in many activities.

Complete the following by using either active or passive infinitive forms of the verbs in parentheses. Be sure to include negatives or subjects (phrases with *for*) when indicated. The first two are done as examples.

STRESS

LOIS: What a stressful day! I need ____to take____ a vacation!
1 (take)

CLARK: You look tired. It would be good ___for you to get away___ for a while.
2 (you / get away)

LOIS: This story had _____ by 10:00 A.M. In order
3 (finish)

_____ it on time, I had _____
4 (I / finish)   5 (stay)

up all last night. It would be terrific _____
6 (have / not)

_____ for the rest of the day.
7 (work)

CLARK: Wouldn't it be great _____ a month off? It would be
8 (take)

nice _____ nothing but relax.
9 (do)

LOIS: It would be even nicer _____ us a raise. Then I
10 (the boss / give)

wouldn't need _____ so much. Well, it's easy
11 (work)

_____, isn't it?
12 (dream)

Make sentences with infinitive phrases of purpose by combining the sentences below. Match the items or events on the left with the purposes for them on the right in order to create new sentences. The first one is done as an example.

example: **Most people play sports to relax, have fun, and keep in shape.**

1. Most people play sports.
2. However, some people will do almost anything.
3. Some athletes save all their extra money.
4. Avid joggers use computerized running shoes.
5. Some joggers also buy watches with special gauges.
6. Golfers watch videotapes of themselves.
7. Rock climbers use specially designed boots, ropes, and hardware.
8. Bicyclists wear expensive, tight-fitting suits.

a. Computerized running shoes can measure distance and speed.
b. Videotapes help golfers to perfect their "swing."
c. People want to relax, have fun, and keep in shape.
d. These suits cut down wind resistance.
e. With their extra money, they can buy "hi-tech" sports equipment.
f. These gauges measure joggers' heart beat and blood pressure.
g. These people want to become "superathletes."
h. With special equipment, rock climbers can make difficult or dangerous climbs.

D. Infinitives Following Adjectives, Adverbs, and Nouns

Adjectives + Infinitives

examples	notes
I am **pleased to see** you. It is **great to see** you.	Many adjective / infinitive combinations follow this pattern: *it* + *be* + adjective + infinitive.
It was **nice of you to come**.	*Of* + an object often follows adjectives such as *nice, good,* and *polite.*
He was **the first** (person) **to leave**.	Infinitives often follow ordinals (*the first, the second,* and so on) or adjectives such as *the last* and *the only.*

Adverbs + Infinitives

examples	notes
This tennis racket is **too** heavy for me to **use**.	*Too* often implies a negative result: *This racket is very heavy; I can't use it.*
This handle is**n't** big **enough to grip** well.	*Not enough* also implies a negative result: *This handle isn't very big, so I can't grip it well.*
This racket is light **enough to use** yet strong **enough to last** a long time.	*Enough* implies a positive result: *This racket is very light, but it will also last a long time.*
I would like to learn **how to play** tennis well. I would like to know **where to buy** a good racket.	Phrases with *what, when, where,* and *how* are reduced forms of noun clauses: *I would like to learn how I can play tennis well. I would like to know where I can buy a good racket.*

Nouns + Infinitives

examples	notes
Is this a good time **to visit** them? That would be a nice thing **to do**.	Infinitives are often used in the following combination: *this / that / it* + *be* + adjective + noun + infinitive.
In order to finish, we have to work faster. (**To finish,** we have to work faster.)	Infinitives are also used to express purpose or goals. *In order* is not necessary for this meaning; it may be omitted.
There is work **to be done**. I have work **to do**. She wants a magazine **to read**. Do you have money **to buy** one?	Similarly, infinitives can be used after nouns to show what should or can be done with the nouns. *There* + *be* + noun + infinitive is a common combination.

exercise 13 Add infinitive phrases to complete the following.

example: I'm interested in learning how _____to ski._____

1. I'm looking for a pair of skis. Can you tell me where . . . ?
2. Have you considered classes? It would be a good idea . . .
3. Many beginners have a hard time because skiing is a difficult sport . . .
4. It usually takes several years . . .
5. Where can I get skis? Do you know of a good place . . .
6. I don't want to go alone. Do you have time . . . ?
7. I don't know anything about skis. Can you tell me what . . . ?
8. You can always rent skis if you don't have enough money . . .
9. Can you tell me where I can rent skis? I don't know where . . .
10. Thanks for your time. It was really nice of you . . .

exercise 14 Complete the following passages by filling in the gerund or the infinitive forms (active or passive) of the verbs in parentheses. Be sure to include negatives or subjects (*for* + noun / pronoun) when indicated. The first one is done as an example.

1. **LEARNING TO RELAX**

   _____Relaxing_____ should be easy, but many people are so accustomed
       1 (relax)

   to _____ a fast pace in their work that it is difficult
       2 (keep up)

   _____. Instead of _____ and
       3 (they / relax)   4 (calm down)

   _____ a free moment, they immediately worry about
       5 (enjoy)

   _____ something else. It is hard _____
       6 (do)   7 (they / not be)

   busy.

2. DANCE

_____ is the best way _____. While
    8 (dance)   9 (some people / relax)

_____, you can forget about _____. Even if you
    10 (dance)   11 (worry)

don't know how _____, you can still enjoy yourself by
                 12 (dance)

_____ to the music. _____ how
    13 (move)   14 (not know)

_____ well shouldn't bother you. It's more important
    15 (dance)

_____ the music and movement.
    16 (you / enjoy)

3. YOGA

Interest in _____ yoga is at an all-time high, and with
              17 (learn)

good reason. In the past decades, millions of people have begun to realize

the effects of _____ with stress and the importance of
             18 (live)

_____. Yoga is a discipline that combines mental, spiritual, and
    19 (relax)

physical well-being. It teaches you how _____ for your health
                        20 (care)

and beauty at the same time. Most yoga exercises consist of

_____ your body in all directions while breathing
    21 (stretch)

regularly and deeply. By _____ disciplines such as
                   22 (practice)

yoga, you can learn how _____ yourself down and
                   23 (slow)

_____ the effects of _____.
    24 (appreciate)   25 (relax)

Using What You've Learned

What do you feel like doing this afternoon? Tonight? Take turns making suggestions with *how about* + gerund. Make a chain around the class. One student can begin: Turn to your neighbor and make a suggestion. Your neighbor will respond and then turn to his or her neighbor with a suggestion. Continue until the whole class has had a turn.

example: A: **How about going to a movie tonight?**
                  B: **Sorry, but I have a lot of homework.**
                  B: **How about ordering a pizza for dinner?**
                  C: **That sounds great!**

In pairs or small groups, use the following phrases in a discussion of your favorite pastimes (sports, hobbies, arts, crafts). After you have finished, choose one member of your group to give a brief summary of your discussion for the entire class.

I'm interested in . . .	It's fun . . .
I'm excited about . . .	It's enjoyable . . .
I'm afraid of . . .	It's boring . . .
I'm good at . . .	It's interesting . . .

example: **I'm interested in photography. I'm not very good at using all the different lenses, but it's fun. For me, it's always enjoyable to take pictures and to develop my own film. And, it's less expensive for me to do it myself.**

TOPIC **two**

Verbs Followed by Gerunds or Infinitives

Setting the Contex

Have you ever studied the stars? What do you know about the sky?

The Sky Above Us

Humans have always been fascinated by the sky, the wind, and the stars. Even in ancient times, men and women imagined flying or traveling through space—long before it was ever possible to do. Through the years, some of the greatest inventions—telescopes, airplanes, radar, satellites, and spaceships—
5   have come from people who hoped to master the sky.

There are people who enjoy simply looking at the sky. For them, it's relaxing to sit quietly and look. They enjoy watching a sunset or cloud formations or gazing at stars on a clear night. Others, though, want to find action, and they try doing all types of air sports, like flying, ballooning, hang gliding, or skydiving.
10   And, finally, there are those who use the sky to learn more about themselves and their futures. The art of reading the stars—astrology—has existed for centuries. Its zodiac is based on some of the brightest constellations in the sky.

Have you ever tried any of the activities mentioned in the passage? Using telescopes or star charts to study the constellations? Doing air sports, such as flying small planes or hang gliding? Learning astrology?

Verbs Followed by Gerunds or Infinitives

Some verbs may be followed by gerunds, some by infinitives, and some by either. Here are two lists. More verbs are covered later in the chapter. See Appendix Five for a complete list of verbs followed by gerunds or infinitives with examples.

Verbs Followed by Gerunds

anticipate	imagine	**examples**
be worth	involve	Can you **imagine traveling** through outer space?
can(not) help	mind	I **can't help wondering** about the universe.
consider	recommend	
enjoy	suggest	

Verbs Followed by Infinitives

appear	have	seem	**examples**
be	hope	want*	Would you **dare to try** skydiving?
be able	know (how)	would like*	I **would like to learn how** to hang glide.
be supposed	learn (how)	would love*	I've **decided to take** a class.
dare*	need*		I **need to register** for the class today.
decide	plan		

*More information about these verbs is in Topic Three.

exercise 1 Underline all the infinitives and gerunds in the "The Sky Above Us" on page 230. What word(s) come before each? Separate the expressions with gerunds or infinitives into the categories shown below.

VERB + GERUND	PREPOSITION + GERUND	VERB + INFINITIVE	ADJECTIVE, ADVERB, OR NOUN + INFINITIVE
imagined flying			

 **exercise 2** Form complete sentences from the following cues.

> **example:** want / study
>
> **He wanted to study medicine.**

> **1.** appear / be   **5.** not mind / help
> **2.** decide / stay   **6.** plan / study
> **3.** enjoy / listen   **7.** want / learn
> **4.** hope / return   **8.** would like / visit

 **exercise 3** Complete the following using gerund or infinitive forms of the verbs in parentheses.

> **example:** They appeared . . . (be angry)
>
> **They appeared to be angry.**

> **1.** We anticipated . . . (get home late)
> **2.** It was worth . . . (wait for him)
> **3.** We decided . . . (leave earlier)
> **4.** She enjoyed . . . (visit Hawaii)
> **5.** He didn't mind . . . (tell about that) (*passive*)
> **6.** He needed . . . (tell about that) (*passive*)
> **7.** They recommended . . . (see a doctor)
> **8.** I would like . . . (see her)

 **exercise 4** Rephrase each sentence using the cues below. Pay attention to the use of infinitives and gerunds.

> **example:** Would you enjoy flying a plane?
>
> **Would you dare to fly a plane?**
> **Can you imagine flying a plane?**

> **1.** Do you want to learn how to fly a plane?
>
>   Would you like . . .
>
> **2.** You need to find a good instructor.
>
>   I recommend . . .
>
> **3.** I hope to begin flight classes soon.
>
>   I anticipate . . .
>
> **4.** Becoming a pilot involves spending a lot of money.
>
>   Someone who is becoming a pilot has . . .
>
> **5.** Some student pilots decide to buy a plane.
>
>   Some student pilots are able . . .
>
> **6.** My instructor wants to rent a plane.
>
>   My instructor suggests . . .

Complete the following using gerund or infinitive forms of the verbs in parentheses. Be sure to include negatives, possessives, or subjects when indicated. The first one is done as an example.

AMATEUR ASTRONOMY

1. Would you like ____to know____ more about the stars but don't know
   1(know)
   where _____? Well, even though there appear
   2(begin)
   _____ millions of stars, only about six thousand are visible.
   3(be)

2. The visible stars are the brightest but not necessarily the closest. Many of
   these seem _____ together. These groupings are called
   4(group)
   constellations, and many have unusual names, such as Taurus the Bull and
   Orion the Hunter. You can learn _____ many of the
   5(recognize)
   constellations by _____ what they represent.
   6(remember)

3. The best time _____ the stars is during cold, clear
   7(you / study)
   nights. It is easier _____ many of the fainter stars then
   8(see)
   because the atmosphere lets more light reach the earth.

4. Don't be discouraged by _____ a telescope. You can
   9(not have)
   always see important stars—like Polaris, the North Star. Early navigators
   knew how _____ direction by _____
   10(tell)   11(find)
   Polaris because it is almost directly over the North Pole. In order
   _____ a steady direction east or west, you have
   12(keep)
   _____ sure Polaris is in the same position each night.
   13(make)
   Explorers have used this method of _____ for over
   14(navigate)
   three thousand years.

5. If you are interested in _____ more, consider
   15(learn)
   _____ in a course or _____ a local
   16(enroll)   17(join)
   group of astronomers. And, of course, before _____ in
   18(invest)
   a telescope or any expensive equipment, ask your local science museum or
   school department for advice.

 Complete the following, using gerund or infinitive forms of the verbs in parentheses. Be sure to include subjects when indicated. The first one is done as an example.

BIRD-WATCHING

There are some things you can do anywhere—like observing birds. Bird

_____*watching*_____ is a pastime, even a competitive sport, for millions
 1 (watch)

of people around the world. To bird lovers, it's thrilling _____
 2 (see)

a rare bird in the wild, but it's equally exciting _____ birds
 3 (observe)

close to home. The sport is a relaxing but rewarding one for anyone who

enjoys _____ outdoors. Bird-watchers recommend
 4 (be)

_____ a guidebook to local birds and _____
 5 (you / buy)   6 (get)

good, comfortable shoes for _____. They suggest
 7 (walk)

_____ your local parks regularly and perhaps _____
 8 (visit)   9 (get)

involved in a bird-watching society. Within a short time, you will learn

_____ many species of birds.
 10 (identify)

HIGH IN THE SKY: BALLOONING

Could you imagine _____ in a basket and _____ in

1 (stand)   2 (float)

the sky with a small tank of gas as your only power source? Some people

would never dare _____ the sport of _____, but others

3 (try)   4 (balloon)

dream of _____ the worry and work below. For those of you who

5 (escape)

dread _____ up high, this is not your sport! But for those of you

6 (be)

who don't mind _____ high above the ground for hours at a time,

7 (be)

hot-air _____ can fulfill your greatest escape fantasies. From up high,

8 (balloon)

you will be able _____, _____, and _____ a

9 (see)   10 (hear)   11 (feel)

whole new world. Perhaps you won't be able _____

12 (help)

_____ a little nervous, but you can anticipate _____

13 (feel)   14 (see)

your world from a whole new perspective.

Balloonists all agree that the pleasure of the sport is worth _____

15 (take)

the risk and _____ one's fears. They believe that many fears come

16 (face up to)

simply from _____ the principles of _____ a balloon.

17 (not understand)   18 (fly)

_____ it fly involves

19 (make)

_____ air inside the balloon

20 (hold)

and _____ it. The air inside the

21 (heat)

balloon is lighter than the surrounding

air, which makes the balloon rise.

If you really want _____,

22 (escape)

_____ may be the sport for

23 (balloon)

you! Plan _____ your troubles

24 (leave)

on the ground as you experience the

skies above.

Using What You've Learned

Have you ever visited an astrologer or a fortune-teller? In many cultures, telling the future is an important art. Some tell the future through the stars, others through tea leaves, coffee grounds, or crystal balls. Today, use your grammar book to tell the future. Work in pairs or in small groups and role-play a visit to a fortune-teller. Use the following with gerunds or infinitives in your role plays.

example: Do you really want . . . ?

Do you really want to know your future?

1. It will involve . . .
2. You seem . . .
3. Your future appears . . .
4. I can't help . . .
5. You can anticipate . . .
6. You had better (not) hope . . .
7. Have you considered . . . ?
8. You must learn . . .
9. You need . . .
10. I suggest . . .

TOPIC three

More Verbs Followed by Gerunds or Infinitives

Setting the Context

Do you like to be indoors? Or would you rather be outdoors?

The Great Outdoors

Some people spend their time relaxing indoors, but other people need to get outside and do things. It's easy if you happen to live in a warm, sunny place like Florida or California or Hawaii!

discussing ideas

In terms of outdoor activities, what are your favorite sports or pastimes? Do you like to play organized sports, such as soccer or baseball? Or do you prefer individual activities, such as camping or hiking?

A. More Verbs Followed by Gerunds

			examples
admit	finish	regret	**I appreciated** your **explaining** the rules.
appreciate	forgive	risk	You should **spend** some **time reading** the rule book.
avoid	keep (on)	spend (time)	
delay	miss	tolerate	
dislike	postpone	understand	
escape	practice		

B. More Verbs Followed by Infinitives

			examples
afford	hesitate	refuse	Can you **afford to buy** that new set of golf clubs?
agree	intend	tend	
care	manage	threaten	I would **hesitate to spend** that much money.
deserve	mean*	volunteer	
fail	offer	wait	
forget	prepare	wish	
happen	pretend		

*See page 248 for more information about *mean*.

 **exercise 1**   Complete the following, using gerund or infinitive forms of the verbs in parentheses. Be sure to include negatives and make other changes when indicated.

> **example:**   We can't afford . . . (buy that car)
> **We can't afford to buy that car.**

1. They agreed . . . (not tell anyone)
2. We appreciated . . . (he / tell us that)
3. He had avoided . . . (tell us)
4. She deserved . . . (tell) (*passive*)
5. I can't forgive . . . (they / not tell us)
6. He happened . . . (mention / the subject)
7. We regretted . . . (not tell) (*passive*)
8. He waited . . . (tell / officially) (*passive*)

 **exercise 2**   Rephrase each sentence using the cues below. Pay attention to use of infinitives and gerunds.

> **example:**   When I was younger, I managed to play soccer almost every day.
> **When I was younger, I spent time playing soccer almost every day.**

1. I miss having time to play soccer.
   I regret not . . .

2. There happens to be a soccer game this afternoon.
   Would you care . . . ?

3. I meant to tell you about the game sooner.
   I intended . . .

4. Let's avoid spending a lot of money.
   I can't afford . . .

5. John has volunteered to buy the tickets.
   John has offered . . .

6. They'll delay starting the game if it rains.
   They'll postpone . . .

C. Verbs That May Be Followed by a (Pro)Noun Object Before an Infinitive

Infinitives may follow these verbs directly, or a noun or pronoun object may come between the verb and the infinitive. The meaning of the sentence changes with the use of a (pro)noun. Note that *for* is not used before the (pro)noun.

Verb [+ (Pro)Noun] + Infinitive

examples	
ask promise beg want dare would like expect use need	She **asked to play** soccer with us. She **asked her friend to play** soccer with us. She **wanted her friend to play**.

D. Verbs That *Must* Be Followed by a (Pro)Noun Object Before an Infinitive

A noun or pronoun object *must* follow these verbs if an infinitive is used. The object comes between the verb and the infinitive. Note that *for* is not used before the (pro)noun.

Verb + (Pro)Noun + Infinitive

examples		
advise* get remind allow* hire require cause* invite teach* convince order tell encourage* permit* urge force persuade warn	The doctor **encouraged him to get** more exercise. She **persuaded him to start** a regular exercise program. She **told him to begin** today.	

*These verbs are followed by gerunds if no (pro)noun object is used after the main verb.

exercise 3   Complete the following sentences by using *for* or X (to indicate that nothing is needed).

> **example:** We asked __X__ Mary to go camping with us.
>
> It was difficult _for_ her to decide.

1. We had expected _____ her to say yes immediately.

2. She promised _____ us to ask for vacation time.

3. It wasn't easy _____ her to get time off from work.

4. We told _____ her to keep trying.

5. We finally convinced _____ Mary to come.

6. Then, she invited _____ her friend to come.

7. In order _____ both of them to come, we had to find a bigger tent.

8. Our neighbor wanted _____ us to use his tent.

exercise 4   Complete the following passage by using active or passive infinitive or gerund forms of the verbs in parentheses. Be sure to include negatives or noun objects when indicated. The first one is done as an example.

1. Bicycles were invented in the early nineteenth century as "toys" for the

rich, the only people who could afford ____*to buy*____ the early models.

                                                                   1 (buy)

Later, bikes became more affordable, but few people would dare

_____ _____ in order
       2 (risk)   3 (fall)

_____ one.
     4 (try)

2. By 1899, one out of every six Americans had managed _____
                                                     5 (buy)

a bike and _____ how _____ it.
            6 (learn)   7 (ride)

The bicycle boom was on! Even the *New York Times* hired

_____ races and encouraged _____
   8 (reporters / cover)   9 (local groups / sponsor)

bicycle events. But then the automobile was invented, and its popularity

threatened _____ the bicycle entirely.
        10 (eliminate)

3. The 1970s and the oil crisis brought new popularity to the bicycle when the

government urged _____ as much. At the same time,
                  11 (Americans / not drive)

doctors were advising _____ more exercise. Bicycle
                      12 (people / get)

sales skyrocketed—from fewer than 7 million in 1970 to over 15 million

in 1973.

4. The popularity of _____ is expected _____
                       13 (bicycle)   14 (keep)

_____ as millions of people worldwide rely on bikes
15 (increase)

for transportation and recreation. In fact, in Washington, D.C., alone over

seventy thousand bicyclists commute to their jobs daily. These cyclists risk

_____ by cars, and they have _____
         16 (hit)   17 (tolerate)

_____ exhaust-filled air. Yet, bicycle commuters have
18 (breathe)

learned _____ with these hazards. They refuse _____
                19 (live)

_____ the exercise and the low cost of _____
20 (give up)   21 (ride)

a bicycle to work every day.

exercise 5 Complete the following passage with gerund or infinitive forms of the verbs in parentheses. Include negatives and objects where indicated. The first one is done as an example.

THE SIMPLE LIFE: CAMPING

_____Camping_____ can teach you many things, such as how
1 (camp)

_____ plants and animals, _____ a
2 (recognize)   3 (set up)

tent, and _____ a map. Most of all, you can anticipate
4 (read)

_____ more about yourself and your place in nature.
5 (understand)

Whether you decide _____ into the wilderness,
6 (hike)

_____ by canoe, or simply _____ to
7 (travel)   8 (drive)

a nearby campground, you are probably looking for some of the same experi-

ences. Most campers hope _____ a simpler lifestyle. They
9 (find)

tend _____ about work and worries while they enjoy
10 (forget)

_____ outdoors.
11 (be)

Because the number of U.S. campers is increasing daily, the National

Park Service advises _____ several things. First,
12 (outdoor lovers / remember)

although it encourages _____ the outdoors, it urges
13 (campers / enjoy)

_____ nature with respect. That involves
14 (everyone / treat)

_____ your campsite _cleaner_ than you found it. It involves
15 (leave)

_____ _____ the natural world of plants
16 (learn)   17 (enjoy)

and animals without _____ it. Remember that wild animals
18 (disturb)

are wild, and they can hurt you, just as you can hurt them.

The park service invites _____ and _____
19 (you / enjoy)   20 (explore)

the world of nature, but at the same time, it expects _____
21 (you / protect)

each area you visit so that future generations may look forward to

_____ similar enjoyable experiences.
22 (have)

Camping in Yosemite National Park

Using What You've Learned

activity

In small groups, make up a story together. One member of your group will begin, and the rest will add to it to create an entire story. Each student must talk continuously for at least thirty seconds. As you tell the story, keep your book open to pages 237 to 239 and use as many of the verbs on the lists as possible. (To make this activity more difficult, you may use the rule that no verb can be repeated!) Try to use an infinitive or gerund with each. You may use your own opening to begin the story, or you may use one of the following lines:

1. "It was a dark and stormy night." (from *Paul Clifford*)
2. "Romeo, Romeo, wherefore art thou Romeo?" (from *Romeo and Juliet*)
3. "As Gregor Samsa awoke one morning from uneasy dreams, he found himself transformed in his bed into a gigantic insect." (from *The Metamorphosis*)
4. "Once upon a time there lived . . ."
5. "This is the tale of a meeting of two lonesome, skinny, fairly old men on a planet which was dying fast. . . ." (from *Breakfast of Champions*)

TOPIC **four**

Verbs Followed by Either Gerunds or Infinitives

Setting the Context

*previewing
the
passage*

Have you ever played any board games? What are your favorites?

Games People Play

Some people love to compete on the tennis court, and others like to compete on the chessboard. Me, I've always preferred playing Monopoly. I remember playing all night quite often, and sometimes I would continue playing into the morning. I just couldn't stop building those hotels!

*discussing
ideas*

What board games are most popular in your culture? Tell the class about some of them, or better yet, bring a game to class and show your classmates.

A. Verbs Followed by Either Gerunds or Infinitives

These verbs may be followed by either gerunds or infinitives without affecting the basic meaning of the sentence.

examples

Verb + Gerund	It **began raining.**	begin	like*
		can't bear	love*
Verb + Infinitive	It **began to rain.**	can't stand	neglect
		continue	prefer
		hate	start

*Remember that *would like* and *would love* are followed by infinitives. See page 231.

B. Verbs Followed by Gerunds or Infinitives, Depending on the Use of a Noun or Pronoun Object

These verbs are followed by gerunds if no noun or pronoun object is used. If a noun or pronoun object is used, they must be followed by infinitives.

examples

Verb + Gerund	We **don't permit smoking** here.	advise	encourage
		allow	permit
Verb + Noun or Pronoun + Infinitive	They **permitted him to smoke** in the other room.	cause	teach

exercise  Complete the following eight items in your own words. Use at least one infinitive or gerund in each.

example: I like <u>to fish a lot</u>. *or* I like <u>fishing a lot</u>.

1. I like _____.

2. I don't like _____.

3. I would like _____.

4. Last year, I began _____.

5. I still haven't started _____.

6. My teachers always encourage me _____.

7. My parents usually allowed me _____.

8. My parents never permitted _____.

 **exercise 2**   Complete the following conversation by using gerund or infinitive forms of the verbs in parentheses. Note any instance where either an infinitive or a gerund is possible. The first one is done as an example.

HELEN: Harry, let's play some tennis today. You know I love <u>to play (playing)</u>

1 (play)

tennis on a nice day.

HARRY: I would love _____ a set or two, but my elbow hurts.

2 (play)

I've decided _____ tennis until it feels better.

3 (not play)

HELEN: But Harry, you haven't played tennis in months!

HARRY: Oh yes, I have. I played a set with you in December.

HELEN: That was five months ago. Well, then, would you like _____

4 (go)

roller-skating?

HARRY: You know that I really like _____, but my knee hurts.

5 (roller-skate)

HELEN: Harry, I'm going to get upset if you continue _____

6 (make)

excuses. You're just plain lazy!

HARRY: No, I'm not. Besides, there's a golf tournament on TV today.

HELEN: Harry, I can't stand _____ any more boring TV shows.

7 (see)

Let's *do* something.

Complete the following conversation by using gerund or infinitive forms of the verbs in parentheses. Add noun or pronoun objects when indicated, paying careful attention to the use of gerunds and infinitives. Note where either an infinitive or a gerund is possible. The first one is done as an example.

DOCTOR: What happened, Harry?

HARRY: Well, Doctor, my knee suddenly began ____to hurt (hurting)____ several

1 (hurt)

weeks ago, but I've neglected _____ anything about

2 (do)

it until now. I prefer _____ to a doctor unless it's

3 (not go)

absolutely necessary.

HELEN: He may not like _____ to the doctor, but he certainly

4 (go)

loves _____ about his aches and pains!

5 (complain)

DOCTOR: I don't find anything obviously wrong, Harry. But I'd advise

_____ it easy for a week: I'd advise

6 (you / take)

_____ heavy exercise.

7 (not do)

HELEN: Doctor, please don't encourage _____ lazy. If he

8 (Harry / be)

continues _____ at home, he'll get even lazier. I just

9 (sit)

can't stand _____ another day of television. It's

10 (watch)

already started _____ me crazy!

11 (drive)

DOCTOR: I said *heavy* exercise. That allows _____ other

12 (Harry / do)

activities. I encourage _____ any form of moderate

13 (he / do)

exercise.

C. Verbs That Change Meaning Depending on the Use of Infinitives or Gerunds

These verbs may be followed by either infinitives or gerunds, but the choice between infinitives and gerunds affects the meaning of the sentence. In general, the infinitive refers to the future and often involves a purpose, while a gerund refers to the past. The clearest example of this is with the verb *remember*.

	examples	meanings
mean + *Infinitive*	I **meant to visit** Brazil.	I planned to visit Brazil, but I couldn't.
mean + *Gerund*	A trip to Brazil **meant spending** much more money.	A trip to Brazil involved spending much more money.
remember + *Infinitive*	I always **remember to buy** the paper.	I never forget to buy the paper.
remember + *Gerund*	I **remember buying** the paper.	I remember that I bought the paper.
stop, quit + *Infinitive*	He **stopped (quit) to smoke.**	He stopped his work in order to smoke a cigarette.
stop, quit + *Gerund*	He **stopped (quit) smoking.**	He does not smoke any more.
try + *Infinitive*	The room was hot, so we **tried to open** the window.	We were not able to open the window.
try + *Gerund*	The room was hot, so we tried the fan, but it didn't work. Then we **tried opening** the window.	Opening the window was another possibility.

 **exercise 4** Complete the following by using the infinitive or the gerund forms of the verbs in parentheses. The first one is done as an example.

1. After the volleyball game, we all stopped ____to have____ a cup of coffee,

   1 (have)

   but Joanie didn't join us. She said that she had stopped _____

   2 (drink)

   coffee because the caffeine bothered her.

2. Everyone at work was surprised when John quit _____ a long

3 (take)

vacation in South America. He said that we should quit _____

4 (be)

so responsible and take off for faraway places too!

3. "I tried _____ the front door, but it seems _____

5 (open)   6 (be)

stuck."

"Have you tried _____ the key? It's locked, you know."

7 (use)

4. "Did you remember _____ a Monopoly game?

8 (buy)

"Of course, I didn't remember _____ one. I didn't know that

9 (buy)

you wanted one."

"You knew, but you forgot _____ one. I distinctly remember

10 (get)

_____ you _____ one this morning. This means

11 (tell)   12 (buy)

_____ our party tonight."

13 (postpone)

"You meant _____ me, but *you* forgot. I didn't forget!"

14 (tell)

---

exercise 5   **Review.**   Complete the following nine sentences by using either the infinitive or gerund form (active or passive) of the verbs in parentheses. Include negatives and subjects where indicated.

example: ___Mastering___   (master) chess may be frustrating, but it can also be rewarding.

CHESS

1. It will take time and patience _____ (you / learn) the game well.

2. _____ (memorize) the moves of each chess piece is the first step.

3. In order _____ (learn) faster, it is best _____ (you / watch) other players.

4. It is also helpful _____ (teach) by a good player.

5. _____ (plan) a sequence of moves, rather than just one at a time, is the secret to good strategy.

6. _____ (not pay) attention to your opponent's moves can be disastrous.

7. _____ (win) the game is important, but

_____ (play) well, _____ (develop)

strategies and _____ (not get) nervous are just as

important.

8. _____ (watch) by spectators distracts some chess players.

9. Some spectators need _____ (tell)

_____ (be) quiet.

 **exercise 6**   **Review.**   Complete the following passage by using infinitive or gerund forms of the verbs in parentheses. The first one is done as an example.

MONOPOLY

Monopoly, Parker Brothers' game of ____buying____ and
                                    1 (buy)

_____ real estate, was invented in 1933 by an unemployed engineer,
       2 (sell)

Charles Darrow. Darrow had lost his job at the beginning of the Depression,

and although he had continued _____ everywhere, he hadn't been
                                   3 (look)

able _____ steady work in three years. During those years, he tried
        4 (find)

_____ dogs and _____ electric irons _____
    5 (walk)   6 (fix)   7 (make)

some money. _____ busy, he invented things.
                 8 (keep)

First, Darrow tried _____ better bridge score pads and
                         9 (create)

_____ jigsaw puzzles. Unfortunately, no one was interested in
   10 (make)

_____ any of his ideas. Finally, he began _____ about the
   11 (buy)   12 (dream)

days before the Depression when he and his wife had been able _____
                                                                  13 (afford)

_____ vacations. He remembered _____ Atlantic City,
   14 (take)   15 (visit)

New Jersey, and he started _____ maps of the streets. From these,
                              16 (draw)

he developed his game.

The Darrows began _____ every evening _____,
                       17 (spend)   18 (buy)

_____, _____, and _____ "real estate." There
   19 (rent)   20 (develop)   21 (sell)

was no television in those days, and they couldn't afford _____ to
                                                              22 (go)

the movies. _____ with large amounts of money and property was
                23 (play)

entertaining, however, even if neither was real.

Soon friends began _____ in the
                          24 (stop by)

evenings _____ _____
           25 (try)   26 (play)

the game.

Darrow's friends and neighbors asked

_____ sets for them. After a while,
27 (he / make)

Darrow could not make enough sets

_____ the demand for them, so he
28 (satisfy)

went to Parker Brothers with his game. At

first, Parker Brothers rejected it, but that didn't discourage Darrow from

_____ again. Soon, Parker Brothers made him an offer.
29 (try)

Today, Monopoly is the most popular game in the world. It is sold in

fifteen languages.

Using What You've Learned

activity **1**

In pairs or in small groups, use as many of the following verbs as possible to talk about and explain your favorite indoor games. You may want to describe card games, board games, puzzles, or parlor games such as charades. As you talk, be sure to explain any rules involved.

allow	hate	remember
begin	like	start
can't stand	love	stop
continue	permit	try
dislike	prefer	

example: **In Monopoly, you begin by dividing the money and by choosing playing pieces. Then . . .**

activity **2**

Are you frustrated about something? How about getting it out of your system? In groups or as a class, vent your frustrations by making complaints with *can't bear, can't stand,* and *hate* + gerund or infinitive or with *be fed up with, be sick of, be tired of,* and *be sick and tired of* + gerund. Make sure that everyone has the chance to make at least one complaint. Some of you may have more!

example: **I can't stand to do any more homework!**

Special Uses of Other Verb Forms

Setting the Context

Have you ever gone sailing? Is is a popular sport in your area?

Sailing

Nothing is more thrilling* than sailing over white-capped waves on a bright blue day. As the wind blows salty air across your sunburned face and the waves crash against your boat, you begin to breathe the richness of the sea. You feel the salt clinging to your skin and the sun burning your cheeks. You watch the seagulls flying and the pelicans diving for fish. Now the boat pitches† and makes you stagger‡ back and forth. You almost get thrown overboard, but you don't care. Trying to regain your balance, you grin. The trip is exciting and you feel exhilarated§. You smile, seeing, smelling, tasting, feeling the life and power of the sea. It makes you feel alive.

5

*thrilling   exciting
† pitches   rolls forward suddenly
‡stagger   walk out of balance
§exhilarated   excited

This passage uses a great deal of descriptive language. Look again at the vocabulary of sights, sounds, feelings, and movements. Can you give additional descriptive words for each category?

A. Causative Verbs and Related Structures

help, let, and make

These verbs are followed by the simple form of a second verb. They are not generally followed by passive constructions. Note that the use of *to* after *help* is optional.

	examples	notes
help	I **helped** (him) **carry** the packages. I **helped** (him) **to carry** the packages.	*Help* may take the simple form or the infinitive of another verb as an object.
let	I **let** him **borrow** my car. I **let** them **help** me.	*Let* is followed by a noun or a pronoun and the simple form of another verb. It does *not* take an infinitive.
make	I **made** him **wash** my car. I **made** them **help** me. The news **made** me **unhappy**. The bad weather **made** us **late**.	*Make* is followed by a noun or pronoun and the simple form of another verb. *Make* + noun or pronoun + adjective is also frequently used.

have, get, and need

These verbs are often followed by the active or passive form of a second verb.

		examples	notes
have			
	Active	I **had** him **wash** my car. I **had** the barber **cut** my hair.	With *have,* the active form is *have* + noun or object pronoun + simple form. The passive form is *have* + noun or object pronoun + past participle. These constructions are often used when you pay for a service. You *have* someone *do* something, or you *have* something *done* by someone.
	Passive	I **had** my car **washed** (by him). I **had** my hair **cut** (by the barber).	

examples	notes
get and need	
Active I **got** him **to wash** my car. I **needed** him **to wash** my car.	With *get* and *need*, the active form is *get / need* + noun or object pronoun + infinitive. The passive form is *get / need* + noun or object pronoun + past participle. The passive form of *get* is similar in meaning to the passive form of *have*. *Get* is frequently used in conversational English.
Passive I **got** my car **washed** (by him). I **needed** my car **washed** (by him).	

Traveling is fun, but both travel and transportation can cause many problems. Imagine that you've been on a long trip and you're telling about a few of the difficulties you had. Use the following cues to form complete sentences with *make*. Then, think about the last trip that you took. What were some of your reactions to the sights, sounds, smells, food, and weather? Add at least four sentences using your own ideas.

example: the boat ride / feel seasick
> **The boat ride made me feel seasick.**

1. the plane ride / get airsick
2. the bus ride through the mountains / feel dizzy
3. the food / sick
4. the altitude / light-headed
5. the taxi drivers / fear for my life
6. the traffic / arrive late everywhere

Answer the following questions in complete sentences.

1. Do you let other people use your camera (records, golf clubs, or other things that you value in your hobby)?
2. In general, do you let other people borrow things from you?
3. Would you let your best friend borrow something you really value?
4. If it were lost or stolen, would you make your best friend replace it?
5. If it were damaged, would you have your friend pay for repairs?

Imagine that you are planning to take a trip. Think of all the preparations before you leave. Complete the following sentences with appropriate past participles.

example: I'll have an itinerary _____planned_____ by a travel agent.

1. I'll have reservations _____ at a hotel.
2. I'll get my car _____.

3. I'll need the mail _____ at the post office.

4. I'll need my plants _____.

5. I'll have my clothes _____ at the cleaners.

6. I'll get my suitcases _____.

exercise 4   When you have your car checked before a long trip, what do you have done? Use the following cues to form complete sentences with *have, need,* or *get.*

example: car / repair

I'll need the car repaired.

1. the oil / change
2. the brakes / adjust
3. the tires / check
4. the spare tire / repair
5. the engine / tune
6. the car / wash and wax

exercise 5   Complete the following passage with appropriate forms of the verbs in parentheses. The first one is done as an example.

BJORN: Jack, this is Bjorn. I'm taking a little trip and I need a few things. Have

someone _____buy_____ me some tennis balls. Oh, and get someone
           1 (buy)

_____ two reservations on the next flight to Rio de Janeiro.
    2 (make)

JACK: Anything else that you want?

BJORN: Yes, get my white suit _____ and my white hat _____.
                                      3 (press)   4 (clean)

Have my bags _____ and ready to go in an hour. Oh, also, I
                          5 (pack)

need a letter _____ to my attorney. Tell her to have a contract
                       6 (send)

_____ for those new TV commercials. I'll let you _____
       7 (write)   8 (take)

care of the details.

JACK: All right. Have a nice time. When are you coming back?

BJORN: Tomorrow. Have someone _____ me at the airport.
                                              9 (meet)

B. Verbs of Perception

The verbs *see, look (at), watch, observe, listen (to), hear, smell, taste, perceive,* and *feel* can be followed by a second verb. The second verb can be in the simple or the present participle form. Often, there is little difference in meaning between the two forms but the *-ing* form usually stresses an action in progress.

	examples	notes
Present Participle	We **heard** the bell **ringing.**	action in progress
Simple Form	We **heard** the bell **ring.**	completed action
Present Participle	We **saw** the building **burning** down.	action in progress
Simple Form	We **saw** the building **burn** down.	completed action

 **exercise 6** Imagine that you have just taken a boat ride. Use the information in parentheses to complete the following sentences describing what you saw, felt, and so forth.

example: While we were on the ocean, we saw (seagulls / fly around the boat).

While we were on the ocean, we saw seagulls flying around the boat. *or* . . . **we saw seagulls fly around the boat.**

1. We watched (pelicans / dive for fish).
2. We heard (waves / crash into the boat).
3. We felt (saltwater / burn our cheeks).
4. We watched (the sail / fill with air).
5. We felt (wind / blow across our faces).
6. We saw (ocean / become stormy).

C. Present and Past Participles Used as Adjectives

The participle forms of many verbs may also be used as adjectives after linking verbs such as *be, become, feel,* and *get.* In particular, verbs that express emotions are often used in this way.

	examples	notes
Verb	The ideas in that book **interested** me. The plot **fascinated** me.	Verbs that are often used in this way include: *amaze, annoy, astonish, bore, confuse, disappoint, excite, fascinate, frighten, inspire, interest, please, relax, satisfy, surprise, thrill, tire,* and *worry.*

Mosaic One • Grammar

	examples	notes
Present Participle	The ideas in that book were very **interesting** to me.	The present participle expresses the effect of the subject on some-one or something.
Past Participle	I was very **interested in** the ideas in that book. I am getting more **excited about** the subject every day. I never feel **bored with** that book.	The past participle expresses the reaction of the subject to someone or something. Note the variety of prepositions used with the past participle.

 Think about a movie that you've seen recently. Give a short review of the movie by answering the following questions.

1. Why were you interested in seeing the movie?
2. Was the plot interesting?
3. Were you surprised by the ending?
4. Was the language confusing?
5. Did you ever get bored during the movie?
6. Were you tired by the end of the movie, or were you relaxed (excited, fascinated, and so on)?

 Complete the following by using either the present or the past participle of the verbs in parentheses.

example: Staying underwater is ___frightening___ (frighten) to many people.

1. Some people get _____ (worry) about staying under-water for a long time.

2. Yet people everywhere are _____ (interest) in trying scuba diving.

3. Scuba diving is _____ (excite) to many people.

4. They are _____ (thrill) about seeing exotic fish and coral.

5. It is _____ (amaze) to see the variety of fish and plant life that exists underwater.

6. Divers are _____ (surprise / often) by the friendliness of some of the sea animals and fish.

exercise 9   Reread the passage "Sailing" on page 252. Look at the variety of verb forms used in the passage. Try to find several examples for each of the categories shown below.

EXPRESSIONS WITH CAUSATIVE VERBS	EXPRESSIONS WITH VERBS OF PERCEPTION	PARTICIPLES USED AS ADJECTIVES
		thrilling

exercise 10   **Review**   Complete the following passage by using appropriate forms (simple, infinitive, gerund, or present or past participle) of the verbs in parentheses. In some cases, more than one form is correct. Try to give all possibilities.

RIDE THE WIND

_____ is the "hottest," coolest, smoothest, and fastest way
1 (windsurf)

_____ across the water. "It's _____," says one wind-
2 (sail)   3 (thrill)

surfer. "When I catch the wind, I let myself _____, and soon I feel
4 (go)

myself _____ across the water! It makes me _____
5 (fly)   6 (want)

_____ on _____ without ever _____. I get so
7 (keep)   8 (go)   9 (stop)

_____ that I forget how far from shore I've gone."
10 (excite)

_____ is the sport for water lovers who want _____
11 (windsurf)   12 (have)

a great time even though they aren't able _____ to the ocean regu-
13 (get)

larly. You can try _____ on a lake or even a pond. If you decide
14 (windsurf)

_____ it, remember one thing: _____ _____
15 (try)   16 (learn)   17 (windsurf)

usually means a lot of falls into the water. Plan _____ very wet
18 (get)

your first day. But, after one day of _____, you can expect
19 (fall)

_____ the art of _____.
20 (master)   21 (windsurf)

_____ is all a matter of _____ balance and position,
22 (windsurf)   23 (practice)

and you can usually have someone _____ you in three to six hours.
24 (teach)

Soon you will begin _____ your body _____ with the
25 (feel)   26 (move)

board. Those who windsurf seem _____: If you know how
27 (agree)

_____ a bike, you can learn _____. Just remember
28 (ride)   29 (windsurf)

_____ a hot day or _____ a wetsuit because there is no
30 (pick)   31 (rent)

way _____ _____ wet.
32 (avoid)   33 (get)

Using What You've Learned

 **activity 1**

What is on your *To Do* list? What are some repairs or services that you need to take care of? What are some that you have had done lately? Go around the room in a chain, giving statements with *get, have,* or *need.*

examples: **TO DO**   **DONE**

             I have to get my   **I had my teeth checked**

             glasses repaired.   **last week.**

 **activity 2**

When your life is busy, it's had to find time to get everything done that you need to do. It can also be very pleasant to have things done for you. First, make a list of things you enjoy having done for you. Try to give at least five. Then, make a list of things you don't like having done for you. After you have made your lists, work in pairs or small groups. Compare your lists, explaining why you do or do not enjoy each.

examples: **LIKE**   **DON'T LIKE**

             I like getting my   **I don't like having my**

             laundry done.   **teeth cleaned.**

 **activity 3**

Think of a place with lots of unusual sights and sounds. It may be a place that you've visited recently, or it may be a place that you remember from the past. In small groups, take turns telling about the place. Use verbs of perception to describe things that you saw, smelled, heard, and so forth. As an alternative, write a short composition about your place and then share it with your classmates.

examples: **There's a beautiful place in the mountains where we used to camp. From the camp, we could see the mountains rising sharply above us. We would sit and watch deer and moose eating in the meadow below us.**

             Last week I went to Disneyland, and it was incredibly crowded. In every direction, I saw thousands of people walking, standing, eating, laughing, arguing, getting sunburned and tired. I heard hundreds of people screaming as they rode on the different rides.

Think about a trip you've taken; a sport you've played; or a restaurant, store, or museum you've visited during the past few weeks. Give several original sentences using either present or past participles. Choose from the following verbs or add your own.

POSITIVE FEELINGS		NEGATIVE FEELINGS	
amaze	interest	annoy	disappoint
amuse	intrigue	bewilder	shock
excite	relax	bore	tire
fascinate	surprise	confuse	worry

activity 5

Traveling to faraway places is one of the most fascinating ways to spend your leisure time. Imagine yourself in the Middle East, in the Amazon, or in Paris. Imagine where you have been and how you arrived at this destination. Imagine what you will do next. As you imagine, describe everything that you see, hear, smell, feel, perceive. Are you excited? Are you nervous? What are the most interesting things around you?

Use of Verb Forms

Gerunds, infinitives, and other verb forms are frequently tested on standardized English proficiency exams. Review these commonly tested structures and check your understanding by completing the sample items below.

Remember that . . .

- Different verbs are followed by different forms. Make sure the appropriate form is used.
- Gerunds, not infinitives, are used after prepositions.
- In lists containing verb forms, make sure that the same form is used whenever possible. Don't mix forms (for example, gerunds and infinitives) unless it is unavoidable. Try to use parallel structures.

Part 1: Circle the correct completion for the following.

example: John appears _____ happy with his work.
    a. to be
    b. be
    c. been
    d. being

1. The pitching of the waves on the open sea caused the small vessel _____.
    a. capsize
    b. capsizing
    c. to capsize
    d. have capsized

2. It will always be helpful _____ a map while hiking in wilderness areas.
    a. to carry
    b. to carrying
    c. carrying
    d. carry

3. Of the various activities she does, Mary likes swimming and _____ the best.
    a. to ride a horse
    b. to horseback ride
    c. horses
    d. horseback riding

Part 2: Circle the letter below the underlined word(s) containing an error.

example: An individual <u>may</u> feel frustrated and <u>confusing</u> if <u>she</u> has

                   A   Ⓑ   C

         doesn't know the language of the country <u>where she is living</u>.

                                                                D

1. The Park Service always advises visitors <u>using</u> extra caution when

                                              A

   <u>hiking</u> or camping in areas <u>where</u> bears <u>have been sighted</u>.

    B   C   D

2. <u>The</u> popularity of bicycles <u>increased greatly</u> during the 1970s, as

  A   B

   more people began to ride them for pleasure and <u>use</u> them for

                                                C

   <u>to commute</u> to work.

     D

3. Polaris, <u>the North Star</u>, has helped <u>guiding</u> seafarers <u>ever since</u>

           A   B   C

   ancient times when <u>sophisticated</u> navigational tools did not exist.

                           D

CHAPTER eight

Creativity

Introduction

In this chapter, you will review the variety of sentence types in English, and you will study both compound and complex sentences. In terms of complex sentences, this chapter focuses on complex sentences with adverb clauses of time and condition. Later chapters cover other types of complex sentences. As you study this chapter, pay close attention to the time frames expressed by the different constructions.

The following passage introduces the chapter theme, Creativity, and raises some of the topics and issues you will cover in the chapter.

The Creative Urge

If an inventor builds an astounding machine or an artist produces a stunningly original work, we call this creative genius. Yet, creativity is not only in the realm of artists and scientists: It is an attribute we all have within us. The creative urge is the most profoundly human—and mysterious—of all our attributes. Without
5 fully understanding how or why, each of us is creative.

Since earliest times, humans have produced marvelous creations. Learning to use fire and to make tools were incredibly creative achievements. Above all, early humans produced our most extraordinary creation: language.

After our ancestors had learned to communicate with each other, a long
10 series of amazing developments began. Creativity flourished among such peoples as the ancient Egyptians, Minoans, Greeks, Mayans, and the Benin of Africa. Long before the modern age of machines, our ancestors had already developed sophisticated techniques and systems in mathematics, astronomy, engineering, art, architecture, and literature.

15 Of course, not every society has made tremendous achievements by today's standards. While the Egyptians were developing mathematics and building libraries, other societies were still learning to use fire. By the time Europe began to use money, China had already been trading with paper currency for hundreds of years. Nevertheless, every new achievement represents human creativity. If
20 one attribute characterizes humans, it is our creative urge to improve, to find new ways of doing things.

discussing ideas

Who are some creative individuals (past or present) from your culture? What has your culture created that is unusual or unique?

TOPIC **one**

Compound Sentences

Setting the Context

*previewing
the
passage*

Creativity is a difficult concept to define because it means different things to different people. What's your own definition of creativity?

What Is Creativity?

To create means "to bring into being, to cause to exist." According to this dictionary definition, ordinary people are creative every day. We are creative whenever we look at or think about something in a new way.

*discussing
ideas*

Can you give some examples of creativity in our day-to-day lives?

A. Review of Sentence Types

Sentences may be simple, compound, complex, or a combination of compound and complex.

	examples	notes
Simple	Creativity is part of everyday life.	Simple sentences have one subject/verb combination.
Compound	Many artists are highly creative, **but** ordinary people can be just as creative. Some people are creative from childhood; **however,** others show their genius later in life.	Compound sentences are two simple sentences connected by *and, but, for, nor, or, so,* or *yet.* A compound sentence may also be formed by joining two sentences with a semicolon. Transition words or phrases are often used with compound sentences.
Complex	**Although** some people are creative from childhood, others show their genius later in life.	Complex sentences consist of two or more clauses: a main clause that is complete by itself and one or more dependent clauses introduced by a connecting word such as *although, because, if, that, when,* or *who.*

Punctuation Guidelines

1. **Coordinate Clauses**

   A comma is normally used before conjunctions that join two independent clauses.

   _____, and _____.

   Note: The comma is optional in short sentences.

2. **Transitions**

   Most transitions are used at the beginning of a sentence or after a semicolon. They are normally followed by a comma. In some cases, transitions may be used in the middle or at the end of a sentence.

   In addition, _____.

   _____; in addition, _____.

3. Subordinate Phrases and Clauses

Most adverb phrases and clauses may begin or end sentences. A comma is normally used after introductory phrases and clauses.

_____ while
_____.

While _____,
_____.

---

exercise 1

Review. Label subject(s) and verb(s) in the following sentences. Then indicate what type of sentence each is (simple, compound, or complex). If the sentence is compound or complex, circle the connecting word. Underline the *dependent* clauses in complex sentences.

example:
             Subject   Verb   Subject Verb   Verb
         We are creative (whenever) we look at or think about something in a new way.   *Complex*

1. First of all, creativity involves an awareness of our surroundings.

2. It is the ability to notice things that others might miss.

3. A second part of creativity is an ability to see relationships among things.

4. Creativity is involved when we remake or reorganize the old in new ways.

5. We might find a more efficient way to study, or we could rearrange our furniture in a better way.

6. Third, creativity means having the courage and drive to make use of our new ideas.

7. To think up a new concept is one thing; to put the idea to work is another.

8. These three aspects of creativity are involved in all the great works of genius; however, they are also involved in many of our day-to-day activities.

Review. Label subject(s) and verb(s) in the following quotations. Then indicate what type of sentence each is (simple, compound, or complex). If the sentence is compound or complex, circle the connecting word. Underline the *dependent* clauses in the complex sentences.

examples:

                                    S   V

In order to create, there must be a dynamic force.

                                             simple sentence

                        S   V   S V

What force is more potent (than) love is? —*Igor Stravinsky*

                                        complex sentence

1. The creative person is both more primitive and more cultivated, more destructive, a lot madder, and a lot saner than the average person is.

   —*Frank Barron*

2. Creative minds always have been known to survive any kind of bad training. —*Anna Freud*

3. All men are creative, but few are artists. —*Paul Goodman*

4. Human salvation lies in the hands of the creatively maladjusted.

   —*Martin Luther King, Jr.*

5. In creating, the only hard thing's to begin; a grass blade's no easier to make than an oak. —*James Russell Lowell*

6. One must still have chaos in oneself to be able to give birth to a dancing star. —*Friedrich Nietzche*

7. He who does not know how to create should not know. —*Antonio Porchia*

8. A creative artist works on his next composition because he was not satisfied with his previous one. —*Dmitri Shostakovich*

B. Coordinating Conjunctions

And, but, for, or, so, yet, and *nor* are used to join two independent clauses into one compound sentence. A comma is normally used between the two clauses. In short sentences, however, the comma can be omitted. Note that *and, but, or,* and *yet* are often used to join words or phrases, also.

and, but, for, or, so, yet

	examples	notes
Martin is easy-going,	**and** he is quite funny.	*and* = addition
	but he sometimes loses his temper.	*but* = contrast
	for he enjoys just about everything.	*for* = reason
	or at least he seems that way.	*or* = choice
	so many people like him.	*so* = result
	yet he gets nervous about tests.	*yet* = contrast

nor

simple sentences	compound sentences	notes
The box is not very big. It is not very heavy.	The box is not very big, **nor is** it very heavy.	*Nor* is used to join two negative clauses. When *nor* begins the second clause, the auxiliary or the verb *be* is placed before the subject. A negative is not used in the second clause.
Ann doesn't like cold weather. She doesn't enjoy snow.	Ann doesn't like cold weather, **nor does she** enjoy snow.	
Ben hasn't done his homework. He hasn't cleaned the house.	Ben hasn't done his home-work, **nor has he** cleaned the house.	

 **exercise 3** Form compound sentences in items 1 to 6 using the coordinating conjunctions indicated for each set. Change word or sentence order when necessary Also change nouns to pronouns and add commas. For sentences with more than one possibility, form two sentences and try to explain any difference in meaning or emphasis.

example: (nor) Some people do not use all their senses very often. They do not have a very great awareness of their surroundings.

Some people do not use all their senses very often, nor do they have a very great awareness of their surroundings.

1. (but / yet) Some people use all five senses often.
Most of us rely heavily on our sight.

2. (nor)   Many people do not pay attention to sounds.
Many people do not take time to listen.

3. (for / so)   Musicians pay attention to all types of sounds.
Musicians want to find interesting new combinations.

4. (and / yet)   A musician can find music in exotic sounds.
A musician may also hear music in ordinary noises.

5. (or / and)   A car horn may produce a new rhythm.
A bird may sing a new sequence of notes.

6. (but / yet)   Another person may not hear these combinations.
A music lover will find these combinations.

C. Transitions

Transitions are words or phrases that link two related ideas. The accompanying list contains some of the most frequently used. In the following chapters, you will study these and other transitions in more detail.

	examples	notes
Provide Examples	Anyone can be creative. **For example,** a cook who tries a new recipe is creative.	*For instance* is also used to give examples. Like *for example,* it is common in conversational English.
Express Emphasis	Each of us is creative and, **in fact,** we are creative more often than we realize.	*In fact* emphasizes important or little-known information.
Give Additional Information	Creativity involves looking at things in a new way; **in addition,** it means trying new things.	*In addition* has the same meaning as "also."
Show Contrast	Everyone can be creative; **however,** many people are afraid to try.	*However* has the same meaning as "but."
	Some people never try new ideas; **on the other hand,** there are many people who constantly try new things.	*On the other hand* refers to the opposite side of an issue. *In contrast* is also common.

	examples	notes
Provide a Reason or Result	Creativity is a mysterious process; **therefore,** it is difficult to define.	*Therefore* means "as a result" or "so."
Show Sequence (by Time or Order)	Creativity involves several steps. **First,** it is being aware of something. **Next,** it involves seeing a relationship with something else. **Then,** it means using the new ideas.	Some of the most common sequence transitions are: *first, second, now, then, next, earlier, later, finally.* Sequence transitions are not normally used with a semicolon.

exercise  Describe the process of taking a picture by putting the following steps in order. Use sequence transitions (*first, second,* and so on) as you reorder the sentences. More than one sequence is possible.

> **example:** First, load your camera with film.

TAKING PHOTOGRAPHS

1. Focus the camera.
2. Choose an appropriate lens.
3. Take the picture.
4. Look at the object from several different angles and compose your picture.
5. Remove the lens cap.
6. Load your camera with film.

Two of this century's most creative musicians have been the jazz greats Louis Armstrong and Miles Davis. Both played the trumpet, but in other aspects, they were two very different individuals. Read the information about them below. Then write sentences with *in contrast* and *on the other hand.*

example:

Louis Armstrong always tried to please his audiences and his fans.

Miles Davis did not seem to care about popularity.

Louis Armstrong always tried to please his audiences and his fans; in contrast, Miles Davis did not seem to care about popularity.

1. Louis Armstrong came from a relatively poor family in New Orleans.

Miles Davis was born into a prosperous middle-class family in East Saint Louis.

2. Louis Armstrong was friendly and fun-loving.

Miles Davis was often called mysterious, rebellious, and even shy.

3. Armstrong was a film star and comedian as well as a musician.

Davis concentrated only on jazz.

4. Armstrong maintained a consistent style throughout his career.

Miles Davis changed his musical style numerous times.

5. There is a simplicity and clarity to most of Louis Armstrong's music.

The music of Miles Davis is often very abstract and complex.

Louis Armstrong

Miles Davis

**exercise 6**

This passage is about the artist Georgia O'Keeffe and her photographer, Alfred Stieglitz. First, read the passage to understand the ideas. Then, complete it by adding transitions: *however, in addition, in fact, therefore*. Use each at least once. You will also need to add punctuation.

Note: In general, a writer would not use this many transitions in one short passage. Other connecting words such as *although, because, but,* and so on would also be used to give more variety.

GEORGIA O'KEEFFE AND ALFRED STIEGLITZ

Georgia O'Keeffe has been the most famous female artist of the twentieth century. She was born and raised on a large farm in Wisconsin ; *therefore,* she felt more at home in wide open spaces than she did in cities. _____
²
O'Keeffe moved to New York City in the 1920s because of the large artist community there.

It was difficult for a woman to be an artist at that time _____ she
³
had to work very hard to support herself. She sold paintings _____
⁴
she worked as a teacher in order to make a living. In her early years, O'Keeffe received little recognition for her work, and her life in New York was difficult.

_____ after her marriage to the famous photographer Alfred
⁵
Stieglitz, she became very well known.

Stieglitz and O'Keeffe were a brilliantly creative couple. _____
⁶
together, they produced more creative works than perhaps any other twentieth-century couple.

Georgia O'Keeffe and Alfred Stieglitz

Jack-in-the-Pulpit #2 by Georgia O'Keeffe

exercise 7 Combine the following sentences, using *for example, however, in addition, in fact, on the other hand,* or *therefore.* Use each transition once. Add appropriate punctuation and make other necessary changes. For example, change nouns to pronouns when appropriate.

> **example:** Being creative involves making the best use of your senses. Being creative means looking at the same object from many different perspectives.
>
> *Being creative involves making the best use of your senses; for example, it means looking at the same object from many different perspectives.*

1. A good photographer looks at the object itself. A good photographer considers the distance, angle, texture, and light.
2. Light is one of the most important aspects of a good picture. The same scene can be either unusual or boring, depending on the light.
3. Creative photographers experiment with light. They may take the same picture at many different times of day.
4. Mornings and evenings give warm light, rich colors, and long shadows. Noon gives harsh, bright light to a picture.
5. Morning and evening light is richer. Most outdoor photographers work between sunrise and 10:00 A.M. and between 4:00 P.M. and sunset.
6. Bright sunlight makes colors seem pale. Good pictures can be produced even on very sunny days by using a "sunlight" filter.

Using What You've Learned

activity 1 In pairs or in small groups, discuss the various quotations from Exercise 2, page 268. After your discussion, choose one quotation that particularly interests you. Express your own thoughts about it in a paragraph or brief composition. You might explain the quotation, or you might describe a person or activity that illustrates the idea of the quotation.

activity 2 Do you have a pastime or hobby that you enjoy? It might be taking pictures or drawing or playing an instrument or making crafts, for example. Think about how you do this activity. Then, work in pairs or small groups, and take turns describing some of the steps involved in the activity. Try to include sequence transitions in your description.

activity 3

Reread your comparisons of Louis Armstrong and Miles Davis in Exercise 5, page 272. Then think of two other individuals who do the same activity but who have very different styles or personalities. The two may be musicians, artists, sports figures, actors or actresses, or politicians, for example. Write a brief composition comparing the two individuals, using transitions when possible. Then work in pairs or small groups and tell each other about these people.

TOPIC **two**

Adverb Clauses of Time and Condition: Unspecified or Present Time

Setting the Context

previewing the passage

In the following quotation, Theodore Levitt talks about thinking versus doing. As you read, try to decide if you agree with his thoughts on creative ideas and innovation.

Creativity and Innovation

*I*f creativity is thinking up new things, innovation is doing them. Ideas are useless unless they are used, and the proof of their value is in their implementation.*

There is no shortage of creativity or creative people. . . . If there is a shortage, it is a shortage of innovators.

5

Theodore Levitt, Harvard University

discussing ideas

Do you agree with Levitt? Is there a shortage of innovators in our world? Can you give some examples?

---

implementation being put into action

A. Clauses of Time: Unspecified or Present Time

Time clauses can relate ideas or actions that occur at the same time or in a sequence. These may be habitual, repeated activities, or they may be occurring in the present. Note that these clauses may begin or end sentences.

Habitual Activities

	examples	notes
when	**When** Tim Astor gets a new idea for a novel, he writes it down immediately.	*When* joins two actions that happen at the same time or in sequence. In many cases, *when* means "at any time" and is the equivalent of *whenever.* The simple present is generally used in both clauses.
whenever	He begins a new book **whenever** he gets an inspiration.	
after	He edits his material **after** he finishes the entire first draft.	*After, before,* and *until* join actions that occur in sequence. Either the simple present or the present perfect may be used in the dependent clause. The present perfect emphasizes the completion of the action.
before	He never starts a new project **before** he has completed the current one.	
until	He works on a project **until** he is fully satisfied with it.	
as	**As** he is writing, he often listens to classical music.	*As* and *while* may join two actions that happen at about the same time. The present continuous can be used in the dependent clause to emphasize continuity. The verb in the main clause shows whether the action is habitual or happening at the moment of speaking.
while	He often listens to music **while** he is writing.	

Present Activities

	examples	notes
as	Tonight he is listening to Beethoven's Fifth Symphony **as** he is writing.	*As* and *while* can join two actions that are happening at the present. In this case, both clauses are in the present continuous.
while	He is humming **while** he is writing.	

Past and Present Activities

	example	notes
since	He has been writing **since** he woke up at six this morning.	*Since* joins a previous action or situation to an action or situation in progress. The main clause is in the present perfect (continuous).

 **exercise 1**   Complete the following with present forms of the verbs in parentheses. The first one is done as an example.

A METHOD TO OUR MADNESS

For most of us, when we _____think_____ of the work of creative artists

1 (think)

and scientists, we _____ a mysterious world of geniuses. When

2 (imagine)

an inventor _____ an amazing new machine, when a musician

3 (develop)

_____ a beautiful piece of music, or when a scientist _____

4 (create)   5 (make)

a major discovery, we _____ in awe. We _____ that these

6 (feel)   7 (assume)

geniuses _____ very different from us. Yet, geniuses or not, we all

8 (be)

_____ a similar creative process whenever we _____ at

9 (use)   10 (look)

something in a new way or _____ new solutions to a problem. It

11 (try)

_____ a process of first looking at a situation carefully and then

12 (be)

making and following a plan of action.

exercise 2   Think about the process of writing a composition. Make a step-by-step plan of action for writing by forming complete sentences from the clauses below. Try to give at least two completions for each step. You may want to add more steps.

example: Whenever you write something. . . .

        you have to concentrate on your ideas.

  or   *you should find a quiet place without distractions.*

1. Before you begin to write a composition, . . .

2. While you are thinking about the topic, . . .

3. After you have gathered your ideas, . . .

4. When you need more information on a topic, . . .

5. . . . as you are writing.

6. After you have finished writing, . . .

7. . . . until you are satisfied with your composition.

8. . . . before you hand in your composition.

 **exercise 3** Describe the following processes by making statements with time clauses. Explain: (a) what you should do before you begin . . . , (b) what you should do while you are . . . , and (c) what you should do after you have finished. Add modal auxiliaries such as *can* or *should* and combine steps when necessary.

example: **Before you begin painting, you should choose a good piece of watercolor paper. After you have sketched your drawing lightly, wet the paper with water . . .**

1. Painting a watercolor
   - Choose a good piece of watercolor paper.
   - Sketch your drawing lightly.
   - Wet the paper with water.
   - Use watery paint for large areas.
   - Catch any drips.
   - Use a drier brush for details.
   - Let your painting dry completely.
   - Mount your picture.

2. Sculpting clay
   - Put a mat down to protect the table.
   - Work the clay with your hands.
   - Add water to soften the clay.
   - Shape individual parts of the sculpture.
   - Attach each part by pinching it on.
   - Smooth the sculpture with water.
   - Use tools to draw any details.
   - Carefully put the sculpture on a piece of paper.
   - Let the sculpture dry at least twenty-four hours.

 # B. Clauses of Condition: Unspecified or Present Time

	examples	notes
if	**If** Tim writes a lot during the week, he usually has time to relax on the weekend.	The main clause is the effect or result of the dependent clause. These sentences refer to habitual activities or activities that are true in general.
	Tim usually has time to relax on the weekend **if** he writes a lot during the week.	
unless	Tim rarely writes on the weekend **unless** he has a deadline.	*Unless* is used similarly to *if . . . not* in many sentences. However, *unless* is more emphatic.
	Unless he has a deadline, Tim doesn't work on the weekend.	

exercise 4 According to Paul Heist in *The Creative College Student,* the following are some of the chief characteristics of creative students and creative people in general. *Creative people are flexible, independent, innovative, spontaneous, and open to a wide range of experiences. They develop their own styles and their own sense of beauty.*

The following deals with some of these characteristics. Form complete sentences from each pair by matching a main clause with a dependent clause. Be sure to pay attention to the difference in meaning of *if* and *unless.*

example: If you develop your own style, . . .   <u>*b*</u>

Unless you develop your own style, . . .   <u>*a*</u>

　　a. you end up imitating other people.
　　b. you don't have to imitate other people.

1. If a person is independent, . . .   _____

Unless a person is independent, . . .   _____

　　a. he or she usually relies on others for support or encouragement.
　　b. he or she doesn't have to depend on others for support or encouragement.

2. If you are flexible, . . .   _____

Unless you are flexible, . . .   _____

　　a. you can adapt more easily to new situations.
　　b. it may be difficult for you to adapt to new situations.

3. If people are open to new ideas, . . .   _____

Unless people are open to new ideas, . . .   _____

　　a. they can take better advantage of unusual opportunities.
　　b. they may miss many unusual opportunities.

4. If you are innovative, . . .   _____

Unless you are innovative, . . .   _____

　　a. it may be difficult for you to find solutions for many problems.
　　b. you can usually find solutions for most problems.

Complete the following sentences in your own words.

example: I feel most creative when . . .
I am relaxed (I am a little tired, I listen to music).

1. It is easiest for me to write (sing, draw, and so on) if . . .
2. Most of my best ideas come after . . .
3. It is hard for me to concentrate unless . . .
4. I have done my best work since . . .
5. I really enjoy listening to music while . . .
6. I am fascinated whenever . . .
7. It is not easy for me to start a project before . . .
8. I am often afraid to . . . until . . .

 **exercise 6**

What type of student are you? What type of person are you? Answer the following questions in complete sentences.

1. When do you do two things at once?
2. Do you watch TV while you are doing your homework?
3. What else do you do while you are doing your homework?
4. Can you concentrate if people around you are talking or doing other things?
5. Are you nervous before you take a test?
6. Do you celebrate after you have turned in a big assignment?
7. Do you always take notes (listen carefully) when you are in class?
8. Do you get depressed if you get less than an A?

Using What You've Learned

 **activity**

Who is someone that you consider creative? Do you have a friend or relative who is good at making or fixing things, at painting, at cooking or baking, at playing or writing music? Give a brief presentation on a creative individual you know. Use the following questions to help you prepare.

1. How is this person creative?
2. When is he or she the most creative? What seems to inspire him or her?
3. Has this person always been creative?
4. What interesting things has he or she done or produced?
5. What is this person doing now? Is he or she still involved in creative activities?

Whistler in the Dark
(self-portrait)

Mosaic One • Grammar

Adverb Clauses of Time and Condition: Past Time with the Simple Past and Past Perfect Tenses

Setting the Context

A Renaissance person is someone who is knowledgeable and accomplished in a wide variety of fields. The following passage is about such a person, Leonardo da Vinci. What do you know about his accomplishments? Can you name any?

Leonardo da Vinci

Most people recognize Leonardo da Vinci as the painter of the *Mona Lisa* and the *Last Supper*. Yet, Leonardo was a master of design, engineering, science, and invention, as well as a master of art.

5   After Leonardo had painted his most famous works, he began to spend more time on his other dreams. As a military engineer, Leonardo had drawn plans for primitive tanks and airplanes long before they were ever dreamed possible. He is also credited with having designed the first parachute and having

10   constructed the first elevator.

In the sciences, Leonardo was equally amazing. He had discovered complex principles of physics nearly a century before Galileo did his own work. In anatomy, Leonardo studied muscle and bone struc-

15   ture to improve his painting, and even after he had tired of painting, he continued to study the workings of the heart. He had even speculated on the circulation of blood a century before William Harvey proved it. Leonardo da Vinci was so far ahead of his time

20   that not until this century did his genius become truly evident.

The *Mona Lisa*

This passage tells about only some of Da Vinci's works. Can you tell about any others? Can you name other individuals who have made great accomplishments in many different fields? Can you name other individuals who have been *ahead of their time*?

A. Clauses of Time: Past Time with the Simple Past and Past Perfect Tenses

	examples	notes
before **by the time (that)** **until** **when**	Leonardo da Vinci **had painted** the Mona Lisa **before he worked** on many of his ideas for inventions.	The past perfect is used to refer to an event or situation that came before another event or time in the past. With *before, by the time that, until,* and *when,* the past perfect is used in the main clause.
after **as soon as** **once**	**After** Leonardo da Vinci **had painted** his major artworks, he **spent** more time on his inventions.	In complex sentences with *after, as soon as,* and *once,* the past perfect (continuous) is used in the dependent (not the main) clause.

B. Adverbs of Frequency with Time Clauses

examples	notes
Leonardo da Vinci **had already worked** as a civil engineer, military engineer, and architect **by the time** he **began** his major paintings.	Adverbs such as *already, hardly, just, scarcely,* and *not . . . yet* are often used with the past perfect. They generally come between *had* and the past participle.

C. after, before, by, and until as Prepositions

After, before, by, and *until* can also be used as prepositions in phrases of time. Sentences with *before, by,* and *until* may use the past perfect tense, while sentences with *after* would generally use the simple past tense. Compare:

examples	
Subordinating Conjunction	**Before** he began his major paintings, da Vinci had already worked as an engineer and architect. **After** da Vinci had painted many of his major artworks, he spent more time on his inventions.
Preposition	**Before** 1495, da Vinci had already worked as an engineer and architect. **After** 1500, da Vinci spent more time on his inventions.

 **exercise 1** Reread "Leonardo da Vinci" on page 281. How many sentences can you find with adverb clauses of time? For each such sentence, find the connecting word. Then, explain which action came earlier and which action came later.

 **exercise 2** Everyone develops special talents during his or her lifetime, but few are able to equal the extraordinary feats of the following individuals. Complete the passages here and on the next page by using simple past or past perfect forms (active or passive) of the verbs in parentheses. Note any case where you feel both tenses are appropriate. The first two are done as examples.

1. IBN SINA

Ibn Sina _____was_____ a Persian who _____wrote_____ *The Canon of*
                    1 (be)   2 (write)
Medicine. This medical encyclopedia _____ very advanced; as
                                              3 (be)
a result, scholars _____ it for five centuries. Before his death in
                       4 (use)
1037, Ibn Sina _____ an additional 150 books on such varied
                   5 (complete)
subjects as philosophy, mathematics, theology, and astronomy. Like many

learned men, he _____ early. By the age of ten, he _____
                    6 (begin)   7 (memorize)
the Koran. By the age of eighteen, he _____ as a physician for a
                                            8 (work)
sultan.

2. SOR JUANA INÉS DE LA CRUZ

Sor Juana, the Great Mexican poet, _____ in Mexico City
$\underset{\text{1 (bear)}}{}$
around 1651. She _____ to read before she _____
$\underset{\text{2 (start / already)}}{}$ $\underset{\text{3 (be)}}{}$
three years old. By her seventh birthday, she _____ to enter
$\underset{\text{4 (try)}}{}$
the university. Because girls _____ in the university, Sor
$\underset{\text{5 (not allow)}}{}$
Juana eventually _____ the convent. During her life,
$\underset{\text{6 (join)}}{}$
she _____ extraordinary prose and poetry. Before she
$\underset{\text{7 (write)}}{}$
_____ in 1695, she _____ a library of over 4,000
$\underset{\text{8 (die)}}{}$ $\underset{\text{9 (collect)}}{}$
books.

3. JOHANN WOLFGANG VON GOETHE

Goethe _____ from 1749 to 1832. He _____ a
$\underset{\text{1 (live)}}{}$ $\underset{\text{2 (be)}}{}$
scientist as well as the greatest of German poets. By age sixteen, he

_____ religious poems, a novel, and a prose epic. While
$\underset{\text{3 (write / already)}}{}$
continuing to write, he _____ both law and medicine. After he
$\underset{\text{4 (study)}}{}$
_____ to live in Weimar, Goethe _____ minister of
$\underset{\text{5 (invite)}}{}$ $\underset{\text{6 (become)}}{}$
state. Because of his position, he _____ himself in agriculture,
$\underset{\text{7 (educate)}}{}$
horticulture, and mining. He then _____ to master anatomy,
$\underset{\text{8 (proceed)}}{}$
biology, optics, and mineralogy.

4. JOHN STUART MILL

Perhaps John Stuart Mill _____ more at age thirteen than most
$\underset{\text{1 (master / already)}}{}$
people learn in their entire lives. He _____ reading Greek at
$\underset{\text{2 (begin)}}{}$
three and Latin at seven. By age twelve, he _____ all the
$\underset{\text{3 (read)}}{}$
masterpieces in both languages. He then _____ to logic and
$\underset{\text{4 (turn)}}{}$
political economy; by eighteen, he _____ articles on these
$\underset{\text{5 (write)}}{}$
topics for the *Westminister Review.*

5. MARGARET MEAD

By the time Margaret Mead _____ twenty-six, she _____
$\underset{\text{1 (be)}}{}$ $\underset{\text{2 (name / already)}}{}$
curator of the American Museum of Natural History. Before she

_____ age thirty, she _____ two major books on
$\underset{\text{3 (reach)}}{}$ $\underset{\text{4 (publish)}}{}$
people of Oceania. Before her death in 1978, she _____
$\underset{\text{5 (write)}}{}$
hundreds of articles and books on topics ranging from anthropology to

nuclear warfare and disarmament.

The following exercise gives you information on Michelangelo Buonarroti (1475–1564) and some of his accomplishments. The sentences are listed in chronological order. Use the cues in parentheses to combine each pair. Change nouns and verb tenses, omit words, and add punctuation when necessary.

> **example:** Artists used methods of fresco* painting for many centuries. The Italians perfected the technique. (before)
>
> *Artists had used methods of fresco painting for many centuries before the Italians perfected the technique.*

1. Both Michelangelo and Leonardo da Vinci worked with fresco. Michelangelo and Leonardo were commissioned for a painting in Florence. (before)
2. Michelangelo began his work on the Council Room in Florence. Michelangelo was called to Rome by Pope Julius II (soon after)
3. Michelangelo left for Rome. The two artists never worked together again. (once)
4. Michelangelo arrived in Rome. The pope commanded Michelangelo to fresco the Sistine Chapel. (as soon as)
5. Michelangelo didn't finish the ceiling. The pope impatiently opened the Sistine Chapel in 1509. (when / yet)
6. Michelangelo, without help, covered 5,800 square feet with fresco painting. Michelangelo finished the Sistine Chapel ceiling. (by the time that)

A detail from the Sistine Chapel ceiling painted by Michelangelo Buonarroti

---

fresco   the art of painting on a moist plaster surface

Using What You've Learned

activity 1

Leonardo da Vinci was "far ahead of his time." He had drawn plans for a number of inventions that were not developed until centuries later. Some of these plans included: an airplane, an elevator, a helicopter, lock gates for canals, a submarine, a tank. In small groups, discuss one or more of these inventions. Try to imagine what da Vinci had been thinking, doing, or feeling before he created his plans and how he arrived at them. You might want to use the following questions to help you. After you have finished, choose one member to give a brief summary for the class.

1. What do you think led da Vinci to these ideas? What problems had he been trying to solve?
2. Can you think of any reasons why he didn't develop the actual invention. (He *did* design and build a type of gate for canal locks.) Were all the necessary materials available at that time?
3. When were these inventions actually developed?
4. How have they changed since then?
5. How have they affected our lives?

Movable derrick

Tank

Submarine

activity 2

Is there someone whom you particularly admire for his or her knowledge or accomplishments? He or she may be a musician, a scholar, a sports figure, a politician, a friend, or a family member. What did this person do? How did he or she accomplish this?

Write a brief composition describing this person's accomplishments. Organize your composition in chronological order, and be sure to pay close attention to use of verb tenses. Later, work in small groups and share your descriptions with your classmates.

Adverb Clauses of Time and Condition: Past Time with the Simple Past and Past Continuous Tenses

Setting the Context

Who was Albert Einstein? What do you know about his work?

Creativity and Genius in Science

One of history's greatest revolutionary thinkers has been Albert Einstein, yet virtually no one foresaw his creativity. When he was a child, his parents actually suspected that he was mentally handicapped. For example, while he was learning to talk, he had great difficulties. When he entered school, he was considered "average" at best. Later, after he had finally graduated from a technical school, he was not able to find a job teaching science. Yet Einstein went on to become one of the world's greatest scientists, and today his name is synonymous with genius.

5

Albert Einstein
in Princeton,
New Jersey

 In many ways, Einstein was what we call a *late bloomer,* someone who develops his or her potential later than other people do. Do you know of other people who began great accomplishments later in life? What about the opposite? Do you know of people who were *precocious,* who produced a great deal early in life and then stopped?

Clauses of Time and Condition: Past Time with the Simple Past and Past Continuous Tenses

	examples	notes
when	**When** Einstein **had** extra time during the day, he **wrote** down his ideas.	The simple past tense is used with *when* to show a direct connection in the time of occurrence of two events.
if **unless**	**If** he **had** enough time, he **wrote** out long mathematical equations. **Unless** he **had** no time, he **would** usually **write** down notes each day.	*If* and *unless* express a cause/effect relationship between two events. The main clause is the effect or result of the dependent clause.
as **while**	**As** Einstein **was doing** his work, he **was** also **thinking**. **While** Einstein **was working** in the patent office, he **had** plenty of time to think.	The past continuous is used to express past actions in progress at a particular time. Both clauses may use the past continuous to emphasize that both activities were in progress at the same time.

 Complete the following passage by using simple past or past continuous forms of the verbs in parentheses. Include adverbs where indicated. The first one is done as an example.

ALBERT EINSTEIN

When Einstein _____was_____ a child, he _____ no early
                        1 (be)   2 (show)

evidence of genius. While he _____ to talk, he _____
                                    3 (learn)   4 (have)

tremendous difficulties, and his parents _____ him of being men-
                                                5 (suspect / even)

tally retarded. In high school, he _____ an average student. When
                                        6 (be)

he _____ from a technical institute in Zurich, Switzerland, he
        7 (graduate / finally)

_____ able to find a teaching appointment in science. He
      8 (not be)

_____ up working in a patent office in Bern, Switzerland.
        9 (end)

Einstein _____ that type of job, but as he _____ in
              10 (not want)   11 (work)

the office, he _____ able to spend time thinking. Several years
                    12 (be)

later he _____ five papers in one year, 1905. These papers
              13 (publish)

_____ an explanation of his special theory of relativity, which
      14 (include)

_____ a worldwide scientific revolution.
    15 (begin)

 **exercise 2** Many of science's greatest findings or events have come as a result of good luck as well as hard work. Complete the passages here and on the next page by using simple past or past continuous forms of the verbs in parentheses. The first verb is done as an example.

1. During the late 1800s, Louis Pasteur ___was experimenting___ with
                                                  1 (experiment)

bacteria. When Pasteur _____ chickens old bacteria by accident,
                              2 (give)

they _____ sick but they _____. When he
        3 (become)   4 (not die)

_____ the injections several times, the chickens
      5 (repeat)

_____ a resistance to infection. This discovery _____
      6 (develop)   7 (begin)

his work on immunization.

2. While von Mering and Minkowski _____ the pancreas (which
                                              1 (study)

helps to metabolize sugar), they _____ the organ from several
                                        2 (remove)

dogs. Later, a laboratory assistant _____ something unusual.
                                            3 (notice)

Flies _____ around the cages of these dogs, but they
          4 (swarm)

_____ near the cages of other dogs. When the two researchers
      5 (not go)

_____ the dogs without pancreases, they _____ that
      6 (test)   7 (discover)

the dogs _____ the symptoms of diabetes. This incident
              8 (have)

_____ medical science the first information connecting the
      9 (give)

pancreas to the cause of diabetes.

3. In 1929, the English bacteriologist Alexander Fleming

_____ with a bacteria culture when it _____

1 (experiment)   2 (become)

contaminated by a mold. When the mold _____ the bacteria,

                                     3 (touch)

the bacteria _____. Fleming _____ this mold and

               4 (die)   5 (save)

_____ it grow in a liquid. While this mold _____, it

      6 (let)   7 (grow)

_____ a substance that _____ able to kill a number of

    8 (produce)   9 (be)

bacteria. Moreover, the substance _____ animals. This

                                    10 (harm / not)

substance later _____ known as penicillin.

                 11 (become)

exercise 3 The following exercise gives you information on Marie Curie and the discovery of radium. Marie Curie is the only person in history to win two Nobel Prizes in science. Complete the passage by using simple past, past continuous, or past perfect forms (active or passive) of the verbs in parentheses.

Marie Curie

1. Born in Poland in 1867, Marie Sklodowska ___was not allowed___

                                                 (not allow)

to attend school there beyond the high school level.

2. After an older brother and sister _____ for university education

                                    (leave)

in Paris, Marie _____ to send them money and to save for her

                         (work)

own education.

3. While she _____, Marie _____ herself from family

                (work)   (teach)

books.

4. As soon as she _____ enough money, she _____

                   (save)   (go / also)

to Paris.

5. While Marie _____ at the Sorbonne, she _____ as

                  (study)   (live)

economically as possible and _____ all her time studying.

                                   (spend)

6. When she _____, Marie Sklodowska _____ at the top

                 (graduate)   (be)

of her class.

7. In 1894, she _____ to Pierre Curie, who

                       (introduce)

_____ somewhat famous for his work in physics.

    (become / already)

8. After Marie _____ Pierre Curie, she _____ to apply

                     (marry)   (begin)

his earlier discoveries to the measurement of radioactivity.

9. Scarcely six years after Marie _____ in Paris, she
   (arrive)
   _____ major discoveries about radioactivity; Pierre
   (make)
   _____ the potential and _____ his own research
   (see)   (drop)
   to join her.

10. In December 1898, the Curies _____ other experiments with
    (conduct)
    uranium ore when they _____ a new radioactive substance:
    (detect)
    radium.

11. In 1903, Marie Curie _____ her dissertation on radioactivity,
    (write)
    and for it, she and Pierre _____ that year's Nobel Prize with
    (give)
    Antoine Becquerel.

12. After Pierre Curie's death in 1906, Marie _____ her study of
    (continue)
    radioactive elements, and in 1911 she _____ the Nobel Prize
    (award)
    in chemistry.

exercise 4 The sentences here and on the next page give a brief chronology of the life of Albert Einstein. Combine each group of sentences by using coordinating or subordinating conjunctions or transitions. You can choose from the following connecting words or you can experiment with others: *after, and, as soon as, as a result, before, for example, in addition, when, while, until.* Change words, phrases, verb tenses, and punctuation when necessary.

> **example:** In 1900, Albert Einstein graduated from the Polytechnic Academy in Zurich. Later that year, Albert Einstein became a Swiss citizen. Later that year, Albert Einstein took a job in a Swiss patent office.
>
> In 1900, after Albert Einstein had graduated from the Polytechnic Academy in Zurich, he became a Swiss citizen and took a job in a Swiss patent office.

1. Albert Einstein worked in the patent office for three years. Then, Albert Einstein married Mileva Marié.

2. Albert Einstein worked in the patent office for several years. During that time, he developed many of his theories.

3. Einstein did not produce any notable scientific work. Then he published five papers in 1905.

4. These papers were published. Einstein immediately became famous in the scientific community.

5. These papers contained many revolutionary ideas. They outlined the "special theory of relativity," the "equivalence of mass and energy $(E = mc^2)$," and the "photon theory of light."

6. Einstein published his papers in 1905. Before then, he had been completely unknown in the scientific community.

7. During the next six years, Einstein continued to develop his theory of relativity. During that time, Einstein continued to study the relationship between mass and energy. During that time, Einstein tried to incorporate gravity into his theory.

8. Einstein taught in Prague for a brief time. Then the Einstein family returned to Switzerland. Einstein was offered a position at the Polytechnic Academy in Zurich.

exercise 5   The following is a continuation of the chronology of Albert Einstein's life. Use the information to write a short paragraph on him. Combine ideas by using coordinating conjunctions, subordinating conjunctions, and transitions. Change words, phrases, verb tenses, and punctuation when necessary.

1914   Einstein accepted a position at the Prussian Academy of Sciences.

The Einstein family moved to Berlin.
Einstein's wife and sons vacationed in Switzerland.
World War I began.
His family was unable to return to Germany.
This forced separation eventually led to divorce.

1916   Einstein published his paper on the general theory of relativity.

This theory was revolutionary.
It contradicted Newton's ideas on gravity.
It predicted irregularities in the motion and light from Mercury.
During this time, Einstein devoted much of his time to pacifism.
Einstein began to write and distribute antiwar literature.

1919   The Royal Society of London verified Einstein's predictions about Mercury.

Einstein quickly became famous.
Einstein married Elsa, the daughter of a cousin of his father.
Einstein stayed in Berlin.
Einstein continued to work for pacifism.

1912   Einstein was awarded the Nobel Prize in physics.

Using What You've Learned

At the library, research the later part of Albert Einstein's life. Use this information along with information from the passage and exercises in this section to write a short biography of Einstein. Pay close attention to use of verb tenses and connecting words when you edit your composition.

activity 2

Use information from the exercises in this section, along with other information you can gather, to write a short composition about one of the following:

- Marie Curie and the discovery of radium
- Alexander Fleming and the discovery of penicillin
- Louis Pasteur and immunization, pasteurization, or other processes

activity 3

Many creative individuals seem to create nothing for years and then suddenly produce a wealth of ideas or creations. Has this experience ever happened to you? Did you ever think and think and think about a problem, but with no results? Then suddenly you found the answer while you were doing something completely different? In a brief composition or in a small group discussion, tell about this experience.

activity 4

M. C. Escher was a Dutch artist who lived from 1902 to 1972. He created some of the most unusual and stimulating drawings in history. The drawing below is his interpretation of *Relativity*. In pairs or in small groups, discuss the following questions about this work. Be sure to include your own questions too.

1. How do you react when you see a drawing like this?
2. Try to imagine what Escher was thinking about while he was planning this.
3. Why do you think he called it *Relativity*?
4. How do you think he drew the picture? For example, do you think he drew several separate pictures and later put them together?

Relativity by M. C. Escher, National Gallery of Art, Washington, D.C. Gift of Mrs. C. V. S. Roosevelt

Adverb Clauses of Time and Condition: Future Time

Setting the Context

previewing the passage

The passage below shows you a decision tree. In business, decision trees are often used to systematically present all the possible causes and effects of an action. Have you ever used one?

Decision Making

Making a good decision is one of the most creative things we do. In many ways, creativity is the ability to see all the alternatives. It can be an analytical process. Using a decision tree can be a great help, especially if the decision is a complicated one.

Car A: $6,000; used, high mileage, needs many repairs
Car B: $13,000; new, excellent condition, warranty

If I don't fix the engine, . . .

If I buy A, I will have $4,000 left, but I will have to make a lot of repairs.

If I fix the engine, it will cost $600.

If I buy new tires, it will cost $300.

I have $10,000.

If I borrow $3,000 from the bank, I will pay 12% interest.

If I buy B, I will need $3,000 more.

If I borrow from my brother, I will pay 8% interest, but I will have to repay it sooner.

Making decisions is often one of the most creative things we do. Think about your own decision making? How do you decide what to do and how to do it?

 A. Clauses of Time: Future Time

	examples	notes
after	**After I finish,** I will take a long vacation!	The verb in the dependent clause is in the simple present or the present perfect tense. The present perfect emphasizes the completion of the action.
as soon as	I'm going to call you **as soon as I finish.**	
before	I won't call you **before I have finished.**	
once	**Once I've finished,** I'll call you.	The verb in the main clause is in a future tense. Modal auxiliaries such as *can* and *should* are often used in either clause.
until	I should work **until I have finished.**	
when	**When I finish,** I'll give you a call.	
as	I'll have to concentrate a lot **as I'm working.**	The present continuous is often used in dependent clauses with *while* or *as* to emphasize an action in progress.
while	**While I'm working,** I won't think about my vacation.	

exercise 1 Complete the following in your own words.

> **example:** After we finish this section, **we are going to review several chapters.**

1. After this class is over, . . .
2. When we have finished this chapter, . . .
3. Tonight, I'm going to finish my work before . . .
4. While I'm studying tonight, . . .
5. As soon as I get home, . . .
6. I'll call them once . . .
7. As we're doing the dishes . . .
8. I will keep on taking the TOEFL until . . .

Think about your next writing assignment and the steps in writing that you listed in Exercise 2, page 277. What are you going to do before you start writing? While you are writing? After you have finished writing? Form complete sentences from the cues. Add specific information about your next writing assignment.

example: think about a topic

Before I start writing, I am going to think about . . . (a topic). While I am thinking about the topic, I'll gather information on. . . .

1. make a list of ideas
2. organize the ideas into logical groups
3. write a rough draft
4. rewrite the rough draft
5. proofread the composition
6. hand it in

B. Clauses of Condition: Future Time

Factual conditional sentences that refer to the future generally express predictions or intentions. The main clause shows the effect or result of the *if* clause.

	examples	notes
if	**If I finish** my work, **I will** (may, might, and so on) go to the party. **I am not going** to go (can't go, shouldn't go, and so on) **if I haven't finished** my work.	The verb in the dependent clause is in a present tense. The verb in the main clause is *be going to* or a modal auxiliary: *will, may, might, should,* and so on.
unless	**Unless I finish** my work, **I am not going** to go (can't go, shouldn't go, and so on) to the party.	*Unless* is similar in meaning to *if . . . not* in many sentences, but *unless* is more emphatic.

Complete the following in your own words.

example: If the weather is nice this weekend, **we'll take a trip.**

1. If I have enough money, . . .
2. If it rains tomorrow, . . .
3. If I finish my homework early, . . .
4. If I don't finish my homework, . . .
5. If my friends invite me to visit, . . .
6. If my parents don't call soon, . . .
7. If I win a scholarship, . . .
8. If I get 600 on the TOEFL test, . . .

Imagine that you are trying to decide about places to live. Use the following decision tree, similar to the one in the opening passage, to help you decide what to do. Use the correct forms of the verbs in parentheses and add more information. Then make your decision and explain why you made that decision.

I can spend up to $500 a month for my expenses (housing, meals, transportation).

Apartment A: with Americans; $280 a month; near school
Apartment B: with people from my own country; $200 a month; far from school

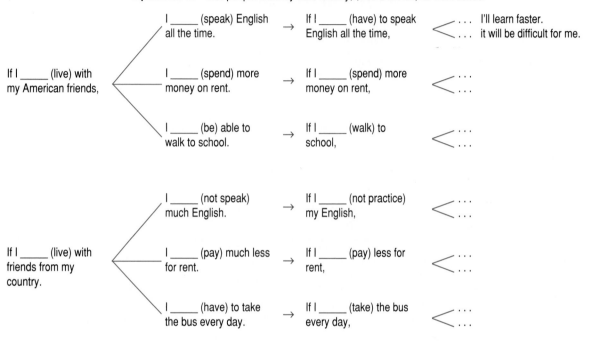

Combine the following pairs to form new sentences with *unless*.

example: I should speak English more often. If I don't, I'll never become fluent.

Unless I speak English more often, I'll never become fluent.

1. I should find a cheaper place to live. If I don't, I'll run out of money soon.
2. We should save more money. If we don't, we'll never be able to take a long vacation.
3. You should send your application for school soon. If you don't, you may not be accepted this year.
4. I should write my parents soon. If I don't, they'll start to get worried about me.
5. You should start your research project soon. If you don't, you may not be able to finish in time.

 **exercise 6**

The following guidelines for excellence in business are from *In Search of Excellence* by Thomas J. Peters and Robert H. Waterman. According to Peters and Waterman, these are the eight attributes of "excellent, innovative companies." After reading the list, think about the causes and effects of these attributes. Then think about the consequences for a company that does not have them. Form sentences using *if, unless, before, after,* and *when* to express your ideas. You may have several opinions for each. The first one is done as an example.

EXCELLENT, INNOVATIVE COMPANIES

1. take action
   They make theories and analyses, but most important, they try new ideas.

   If a company is innovative, it will try new ideas.

   When a company takes action, it will be able to see results, rather than guess the results.

   If a company doesn't try something new, another company will probably try it first.

   Unless a company tries new ideas, it won't make any progress.

2. are close to the customer
   They get their ideas from the people they serve; they listen carefully to their customers.

3. encourage independence and ingenuity
   They don't hold people back. They encourage employees to be creative and to take risks. They support experimentation.

4. work for productivity through people
   They treat everyone in the company as an important source of ideas. They never encourage a "we/they" management/worker situation.

5. keep "quality" as the basic philosophy of the organization
   Quality is the most important thing, not status, organization, resources, or technology.

6. stick to their own business
   They don't get involved in things that are outside of their area of expertise. They don't acquire jobs or businesses they don't know how to run.

7. keep their organization simple and their staff to a minimum
   Their structures and systems are simple; they avoid having too many managers.

8. are both centralized and decentralized
   Control is loose because workers at all levels have authority and responsibility; on the other hand, control is tight because top management decides the basic direction of the company.

C. Sentence Problems: Fragments, Comma Splices, and Run-ons

Fragments, comma splices, and run-on sentences are some of the most common errors in writing. These errors involve incomplete ideas or incorrect punctuation.

	examples	notes
Fragment	Thinking up new ideas.	Fragments are incomplete sentences.
Comma Splice	Thinking up new ideas can be difficult, it is important.	A comma splice is two sentences combined with a comma but without a connecting word.
Run-On Sentence	Thinking up new ideas can be difficult it is important.	A run-on sentence is two sentences combined without proper punctuation.

Error Analysis. Some of the following sentences are well written. Others are incomplete or are punctuated incorrectly. For each sentence, indicate: complete (C), incomplete (I), or punctuation error (PE). Then, rewrite the incorrect sentences correctly.

example: ___I___ If a scientist makes an outstanding discovery.

A scientist may make an outstanding discovery.

or   If a scientist makes an outstanding discovery, we call this creativity or genius.

1. _____ When an artist produces a masterpiece.

_____

2. _____ People are creative not only in art or science, they are also creative in their daily lives.

_____

3. _____ Ordinary people are creative every day.

_____

4. _____ Creativity involves awareness it means noticing the world around us.

_____

5. _____ To think up a new concept.

_____

6. _____ It is the courage and drive to make use of new ideas.

_____

7. _____ Creativity combining old ideas in new ways.

_____

8. _____ According to an old saying, there is nothing new under the sun.

_____

9. _____ Is not always easy to look at the same ideas in a different way.

_____

10. _____ Being open to new ideas is sometimes difficult, however, everyone of us has the ability to do it.

_____

 **Error Analysis.** The following passage contains errors in punctuation: sentence fragments, comma splices, and run-on sentences. First, read the passage once to understand the ideas. Then, correct the passage by changing or adding punctuation when necessary.

CREATIVITY

One form of creativity is the sudden flash of insight. When an idea pops into your head. This is what Arthur Koestler called the Eureka process. *Eureka* comes from the story of the ancient Greek scientist Archimedes. Archimedes supposedly leapt naked from his tub. Shouting "Eureka!" *Eureka* mean "I have found it." He had suddenly figured out why some things float.

Not all creative discoveries come like a flash of light, however. In fact, Thomas Edison, the inventor of the light bulb, tried hundreds of metal combinations in his laboratory. Before he found the right one to conduct electricity. Edison was able to create something new and valuable because of his energy and tenacity. He gave his own definition of genius it is 1 percent inspiration and 99 percent perspiration.

Despite their differences, Edison and Archimedes had much in common, they followed the same process. First, both recognized a problem. And were aware of previous steps to solve it. Both consciously or unconsciously worked toward a solution. Finally, both arrived at a solution, this was the creative idea.

Using What You've Learned

activity 1

Look a little into the world of myths and superstitions. In small groups, share some of the traditional beliefs and/or superstitions from your culture. Use these ideas and add some of your own. Then, share your information with the whole class.

What will happen . . .
- if you break a mirror?
- if you step on a crack in the sidewalk?
- if you walk under a ladder?
- if a black cat crosses your path?

activity 2

Rube Goldberg was a creative American cartoonist. He "created" some of the world's most amazing "inventions." The invention in the accompanying cartoon is designed to attract a waiter's attention. Read the text and then follow the drawing to give the step-by-step process involved. Use *if, when, before,* and *after* to join the steps.

> **example:** **If you light the skyrocket, the string will open the jack-in-the-box. When the skyrocket goes off, . . .**

activity 3

Think about the various descriptions of creativity, innovation, and excellence in this chapter. Try to put these ideas to use as you consider the problems of teaching and learning a language. Imagine that you and your classmates are educational consultants. You have been asked to design a program for a language school.

Separate into small groups. Discuss your ideas on the best ways to learn languages. Then, as a group, make a list of recommendations for planning a language program. Be sure to consider the following four ideas and to add any of your own:

1. How many students should there be per class? How many different teachers should students have?

2. How many hours a day should students have classes? When should the classes be offered?
3. What kinds of classes should be offered?
4. Should there be a language lab? Should use of the lab be optional or mandatory?

Remember that both money and time may be problems for the students. Some may be working. Some may have families. Many will not be able to afford expensive classes. How should you plan if you want to offer economical and effective classes?

activity 4

"Poetic license" is the poet's "permit" to break rules of grammar or punctuation in order to be creative. In small groups, try to find any instances where rules are broken. Would the piece still be poetry if it followed all the rules?

TO LOOK AT ANYTHING

To look at any thing,
If you would know that thing,
You must look at it long:
To look at this green and say
"I have seen spring in these
Woods," will not do—you must
Be the thing you see:
You must be the dark snakes of
Stems and ferny plumes of leaves,
You must enter in
To the small silences between
The leaves,
You must take your time
And touch the very peace
They issue from.

—John Moffit, *The Living Seed*

TOPIC SIX
Review: Chapters Five to Eight

exercise 1

Review. First read the passage on page 303 for meaning. Then complete it by choosing the appropriate word(s) from each set in parentheses. If nothing is needed, choose *X*. The first three are done as examples.

In 1790, only a few years after the Revolutionary War (ended /(had ended)
in the United States, a new revolution (began)/ had begun). This revolution
((was)/ is) fairly peaceful, but it involved large amounts of (the / X) money,
creativity, and emotion. It involved patents.

According to the dictionary, (a / an) patent is a government grant to
(a / an) inventor for a specific period of time to make, use, and (sell / to sell)
an invention. Every part of this definition (changes / has changed) since the
beginning of the patent system in (the / X) 1790. In the beginning, an invention (can be / could be) almost anything. The invention simply had (to be / be)
unusual. Later it (became / was becoming) something "new and useful." By
1880, it had to be (the / X) result of a "flash of genius." In (the / X) 1950s, a
patented invention (defined / was defined) as something that (might not have
occurred / should not have occurred) to the ordinary person.

Patents gave inventors rights to the invention for a period of years, usually
seventeen. Inventors had to explain their inventions publically, however. (Until /
After) the patent had expired, anyone (can / could) make the invention.

Since it (begins / began), the patent system has encouraged (many / much)
inventors (developing / to develop) their ideas, but it has made (few / little)
inventors (become / to become) rich. Many inventors have had serious financial problems, and (other / others) people—not the inventors—have often
made fortunes from their ideas.

During (the / X) 19th century, a tremendous number of patents (was given /
were given). For example, Cyrus McCormick (gave / was given) the patent
for the McCormick reaper and Charles Goodyear (awarded / was awarded) the
patent for (vulcanizing / to vulcanize) rubber. But the giant of all inventors
was Thomas Alva Edison. Edison (holds still / still holds) the record for the
number of patents given to a single inventor. He (has / is having) a total of
1,093. Edwin Land, who (invented / was invented) the Land camera and
(founded / was founded) Polaroid, is second with 533.

Review. Following is information about Thomas Edison and some of his accomplishments. The pairs of sentences are listed in chronological order. Use the cues in parentheses to combine each pair. Use a past perfect verb in each new sentence. Change nouns, and adverbs, omit words, and add punctuation when necessary.

example: Thomas Edison ended his formal education.
Thomas Edison became a teenager. (long before)

Thomas Edison had ended his formal education long before he became a teenager.

1. Thomas Edison invented dozens of practical tools and machines.
Thomas Edison reached his early twenties. (before / already)

2. Edison made some money from an invention for the stock market.
Edison set up a factory in Newark, New Jersey. (soon after)

3. Edison ran the factory for just two years.
Edison decided to organize the first U.S. industrial research park in Menlo Park, New Jersey. (when)

4. In his attempts to create a light bulb, Edison tried hundreds of metal combinations.
Edison finally found the right one to conduct electricity. (before)

5. Edison developed the first commercial light bulb.
Edison created the mimeograph, dictating machines, early motion picture cameras and projectors, and an iron-alkaline battery, among other inventions. (after)

6. Edison received over 1000 patents for practical applications of scientific principles.
Edison died. (by the time that)

Review.   Work in pairs for this exercise. Half of the pairs should use charts 1 and 2 and half should use charts 3 and 4. In your pairs, take turns asking and answering questions in order to complete the following charts. Do not look at each other's charts. Here are some sample questions. Try to add your own questions too.

Who invented _____ ?
Who was _____ invented by?
By whom was _____ invented?
What did _____ invent?
When was _____ invented?
What could _____ do?
What impact has _____ had on our lives?
What are some of the effects of _____ ?

Inventions: Chart 1

			Joseph Glidden	Alexander Graham Bell	
Inventor with patent			Joseph Glidden	Alexander Graham Bell	
Invention	cotton gin	sewing machine		telephone	
Year of patent			1874		1880
Function	took seeds out of the cotton		provided cheap, practical fencing material		provided economical and safe lighting
Impact on the world		built the garment industry; created the first millionaire inventor		began a communications revolution; produced the world's largest company—ATT—until it was broken up in 1984	

Inventions: Chart 2

Inventor with patent	Eli Whitney	Elias Howe			Thomas Edison
Invention			barbed wire		light bulb
Year of patent	1794	1846		1876	
Function		mechanized sewing		allowed long-distance communication	
Impact on the world	made cotton the world's most important crop; made slavery profitable in the United States; helped start the Civil War		allowed ranchers to close the plains of the American west		gave a new dimension to life around the world; began the electronic age

Inventions: Chart 3

Inventor with patent		George Selden		Chester Carlson	
Invention	machine gun		airplane		transistor
Year of patent	1890	1895			
Function	allowed bullets to be fired rapidly		allowed humans to fly	created a "dry" process for copying paper documents	could change weak electrical signals into strong ones
Impact on the world		did not invent the automobile, but got the patent and delayed the development of cars in the United States until 1911, when Henry Ford won in court			became the basis for all solid state technology; formed the basic device in miniature electronic systems like radios; led to development of the silicon chip for computers

Inventions: Chart 4

Inventor with patent	Hiram Maxim		Orville and Wilbur Wright		John Bardeen, Walter Brattain, William Shockley (ATT)
Invention		automobile		xerography	
Year of patent			1906	1942	1950
Function		provided a motor-ized vehicle for rapid transportation			
Impact on the world	completely changed wars and ways of fighting		changed transport-ation forever; was the beginning of hundreds of indus-tries connected with flight	allowed documents to be copied easily using electricity; began a multibillion dollar company named Xerox	

Review of Problem Areas: Chapters Five to Eight

A variety of problem areas are included in this test. Check your understanding by completing the sample items below.

Part 1: Circle the correct completion for the following.

example: When John _____ satisfied with his work, he will submit the project.
    a. is being
    (b.) is
    c. will be
    d. is been

1. By 1911, Marie Curie _____ two Nobel Prizes in science.
    a. had been awarded
    b. had being awarded
    c. awarded
    d. was being awarding

2. Professional musicians often rehearse their music mentally in order _____ better.
    a. performing
    b. being performed
    c. to perform
    d. to be performed

3. Until barbed wire was invented, _____ land in the Great Plains had been fenced.
    a. few of
    b. few of the
    c. little of
    d. little

4. Most minerals near the earth's surface are located in _____ amounts.
    a. a small
    b. small
    c. the small
    d. the very small

5. The light bulb, along with over 1,000 other useful items, _____ by Edison.
    a. were patented
    b. patented
    c. patenting
    d. was patented

Part 2: Circle the letter below the underlined word(s) containing an error.

example: An individual often <u>feels frustrated</u> <u>unless</u> she has difficulties
                          A   Ⓑ

in speaking the language of the country <u>where she is living</u>.
   C   D

1. <u>Physically fit</u> people <u>should be</u> able <u>to stay</u> the same weight over
        A   B   C
    a period of several years <u>unless</u> they maintain good health habits.
                                   D

2. Keynesian economics <u>has influenced</u> a number of <u>key govenmental</u>
                              A   B
    policies and policy makers involved with <u>monetary decision</u> making
                                                   C
    during the last five <u>decade</u>.
                            D

3. The <u>physiological and psychological</u> benefits of exercise <u>has been</u>
            A   B
    <u>shown</u> through numerous studies <u>done</u> on <u>stress reduction</u>.
       C   C   D

4. <u>When</u> Einstein's five papers, <u>including</u> his special theory of
       A   B
    relativity, <u>were published</u> in 1905, a scientific revolution began
                     C
    <u>to unfolding</u>.
       D

5. After Leonardo da Vinci <u>had painted</u> the *Mona Lisa,* he <u>had gone</u> on
                                A   B
    to pursue research in <u>such</u> varied fields as physics, anatomy, and
                              C
    <u>military science</u>.
       D

CHAPTER **nine**

Human Behavior

Buddhist temple

Introduction

In this chapter, you will review basic word order of modifiers, and you will study adjective clauses. As you study the chapter, pay close attention to the role of punctuation with these clauses.

The following passage introduces the chapter theme, Human Behavior, and raises some of the topics and issues you will cover in the chapter.

previewing the passage

Many things affect the way we think and act, but perhaps the most powerful and pervasive force in people's lives worldwide is religion. Has religion influenced your own development and way of life? In what ways?

Religion and Human Behavior

Does life have meaning? What gives it meaning? Why do we act the way we do? What is the best way to live? How can we be happy? How can we find peace?

5   These are questions that people have struggled with throughout history. Philosophers, psychologists, sociologists, and physicists are among the many thinkers who have tried to give us answers. We look for answers within ourselves, but few are satisfactory. In the end, it is religion that gives most of the world answers to these questions.

Hundreds of religions exist in the world, yet all religions try to answer the
10   same questions. Every religion teaches basic ideas that help humans understand their nature and their behavior. Every religion describes two sides of human nature—the animal and the divine. It is these opposing sides that cause conflicts. Every religion gives people a method that they can follow to resolve the conflicts. All religions have a goal, which is in one form or another the trans-
15   formation of humans from the animal to the divine. This transformation to inner peace is common to all religions, though it has many names: nirvana, heaven, salvation.

All cultures in the world have religious beliefs. For that reason, every part of life is affected by religions, whose teachings offer guidelines on ways to live.

discussing ideas

Think about religion in your culture. Is there one major religion? Or are there several? Is religion an important influence in your culture? To what extent does it affect or control the way people think and behave?

Islamic mosque

Christian church

Jewish synagogue

Hindu temple

Chapter Nine • Human Behavior

TOPIC **one**

Review of Modifiers and Introduction to Adjective Clauses

Setting the Context

previewing the passage

This chapter talks about five of the major world religions. It begins with Hinduism, the oldest of the five. What do you know about Hinduism? Is it practiced in your area or country?

Hinduism

The religious tradition that we call *Hinduism* is the product of 5000 years of development. The name, however, dates only from about A.D.* 1200, the time when the invading Muslims wished to distinguish the faith of the people of India from their own.

5   *Hindu* is the Persian word for *Indian*. Hindus themselves, however, call their religious tradition the eternal teaching or law *(sanatana dharma)*.

Hinduism has no founder and no prophet.[†] It has no specific church structure, nor does it have a set system of beliefs defined by one authority. The emphasis is on a way of living rather than on a way of thought.

10   Radhakrishnan, a former president of India, once remarked: "Hinduism is more a culture than a creed."

discussing ideas

Where did the name *Hindu* come from? Who founded Hinduism? Does Hinduism have a strictly organized system of beliefs? Do you think Hinduism is somewhat different from other religions in these regards?

A. Review of Modifiers

Remember that English has fairly strict rules for the word order of modifiers in a sentence. To review the order of modifiers, see Chapter One, page 11.

---

*A.D.   *anno Domini,* "in the year of the Lord"—that is, after Christ
[†]*prophet*   a person who claims to speak for God

Look at the italicized modifiers in the following sentences and indicate which word(s) each modifies. Try to identify the modifiers (adjective, adverb, article, and so on).

article   preposition   preposition
               noun   noun

example: *The* majority *of Hindus* believe *in karma.*

1. *An important* concept *of Hinduism* is karma, *which means "action" or "work."*
2. Because *most* Hindus believe *in reincarnation,* karma *also* means the consequences *of actions from one life to the next.*
3. To *some* social scientists, karma is *heredity,* or genetic inheritance, and dharma is *free will,* the ability to make choices.
4. Reincarnation means *an* individual has lived *many* lives and will live many more until the *final* liberation.
5. Because of karma and reincarnation, respect *for life, customs, and laws* is very important to Hindus.
6. *Some* Hindus believe that being a vegetarian is *the best way* to show respect *for life.*

Hindus at a temple in India

The Ganges River

Quickly reread the passage "Hinduism" on page 312. Then do the following:

1. Read the first sentence of the passage. Name the subject, verb, and complement in the main clause. Name the subject, verb, and connecting word in the dependent clause.
2. In the same sentence, name the parts of speech of the following:
   - **a.** *religious*
   - **b.** *Hinduism*
   - **c.** *the*
   - **d.** *of*
   - **e.** *development*

Introduction to Adjective Clauses

An adjective clause is a dependent (relative) clause that modifies a noun or pronoun. An adjective clause usually comes immediately after the word(s) it modifies. In some cases, a pronoun or prepositional phrase may come between the (pro)noun and the clause. English has several different types of adjective clause constructions. You will study each one in detail in later sections.

examples	
Subject Clauses: that, which, *and* who	Hinduism is a religion **that** did not have one founder.
Object Clauses: that, which, *and* who(m)	The man **whom** I met yesterday is a Hindu. The man **to whom** I was introduced is a Hindu.
Possessive Clauses: whose	Hinduism is a religion **whose** beliefs form a major part of Hindu culture.
Time and Place Clauses: when *and* where	India is a country in Asia **where** a majority of the population is Hindu.

exercise  Each of the following sentences has an adjective clause. Underline the dependent clauses and circle the word(s) they modify.

example: The Ganges is a (river) that flows through northern India.

1. It is a river whose water is sacred to Hindus.

2. Hindus from all over the world travel to the Ganges, which is the symbol of life without end.

3. Every day, the Ganges is filled with hundreds of thousands of people who come to drink or bathe in the sacred water.

4. Millions of people come for the great Kumbh Mela Festival, which is held once every twelve years.

5. This festival takes place at Allahbad, where the Ganges and the Jumna rivers join.

6. The Kumbh Mela Festival is a special time when all Hindus hope to bathe in the sacred waters of the Ganges.

7. A very important festival is the Kumbh Mela Festival, during which millions of people drink or bathe in the sacred river.

8. Varanasi, which is another city on the Ganges, is the most sacred for Hindus.

9. Varanasi is the city that Hindus believe to be the most sacred.

10. All Hindus hope to die at Varanasi, where the sacred water gives eternal life.

11. A hope that all Hindus have is to die at Varanasi.

12. The sacred ashes of those who have died at Varanasi are thrown on the river, and their lives will continue forever.

Using What You've Learned

activity

The word *holiday* originally was "holy day," and it had a strictly religious meaning. Today, we use *holiday* to mean any vacation day. Just as religions celebrate special holidays, so do cities, states, countries, and cultures.

In groups, look at the types of holidays celebrated in the various countries, cultures, and religions represented in your class. First, separate into four groups. Each group will take a season (spring, summer, winter, or fall). In your group, make a list of the holidays celebrated during that season. Include a brief description of how and where they are celebrated. Are there similar holidays in several cultures? Are they celebrated in similar ways? After you have finished, share your information with the rest of the class. Later, you will be asked to give a brief presentation about one holiday from your religion or culture.

TOPIC **two**

Clauses with that, when, and where: Replacement of Subjects, Objects, and Adverbials of Time or Place

Setting the Context

previewing the passage

Hinduism and Buddhism are closely related in many ways. Siddhārtha Gautama was a Hindu who sought knowledge throughout his life, and his teachings developed into Buddhism. Why do you think Buddhism became a separate religion? Has this happened in other religions?

Buddhism

Buddhism developed from the teachings of Siddhārtha Gautama (the Buddha or "enlightened one"). However, it is not a religion that honors one person, human or divine. Buddha is neither a god nor a god-sent mediator. He is not a "redeemer" who can save others.

5   In Buddhism, teaching *(dharma)* and knowledge are more important than the person, Buddha. This knowledge is a special religious knowledge that people attain through transcending human limitations. It is knowledge that goes far beyond the limits of thought. It leads to the ultimate goal, where the personality is transformed. The path to this transformation is a method of forming "right"

10   habits.

Today, Buddhists refer to Buddha as the great example, but every person has to seek his or her own enlightenment. Selflessness and the seeking of peace on earth are the ways to enlightenment.

The Great Buddha of Kamakura, Japan

***discussing
ideas***

According to the passage, every person has to seek his or her own enlightenment. What does *enlightenment* mean to you?

A. Clauses with *that:* Replacement of Subjects

That can replace the subject of a simple sentence. It is used for ideas and things. In informal English, *that* is sometimes used to refer to people; *who* is generally preferred, however. Commas are *not* used with adjective clauses beginning with *that.*

examples	
Simple Sentences	Buddhism is a **religion. This religion** teaches a way of life.
Complex Sentence	Buddhism is a religion **that** teaches a way of life.
Simple Sentences	Siddhārtha was a **person. This person** tried to overcome suffering.
Complex Sentence	Siddhārtha was a person **that (who)** tried to overcome suffering.

 **exercise 1**   Combine the following sentences to form adjective clauses with *that*. Make any necessary changes in the sentences.

> example: We visited a Buddhist temple. The temple was in Tokyo.
>
> **We visited a Buddhist temple that was in Tokyo.**

1. I bought a book. The book was about Buddhism.
2. Buddhism is a religion. It has over 300 million followers.
3. Buddhism has many beliefs. These beliefs help people to deal with their problems.
4. I have a problem. It has been bothering me for a while.
5. I talked about it with a friend. The friend had a similar problem.
6. My friend had some ideas for me. These ideas were very helpful.

exercise 2   Combine the following sentences to form adjective clauses with *that*. Make any necessary changes in the sentences.

> example: Buddha is a word from Sanskrit. This word from Sanskrit means "the enlightened one."
>
> **Buddha is a word from Sanskrit that means "the enlightened one."**

1. Through meditation, Buddha learned laws of life. Laws of life include the "Four Noble Truths" of Buddhism.
2. The first law is about suffering. The suffering comes from our past actions or "karma."
3. The second law talks about desires. The desires are for the wrong things.
4. The third law says changing our lives will solve the problems. The problems come from desires.
5. The fourth law describes a way of living. The way of living is Buddha's path to inner peace.
6. According to Buddha, these four "Noble Truths" are the laws. These laws will lead us to enlightenment.

 Summarize the information given in Exercise 2 by completing the following in your own words:

Buddha taught a way of thinking and acting that . . .

B. Clauses with *that:* Replacement of Objects of Verbs

To form an adjective clause, the relative pronoun *that* can replace the object of the verb in a simple sentence. *That* normally refers to things or ideas, and in informal English it may be used to refer to people. In addition, *that* is sometimes omitted in informal English; this is possible only when *that* replaces an object (not the subject).

examples

Simple Sentences	The **ideas** helped relieve suffering. Siddhãrtha taught **these ideas**.
Complex Sentences	The ideas **that** Siddãrtha taught helped relieve suffering.
	The ideas Siddhãrtha taught helped relieve suffering.

C. Clauses with *when* or *where:* Replacement of Adverbials of Time or Place

When and *where* can be used as relative pronouns that replace adverbials of time or place. Do not confuse adjective clauses with *when* or *where* [which follow the noun(s) they modify] with adverb clauses (which may begin or end sentences).

examples

Simple Sentences	Siddhãrtha lived at a **time**. People suffered tremendously **then**.
Complex Sentence	Siddhãrtha lived at a time **when** people suffered tremendously.
Simple Sentences	Nepal is a **country**. Buddhism and Hinduism are practiced **there**.
Complex Sentence	Nepal is a country **where** Buddhism and Hinduism are practiced.

exercise 4 Combine the following sentences by using *that, when,* or *where.* Eliminate words whenever necessary.

> **example:** Nirvana is a state of being. People can reach nirvana through learning.
>
> **Nirvana is a state of being that people can reach through learning.**

1. The word is *nirvana.* Buddhists use this word to describe inner peace.
2. Nirvana is the goal. Every Buddhist hopes to achieve this goal.
3. It is a feeling. People describe the feeling as inner peace.
4. According to an early Buddhist scripture, nirvana is a place. There is no earth, water, fire, and air there.
5. It is a time. An individual achieves the end of suffering then.
6. The way is through meditation. People can reach nirvana this way.

Buddist monk meditating

exercise 5 Whenever you study a new subject, you need to define and understand key words. Definitions often use adjective clauses. In order to understand Exercise 6, which follows, you will need to know the meanings of the following words. Complete their definitions by choosing the appropriate adjective clause.

1. Our lifestyle is the way . . .
2. Our livelihood is the way . . .
3. Discipline is the effort . . .
4. Wisdom is knowledge and and understanding . . .
5. Our intentions are actions . . .
6. Our morals are the guidelines . . .

    a. that we gain through study and experience
    b. that we choose to live, act, and think
    c. that we plan to do
    d. that we earn money
    e. that we use to determine right from wrong
    f. that we use to control our thoughts and actions

Error Analysis. Many of the following sentences have errors in the formation of adjective clauses. Find the errors and correct them. Indicate sentences that have no errors.

examples: The way to nirvana is a method that Buddhists call the
              "Eightfold Path."   *correct*

              People who follow the Eightfold Path reach a point ~~that~~ *where*
              extremes and impulses are avoided ~~there.~~

1. The Eightfold Path gives a moral way of living that ~~it~~ includes "right speech, action, and livelihood."

2. It has instructions on discipline that ~~they~~ involve "right effort, mindfulness, and concentration."

3. The Eightfold Path also discusses the wisdom that we develop ~~this wisdom~~ through "right views and intentions."

4. It is not a set of teachings that emphasizes strictness or severity.

5. It teaches a moderate lifestyle where avoids strong feelings.

6. The Eightfold Path leads to Nirvana, a feeling of peace when a person no longer has inner conflicts or suffering.

Summarize the information given in Exercise 6 by completing the following in your own words:

The lifestyle that Buddha . . .

Have you felt moments of real inner peace? Describe one by completing the following sentences. Add other information if you wish.

1. I've felt the kind of peace that . . .
2. It was at a time (in my life) when . . .
3. I had reached a point (in my life) where . . .
4. It gave me the sensation that . . .

Quickly reread the passage "Buddhism" on page 316. Then answer the following:

1. What is the function of *that honors one person* in line 2?
2. What is the function of *that people attain through transcending human limitations* in lines 6 to 7?
3. Compare these two clauses. How do they differ structurally?

Using What You've Learned

activity

After you have completed this section, there still may be words that confuse you. Make a short list of new vocabulary that you don't completely understand. Then, in small groups, write your own definitions for them.

After you have written your own definitions, check with other groups, with your teacher, or with your dictionary to see if the definitions are correct. You may also want to define some of the following words:

atheism	festival	ritual
belief	prayer	sin
doctrine	prophet	tradition
faith	religion	worship

TOPIC **three**

Restrictive and Nonrestrictive Clauses; Clauses with who, which, and whose: Replacement of Subjects and Possessives

Setting the Context

previewing the passage

The following passage tells about the third major world religion, Judaism. What do you know about Judaism? Are you familiar with any of its customs, traditions, or teachings?

Judaism

Judaism, which is the parent of both Christianity and Islam, is the oldest of the world's three great monotheistic * religions. The core of Judaism is the belief in only one God, who is the creator and ruler of the whole world. He is transcendent[†] and eternal.[‡]

5   Judaism was founded by Abraham. According to Jewish tradition, Abraham made an agreement with God that he and his family would teach the doctrine

---

*monotheistic   believing in one God
[†] *transcendent*   going beyond the limits of time and space
[‡] *eternal*   forever

of only one God. In return, God promised Abraham the land of Canaan for his descendants.

10   Judaism is based on two fundamental texts: the Old Testament of the Bible (the Torah) and the Talmud, which is a collection of poetry, anecdotes, laws, traditions, biographies, and prophecies of the ancient Jews. All of Judaism's teachings, laws, and customs are also called the *Torah,* which means "to teach."

Passover Seder

discussing ideas   About one-half of the world's religions are monotheistic (believing in one God), while the others are polytheistic. In your opinion, is this a major difference in beliefs? Is this more important than any similarities among religions?

A. Restrictive and Nonrestrictive Clauses

Restrictive clauses identify the nouns they describe. Restrictive clauses give *essential* information about these nouns. *No* commas are used with restrictive clauses.

Nonrestrictive clauses do *not* define or identify the nouns they describe. Nonrestrictive clauses give *extra* information: the identity of the noun is already known. A comma is used at the beginning and at the end of a nonrestrictive clause. *That* may not be used with nonrestrictive clauses (with commas).

	examples	notes
Restrictive	I met a professor **who teaches a religious studies course at the college.**	Restrictive clauses explain *which* people, places, things, or ideas: not everyone or everything; only what is described in the clause.
Nonrestrictive	I met Dr. Chang, **who teaches a religious studies course at the college.**	Nonrestrictive clauses add information. They do *not* explain *which* people (places, and so on). Clauses that modify proper names, entire groups, or nouns that are unique (the sun, and so on) are normally nonrestrictive.

In some cases, the same clause may either identify or give extra information, depending on the situation. Compare the examples below.

	examples	notes
Restrictive	My brother **who lives in Iowa** is a teacher. (I have several brothers; the brother in Iowa is a teacher.)	This clause tells *which* brother. No commas are used.
Nonrestrictive	My brother, **who lives in Iowa,** is a teacher. (I have only one brother, or I'm talking about one brother now. By the way, he lives in Iowa.)	This clause gives extra information. Commas are used.

Note: In spoken English, speakers often pause before and after a nonrestrictive clause. This tells you that the information is *extra.* Thus, pauses are likely in the second sentence but not in the first.

exercise  As your teacher reads sentences 1 to 8 aloud, underline the adjective clause in each. Then, decide whether the information is *essential* (telling *which* person, thing, and so on) or *extra.* Add commas if the information is extra.

example: People <u>who believe in Judaism</u> are called Jews.
essential information; no commas

1. Steve Wise who comes from Maryland is Jewish.

2. Steve's brother who lives in Chicago is a rabbi. (Steve has only one brother.)

3. Joan's brother who lives in Chicago is a rabbi. (Joan has several brothers.)

4. Judaism is based on the Talmud and the Old Testament which is also part of the Christian Bible.

5. The Bible which has two parts is the basis for both Judaism and Christianity.

6. A synagogue is a place where Jews worship and study.

7. The Touro Synagogue which is in Rhode Island is the oldest in the United States.

8. The synagogue which is in Rhode Island is the oldest in the United States.

B. Clauses with *who* or *which*: Replacement of Subjects

To form an adjective clause, the relative pronoun *who* or *which* can replace the subject of a simple sentence. *Who* refers to people only. It may be used in both restrictive and nonrestrictive clauses. *Which* refers to things or ideas. In nonrestrictive clauses (with commas), *which* (not *that*) must be used. In restrictive clauses (without commas), either *which* or *that* may be used, but *that* is preferred.

examples	
Simple Sentences	We spoke with **Dr. Chang. Dr. Chang** is an exchange scholar.
Complex Sentence	We spoke with Dr. Chang, **who** is an exchange scholar.
Simple Sentences	Dr. Chang will lecture on **Judaism. Judaism** is his specialty.
Complex Sentence	Dr. Chang will lecture on Judaism, **which** is his specialty.
Simple Sentences	Dr. Chang will lecture on a **topic. This topic** is very interesting.
Complex Sentence	Dr. Chang will lecture on a topic **that (which)** is very interesting.

 *exercise* 2   Use *who* or *which* to form an adjective clause from the second sentence in each pair. Combine the sentences, omitting words and adding commas when necessary.

example: Yesterday I met Mr. Preston. Mr. Preston is a world-famous scholar.

Yesterday I met Mr. Preston, who is a world-famous scholar.

1. Mr. Preston will give a talk about archeology. Archeology is the study of past human life and activities.
2. Mr. Preston will speak about various ruins in the Middle East. Mr. Preston has spent many years doing archeology.
3. The Middle East includes countries in Southwest Asia and North Africa. The Middle East is also called the Mideast.
4. The Middle Eastern countries are Egypt, Israel, Jordan, Saudi Arabia, and Yemen. These Middle Eastern countries are on the Red Sea.
5. Mr. Preston used to live in Jerusalem. Jerusalem is a very important center for Judaism, Christianity, and Islam.
6. Mr. Preston told me about several archeologists. These archeologists are doing interesting work in Jerusalem.

Archeological dig in Israel

 **exercise 3**   Use *who* or *which* to form an adjective clause from the second sentence in each pair. Combine the sentences, omitting words and adding commas when necessary.

> **example:**   Many religions have spring festivals like Passover. Passover marks the end of winter.
>
> *Many religions have spring festivals like Passover, which marks the end of winter.*

1. Passover commemorates the Jews.
   These Jews made the Exodus from Egypt.

2. Rosh Hashanah celebrates the "birthday of the world."
   Rosh Hashanah is the Jewish New Year's festival in the fall.

3. The Shofar is a trumpet.
   This trumpet is blown at Rosh Hashanah.

4. The ten days are a time for confessing sins and asking forgiveness.
   These ten days follow Rosh Hashanah.

5. This period ends with Yom Kippur.
   Yom Kippur is the "Day of Atonement."

6. On Yom Kippur, the synagogues are filled with people.
   These people are praying and asking forgiveness for their sins.

 Summarize the information given in the preceding exercise by completing this sentence in your own words: *Three important Jewish holidays are Passover, which . . . ; Rosh Hashanah, which . . . ; and Yom Kippur, which . . .*

exercise 5 In the following sentences, decide whether you may change *who* or *which* to *that*. If you cannot, explain why not.

> **examples:** A rabbi is a person who teaches and leads worship.
>
> *A rabbi is a person that teaches and leads worship.*
>
> *You can change* who *to* that *because the clause is restrictive (no commas are necessary).*

1. *Rabbi* is a Hebrew word which means "teacher" or "my master."
2. Only a person who has learned the Torah may be called a rabbi.
3. A rabbi has many duties, which include interpreting Jewish law and giving spiritual guidance.
4. Originally, rabbis were scholars who lived and studied at the synagogues.
5. Rabbis were the people who taught young children the Jewish faith.
6. Rabbi Gordon, who is a friend of ours, teaches several classes each week.

 # C. Clauses with *whose:* Replacement of Possessives

The relative pronoun *whose* can be used to form an adjective clause. It replaces a possessive. *Whose* normally refers to people, but it may also refer to places, ideas, or things.

examples	
Simple Sentences	I never miss a class with **Dr. Chang. Dr. Chang's (his)** lectures are always fascinating.
Complex Sentence	I never miss a class with Dr. Chang, **whose** lectures are always fascinating.
Simple Sentences	I particularly enjoyed **the last lecture. Its** topic was "Judaism and the Legal System."
Complex Sentence	I particularly enjoyed the last lecture, **whose** topic was " Judaism and the Legal System."

exercise 6   The following sentences include adjective clauses with *whose.* Rephrase these sentences to form two complete sentences by eliminating *whose* and adding a possessive (or a prepositional phrase).

> **example:** The Jewish tradition of learning comes from the Bible, whose chapters stress the importance of education.
>
> **The Jewish tradition of learning comes from the Bible. The Bible's chapters (the chapters of the Bible) stress the importance of education.**

1. The tradition of learning centers around children, whose education begins at an early age.
2. Education begins with the parents, whose duty is to teach the commandments.
3. The education of the child continues with the rabbi, whose teaching includes both religious and social ideas.
4. Traditionally, all rabbis were scholars whose studies and teachings have shaped modern Judaism.
5. Religious education follows a strict progression whose order and methods have changed little over centuries.
6. Countries everywhere have been influenced by Judaism, whose teachings form the basis of many legal systems.

A rabbi teaching a class of children in North Carolina

exercise 7   Complete the following ten sentences with *who, which, that, whose,* or *X* to indicate no relative pronoun is needed. In some cases, more than one relative pronoun may be used. In other cases, the relative pronoun may be omitted. In these cases, give all possibilities, but indicate the preferred form.

> **examples:**   The Talmud, ____which____ is a sacred Jewish text, gives detailed rules about daily life.   *only one possibility*
>
> The Talmud was developed by ancient rabbis ___who (that)___ wrote stories and parables about daily life.   *who is preferred*

1. The Talmud explains rituals _____ many Jews perform every day.

2. Children learn Jewish rituals from their parents and from the rabbi,

   _____ work includes teaching as well as leading worship.

3. The first rituals _____ Jews perform in the morning are to thank God and to wash their hands.

4. Washing the hands is a ritual _____ symbolizes purity.

5. Cleanliness, _____ is very important in Judaism, is the basis for many Jewish customs.

6. The Talmud gives many rules _____ cover food preparation.

7. Food _____ has been prepared in special ways is called "kosher."

8. Foods like pork, _____ spoils easily, have traditionally been forbidden.

9. This is an example of a religious custom _____ basis was practical. It protected against food poisoning.

10. Jews _____ follow these rules strictly are called "orthodox."

exercise 8

Error Analysis. Many of the following sentences have errors in their use of adjective clauses. Correct the errors. Then look for the sentences in the passages "Hinduism" on page 312, "Buddhism" on page 316, and "Judaism" on page 321 to see if your answers are correct.

example: Judaism which is the parent of both Christianity and Islam is the oldest of the world's three great monotheistic religions.

The clause is nonrestrictive and needs commas.

Correction: Judaism, which is the parent of both Christianity and Islam, is the oldest of the world's three great monotheistic religions.

1. The religious tradition that we call *Hinduism* is the product of 5000 years of development.

2. Buddhism is not a religion that it honors one person.

3. Knowledge in Buddhism is a special kind of religious knowledge people attain through transcending human limitations.

4. It is knowledge goes far beyond the limits of thought.

5. In Buddhism, knowledge leads to the ultimate goal where the personality is transformed there.

6. The core of Judaism is the belief in only one God, who is the creator and ruler of the world.

7. Judaism is based on the Old Testament and the Talmud, which it is a collection of poetry, anecdotes, and so on.

8. All of Judaism's teachings are also called the *Torah* which means "to teach."

Using What You've Learned

activity **1**

What is your favorite holiday? Is it a religious, cultural, or national holiday? How is it celebrated? Is there special food, clothing, dancing, or music? Prepare a brief (three- to five-minute) presentation on the holiday of your choice. If possible, bring any special clothing, music, or pictures to show the class as you are describing the holiday.

> **example:** This is a picture of the Passover celebration at my parents' home. My father is the man who . . . . He is wearing a yarmulke, which symbolizes . . .

activity **2**

Try some additional definitions for words and expressions from American popular culture. You may need to ask people outside your class for help. When you prepare your definitions, use adjective clauses whenever possible. Then, try to add one or two other expressions you are familiar with. Finally, work in small groups and share your definitions.

> **example:** What is a yuppy?
>
> A yuppy is a "young urban professional." It is someone who might be single or married, but who probably doesn't have children. It's a person who has a good job and a fair amount of money. . . .

- What is a potluck?
- What is a fender bender?
- What is a nerd?
- What are jelly beans?
- Who is Oscar the Grouch?
- What was November 22, 1963?
- What is an all-nighter?

- What is a hoola-hoop?
- What is the tooth fairy?
- What are "jammies"?
- What is leap year?
- What is and was Watergate?
- What was the Twist?
- What is a WASP?

activity **3**

Write at least three sentences describing one of your classmates. Use adjective clauses in your descriptions. Then, read your descriptions to the class, but don't say the person's name. Can the other students guess who you are describing? (Don't make your description too easy!)

> **example:** I'm thinking of someone who is in this class. She's a woman who has been in this city only a few months. She's someone who wants to study business. I think she will succeed because she's responsible and hardworking.

Clauses with whom and which: Replacement of Objects

Setting the Context

previewing the passage

The teachings of Jesus have had a tremendous impact on our world. What do you know about his teachings?

Christianity

*C*hristianity is based on the teachings of Jesus Christ, whom Christians call the "Son of God." At the same time, Christians commemorate Jesus as an actual historical figure. He was a man of lowly social standing who was unknown outside of the small part of the Roman Empire where he lived and died.

5   Jesus was born in Bethlehem, in Judea, in about 4 B.C.* and was raised in Galilee, where he spent most of his short life. Little is known about Jesus' early years. Our knowledge of Jesus comes from the last three years of his life, which he spent preaching a doctrine of brotherly love and repentance. During these three years of teaching, he and his closest followers traveled throughout Palestine. Wherever Jesus went, he drew large crowds. Before long, he was known

10   as a healer, and people came from far and wide to ask his help.

    As Jesus grew popular with the common people, who saw him as their long-awaited savior, he become a political threat. Within a short time, Jesus was arrested as a political rebel and was crucified.

Easter Sunday
mass at St. Peter's
Cathedral, Rome, Italy

*B.C.   before Christ

 **discussing ideas** Christianity has many different sects (or divisions). Are you familiar with any of them? Which?

 A. # Clauses with *whom* and *which*: Replacement of Objects of Verbs

The relative pronouns *who(m)* and *which* can replace the object of a verb in a simple sentence. *Whom* is used to refer to people only. Note that *whom* is used in formal speaking and writing; *who* is often substituted in informal English. *Which* is used to refer to things or ideas. *Which* must be used in nonrestrictive clauses (with commas). *That* is preferred in restrictive clauses (without commas) that describe things or ideas.

examples

Simple Sentences	**Dr. Gill** will teach a class on the early Christians. I met **Dr. Gill** last week.
Complex Sentences	Dr. Gill, **whom** I met last week, will teach a course on the early Christians. (formal)
	Dr. Gill, **who** I met last week, will teach a course on the early Christians. (informal)
Simple Sentences	**History 410** covers early Roman history. Dr. Gill teaches **History 410**.
Complex Sentence	History 410, **which** Dr. Gill teaches, covers early Roman history.

 **exercise 1** Underline the adjective clauses in the following eight sentences. Then decide whether the clauses are restrictive or nonrestrictive. Add commas if the clauses are nonrestrictive.

example: After Christ's death, the followers whom Jesus had chosen met privately. *no commas needed*

1. Peter was a fisherman whom Jesus had selected to lead his new religion.

2. Peter whom Jesus had chosen as leader kept the followers together.

3. The followers of Jesus were Jews, and they believed in Judaism which they continued to practice.

4. Christianity as a separate religion actually began with Saint Paul whom many scholars consider to have been the main organizer of the new movement.

5. Both Peter and Paul were probably executed around 60 A.D. in Rome which Christians had made the center of the new religion.

6. At that time, only a small sect of "fanatics" believed in Christianity which most people ignored.

7. By 400 A.D., however, Christianity was the official religion of the Roman Empire which the Emperor Trajan had extended throughout the Mediterranean.

8. Today over 1 billion people believe in the group of religions which we call Christianity.

exercise 2 Combine the following sentences by using *whom* or *which*. Form an adjective clause from the second sentence in each pair. Change words and add punctuation when necessary.

example: The word *holiday* actually came from the words *holy* (religious) and *day*. We use the word *holiday* to mean a vacation day.
The word holiday, which we use to mean a vacation day, actually came from the words holy and day.

1. Holidays such as Christmas have become more like social occasions than religious events. Christianity instituted Christmas.

2. Christmas originally honored only the birth of Jesus Christ. People of many religions now celebrate Christmas.

3. Perhaps the best-known character in the Christmas celebration today is Santa Claus. We see Santa Claus in every store window.

4. The symbol, Santa Claus, came into being in 1822 in the poem *The Night Before Christmas*. Clement Clark Moore wrote this poem.

5. The Christmas tree is a popular tradition. German farmers began this tradition many, many years ago.

6. The custom of decorating the tree began in the 1800s. Bohemians started this custom.

7. The manger or nativity scene is one of the oldest Christmas symbols. St. Francis of Assisi first created a manger in 1223.

Decorating a Christmas tree

8. The birth of Jesus Christ marks the beginning of the Roman calendar. Much of the world uses the Roman calendar.

9. A Roman abbot and astronomer set Christ's birth as the beginning of the calendar. The Catholic Church commissioned this person.

10. Other calendars include the Islamic, the Chinese, and the Jewish calendars. Many groups or countries follow these calendars.

B. Clauses with *whom* and *which:* Replacement of Objects of Prepositions

Relative pronouns may replace the object of a preposition. Several constructions are possible, depending on how formal or informal the statement should be. In formal English, the preposition begins the adjective clause. In informal English, the preposition usually follows the verb in the adjective clause. If the preposition begins the clause, *whom, which,* or *whose* must be used. In restrictive clauses with the preposition at the end, the relative pronoun may be dropped.

examples

Simple Sentences	**Dr. Church** teaches a course in Roman history.
	I was introduced to **Dr. Church** yesterday.
Complex Sentences	Dr. Church, **to whom** I was introduced yesterday, teaches a course in Roman history. (*formal*)
	Dr. Church, **who(m)** I was introduced **to** yesterday, teaches a course in Roman history. (*informal*)
Simple Sentences	**Bascom Hall** is the building.
	The course is taught in **Bascom Hall.**
Complex Sentences	Bascom Hall is the building **in which** the course is taught. (*formal*)
	Bascom Hall is the building **which** the course is taught **in.** (*informal*)
	Bascom Hall is the building **that** the course is taught **in** (*or* **where** the course is taught). (*informal*)
	Bascom Hall is the building **the course is taught in.** (*Note:* This construction is possible only with restrictive clauses with the preposition at the end.)

Combine the following sentences by using *whom* or *which* with prepositions. Form adjective clauses from the second sentence in each pair. Use the adjective clause to modify the italicized word(s). Change words and add commas when necessary.

example: The Greek word *biblia* simply means "the books." The word *Bible* is derived from *biblia*.

The Greek word biblia, from which the word Bible is derived, simply means "the books."

1. The Bible is a collection of *books.* Both Christians and Jews take their doctrines from these books.
2. These books were written over a period of more than one thousand *years.* During that time, numerous authors contributed their own styles and perspectives.
3. The *Old Testament* is the longer of the Bible's two sections. Judaism is based on the Old Testament.
4. The Old Testament has given us many rules of behavior such as *the Ten Commandments.* Most Western legal codes are founded on the Ten Commandments.
5. The *New Testament* consists of twenty-seven writings completed during the first century A.D. Christianity derives its teachings from the New Testament.
6. Its gospels, revelations, and letters were written by *many authors.* We get a variety of perspectives on the life and teachings of Jesus from these authors.

Review.   Complete the following sentences by adding *which, whose, that,* or *X* to indicate that no relative pronoun is needed. Give all possibilities, but indicate the preferred form. Add commas when necessary.

1. The name *Christianity* _____ includes all Christian sects was not used during the lifetime of Jesus.

2. *Jesus* is the Greek name for Joshua _____ means "Jehovah is salvation" in Hebrew.

3. *Christ* comes from a Greek word _____ means "messiah" or "anointed one."

4. *Christ* was a name _____ the people of Antioch, Syria, gave to Jesus.

5. The ending *-ian* _____ comes from Latin was added to Christ.

6. The name *Christian* _____ was soon adopted by the followers of Jesus appeared in later portions of the New Testament.

7. Many words in Christianity come from Greek _____ the Romans used as the common language of their empire.

8. Greek was the language of the great missionary Saint Paul _____ thirteen letters (or *epistles*) are an important part of the New Testament.

Review.   Combine the following sentences by using *who, which, whose, that,* or *when.* Form adjective clauses from the second sentence in each pair. Omit or change words when necessary and pay close attention to punctuation.

1. Christianity consists of three major branches: Roman Catholic, Eastern Orthodox, and Protestant. Christianity has over 1 billion followers.
2. The largest branch is the Roman Catholic church. The Roman Catholic church is headed by the pope, the bishop of Rome.
3. The origins of Christianity's major branches were two historic movements. The attempts of these movements to make reforms divided the Roman Catholic church.
4. The second branch, Eastern Orthodox, dates from 1054. The "great schism" occurred between East and West (Greek and Latin Christianity) in 1054.
5. Actually, differences had begun centuries before 1054. These differences centered around authority and control.
6. The third branch developed from a sixteenth-century movement. The movement is called the Reformation.
7. The Protestant Reformation began as a protest against some practices. German Catholics opposed these practices.
8. Protestants had hoped to reform the Catholic church. Protestants saw abuse of faith, power, and money in the Catholic church.
9. The Protestant Reformation was led by Martin Luther. The Catholic church excommunicated Martin Luther.
10. Martin Luther then founded his own religion. This religion became known as Lutheranism.
11. Eventually, other divisions led to the formation of over 250 Protestant sects. The divisions concerned specific beliefs and practices.
12. Lutheranism is the largest branch of Protestantism. The various churches of Protestantism are now loosely united by the World Council of Churches.

Summarize the information given in the preceding exercise by completing this sentence in your own words: *Christianity has three major branches: Roman Catholic, which . . . , . . .*

Using What You've Learned

activity 1

Most religions and cultures have special ceremonies to mark important stages in life. Birth, adolescence, and death are commemorated in special ways around the world. In pairs or in small groups, discuss one or more of these ceremonies and prepare a brief presentation for the entire class. Make sure to include descriptions of actions, food, special clothing or music, and so forth.

example: Baptism, or christening, is the ceremony that Christians use to welcome a child into the world and into the faith. The ceremony often uses a baptismal font, which is a large basin filled with holy water.

activity 2

Think about the high points and low points of your life. Think about the best and worst, the most interesting, and the most frightening. Tell or write several brief stories about them. Below is some vocabulary to give you ideas. Begin your story with *The (adjective + noun) that (whom) I have ever . . .*

examples: The strangest dream that I have ever **had was when I was about seventeen . . .**

or   The most embarrassing situation **that I have ever been in was during eighth grade . . .**

or   The most interesting teacher whom I have ever **known was . . .**

ADJECTIVES		NOUNS	
best	funny	dream	person
bizarre	interesting	experience	situation
embarrassing	strange	friend	teacher
exciting	worst	meal	trip
frightening		nightmare	

Clause to Phrase Reduction; Agreement with Adjective Phrases and Clauses

Setting the Context

Islam is the "youngest" of the five major world religions. What do you know about Islam? Who founded it? When?

Islam

Beginning in Mecca about A.D. 610, Islam is the youngest of the great religions. It was founded by Muhammad, a respected and influential citizen of Mecca. Not feeling satisfied with success and security, Muhammad continued to search for answers to the many questions that bothered him. Finally, leaving

5   friends and family, Muhammad sought the desert and its solitude. In the desert, an event occurred which changed his life and affected the history of the world. According to Islamic tradition, on a lonely night, the angel Gabriel appeared to Muhammad. Muhammad returned from the desert to proclaim the words of Allah, revealed to him by the angel. This event began the religion we now call

10   Islam.

Millions of pilgrims at midday prayer at the mosque in Mecca, Saudi Arabia

A page from a thirteenth century koran

discussing ideas

Most religions have some form of meditation. Many great thinkers have gone to the desert or the mountains in order to be alone, to think, and to search for answers. What is the role of solitude in this search?

A. Appositives

Appositives are nouns or noun phrases that describe nouns. Nonrestrictive adjective clauses (clauses that use commas) can be shortened to appositives by eliminating the relative pronoun and the verb *be*. The order of the noun and the appositive can usually be reversed without affecting the meaning of the sentence. Appositives, like nonrestrictive clauses, are normally preceded—and may be followed—by commas.

examples

Clause	We recently met Dr. Carlson, **who is a professor of Islamic studies.**
Appositive Phrases	We recently met Dr. Carlson, **a professor of Islamic studies.**
	We recently met a professor of Islamic studies, **Dr. Carlson.**

exercise 1   In the following sentences, change the adjective clauses to appositive phrases.

> **example:** The Koran, which is the sacred book of the Muslims, takes its name from the Arabic word meaning "recite."
>
> The Koran, the sacred book of the Muslims, takes its name from the Arabic word meaning "recite."

1. The Koran is based on revelations to Muhammad, who was the founder of Islam.

2. The whole book, which is the length of the Christian New Testament, is memorized by many Muslims.

3. Those who memorize the Koran earn a special title, which is "Hafiz."

4. The first chapter, which is *Sura 1,* is the most common prayer among Muslims.

5. The followers of Islam, who are perhaps 600 million worldwide, say prayers from the Koran five times each day.

exercise 2   Summarize the information given in the preceding exercise by completing this sentence in your own words: *The Koran, . . .*

B. Past Participial Phrases

Adjective clauses with verbs in the passive voice may be shortened to phrases that use the past participle. To form a phrase with a past participle, eliminate the relative pronoun and the verb *be* from an adjective clause.

examples

Clause	Dr. Carlson recently taught a course **that was called "Islam and the Arts."**
Phrase	Dr. Carlson recently taught a course **called "Islam and the Arts."**

 **exercise 3** In the following sentences, change adjective clauses to phrases with past participles.

example: Muslims follow a set of rules and traditions that is called the "Five Pillars of Islam."

Muslims follow a set of rules and traditions called the "Five Pillars of Islam."

1. The *shahada,* which is repeated each day, is the Muslim's statement of faith.

2. The second pillar consists of prayers that are said five times a day while facing toward Mecca.

3. The third pillar is a donation of money that is determined by a Muslim's income.

4. The fourth pillar is to fast during the ninth month of the Muslim calendar, which is known as Ramadan.

5. The last pillar of Islam is a pilgrimage to Mecca, which is made at least one time in a person's life if health and finances permit.

C. Present Participial Phrases

Some adjective clauses with verbs in the active voice may be shortened to phrases using present participles. The adjective clause must have *who, which,* or *that* in the subject position. To form a phrase, omit *who, which,* or *that* and use the present participle of the verb. The order of the noun and the phrase can often be reversed.

	examples
Clause	Over 600 million people, **who represent** every race and continent, believe in Islam.
Phrase	Over 600 million people, **representing** every race and continent, believe in Islam.
Clause	Islam, **which began** in Arabia, spread quickly throughout the world.
Phrases	Islam, **beginning** in Arabia, spread quickly throughout the world.
	Beginning in Arabia, Islam spread quickly throughout the world.

In the following sentences, change the adjective clauses to phrases with present participles.

example: Islam, which spread from Spain to Indonesia, brought new art forms to many parts of the world.

Islam, spreading from Spain to Indonesia, brought new art forms to many parts of the world.

or   Spreading from Spain to Indonesia, Islam brought new art forms to many parts of the world.

1. Islam contributed to numerous art forms, which included weaving, painting, metalwork, literature, and architecture.

2. Islamic architects, who followed the plan of Muhammad's seventh-century house in Medina, designed magnificent mosques such as the Great Mosque in Córdoba, Spain, and the Royal Mosque in Isfahan, Iran.

3. A Muslim who travels in a foreign country will find the same design in all mosques.

4. Mosques may be large or small, but they have the same design, which consists of an open courtyard and enclosed prayer halls.

5. Artisans who work with ceramic, wood, and metal have created magnificent decorations, such as at the mosque in Medina.

Interior of mosque dome, Córdoba, Spain

Review.   First, underline the appositive or participial phrase in each of the following sentences. Then expand the sentences by changing the phrases to adjective clauses.

example: Modern science owes a tremendous debt to the Islamic Empire, <u>the center of Western learning from the ninth to the fourteenth centuries.</u>

Modern science owes a tremendous debt to the Islamic Empire, which was the center of Western learning from the ninth to the fourteenth centuries.

1. Islam has given us the knowledge of Greek science, preserved and developed by the Muslims.

2. Much of Islam's scientific development was done at Baghdad, the capital of the Islamic Empire.

3. Caliph Ma'mum, ruler from 813 to 833, created the "House of Wisdom."

4. The House of Wisdom, containing a library, a translation bureau, and a school, was a sophisticated center of learning.

5. At the House of Wisdom, scholars studied Greek, Persian, and Indian scientific works translated into Arabic.

6. Scientists studying ancient Greek manuscripts developed the foundations for modern medicine.

7. Muslim scientists experimenting with a variety of laboratory techniques developed the foundation for modern chemistry.

8. In mathematics, Muslims gave us three extremely important ideas—the use of numerals, the decimal system, and the concept of zero.

D. Agreement with Adjective Phrases and Clauses

The subject of a sentence determines if the verb should be singular or plural. Adjective phrases and clauses that come between the subject and verb do not affect the agreement. Adjective clauses are singular or plural, depending on the noun(s) they modify. In adjective clauses with their own subjects (object clauses), however, the subject and verb of the clause should agree.

	singular verb	plural verb
With Adjective Phrases	The **Koran,** the sacred book of the Muslims, **comes** from the Arabic word "recite."	**Muslims,** followers of Muhammad, **recite** from the Koran each day.
With Adjective Clauses	The **Koran,** which **is** the sacred book of the Muslims, **comes** from the Arabic word "recite."	**Muslims,** who **are** followers of Muhammad, **recite** from the Koran each day.
	Sura I, which **a believer** in Islam **recites** daily, comes from the Koran.	*Sura I,* which **Muslims recite** daily, comes from the Koran.

Choose the correct form of the verbs in parentheses to complete the following sentences.

1. The Koran, the sacred book of the Muslims, (take /(takes))its name from the Arabic word meaning "recite."

2. Many scholars who study Christianity (consider / considers) St. Paul to have been the main organizer of Christianity as a separate religion.

3. Peter, who was one of the fishermen, (was / were) chosen by Jesus to be a leader.

4. Traditionally, all rabbis were scholars whose knowledge (has / have) shaped modern Judaism.

5. Rituals which are explained in the Talmud (is / are) performed by many Jews every day.

6. Judaism, which is the parent of both Christianity and Islam, (is / are) the oldest of the world's three great monotheistic religions.

7. Muslims follow a set of rules and traditions that (is / are) called the "Five Pillars of Islam."

8. Mosques may be large or small, but they have the same design, which (consist / consists) of an open courtyard and enclosed prayer halls.

9. The House of Wisdom, containing a library, a translation bureau, and a school, (was / were) a sophisticated center of learning.

10. Santa Claus, whom we see in store windows and television commercials, (is / are) one of the most popular Christmas symbols.

Using What You've Learned

 **activity 1**

In many countries and cultures, marriage has both a civil and a religious ceremony. How is marriage performed in your religion or in your culture? What is the typical clothing, music, or dance? Is there a party or a dinner after the ceremony?

Form small groups and give a brief description of marriage rites. You may choose to work in groups from the same religion or from the same culture. Or you may choose groups of all men and all women, to give the male and female points of view. If you wish, you can include a role play of a typical marriage, translating the words said in the ceremony into English.

George Bernard Shaw said, "There is only one religion, though there are a hundred versions of it." After studying this chapter, do you agree with Shaw's thoughts? If this is true, why have the religions of the world created so many divisions among people? How would the world be different if everyone believed in only one religion? Use information from this chapter and your own ideas and opinions to write a short essay agreeing or disagreeing with Shaw's thoughts.

activity 3

How many adjective clauses can you put in one sentence? While this may be very poor writing style, it certainly is a test of your knowledge of adjective clauses!

First read the following attempt by one student. How many clauses do you find? (The answer is on page 344.) Then try an original one. *But remember that this is only for practice.* We do not recommend using dozens of adjective clauses in your sentences!

There was an old man who lived in Mexico City, which is the capital of Mexico, which is situated between North and South America, who had a big house that was surrounded by a large garden in which a lot of old trees grew and where sat the old Rolls-Royce, in which the old man had driven through the city until he had an accident in which he hurt his legs and arms, which were then put in casts by a doctor who came from the hospital that had been built by the father of the old man who had the accident, and it is now the best hospital in Mexico, the one in which all the most talented surgeons work, most of whom come from the University of Mexico City, which has a large painting on its front wall that was done by Salvador Dali, who is a Spanish surrealistic painter and who is, unbelievably, related to our old man who had the accident in Mexico City, which is, as mentioned above, the capital city of Mexico.

—Hans Jurgen

focus on testing

Use of Adjective Clauses and Phrases

Modifiers such as adjective phrases and clauses are frequently tested on standardized English proficiency exams. Review these commonly tested structures and check your understanding by completing the sample items below.

Remember that . . .

- *That* may not be used in nonrestrictive clauses (with commas).
- In formal English, *who* (not *that*) is preferred when describing people.
- In formal English, *whom* (not *who*) must be used with object clauses.
- When adjective clauses are reduced, the appropriate participle form must be used.
- Subjects and verbs must agree in number.

Part 1: Circle the correct completion for the following.

example: John appears happy with his new boss, _____ is from Spain.
    a. that   **c.** whose
    b. whom   **(d.)** who

1. *Hindu* is a word _____ Persians gave to the people of India.
    a. that   **c.** who
    b. that was   **d.** whose

2. The Old Testament, _____ Judaism is based, is the longer of the Bible's two sections.
    a. which   **c.** on whom
    b. on which   **d.** what

3. The gentleman _____ we were introduced is an archaeologist.
    a. to whom   **c.** who
    b. whom   **d.** to who

Part 2: Circle the letter below the underlined word(s) containing an error.

example: <u>Overseas</u> travelers <u>often</u> experience culture shock, <u>which are</u>
         A   B   Ⓒ
often a combination of <u>confusion</u>, frustration, and depression.
                     D

1. *Nirvana* is the word <u>that</u> Hindus <u>use it</u> <u>to describe</u> <u>a</u> sense of inner
                    A   B   C   D
peace.

2. Sociologists are researchers <u>who</u> <u>studies</u> the science of society,
                            A   B
<u>along with</u> <u>its</u> social institutions and social relationships.
    C   D

3. Mosques <u>may be</u> large or small, but <u>they</u> have the same design
           A   B
<u>consist of</u> an open courtyard and <u>enclosed</u> prayer halls.
    C   D

Answer: 21 clauses

Crime and Punishment

in this chapter

Introduction

In this chapter, you will look at the difference in expressing hopes, wishes, and dreams, in contrast to describing reality. To do so, you will review the modal auxiliaries, and you will study the verbs *hope* and *wish* and various conditional sentences.

The following passage introduces the chapter theme, Crime and Punishment, and raises some of the topics and issues you will cover in the chapter. Note that many of the selections in this chapter come from people who have spent time in prisons for a variety of crimes—both violent and nonviolent.

previewing the passage

Have you been the victim or the witness to a crime? What happened?

Crime in our Society

Imagine what you would do if you were in the following situations. If you didn't have enough money to pay your income taxes, would you cheat on them? If you were drunk, would you drive your car? If you were the president of a corporation, would you allow your employees to dump waste into the ocean? Would you ever take something from a store without paying if you didn't have the money for it? Would you become violent if you were angry with your friends or family? These are just some examples of the types of situations in which people may make a decision which can lead to criminal behavior.

5

Why do people do things which are illegal and can hurt others? Criminologists suggest that the reason we have so much crime is that it is a symptom of other social problems, such as a poor educational system, lack of family values, unemployment, and drug use.

10

Everybody hopes that crime will decrease, but what can we do to prevent it? Some people wish that we had tougher judges and mandatory sentences for those people who break the law. Others wish that more tax money were spent to fight crime; they wish we had more police on the streets. Still others believe we need to work on changing society. These people hope that social change will lead to a reduction in crime. No matter how we choose to fight crime, everyone wishes we could feel safer in our homes and on the street.

15

discussing ideas

In your opinion, what causes crime? If you were working on a crime prevention committee, what would you suggest we do to prevent crime?

hope and wish

Setting the Context

What does *doing time* mean?

Doing Time

When I was a child, my ma* always talked about taking responsibility for your own actions. Sometimes I don't care anything about what she said, but many days I wish I'd listened to her and I'd thought about what she was trying to teach me. Here I am—doin' time in the joint.† I'm caged like an animal because
5   I did some horrible things to some people who were probably nice. Sure, I wish I weren't here. Sure, I wish they'd never caught me.

    But that ain't‡ all. I wish this life I've got now had never happened. I wish I'd done it differently. I wish I'd believed that someday I'd be responsible for what I'd done. I hope somebody will look at my life and will learn from it. I hope some-
10   body will pay attention to the words of people like my ma.

    I wish I'd known . . . I wish I'd listened. And I wish I were out on the street.

Phillip Moton, A Quad, California Men's Colony

---

*Ma   Mother, Mama
†the joint   slang for *the prison*
‡ain't   slang for *isn't* or *aren't*

discussing ideas Have you ever known any prisoners? Did you ever know anyone who worked in a prison? What are prisons like in your native country?

A. *hope* Versus *wish*

The verb *hope* is generally used to express optimism; the speaker feels that something is possible. The verb *wish* is often used to express impossibility or improbability; the speaker wants reality to be different than it is. To show the contrast to reality, *would, could,* or a special verb form—the subjunctive mood—is used after *wish*. The subjunctive mood shows that the ideas are imaginary, improbable, or contrary to fact.

	examples	implied meaning
hope	I **hope** (that) he **will visit** us.	It is quite possible that he'll visit us.
wish	I **wish** (that) he **would visit** us.	It is doubtful that he'll visit.
hope	I **hope** (that) they **are going**.	I think that they are going to go.
wish	I **wish** (that) they **were going**.	I don't think they're going to go.

B. The Subjunctive with *wish*

Wishes are expressed by using *would, could,* or a subjunctive verb form in the dependent clause. For present and future wishes, in most cases the subjunctive is the same as the simple past tense. However, in formal English, *were* is used for all forms of the verb *be*. In informal English, *was* is often used with *I, he, she,* and *it,* although this is considered incorrect.

Past wishes are also expressed by using a subjunctive verb form in the dependent clause. In all cases, this form is the same as the past perfect tense (*had* + past participle).

	examples	implied meaning
Wishes About the Future	I **wish** (that) I **could go** home soon.	I can't go home soon.
	I **wish** (that) things **would change**.	Things probably won't change.

	examples	implied meaning
Wishes About the Present	I **wish** (that) I **weren't** here.	I am here, but I'm not happy about it.
	I **wish** (that) I **weren't living** here.	I am living here, but I don't like it.
	I **wish** (that) I **didn't have** to be here.	I have to be here, but I don't like it.
Wishes About the Past	I **wish** (that) my life **had been** different.	I don't like the way my life has been.
	I **wish** (that) I **had known** better.	I didn't know better then, and I regret it.

exercise 1 Underline the verbs in the dependent clauses. Do the verbs refer to the present, past, or the future? Indicate the time frame of each. Then rephrase each sentence to show its meaning.

examples: I wish I <u>were going</u> to see my family soon.   (I'm probably not going to see my family soon, but I would like to.)
I wish that you <u>were</u> here.   (You're not here, and I miss you.)
I wish that I <u>hadn't done</u> it.   (I did it, but I regret it now.)

1. I wish that I had worked harder.

2. I wish that I had more free time.

3. I wish that I were sleeping.

4. I wish that my friends lived closer to me.

5. I wish that I hadn't stolen the money.

6. I wish that my landlord would lower the rent.

exercise 2 Quickly reread the passage "Doing Time" on page 347. Underline the dependent clauses that follow the verbs *hope* and *wish*. Identify the verb(s) in these clauses and tell the time frame (past, present, or future) for each.

exercise 3 Anyone who is spending time in prison would most likely rather be somewhere else and be doing something else. Rephrase the following sentences to use *wish*.

example: I'd rather be with my friends.
I wish I were with my friends.

1. I'd rather be outside in the fresh air.
2. We'd rather be jogging.
3. I'd rather be home.
4. I'd rather be at the beach.

5. I'd rather be driving.
6. We'd rather be playing soccer.
7. I'd rather be with my children.
8. I'd rather be free.

In pairs, take turns making statements and responses. Use the example as a model.

example: My cousin graduated last year.

> A: **My cousin graduated last year.**
> B: **Don't you wish that you had graduated last year too?**
> A: **Of course.** (*or:* **Not really.**)

1. My friend traveled around the world last year.
2. My sister will get married next year.
3. My brother got a scholarship at the university.
4. My father learned to speak German.
5. My mother is a computer whiz.
6. My brother-in-law is trilingual.

 **exercise 5**

The following are quotes from people who have been convicted of crimes and who have spent time in prison. Complete them by adding appropriate forms of the verbs in parentheses. Add modal auxiliaries when necessary.

1. You don't want to know about what I've done. I wish I _____
(do / never)

it, that's for sure. Look at me. Do I look like a criminal? No, but I am.

I wish I _____ in prison, but that's only part of it. I wish I
(not / be)

_____.   —Jack B., bank robber
(be born / never)

2. I did something I believed was right. I still don't know if it was the right

thing to do. I wish that I _____. I kidnapped someone. I kid-
(know)

napped someone important. I wanted to create a revolution because I

wanted social justice. Here I am behind bars, and the revolution never

came. I hope someday we _____ justice in our society. I wish
(have)

I _____ the answers because what I did hasn't seemed to help.
(know)

                                             —Bill H., kidnapper

3. I carried drugs across the border. For that, I got five years to life here in the

U.S. I wish I _____ what was going to happen. I thought I was
(know)

going to make some money. Now here I am and my wife's alone with my

kids and they don't even remember their father. I hope that someday they

_____ me again. I wish I _____ them. I am so sad
(love)   (see)

and lonely.   —Ramón G., drug smuggler

4. I killed some people, famous people. The family—we killed some people. I

don't think about it much now. I have asked forgiveness from my God, and

I hope he _____ me. Many people in the joint, we find religion. I
          (forgive)

found it here. Today, I can hope that tomorrow I _____, tomorrow
                                                              (sleep)

I _____. I wish I _____ to be here, but it has led me to
      (rest)   (not have)

some hope.

—Tex W., murderer

Using What You've Learned

activity 1 Each one of us has choices to make, and sometimes we make the wrong ones. Think of three bad choices you have made: in your studies, your career, or your personal life, for example. Looking back, what do you wish that you had done? Write a short paragraph telling what you wish had happened. Later, in a small-group discussion, share your composition with your classmates.

activity 2 Aladdin found his Genie of the Lamp. Imagine that you've found yours! What three wishes would you wish for? Orally or in writing, tell what you desire and why you'd like to make those particular wishes.

activity 3 North Americans love to put bumper stickers on their cars. One popular type of bumper sticker begins, "I'd rather be . . . ," meaning "I wish I were . . . " Such bumper stickers usually tell about our hobbies and interests. In pairs or small groups, create your own bumper stickers with *wish*. Try to create at least five slogans beginning with *I wish I were* or *I wish we were*.

examples: We wish we were sailing.

              We wish we could be studying more grammar.

activity 4

The verbs *hope* and *wish* often represent the attitudes of the optimist and the pessimist. The optimist hopes that everything will work out, while the pessimist *wishes* it would. In small groups, write short dialogues that include people who are optimistic and people who are pessimistic. The dialogue may be serious or it may be comical. Here are some suggestions for topics:

1. The menu at the dormitory tonight: Imagine that you all live in a dormitory. The food is notoriously bad! Some of you would like to send the cook to the moon or at least to a cooking school. Yet a few of you try to be kind in your attitude toward the cook. You optimistically hope for a miracle.
2. The first date with a new boyfriend/girlfriend: Imagine that you are going out with a new person tonight. You will have to meet his or her family, and you hope to make a good impression on everyone. You are worried about not saying and doing the right things. The people in the family are nervous, too. You imagine that your evening could be a complete disaster, or perhaps it could be the beginning of a wonderful relationship.

Be sure to include a role for everyone in your group. After you have finished, role-play your dialogues for the class.

TOPIC two

Conditional Sentences: otherwise; Imaginary Conditionals: Present or Unspecified Time

Setting the Context

previewing the passage

Do you feel safe? What can you do to lower your risk of becoming a victim of crime?

Woman shoplifting gloves

352 Mosaic One • Grammar

The Risk of Being a Victim

In a recent survey, 17 percent of the people interviewed said that at least one member of their household had been either a victim or a witness to a crime in the past year. However, if you had been a victim of a crime, it most likely wouldn't have been a violent one. Even though a violent crime is three times more likely to occur now than it was thirty years ago, today 94 percent of all crimes don't involve any threat of violence. Most crimes are not the sensational type that become headlines or top stories on the evening news.

So what are your chances of being involved in a crime? If it were 1960 and you were living in the United States, the chances of your experiencing a crime would be low. Today, the odds of experiencing a crime vary. For example, if you lived in an impoverished household, you would be at a greater risk than if you lived in a well-to-do household. If you were an adult, you would be less likely to be victimized than if you were a youth. If you used drugs and committed crimes yourself, you would raise your chances. Interestingly, the odds of being a victim are highest for criminals themselves.

discussing ideas Why do you think youths, criminals, and people living in poverty have the greatest chances of being victims of crimes? What does this tell us about how we can prevent crime?

A. *otherwise*

Otherwise is a transition that contrasts reality with wishes and dreams. It means "If the situation were different" or "under other circumstances." The auxiliaries *could, might,* and *would* are often used after *otherwise*. Notice the possible placement and punctuation of *otherwise* in the following examples:

examples	implied meaning
I'm scared to walk alone at night; **otherwise,** I would go to the party.	I am scared to walk home alone at night, so I won't go to the party.
I don't have any money. **Otherwise, I** might buy a new car.	I don't have any money, so I can't buy a new car.
No one knows where the criminal is hiding. We could arrest him, **otherwise.** *	We don't know where the criminal is hiding. As a result, we cannot arrest him.

*This placement of *otherwise* is informal. It is used in conversation only.

 **exercise 1**   Complete the following sentences in your own words.

> **example:**   I don't have a car; otherwise, I could **take a trip to the mountains.**

1. I don't have much money this month. Otherwise, I might . . .
2. I have a lot of homework tonight; otherwise, we could . . .
3. The reviews of that movie weren't very good; otherwise, . . .
4. I have to work during vacation. Otherwise, . . .
5. I'm out of shape. Otherwise, I . . .
6. I'm afraid of the ocean; otherwise, . . .
7. My roommate is taking a test on Saturday. Otherwise, . . .
8. I don't know how to . . . ; otherwise, . . .

B. Imaginary Conditionals: Present or Unspecified Time

Imaginary conditions express ideas that the speaker or writer thinks are unlikely, untrue, or contrary to fact. They may be wishes or dreams, or they may express advice to others. To show this, *could, might,* or *would* is used in the main clause, and a subjunctive form is used in the *if* clause. In most cases, the subjunctive form is the same as the simple past tense, but with the verb *be,* *were* is used for all persons in formal English.

examples	implied meaning
If I **had** more money, I **could take** some trips.	I don't have much money, so I am not able to take many trips.
If I **were** rich, I **would** never **worry.**	I'm not rich, so I worry sometimes.
If I **were** you, I **would save** money.	My advice to you is that you should save money.
If I **was** you, I **would save** money.*	My advice to you is that you should save money.

*This form is incorrect but is frequently used in conversation.

   Combine the ideas in the following sentences by forming sentences with *if.* Use the example as a model.

> **example:**   I wish this town were stricter about drinking and driving. Then I wouldn't worry so much about driving at night.
>
> **If this town were stricter about drinking and driving, I wouldn't worry so much about driving at night.**

354   Mosaic One • Grammar

1. I wish that there weren't so much crime in this neighborhood. Then I wouldn't feel so nervous about living here.
2. I wish the streets were safer here. Then I could walk home at night.
3. I wish that there weren't so many robberies. Then I wouldn't need five locks on my door.
4. I wish there were more police walking through this neighborhood. Then I would feel safer.
5. I wish that this town were stricter about drinking and driving. Then I wouldn't worry when I drive at night.
6. I wish there weren't so many bike thefts. Then I could park my bike outside.
7. I wish apartments weren't so expensive here. Then I could get a bigger place.
8. I wish that I had a car. Then it would be much easier to get around.

 **exercise 3**   Crime isn't the only way to get money or things without working long and hard. Imagine that the following situations happened to you through good luck. How would you feel? What would you do? What wouldn't you do? Make at least three statements for each, using *if* clauses.

example: Imagine that you were awarded a one-year scholarship at your school—all expenses paid.

If I were awarded a scholarship, I would feel very proud.

If I had a full scholarship, my parents wouldn't have to send me more money.

If I didn't have to pay tuition, I could concentrate more on my work because I wouldn't be worried about money all the time.

1. Imagine that you were offered a special promotion by the phone company for one month's long distance calls—*free.*
2. Imagine that you were the winner of a sweepstakes at your grocery store—for $500 worth of purchases.
3. Imagine that you won a shopping spree at the mall—for everything you could purchase in three hours.
4. Imagine that you had a winning ticket in the local lottery—for $10,000.
5. Imagine that you won an unlimited mileage air pass from an international airline—for one month of travel to anywhere.
6. Imagine that you hit the jackpot in Las Vegas—for $1 million.

We often use *If I were you* . . . instead of *you should* . . . or *you'd better* as a way of giving advice. In pairs, take turns giving advice for the following. If possible, give two pieces of advice for each.

example: A: I often leave my room unlocked.
B: **If I were you, I wouldn't do that. I would lock the door whenever I left.**

1. I don't feel very safe in my apartment. The windows are very low, and the locks are not very good.
2. I worry about parking my car on the street.
3. I usually leave my backpack (briefcase, purse, and so on) in my office near my desk, but I often forget to lock the door when I go out.
4. I often stay late at the lab. Sometimes I work until 12:30 or 1:00 A.M. and then I walk home by myself.
5. All my important documents, such as my passport, are in a box in my closet, I think. I'm not really sure where I put them.
6. I don't believe in banks, so I keep all my cash in my home.

Using What You've Learned

activity 1

Both crimes and punishments vary from culture to culture. Consider the following crimes:

burglary	littering
tax evasion	kidnapping
speeding	drug possession
assault	vandalism

Do you know how these crimes would be punished in your native country? In small groups or as a class, share any information you have on your native country's justice system.

activity 2

Is crime a serious problem in your hometown or in the town where you live now? If you had the chance, how would you deal with the problem? In a short composition, explain how you would handle it. Begin with *If I were the chief of police in (your city)* . . . Then, in pairs, small groups, or as a class, share your ideas.

activity 3

Check your local newspaper, watch the television news, or listen to the radio. Make notes about any recent crimes. Come to class prepared to discuss crime in your town or in the nation.

activity 4

Are you talkative, shy, impatient, calm? Are you a good listener? Do you have a good memory? Reflect for a moment on your personality. Is there anything about yourself that you'd like to change? What are some characteristics or traits that you wish you had? Are there any you wish you didn't have? Give several original sentences using *If I were . . .* or *If I weren't . . .*

example: **If I weren't so careless, I would do better on tests.**
If I were more patient, I'd have less stress.

activity 5 In a speech at Harvard University in 1953, future president of the United States John F. Kennedy said, "If more politicians knew poetry, and more poets knew politics, I am convinced the world would be a better place in which to live."

In your opinion, how might the world be a better place? Share your ideas in a discussion with your classmates or in a brief composition.

TOPIC three
Perfect Modal Auxiliaries

Setting the Context

previewing the passage

Crimes do not always involve hurting someone or damaging property. What other types of crime are there?

Crimes Without Violence

WIFE: I can't believe this!

HUSBAND: What happened? What's wrong?

WIFE: Someone must have gotten my credit card number and used it. I've got charges here that I never made!

5 HUSBAND: But how could it have happened?

WIFE: Well, lately, I haven't asked for the carbon paper when I've made charges. Someone may have gotten my number out of a wastebasket in some store. I should have been more careful. . . .

HUSBAND: No matter what, these things shouldn't happen. It's wrong. Well, let's
10 call the credit card company and put a stop on the card. . . .

Unfortunately, this scenario is not unusual. Worldwide, nonviolent but equally reproachable criminal acts take place all too frequently. These nonviolent crimes are often called white collar crimes. They do not hurt us physically, but they can have other terrible effects.

discussing ideas

Have you ever been a victim of a nonviolent crime, such as the one described in the reading? What happened? What did you do about it?

A. Perfect Modal Auxiliaries

Perfect modal auxiliaries express past activities or situations that were not real or that did not occur. Often, they express our wishes in hindsight.

	examples	notes
UNFULFILLED INTENTIONS AND PREFERENCES		
would	I **would have gone,** but it was impossible.	*Would have* refers to past intentions that were not fulfilled.
would rather	I **would rather have gone** with you than stay here.	*Would rather have* refers to past preferences that were not fulfilled.
UNFULFILLED ADVICE		
should	You **should have gone** too.	*Should have* and *ought to have* refer to actions that were advisable but did not take place.
ought to	He **ought to have stayed** longer.	*Ought to have* is less common than *should have.*
PAST POSSIBILITIES		
could	I **could have gone** later.	*Could have, may have,* and *might have* refer to past possibilities. In many cases, the speaker or writer is uncertain whether the action took place. In some contexts, *could have* also refers to past abilities.
might	He **might have called.**	
may	He **may have left** already.	
PAST PROBABILITIES		
must	He **must have left.**	*Must have* refers to past probabilities. The speaker or writer is fairly certain that the action took place.

 Quickly reread "Crimes Without Violence" on page 357. Underline all the modal auxiliaries in the passage and give the function and time frame of each.

 Change the modals to perfect forms in the following sentences. Then listen carefully as your teacher reads both the present and past forms rapidly. Try to distinguish between the two. What clues can you find to help you distinguish the two forms in rapid speech?

example: He may go to jail.

He may have gone to jail.

1. She may get fired.
2. Someone might steal your bike.
3. It must be dangerous to walk on that path.
4. He must cheat on his taxes.
5. John must be worried.
6. John should be more careful.
7. Sandy could have an accident.
8. They might rob a bank.

exercise 3 We often use responses with modal auxiliaries as a way of empathizing, saying that we understand how someone else feels. In pairs, take turns making statements and responses based on the model. Use *would (not) have* and *too* or *either* in your responses.

example: Someone found out my credit card number and used it. I was really shocked.

A: **Someone got my credit card number and used it. I was really shocked.**
B: **I would have been shocked too!**

1. Someone stole my bicycle. I felt just awful.
2. Someone broke into our apartment, and it scared me to death. I wasn't able to sleep for a week.
3. Another student took my ideas for a project. I was so upset!
4. Someone stole my purse with my address book in it. I felt terrible.
5. Someone got access to my computer and erased several files. I was furious.
6. Someone picked my pocket on the bus. I got so angry!
7. My landlord wouldn't fix the plumbing, so I had to pay the plumber. I was not very happy about that.
8. I had to go to the police station to file a complaint. I felt really nervous.

In each of the following statements, a person had a problem but did something wrong to solve it. What could, should, or might the person have done instead? Give at least two alternative actions for each. Use *could have, should have,* or *might have* in your suggestions.

> **example:** Pedro didn't study for his math exam, so during the exam he cheated and copied down the answers from the test of the woman sitting next to him.
>
> **He should have studied for his exam.**
>
> **He could have tried his best on the exam.**

1. Jack was failing his history course and needed a high score on his final exam. The class was very large, and the final exam was given in a large hall. He paid someone to take his test for him.
2. Mary had a term paper due for a history class. She would fail the course if she didn't complete it. She did not finish her work, so instead, she bought a term paper from another student.
3. Taka did not want to pay for a book for his class, so he photocopied it chapter by chapter, even though the photocopies cost almost as much as the book.

 B. Perfect Modal Auxiliaries and Past Advice

In the present, English has words to express advice, such as *ought to* and *should.* When you want to show that the advice was not taken in the past, use *ought (not) to have* + past participle or *should (not) to have* + past participle.

present to future advice	past advice not taken
He **ought to go.**	He **ought to have gone.**
He **ought not to say** that.	He **ought not to have said** that.
He **should go.**	He **should have gone.**
He **should not say** that.	He **should not have said** that.

 **exercise 5**

In pairs, take turns making the following statements and responding to them. Use *should (not) have* or *ought (not) to have* in your responses. Then add a few original statements and your partners will respond to them.

example: A: Eun didn't want to wrinkle her blouse, so she didn't wear her seatbelt.

B: **She really should have worn her seatbelt.**

A: **Yes, if she had worn her seatbelt, she might not have been injured in the accident.**

B: **Right, maybe she would be home and not in the hospital right now.**

1. Miki was in a hurry, so she parked her car in a "handicapped" zone.
2. Bill wasn't paying attention and ran a red light. He almost hit another car.
3. Dorothy didn't have any change, so she didn't put any money in the parking meter.
4. Abdul didn't pay any of his parking tickets, and one day his car was impounded.
5. While David was driving, he didn't notice his children were throwing candy wrappers out of the car window.
6. Maria was late for an appointment, so she drove 50 miles per hour through a residential area in order to get to a freeway.

Rephrase the following sentences to use *otherwise*. Use *may have, might have, could have,* or *would have* in your new sentences.

example: He was a dangerous criminal, so I was nervous to be near him.

He was a dangerous criminal; otherwise, I wouldn't have been nervous to be near him.

1. There was a lot of crime in that part of town, so I didn't go there very often.
2. The man knew she was a thief, so he didn't hire her.
3. Her boyfriend never paid his parking tickets, so the police towed his car.
4. There are so many social problems; that's why we have so much crime.
5. The prisons are overcrowded, so we need to build more jails.

Using What You've Learned

We often use *otherwise* to make excuses when we haven't done something. What haven't you done recently that you should have done? Think of at least six original sentences that use *otherwise* and perfect modals. Some ideas for topics are: assignments, trips or vacations, calls or letters home, problems with a roommate or friend, cleaning, and fixing things.

example: **I didn't have much free time last weekend; otherwise, I would have written my family.**

The American poet Robert Frost wrote about choices in his poem *The Road Not Taken.* He wrote:

THE ROAD NOT TAKEN

Two roads diverged in a yellow wood,
And sorry I could not travel both
And be one traveler, long as I stood
And looked down one as far as I could
To where it bent in the undergrowth;

Then took the other, as just as fair,
And having perhaps the better claim,
Because it was grassy and wanted wear;
Though as for that the passing there
Had worn them really about the same,

And both that morning equally lay
In leaves no step had trodden black.
Oh, I kept the first for another day!
Yet knowing how way leads on to way,
I doubted if I should ever come back.

I shall be telling this with a sigh
Somewhere ages and ages hence:
Two roads diverged in a wood, and I—
I took the one less traveled by,
And that has made all the difference.

What do you think Frost is telling us about choices in this poem? What does this poem tell us about his life?

Whenever we make a choice, it gives us new possibilities, but at the same time, it usually eliminates others. Think about the "crossroads" in life, when several "roads" are possible. In small groups, discuss some of these. You may want to use your ideas for the basis of a composition too.

TOPIC **four**

Conditional Sentences: Past and Past-to-Present Time

Setting the Context

previewing the passage

Do you believe that abuse of the environment is a criminal act? Can you give any specific examples?

Crimes Against Our Environment

Ok, it's true. We humans have made a mess of our world. We've committed many criminal acts against our environment. If we'd been a little smarter, if we had done more planning, if we hadn't been so greedy, our world would be a much better place. We wouldn't have created giant cities without efficient trans-
5 portation systems. We wouldn't have polluted our air, land, and water. We wouldn't have let people become so desperate that drugs and crime were their only escape. We would have created healthy, *livable* cities that showed respect for humanity and for the environment.

Is it too late? Absolutely not! We got ourselves into this mess; we can
10 certainly get ourselves out.

Jack Powers, age fortyish

discussing ideas Can you give any examples of cases where individuals or companies have been found guilty of environmental crimes?

A. Imaginary Conditionals: Past Time

Conditional sentences with *if* can be used to describe past situations or events that did *not* take place. A subjunctive form, which is the same as the past perfect tense, is used in the *if* clause, and perfect modal auxiliaries are used in the main clause.

examples	implied meaning
If I **hadn't needed** the money, I **wouldn't have done** that.	I did something because I needed the money.
We **would have taken** better care of our environment if we **had been** wiser.	We didn't take good care of our environment because we were not wise.

 **exercise** Complete the following sentences with the appropriate form of the verbs in parentheses.

examples: If I have time, I ___will go___ (go) to the party.

If I had time, I ___would go___ (go) to the party.

If I had had time, I _would have gone_ (go) to the party.

1. If she _____ (be) here, I'm sure she will help us.

If she were here, I'm sure she _____ (help) us.

If she _____ (be) here, I'm sure she would have helped us.

2. If he _____ (want) a raise, he would have worked hard.

If he wants a raise, he _____ (work) hard.

If he wanted a raise, he _____ (work) hard.

3. We _____ (visit) him in prison, if you tell us the address.

We _____ (visit) him in prison, if you had told us the address.

We _____ (visit) him in prison, if you told us the address.

4. If they _____ (need) money, they will rob a bank.

If they needed money, they _____ (rob) a bank.

If they _____ (need) money, they would have robbed a bank.

5. If I _____ (study) harder, I'd get better grades.

If I _____ (study) harder, I'd have gotten better grades.

If I _____ (study) harder, I'll get better grades.

 B. Imaginary Conditionals:
Past-to-Present Time

Conditional sentences with *if* can be used to describe past actions or situations that have affected the present. A subjunctive form (*had* + past participle) is used in the *if* clause, and a simple modal auxiliary is used in the main clause.

examples	implied meaning
If we **hadn't bought** the house, we **might** still **be** in an apartment.	We bought a house, so we don't live in an apartment now.
If we **hadn't bought** the house, we **would** still **have** to pay rent.	We bought a house, so we don't have to pay rent.
We **would have** much less space if we **hadn't bought** the house.	We have much more space now because we bought a house.

 **exercise 2**   Imagine the following possible situations and how they might have affected your life. Complete the following sentences in your own words. Give at least two sentences for each item.

example: If I had been born a millionaire, . . .

If I had been born a millionaire, my money problems today would be completely different! I would have trouble spending it, not making it.

1. If I had never studied English, . . .
2. If I had not come to this school, . . .
3. If I had been born the opposite sex, . . .
4. If I had been born thirty years ago, . . .
5. If I had been elected president of my country ten years ago, . . .
6. If I had gotten married at age 15, . . .

Imagine how our lives might be different today if these events had not occurred. Make notes in the chart below. Try to give at least one negative and one positive effect or result for each event. Then write complete sentences with *if*.

	NEGATIVE	POSITIVE
example: If internal combustion engines hadn't been developed, . . .	If internal combustion engines hadn't been developed, we wouldn't have cars, buses, and taxis. Transportation and travel would be much more difficult.	If they hadn't been developed, however, we also wouldn't have so much air pollution.
1. If petroleum hadn't been discovered, . . .		
2. If cars hadn't been invented, . . .		
3. If no one had invented paper clips, . . .		
4. If zippers hadn't been created, . . .		
5. If computers hadn't been invented, . . .		

exercise 4 Boston is a very "livable" city. In recent years, it has made major improvements. The following sentences tell about some of the changes that have made Boston more pleasant. Rewrite them to show what *might, could* or *would (not)* have occurred if things had been the opposite. Use clauses with *if* and appropriate modal auxiliaries.

example: Bostonians valued their past; as a result, they restored their historic buildings.

If Bostonians had not valued their past, they would not have restored their historic buildings.

Faneuil Hall, a preserved historic site in Boston

1. Bostonians were concerned about historic parts of the city; as a result, they fought very hard to preserve them.
2. Bostonians cared about the beauty of the city; as a result, they preserved many historic areas.
3. The city made major improvements in the old waterfront area; as a result, it is a great attraction today.
4. The old waterfront warehouses in Boston were renovated; as a result, a wide variety of shops and restaurants opened there.
5. The city developed parks and gardens along the harbor; as a result, the waterfront area is very attractive.
6. The city needed new income to pay for some of the improvements; as a result, it tried to attract more tourists.
7. Boston wanted to attract more visitors; as a result, it promoted the development of hotels and tourist facilities.
8. The Boston community was very proud of its history and beauty; as a result, citizens invested in its preservation.

Review.   Complete the following passage with the appropriate forms of the verbs in parentheses. Be sure to add modal auxiliaries when necessary. The first one is done as an example.

CITY LIVING

My name's Mario. I live in a big city. It's a beautiful city in a lot of ways,

but our neighborhood is pretty tough. I wish things _____*were*_____ a lot
                                                          1 (be)

different. For example, I live a long way from school. I wish that I

_____ to get up at 6:00 A.M. to take a bus to school. I wish my
   2 (not have)

school _____ right next door. And I wish the whole neighborhood
          3 (be)

_____ nicer and cleaner. I wish people _____ up around
   4 (be)   5 (clean)

here—and not just the garbage! I wish there _____ any drugs on the
                                                6 (not be)

streets. I wish I _____ out alone at night. Sometimes I wish that my
                     7 (go)

parents _____ here. I hope things _____. I hope I
         8 (never move)   9 (change)

_____ to college and help my family.
   10 (go)

Review.   First read the following quote for meaning. Then choose the appropriate form from the words in parentheses to complete the passage.

At the beginning of this century, Los Angeles (was / were) a sleepy little
town, and even as recently as the 1950s and early 1960s, there (was / were)
farms and orchards close to our house. Gardens (thrived / had thrived) here,
and you (could find / could have found) an incredible variety of exotic plants
and shrubs. Of course, there (wasn't / weren't) any freeways, and there (used
to be / used to being) a good transportation system of electric trains. The air
(was usually / usually was) very clear, and as a young child, I (could see /
could have seen) the mountains to the north and east almost every day.

Now, we (get / have got) freeways, traffic, and pollution. What a shame! If
you (had seen / would have seen) Los Angeles forty years ago, you (had been /
would have been) amazed.

If the city (knew / had known) what (was / was going to) happen. . . . If
Los Angeles (kept / had kept) its train system, we (might / should) have
avoided some of the traffic problems. If city planners (had only thought / had
thought only) more about the future, they could (have put / had put) more
money into public transportation. If fewer people (have / had) moved to southern California, the population wouldn't have (grew / grown) so fast. If L.A.
(didn't grow / hadn't grown) so fast, we (might not have / might not have had)
so many problems today. No one (anticipates / anticipated) all these things;
otherwise, we (had been / might have been) a lot more careful. I certainly
(hope / wish) that we (had / had had) better foresight and planning. I (hope /
wish) that things (will improve / would improve) in the future. Otherwise, we
(might have / might have had) even worse problems in the upcoming years.

—Debra Love, 45, second-generation native of Los Angeles

Using What You've Learned

Think about your hometown or the town where you are living now. Have changes
taken place in recent years? Have these been good or bad? What if these changes
hadn't taken place? What would your area be like? Make at least four statements
using conditional sentences with both past and present time.

activity 2

"What if" you had been born at a different time? How would your life be different? "What if" you had been born in a different place? How would your life be different today? Test your knowledge in a game like Trivial Pursuit. Separate into four different groups. In your groups, make up questions about history, geography, languages, social customs, and so on. (Be sure that you know the answers!) The questions should use clauses with *if.*

> **example:** If you had lived in London in 1900, who would have been the ruler of your country? (Queen Victoria)
>
> If you had been in Buenos Aires in 1930, what kind of music might you have listened to? (tangos)

When you have prepared eight to ten questions, get together with another group. Take turns asking the other group your questions and answering theirs. Keep a count of correct answers, and the group with the highest score wins.

activity 3

Read the following passage, and think about *second chances,* the opportunities to try again.

If I Had My Life to Do Over

I'd make a few more mistakes next time. I'd relax. I would limber up. I would be sillier than I had been this trip. I would take fewer things seriously. I would climb more mountains and swim more rivers. I would eat more ice cream and less beans. I would perhaps have more actual troubles, but I'd have fewer imag-
5   inary ones.

You see, I'm one of those people who live sensibly and sanely hour after hour, day after day. Oh, I've had my moments, and if I had it to do over again, I'd have more of them. In fact, I'd try to have nothing else. Just moments, one after another, instead of living so many years ahead of each day. I've been one
10   of those persons who never goes anywhere without a hot water bottle and a parachute. If I had it to do again, I would travel lighter.

If I had my life to do over again, I would start barefoot earlier in the spring and stay that way later in the fall. I would go to more dances. I would ride more merry-go-rounds. I would pick more daisies.

Nadine Stair, 85, Louisville, Kentucky

Is this passage about reality or dreams? How do you know? Look at the title of this passage. What verb is used? Does it refer to the past or the present? Most of the passage is written in the conditional with *would.* What is the meaning of *would* in these sentences?

Are there things you would do differently if you had the chance? Tell or write about your ideas.

focus on testing

Use of Conditional and Subjunctive Forms

Conditional and subjunctive forms of verbs are frequently tested on standardized English proficiency exams. Review these commonly tested structures and check your understanding by completing the sample items below.

Remember that . . .

- *Hope* is followed by an indicative verb form but *wish* is generally followed by a subjunctive form.
- In formal English, *were* (not *was*) is used with *I, he, she,* and *it* in present *if* clauses.
- In formal English, modal auxiliaries are used in *if* clauses only in specific cases.

Part 1: Circle the correct completion for the following.

example: John wishes that his boss _____ him a long vacation.
    a. gave
    b. would give
    c. will give
    d. was giving

1. If she _____ chosen to study in San Francisco, she would have had to find a new house.
    a. has
    b. would have
    c. will have
    d. had

2. If Los Angeles had not dismantled its system of electric trains, mass transportation there _____ better today.
    a. might be
    b. might
    c. might have been
    d. might had been

3. John's roommate wishes that John _____ a set of drums.
   a. would never have bought
   b. would have never bought
   c. had never bought
   d. never bought

Part 2: Circle the letter below the underlined word(s) containing an error.

example: It's a good idea <u>for overseas</u> travelers <u>to know</u> something of the
                              A   B

language of the new country; <u>otherwise</u>, they <u>might have had</u>
                                   C   Ⓓ

many difficulties in adapting.

1. If Einstein, <u>perhaps</u> the greatest scientist of the twentieth century,
                    A

<u>did not</u> propose his theories of <u>atomic</u> structure, production of the
   B   C

atomic bomb <u>might have been</u> delayed another ten or fifteen years.
                 D

2. Companies <u>may have</u> <u>respond</u> more quickly if the United States
                    A   B

<u>had imposed</u> stricter penalties for pollution much <u>earlier on</u>.
   C   D

3. One of <u>the greatest</u> wishes of <u>humans</u> today is that we <u>could have</u>
               A   B   C

<u>discovered</u> a cure for cancer in the <u>upcoming</u> few years.
   D

CHAPTER eleven
The Physical World

Introduction

In this chapter, you will study compound and complex sentences that show cause, comparison, contrast, effect or result, and purpose. As you study the chapter, note the relationships between ideas and the variety of ways these relationships can be expressed. Also pay attention to the ways these sentences are punctuated and how the sentence focus can change, depending on the choice of connecting word.

The following passage introduces the chapter theme, The Physical World, and raises some of the topics and issues you will cover in the chapter.

The Hydrologic Cycle

Every day, approximately 4 trillion gallons of fresh rainwater or snow falls on the United States. Americans use only one-tenth of this fresh water, and most of the water returns to the system, to be recycled and used again. The renewal process is called the *hydrologic cycle.* Each day the sun evaporates* 1 trillion
5   tons of water from the oceans and land and lifts it as vapor into the atmosphere. This is the greatest physical force at work on earth.

Nevertheless, the United States, as well as most of the world, faces serious water problems, of both quality and quantity. Because rain and snow do not fall evenly across the land, the western United States, with 60 percent of the
10   land, receives only 25 percent of its moisture. Although the East receives a tremendous amount of moisture, it faces problems of quality. Because of large population centers, old sewage systems,[†] and pollution, most of the East—from New England to Florida—faces a lack of *clean* water.

As our population grows, demands for clean water will be greater than ever
15   before. Even if an increased population uses the same amount of water as we do now, the United States will face severe shortages. Because water—clean water—is essential to all life, we must begin now to care for this resource adequately.

In your native country, what are the primary sources of water for human use? In the area where you are living now? Is the water supply adequate for the population?

---

evaporates   changes from liquid to gas
†*sewage systems*   water purification systems

Clauses and Related Structures of Cause, Purpose, and Effect or Result

Setting the Context

What is the climate of the area where you live now? What is the climate of your hometown or region?

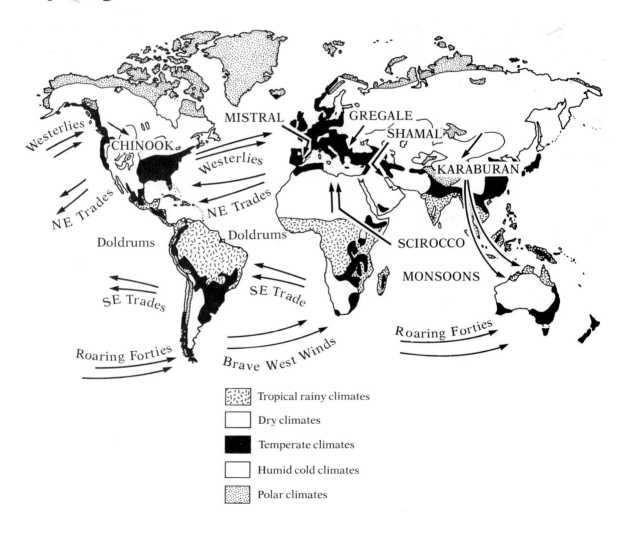

Tropical rainy climates

Dry climates

Temperate climates

Humid cold climates

Polar climates

World Weather Patterns

Because all weather is interconnected, a change in one area affects other areas. Today, scientists collect information worldwide so that they can understand and predict changes in the weather more accurately. Due to technological advances in the last several decades, meteorologists can now gather detailed
5   information on cloud cover, precipitation, temperature changes, wind speed and direction, and energy from both the sun and earth.

This collection of data reveals some interesting facts. For example, winds in one region are accompanied by opposite winds in another; therefore, if north winds are extremely cold in one part of the world, south winds are abnormally
10   warm in another part. Since winds affect precipitation, changes in wind patterns alter the amount of rainfall.

discussing ideas   What kinds of data do scientists collect to study the weather? Why is it important to have information about weather from other parts of the world?

A. Clauses and Phrases of Cause

	examples	notes
WITH CLAUSES		
because	**Because** there was a drought, Californians had many problems with water.	Most adverb clauses may begin or end sentences. Introductory clauses are generally followed by a comma. A comma is not usually used when the main clause begins the sentence.
since	California had many problems with water **since** there was a drought.	
WITH PHRASES		
because of	**Because of** the drought, California had many water shortages.	Prepositions are followed by phrases, *not* clauses. A comma is generally used after an introductory phrase.
due to	California had many water shortages **due to** the drought.	

 **exercise 1** Complete the following in your own words.

> **example:** Because the weather was terrible, **I decided to stay home and study.**

1. Because of the bad weather . . .
2. The electricity went out due to . . .
3. My telephone isn't working because . . .
4. Due to the heat . . .
5. Because the weather in southern California is great . . .
6. I couldn't finish my assignments because of . . .

exercise 2 Complete the following passage by adding *because, because of, due to,* and *since.* Use each word once.

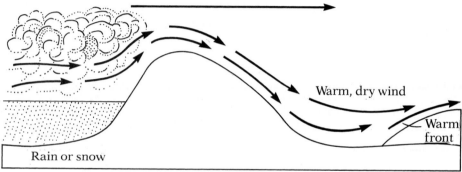

General movement of weather systems

Warm, dry wind

Warm front

Rain or snow

MOUNTAINS AND WEATHER

_____ their height, mountains are important in the making of
_1_
weather. When moisture-filled air encounters mountains, it is forced upward.

_____ the air cools at higher altitudes, water vapor in the air
_2_
turns to rain or snow. By the time the air passes over the mountaintops it has

lost its moisture.

_____ the air is much cooler and thinner then, it sinks.
_3_
_____ the dryness of these downward winds, Indians in the western
_4_
United States call them "snow eaters." They can evaporate snow at the rate of

two feet a day.

B. Clauses and Phrases of Purpose

examples		notes
WITH CLAUSES		
so that	During droughts, governments often set monthly limits **so that** they can control water use.	*So that* is used only between clauses. Clauses with *so that* use modal auxiliaries *(can, could, may, might, will, would)*. Commas are not used with *so that*.
	Los Angeles sets limits **so that** it could control water use.	
WITH PHRASES		
in order to	The city has begun rationing **in order to** conserve more water.	In written English, *in order to* is used more frequently than *so that*. *In order* can usually be omitted; using *in order* emphasizes the idea of purpose.
	The city has begun rationing **to** conserve more water.	

Note: That is sometimes omitted and *so* is used alone in conversational English. Do not confuse *so (that)*, meaning purpose, with the conjunction *so*, meaning result. Compare: *I went to the store so (that) I could buy bread.* (purpose) *I needed bread, so I went to the store.* (result)

 **exercise 3**   Complete the following passage by adding *so that* or *in order to*.

WEATHER RESEARCH

The years 1988–1989 produced extremes of weather in much of the world. Since then, meteorologists have been watching many parts of the world _____ they can learn more about the causes of the unusual weather.
₁
Some scientists have studied volcanoes _____ see their effect on
₂
temperature. Others are researching "El Niño," a warm-water current near the equator, _____ learn its role in weather. In addition, meteorologists
₃
are studying air pollution _____ they can understand its effect on
₄
weather, as well as its role in "acid rain." Most importantly, scientists are collecting data worldwide _____ they can learn the interrelationships
₅
in global weather.

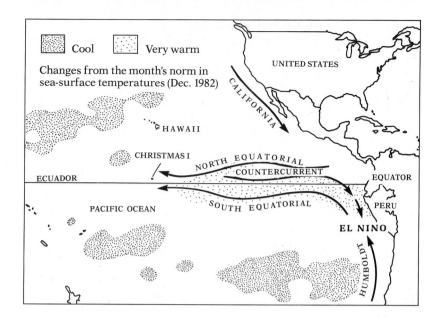

Cool ☐ Very warm ☐

Changes from the month's norm in sea-surface temperatures (Dec. 1982)

exercise 4

In the following sentences, change *so that* to *in order to* or *in order to* to *so that*. Make all other necessary changes.

example: Meteorologists collect data in order to find patterns in the weather.

Meteorologists collect data so that they can find patterns in the weather.

1. Meteorologists study mountainous regions so that they can learn how mountains affect weather.
2. Meteorologists take smog samples in order to study the effects of air pollution on weather.
3. Meteorologists work with oceanographers and geologists so that they can understand the roles of oceans and land formations in weather.
4. Geologists gather rock samples in order to analyze the earth's crust.
5. Astronomers use high-powered telescopes in order to view distant stars.
6. Oceanographers analyze ocean currents and temperatures so that they can understand changes in fish population.

exercise 5

Complete the following eight items in your own words.

example: Astronomers use telescopes so that **they can see farther into the sky.**

1. Doctors use stethoscopes so that . . .
2. Doctors take X rays in order to . . .
3. Dentists use drills in order to . . .

4. Plumbers use wrenches so that . . .
5. People use computers in order to . . .
6. I bought a computer so that . . .
7. People use dictionaries in order to . . .
8. I bought a good dictionary so that . . .

C. Transitions of Effect or Result

	examples	notes
consequently therefore thus as a result for this reason for that reason	During the drought, rainfall was far below normal; **therefore,** farm production fell dramatically. Rainfall was far below normal. **Consequently,** farmers lost many crops. Everyone used less water. **As a result,** we were able to survive the drought.	Transitions may be used to relate the ideas in two different sentences, or they may be used with a semicolon (;) in a compound sentence. *Consequently, thus,* and *therefore* are more common in formal English. The other transitions are used in both formal and informal English.

 Change the following sentences from complex to compound. Rewrite them to use *consequently, therefore, thus, as a result,* and *for this reason.* Use each transition once.

example: Because the equator is closest to the sun, the atmosphere there absorbs the most solar energy.

The equator is closest to the sun; consequently, the atmosphere there absorbs the most solar energy.

1. Because the air at the equator absorbs the most solar energy, it is much hotter than the air near the poles.
2. Since hot air rises, low-pressure areas develop at the equator.
3. Because low-pressure areas are like holes in the atmosphere, cold air moves in from the poles to fill them.
4. Because this pattern is a cycle, air almost always moves toward the equator on the surface and away from it at high altitudes.
5. Since hot and cold air flow in this cycle, our atmosphere is continually in motion.

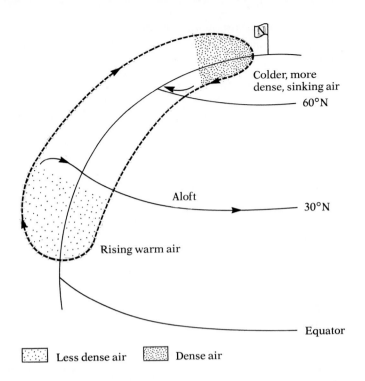

Colder, more
dense, sinking air
60°N

Aloft
30°N

Rising warm air

Equator

:::::::: Less dense air   ▒▒▒▒ Dense air

D. Sentence Focus in Compound and Complex Sentences

In complex sentences, the main clause usually carries the idea that the speaker or writer wants to emphasize. The main clause is, therefore, the focus of most complex sentences. It gives the topic or main idea, while the subordinating clause gives additional information. In contrast, in compound sentences, both clauses generally have equal importance. Compare:

examples	focus
COMPLEX SENTENCES	
Because there was a drought, California had serious water shortages.	serious water shortages in California
Because California was experiencing water shortages, the state imposed limits on daily consumption.	limits imposed by the state on daily consumption
COMPOUND SENTENCE	
California suffered from a long drought; therefore, the state had serious water shortages.	the long drought in California *and* the serious water shortages.

Read the following sets of sentences and underline the main clause in each. Discuss the differences in focus in each set. In some cases, there may be only main clauses.

example: The equator is closest to the sun; therefore, the atmosphere around it absorbs the most solar energy.

Focus: both the equator and the atmosphere around it

Since the equator is closest to the sun, the atmosphere around it absorbs the most solar energy.

Focus: the atmosphere around the equator and the energy it absorbs

1. Since hot and cold air flow in a cycle, our atmosphere is continually in motion.

Hot and cold air flow in a cycle; as a result, our atmosphere is continually in motion.

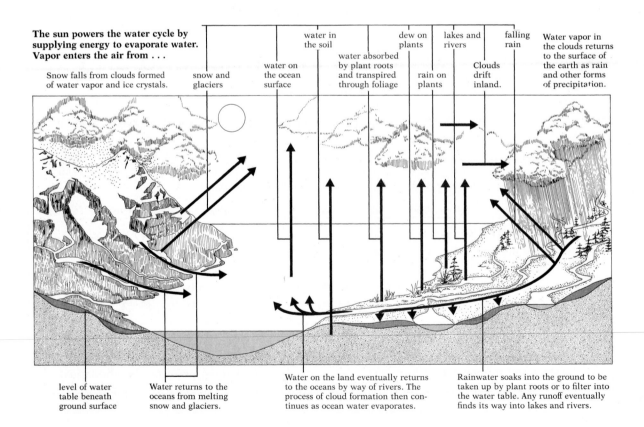

The sun powers the water cycle by supplying energy to evaporate water. Vapor enters the air from . . .

Snow falls from clouds formed of water vapor and ice crystals.

snow and glaciers

water on the ocean surface

water in the soil

water absorbed by plant roots and transpired through foliage

dew on plants

rain on plants

lakes and rivers

Clouds drift inland.

falling rain

Water vapor in the clouds returns to the surface of the earth as rain and other forms of precipitation.

level of water table beneath ground surface

Water returns to the oceans from melting snow and glaciers.

Water on the land eventually returns to the oceans by way of rivers. The process of cloud formation then continues as ocean water evaporates.

Rainwater soaks into the ground to be taken up by plant roots or to filter into the water table. Any runoff eventually finds its way into lakes and rivers.

2. Because air cools at higher altitudes, water vapor in the air turns into rain or snow.

Air cools at higher altitudes; therefore, water vapor in the air turns into rain or snow.

3. Meteorologists study mountainous regions to learn their effect on weather.

Meteorologists study mountainous regions so that they can learn the effect of mountains on weather.

4. The mountains in California absorb much of the moisture coming from the Pacific Ocean; as a result, the states to the east—Utah, Nevada, and Arizona—are extremely dry.

Because the California mountains absorb much of the moisture from the Pacific Ocean, the states to the east—Utah, Nevada, and Arizona—are extremely dry.

5. Due to its scarcity in many populated areas, control of water is becoming a major political and economic issue worldwide.

Fresh water is scarce in many populated areas; consequently, control of this valuable resource is becoming a major political and economical issue worldwide.

 **exercise 8**   Complete the following sentences in your own words.

example: We had to cancel the soccer games due to **the terrible weather.**

1. In extremely cold weather, you shouldn't stay outside for very long because . . .
2. During electrical storms, it is not recommended to be in open areas due to . . .
3. When a tornado has been spotted, people are told to take cover in their basements so that . . .
4. I wouldn't like to live near a volcano because . . .
5. That region is suffering from a serious drought. Therefore, . . .
6. She studied meteorology because of . . .
7. During a flood, people often use sand bags in order to . . .
8. Air pollution can strongly affect the elderly and the very young. For this reason, . . .

exercise 9 Combine the following sentences, using *because, since, therefore, thus, as a result, consequently,* and *for this reason.* Use each at least once. Change words and add punctuation when necessary.

> **example:** The rotation of the earth and its atmosphere affects air patterns. Air does not move directly north and south.
>
> The rotation of the earth and its atmosphere affects air patterns; as a result, air does not move directly north and south.

1. Outer space is frictionless. The earth's atmosphere moves at the same speed as the earth.
2. The earth's circumference at the equator is almost 25,000 miles. The air at the equator travels 25,000 miles each day.
3. There is little surface wind at the equator. The earth and the air move at the same speed.
4. Away from the equator, the surface speed of the earth decreases. The earth's circumference grows smaller toward the two poles.
5. Away from the equator, the air and the earth do not move at the same speed. The midlatitude winds are born.
6. The earth's surface often affects wind patterns. Wind patterns become extremely complicated.
7. The oceans and mountains break wind patterns. High-altitude winds going to the poles can lose their heat.
8. These high-altitude winds lose their heat. These high-altitude winds sink and mix with the surface winds below.

Using What You've Learned

activity 1  Every culture has topics for conversation that are *taboo* (considered inappropriate) and others that are *safe.* Generally speaking, the weather is one of the safest topics for conversation worldwide. In pairs, practice the skill of *small talk*—conversation on a safe topic with strangers or people you don't know well—by talking about the weather. Be creative and see just how long you can keep the conversation going. Your teacher will time you, and the pair who can talk the longest may win a prize—a weather map!

activity 2  Doctors take X rays in order to look for broken bones. A businesswoman buys a computer program so that she can manage her personal finances. Scientists world-wide use e-mail so that they collaborate on research. What equipment or processes are used in your career or hobby? Choose an area of interest to you—your work or your pastimes—and write a short paragraph about it. Tell some of the tools or processes you use and explain the purpose of each. Then work in small groups and take turns telling (not reading) your information. Use structures covered in this section whenever possible.

activity **3**   Choose one of the following questions to answer in a brief composition. Use information from this section to help you, but try to use your own words.

- Why is our atmosphere continually in motion?
- Why do winds develop away from the equator?
- Why is there normally little wind at the equator?
- How do mountains and other geographical features affect the weather?
- What types of weather data do meteorologists study? Why?

TOPIC **two**

Clauses and Related Structures of Contrast: Concession and Opposition

Setting the Context

previewing the passage

How much water is there on earth? Where is it located?

Consumable Water

Of the total surface of the earth, 75 percent is covered by water. Nevertheless, only a small portion can be used for human needs. Only about 3 percent of the water on earth is fresh water, whereas 97 percent is saltwater. And, although 3 percent is fresh, three-quarters of that is ice, primarily in the polar

Most freshwater is frozen in glaciers and polar ice caps.

5　　　ice caps. Thus, just less than 1 percent of the earth's water is available for
human use.

Despite its lack of taste, color, odor, and calories, water is a powerful
beverage. It is the only substance necessary to all life. Many organisms can
live without oxygen; however, none can survive without water. The human
10　　body itself is 78 percent water.

Even though water is critical to all life, it is often taken for granted until a
disaster occurs. Some may be natural disasters, such as droughts or floods;
on the other hand, many are human caused, such as pollution of surface water
or groundwater.

**discussing
ideas**

Either too much or too little water can be a disaster. Has drought or flooding been
a serious problem in your area or country? Is water pollution a serious problem? Is
clean drinking water available for most people?

A. Clauses, Phrases, and Transitions of Concession

The following clauses, phrases, and transitions are used to express ideas or information that is different from our expectations.

	examples	notes
WITH CLAUSES		
although **even though** **though**	**Although** water covers much of the earth, very little is usable.	These conjunctions are commonly used in speaking and writing, but *although* is preferred in formal English.
WITH PHRASES		
despite **in spite of**	**Despite** technological advances, removing salt from ocean water is still very expensive.	*Despite* and *in spite of* are followed by phrases, not clauses. The phrases may contain nouns, pronouns, or gerunds.
WITH TRANSITIONS		
however **nevertheless**	Several countries have large desalinization projects; **however,** no country gets the majority of its water through this process.	*Nevertheless* is used in formal English. *However* is frequently used in both speaking and writing. *However* may appear at the beginning or end or in the middle of a sentence.

   Complete the following in your own words.

> **example:**   I like winter despite **the cold and snow.**

> **1.** Although snow can be beautiful, . . .
> **2.** The weather was perfect that day; nevertheless, . . .
> **3.** Even though it was raining, . . .
> **4.** I enjoy hot weather though . . .
> **5.** Many people dislike humid weather. However, . . .
> **6.** We decided to go camping in spite of . . .

 **exercise 2**   Combine each of the following pairs of sentences in two ways. First, combine them with *although* or *even though*. Then combine them with *however* or *nevertheless*. Be sure to change or omit words and to add punctuation when necessary. Finally, tell the primary focus of each of your new sentences.

> **example:**   We usually think of water as a liquid. Water exits in three forms: gas, liquid, and solid.
>
> Although we usually think of water as a liquid, it exists in three forms: gas, liquid, and solid.
>
> Focus: the three forms of water
>
> We usually think of water as a liquid; however, it exists in three forms: gas, liquid, and solid.
>
> Focus: water as a liquid and the three forms of water

> **1.** All precipitation begins with the cooling and condensing of water vapor. Precipitation may reach earth as rain, sleet, snow, or hail.
> **2.** The actual locations of rainfall depend on geography and winds. The total annual rainfall in the world is enough to provide every human with about 22,000 gallons of fresh water every day.
> **3.** Meteorologists do not know all the effects of air pollution. Many fear that pollution is changing rainfall worldwide.
> **4.** Some countries are finally beginning to react to the problem. Acid rain has already damaged buildings, forests, lakes, and streams around the world.

B. Clauses, Phrases, and Transitions of Opposition

The following clauses, phrases, and transitions are used to express an opposite view of the same idea or information.

	examples	notes
WITH CLAUSES **whereas** **where** **while**	**While** some countries rely on water conservation, others find ways to increase the water supply. Some countries rely on water conservation, **whereas** others find ways to increase their water supply.	*While, where,* and *whereas* are usually used to contrast direct opposites. *Whereas* is used in formal English. Note that in many cases the connecting word may begin either clause. The focus of the sentence changes, but not the general meaning.
WITH PHRASES **instead of**	**Instead of** importing water, some Middle Eastern countries are importing icebergs from the Arctic.y	*Instead of* is followed by a noun phrase or a gerund, not a clause.
WITH TRANSITIONS **in contrast** **on the other hand** **on the contrary**	This is not the most practical way to get more water; **on the other hand,** it is creative. This is not an economical way to get more water; **on the contrary,** it is very expensive.	*In contrast* and *on the other hand* relate different points that are not necessarily direct opposites. *On the contrary* is used differently than other transitions of contrast. It often reinforces a negative idea in the preceding sentence. In many cases, it means the opposite of *in fact.*

 **exercise 3**   Complete the following in your own words.

> **example:** Despite the rain, **we decided to take a long walk.**

1. Although summer weather can be great, . . .
2. Despite the bad weather, . . .
3. While some people enjoy the snow, . . .

4. Even though we are learning more and more about the weather, . . .
5. In the middle latitudes of the earth, four distinct seasons exist. In contrast, . . .
6. I don't like hot weather. On the other hand, . . .
7. I don't enjoy hot weather. On the contrary, . . .
8. Instead of drinking water from the tap, my family . . .
9. Even though much of the earth is covered with water, . . .
10. Meteorologists don't know all the effects of air pollution. On the contrary, . . .

exercise 4 Combine each of the following pairs of sentences in three ways. First, combine them in two different ways with *while* or *whereas*. Then, combine them with *in contrast* or *on the other hand*. Change or omit words and add punctuation where necessary. Finally, tell the primary focus of each of your new sentences.

example: Each year, 80,000 cubic miles of water evaporates from the oceans. Only 15,000 cubic miles of water evaporates from the land.

Each year, while 80,000 cubic miles of water evaporates from the oceans, only 15,000 cubic miles of water evaporates from the land.
Focus: water evaporation from the land

Each year, 80,000 cubic miles of water evaporates from the oceans, while only 15,000 cubic miles of water evaporates from the land.
Focus: water evaporation from the oceans

Each year, 80,000 cubic miles of water evaporates from the oceans; in contrast, only 15,000 cubic miles of water evaporates from the land.
Focus: water evaporation from both the oceans and the land

1. The oceans cover 71 percent of the earth's surface. Land covers only about 25 percent of the earth's surface.
2. Less than 15 percent of the water vapor in the air evaporates from the land. Over one-quarter of the world's annual rainfall (approximately 24,000 cubic miles) falls on the land.
3. Mt. Waialeale in Hawaii receives 470 inches of rain annually. Desert regions in Africa receive less than 1 inch of rain each year.
4. Only 1.7 inches of rain fall annually in California's Death Valley. A few hundred miles north along the coast of the Pacific Ocean, 140 to 150 inches of rain fall.

Complete the following with *instead of, despite, although,* and *while.* Use each one time.

example: In clear air, only temperature and humidity determine when vapor

condenses* into water, ____*while*____ in polluted air, chemicals

and dust affect this process.

1. _____ research on pollution is incomplete, scientists now know that it affects weather.

2. In clear air, condensation happens slowly, _____ in particle-filled air it occurs much more rapidly.

3. _____ serious problems with pollution worldwide, many countries have not yet begun to look for solutions.

4. _____ investing money in mass transportation systems, many countries continue to promote the use of automobiles, a major source of pollution.

Each of the following selections uses both conjunctions and transitions of contrast. Rewrite the sentences shown in bold type, changing transitions to subordinating conjunctions and subordinating conjunctions to transitions. Be sure to make all necessary changes.

example: **CIRRUS CLOUDS**
Pulled apart by winds, the wispy cirrus often look like spider webs. **Cirrus clouds often mean warm weather is on the way;** *however,* **they are actually the coldest clouds of all.** Cirrus can rise to over 40,000 feet, and the moisture in them is frozen into ice crystals.

Even though cirrus clouds often mean warm weather is on the way, they are actually the coldest clouds of all.

1. FOG
When the earth cools at night, water vapor condenses in damp areas, such as river valleys, producing fog. **We call it by a different name;** *never-theless,* **fog is simply a cloud that forms near the ground. Clouds are formed when warm air rises and is cooled,** *whereas* **fog is formed when air cools near the ground or ocean.**

2. CLOUDS AND OCEANS
Because the land and the sea affect clouds differently, sailors often use clouds to help navigate. **Clouds will often form over land; the skies out at sea,** *in contrast,* **will remain cloudless.** *Although* **early Polynesian navigators did not have compasses, they could sail from island to island by reading the clouds.**

_____

*condense   change from gas to liquid or liquid to solid

3. LIGHTNING

Lightning is not entirely understood; *however,* **we do know that power-ful electrical charges build up inside a thundercloud.** *While* **a positive electrical charge builds up near the top of the cloud, a negative charge builds up near the bottom.** The negative charge is attracted to the ground below. When enough voltage builds up, a powerful electric current travels between the earth and sky. This current is lightning.

4. DOES LIGHTNING STRIKE TWICE?

Many myths exist about lightning. **For example, an old saying tells us that "lightning never strikes twice."** *On the contrary,* **almost every bolt of lightning strikes the same place several times. Each bolt is actually a series of "strokes" traveling to and from the earth,** *even though* **we perceive only a single flash of light.**

5. SNOWFLAKES

Although **all snowflakes are six-sided, they have an infinite variety of forms. The most beautiful are delicate star-like flakes.** *In contrast,* **others may look like flat plates, needles, cups, or spools.**

 **Error Analysis.** Many of the following ten sentences contain errors in the use of connecting words or phrases or in punctuation. Find and correct all errors.

                Although

examples: ~~Despite~~ water exists in three forms—gas, liquid, and solid—the most common freshwater form on earth is ice.

         Around three-quarters of the earth's surface is water; however, we cannot use most of it easily.   *correct*

1. Although we call the earth "the water planet," most of its water is not easily used.

2. Even though the amount of water on earth, most of it would be very difficult to recover for human use.

3. Seventy-one percent of the earth's surface is covered by oceans however humans cannot drink untreated saltwater.

4. Saltwater cannot be used easily; on the contrary, consuming saltwater can be very harmful to humans.

5. However in theory fresh water is plentiful 75 percent of it is frozen in glacial ice.

6. The Arctic is a frozen ocean, covered by sea ice and surrounded by land, on the other hand, the Antarctic is a frozen continent, covered by glacier ice and completely surrounded by sea.

7. Water normally freezes at 32° F (0° C) the presence of snow and ice depends on other facts that influence temperature, such as altitude.

8. Although snow and ice cover the peaks of many mountains the regional "snow line" varies greatly according to latitude.

9. Near the poles, the snow line is at sea level. While in the tropics, the snow line is above 20,000 ft (6,000 m).

10. Glaciers can exist on moderately high mountains in the middle latitudes. In contrast, near the equator they exist on only the highest peaks, such as Chimborazo, Kilimanjaro, and Mount Kenya.

 **exercise 8**

Complete the passage with appropriate connecting words. Then look back at the passage "Consumable Water" on pages 385 and 386 to check your answers. Of course, in some cases, more than one possibility exists.

CONSUMABLE WATER

Of the total surface of the earth, 75 percent is covered by water.

_____, only a small portion can be used. Only about 3 percent of
the water on earth is fresh water, _____ 97 percent is saltwater. And,
1 ... 2
_____ 3 percent is fresh, three-quarters of that is ice, primarily in
3
the polar ice caps. _____, just less than 1 percent of the earth's
4
water is available for human use.

_____ its lack of taste, color, odor, and calories, water is a
5
powerful beverage. It is the only substance necessary to all life. Many
organisms can live without oxygen; _____, none can survive
6
without water. The human body itself is 78 percent water.

_____ water is critical to all life, it is often taken for granted
7
until a disaster occurs. Some may be natural disasters, such as droughts or

floods; _____, many are human caused, such as pollution of
8
surface water or groundwater.

Using What You've Learned

activity 1

In pairs or small groups, use the following diagram to learn how to read a weather map. Then, check the weather in your local paper and prepare a short forecast of upcoming weather. Tell what you are basing your predictions on, using as many connecting words of cause, contrast, purpose, or result as you can.

HOW TO READ THE WEATHER MAP

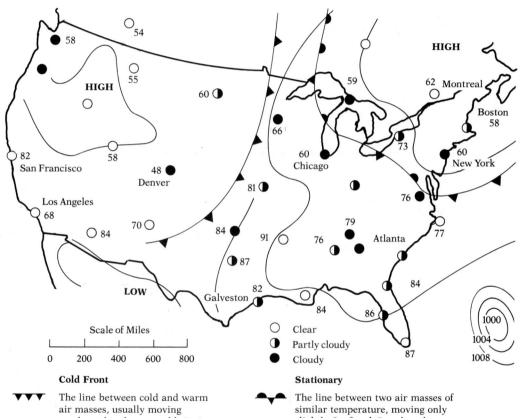

Cold Front

▼▼▼ The line between cold and warm air masses, usually moving southward and eastward bringing brief storms and cooler weather.

Warm Front

●● The line between a mass of warm air and retreating cold air, usually moving northward and eastward and led by rain or snow.

High

A high pressure system usually means clear weather.

Stationary

▲▼ The line between two air masses of similar temperature, moving only slightly. It often brings lengthy periods of precipitation.

Occluded

▲▲▲ The line on which a warm front has been overtaken by a cold front. It usually moves eastward, bringing precipitation.

Low

A low pressure system produces cloudy and often stormy weather.

 **activity 2**

Let's forget the weather and talk about English! First, complete the following by writing your own ideas. Then, get together with a partner and share how you feel about English and your experiences learning it. Try to express your feelings without looking at the sentences you wrote, though.

- I'm study English because . . .
- Although my English isn't perfect, . . .
- Instead of studying English, . . .
- In spite of all the hours I've been studying English, . . .
- Because I want to improve my English, . . .
- I've got to work hard so that . . .
- I need English in order to . . .

TOPIC three

Comparative and Superlative Adjectives and Adverbs

Setting the Context

previewing the passage

What are the major bodies of water in the world? What are the major bodies of water in or surrounding your region or country?

The World's Oceans

Geographers and mapmakers recognize four major oceans: the Pacific, the Atlantic, the Indian, and the Arctic. The Pacific is the largest of the four oceans. At 64,186,300 square miles,* it is almost twice as large as the Atlantic Ocean (33 million square miles) and more than twice as large as the Indian Ocean (28 million square miles). The Arctic Ocean is much smaller than the other three major bodies of water. At 5 million square miles, the Arctic Ocean is only one-twelfth the size of the Pacific. It is much shallower than the Pacific too. The average depth of the Pacific is 13,739 feet, whereas the average depth of the Arctic Ocean is 4,362 feet. In averages, the Atlantic and Indian Oceans are almost as deep as the Pacific. Although the Indian Ocean is smaller than the Atlantic, its average depth is greater than that of the Atlantic.

Other major bodies of water include the South China Sea, the Caribbean Sea, the Mediterranean Sea, and the Bering Sea. In total, 75 percent of the world's surface is covered by water.

5

10

*square mile   a square area measuring 1 mile on each side

 **discussing ideas** Of the oceans and other bodies of water mentioned in the passage, which have you seen? Have you lived near one? If so, describe it for your classmates.

Comparisons with Adjectives and Adverbs

The positive forms of adjectives and adverbs are used in expressions with *(not) as . . . as (as slow as, not as slowly as)*. Comparative forms are used to compare two things. Superlative forms are used to discuss three or more things. *The* is normally used with superlative forms. Note that spelling rules for adding *-er* and *-est* are the same as for adding *-ed* (see Appendix One).

	positive	comparative	superlative
ADD *-er* AND *-est* TO:			
One-Syllable Adjectives	nice	nicer	the nicest
	young	younger	the youngest
Adjectives and Adverbs that Have the Same Form	early	earlier	the earliest
	fast	faster	the fastest
	hard	harder	the hardest
	late	later	the latest
ADD *-er* AND *-est* OR USE *more, less, the most, the least* WITH:			
Most Two-Syllable Adjectives	clever	cleverer more clever	the cleverest the most clever
	funny	funnier more funny	the funniest the most funny
	shallow	shallower more shallow	the shallowest the most shallow
	simple	simpler more simple	the simplest the most simple

Note: With words ending in *-y* and *-le,* the *-er* and *-est* forms are more common than forms with *more, less,* etc.

positive	comparative	superlative

USE *more, less, the most, the least* WITH:

	positive	comparative	superlative
Two-Syllable Adjectives That End in -ed, -ful, -ing, -ish, -ous, -st, and -x	worried	more worried	the most worried
	harmful	more harmful	the most harmful
	caring	more caring	the most caring
	selfish	more selfish	the most selfish
	joyous	more joyous	the most joyous
	robust	more robust	the most robust
	complex	more complex	the most complex
Longer Adjectives and Most -ly Adverbs	difficult	more difficult	the most difficult
	quickly	more quickly	the most quickly
	slowly	more slowly	the most slowly

Irregular Adjectives and Adverbs

adjective	adverb	comparative	superlative
bad	badly	worse	(the) worst
good	—	better	(the) best
well	well	better	(the) best
far	far	farther	(the) farthest (*distance*)
		further	(the) furthest
little	little	less	(the) least
many	—	more	(the) most
much	much	more	(the) most

exercise 1   For each word shown below, give the two forms that are missing.

example: far_____   farther   _the farthest_

POSITIVE	COMPARATIVE	SUPERLATIVE
1. good	_____	_____
2. simple	_____	_____
3. _____	_____	the worst
4. _____	younger	_____
5. handsome	_____	_____
6. _____	later	_____
7. _____	_____	the least

	POSITIVE	COMPARATIVE	SUPERLATIVE
8.	carefully	_____	_____
9.	_____	further	_____
10.	early	_____	_____
11.	_____	_____	the nicest
12.	much	_____	_____
13.	quickly	_____	_____
14.	_____	_____	the fewest
15.	worried	_____	_____
16.	_____	harder	_____

exercise **2** Reread the passage "The World's Oceans" on page 394. Then do the following:

1. Underline all the comparatives (*more . . . than, less . . . than, -er than,* and so on) and superlatives (*the . . . -est*) in the passage.
2. How many bodies of water are being compared in sentence 2? Which form of the adjective is used?
3. How many bodies of water are being compared in the sentence in line 7? Which form of the adjective is used?
4. Can you explain the comparison in the sentence in lines 9 to 10? Which form of the adjective is used?

exercise **3** Complete the following superlative forms of the words in parentheses.

example: <u>The greatest</u> tides in the world occur in the Bay of Fundy.
             (great)

1. _____ waterfall in the world is Salto Angel (Angel Falls) in
   (high) Venezuela.

2. _____ active geyser in the world is Steamboat Geyser in
   (tall) Yellowstone National Park.

3. _____ fjord (inlet) in the world is in eastern Greenland,
   (long) extending inland 195 miles from the sea.

4. _____ water currents in the world are the Nakwakto Rapids in
   (strong) British Columbia, Canada, which may reach 18.4 mph.

5. _____ waterfall in the world is Khone Falls in Laos.
   (wide)

6. _____ place in the world is the Atacama Desert in Chile, which
   (dry) had no measurable rainfall for 400 years.

7. _____ port in the United States is the Port of South Louisiana.
   (busy)

8. _____ inland waterway in North America is the St. Lawrence
   (large) and Great Lakes waterway.

Complete the following with comparative (+) or superlative (++) forms of the words in parentheses. Be sure to add *the* when necessary. The first one is done as an example.

WATERFALLS: WONDERS OF THE WORLD

In 1935, Jimmy Angel, an American looking for gold in Venezuela, discov-

ered ___the highest___ waterfall in the world, Salto Angel (Angel Falls). Angel
1 (++ high)

Falls (3,212 ft) is only slightly _____ than its _____ rival,
2 (+ high)   3 (++ close)

Tugela Falls (3,110 ft) in South Africa. At about 700 feet _____
4 (+ low)

than Tugela Falls is Yosemite Falls (2,425 ft) in California.

High waterfalls may be _____ than _____
5 (+ spectacular)   6 (+ low)

falls, but _____ and _____ falls are in general
7 (+ short)   8 (+ wide)

_____. For example, Khone Falls in Laos drops only 72
9 (+ powerful)

feet, yet it often discharges _____ than 400,000 cubic feet of water
10 (+ many)

per second.

Perhaps _____ "falls producer" of all is the Rio Paraná
11 (++ great)

in South America. It produces Iguassú Falls and Guaíra Falls. Many visitors

Vernal Falls, Yosemite
National Park

Lake Michigan and the Chicago skyline

say that Iguassú Falls is _____ on earth. At _____

                                      12 (++ beautiful)   13 (+ many)

than 2 miles wide, it certainly is one of _____ in the world.

                                           14 (++ awe-inspiring)

And Guaíra Falls is definitely _____ worldwide, with an

                                       15 (++ mighty)

average of 470,000 cubic feet of water per second thundering through a series

of 18 cascades.

 The Great Lakes of North America form the largest body of fresh water in the world and, with their connecting waterways, are the largest inland water transportation system. Use the following chart to complete the following exercise. Be sure to add *the* when necessary.

The Great Lakes					
	LENGTH *(miles)*	WIDTH *(miles)*	DEEPEST POINT *(feet)*	VOLUME *(cubic miles)*	UNITED STATES AND CANADA *total area (square miles)*
Erie	241	57	210	116	32,630
Huron	206	183	750	850	74,700
Michigan	307	118	923	1,180	67,900
Ontario	193	53	802	393	34,850
Superior	350	160	1,330	2,900	81,000

example: **LENGTH**

Lake Erie is ____*shorter*____ than Lake Michigan, but it is

____*longer*____ than Lake Huron or Lake Ontario.

1. **WIDTH**

    a. Lake Superior is a little _____ than Lake Huron.

    b. Lake Ontario is _____ of the five lakes.

    c. Lake Huron is _____ of the five lakes.

2. DEPTH

    a. Lake Superior is by far _____ of the five lakes.

    b. Lake Erie is _____ of the five lakes.

    c. Lake Ontario is _____ than Lake Huron, but it is

    _____ than Lake Michigan.

3. VOLUME

    a. Lake Erie holds _____ water of the five lakes.

    b. Lake Huron holds _____ water than Lake Michigan.

    c. Lake Superior holds over twice as _____ water as Lake
Michigan.

    d. Lake Michigan holds _____ water than Lakes Erie and
Huron combined.

4. TOTAL AREA

    a. Lake Erie covers _____ area of the five lakes.

    b. Lake Superior covers _____ area of the five lakes.

exercise **6**   Without looking back at the opening passage, try to complete the following, using
the appropriate adjectives. Be sure to add *the* when necessary.

    example: The Pacific is <u> *the largest* </u> of the four oceans.

    1. The Pacific is almost twice as _____ as the Atlantic.

    2. The Pacific is _____ than twice as _____ as the
Indian Ocean.

    3. The Arctic Ocean is _____ than the other three oceans.

    4. At an average depth of 4,362 feet, the Arctic is _____ than the
Pacific.

    5. The Atlantic and Indian Oceans are almost as _____ as the
Pacific Ocean.

    6. At an average depth of 13,739 feet, the Pacific is _____ of the
four oceans.

    7. The Indian Ocean is _____ in size than the Atlantic.

    8. The average depth of the Indian Ocean is _____ than that of the
Atlantic.

Complete the following with comparative or superlative forms of the words in parentheses. Be sure to use *the* when necessary.

LAKE BAIKAL

Lake Baikal is a place of superlatives. It is _____,

                                              1 (++ deep)

_____, and _____ lake in the world. It is also

2 (++ old)   3 (++ voluminous)

the home of _____ than a thousand species found nowhere else,

                    4 (+ much)

including the world's only fresh water seal.

Baikal's volume of 5,500 cubic miles is _____ than the com-

                                  5 (+ great)

bined volume of the Great Lakes. However, its surface area is _____

                                                   6 (– little)

than half of Lake Superior's. All together, Lake Baikal and the five Great

Lakes hold _____ than 40 percent of the world's freshwater.

                    7 (+ much)

Lake Baikal is _____ and _____ than

                   8 (+ clear)   9 (– polluted)

almost any other major lake in the world. Overall, its water is, perhaps,

_____ of all major lakes and can be drunk without treatment.

10 (++ pure)

Some problems with pollution in Lake Baikal do exist, however.

_____ threat is from manufacturers on the shores of the

             11 (++ immediate)

lake. However, Russians have responded very quickly to the concerns, perhaps

_____ than to any other issue. In fact, concerns about Lake
12 (+ quickly)

Baikal have drawn _____ reaction from citizens to almost
13 (++ strong)

any environmental concern in the last 30 years.

Of the world's natural resources, Lake Baikal is one of our _____
14 (++ important)

_____ treasures. Its unique environment and its wealth of clean water

should be protected. It is one of the world's _____ sources
15 (++ valuable)

of life-giving water.

Adapted from *Horizons,* Sigurd Olson Environmental Institute

Lake Baikal

Comparison of Lake Baikal and Lake Superior		
	LAKE BAIKAL	**LAKE SUPERIOR**
Surface area *(square miles)*	12,160	31,820
Volume *(square miles)*	5,550	2,900
Average depth *(feet)*	5,313	1,333
Retention time *(years)*	317	191

exercise 8 Use the chart above to write at least five sentences comparing Lake Superior and Lake Baikal.

> **example:** Of the two lakes, the surface area of Lake Baikal is much smaller.

Using What You've Learned

activity 1 Look back at the world map on page 375. Can you label all the oceans? Can you name the most important rivers, lakes, and mountains on each continent? Work in small groups, preferably with classmates from other parts of the world. Combine your knowledge of geography to make lists for each continent. Write as many "superlatives" as you can. Then compare your lists with those of other groups. As a class, are you fairly knowledgeable about geography?

> **example:** Asia: the highest mountain   Mt. Everest

activity 2 Choose a topic that interests you and do some comparison research. Use your local library to learn more about this topic. Gather data that you can later share with your classmates. Choose at least three items to study and prepare a comparison for your classmates in terms of distances, longevity, sizes, shapes, speed, and so on. Prepare a brief report to give in a small group or for the whole class. Here are some topics that may interest you:

- Architecture or engineering: bridges, buildings, dams, tunnels, and so on
- Biology: animals, birds, plants, trees, and so on
- Geography: lakes, mountains, rivers, and so on

> **example:** I like birds, so I researched the three that interest me most. The first is the hummingbird, which is the smallest bird in the world. The second is the ostrich, which is the largest bird in the world . . .

activity 3

In pairs or in small groups, make up quizzes based on information given in this section. Try to write at least ten questions per quiz. In your quizzes, make statements that compare two or more items. Set a time limit for completing the quizzes, and then exchange them with a classmate or with another group. Return your quiz to the author(s) to be corrected.

example: T /(F) Yosemite Falls in California is higher than Tugela Falls in South Africa.

TOPIC four

Comparisons with as and than

Setting the Context

previewing the passage

The world has a tremendous variety of climates. Which do you prefer?

World Climates

Climates can change greatly. Even in a "steady" climate, an area can receive much more rain in some years than it does in others. Too, some areas may get less rain in an entire year than they normally get in one month. Temperature sometimes varies as much as rainfall does. An area with winters that are
5   normally severe may have temperatures above freezing during an entire winter season.

discussing ideas   Is the climate where you live now similar to or different from that of your hometown or region? Are lifestyles of people in the two places similar? Or are they different? Do you think different climates produce differences in lifestyles, even differences in cultures?

Clauses and Phrases with *as* and *than*

Clauses of comparison can be formed with *as* or *than*. Positive adjectives and adverbs are used with *as,* while comparative forms are used with *than.* The clause may use an appropriate auxiliary verb, or it may repeat the first verb. In conversational English, these clauses are often shortened to phrases. In formal English, subject pronouns follow *than* or *as.* In informal English, object pronouns are often used, though this is considered incorrect.

	with clauses (more formal)	with phrases (less formal)
as . . . as	Al likes winter **as much as he likes** summer.	Al likes winter **as much as** summer.
	Al likes winter **as much as he does** summer.	
	Al likes winter **as much as I do**.	Al likes winter **as much as me**.

	with clauses (more formal)	with phrases (less formal)
not as . . . as	I **don't like** the heat **as much as Al likes** the heat. I **don't like** the heat **as much as Al does** the heat. Summer is**n't as pleasant as** fall or spring is.	I **don't** like heat **as much as Al.** I **don't** like heat **as much as him.** Summer is**n't as pleasant.**
more . . . than -er . . . than	The weather here gets **more humid than it gets** in my hometown. The weather here gets **hotter than it does** in my hometown.	The weather here gets **more humid than** in my hometown. The weather here gets **hotter.**
less . . . than -er . . . than	This year, we have gotten **much less rain than we got** last year. This year, we have gotten **much less rain than we did** last year. This year, we've had **many fewer storms than we did** last year.	This year, we've gotten **much less rain than** last year. This year, we've had **many fewer storms than** last year.

Note: *Many, much,* and *even* are often used to intensify *more* or *less: He has much more money. I've written many fewer checks. I wrote even fewer than last month. Not quite* is often used with *as* when the difference between the two items is not great: *It's not quite as hot today as it was yesterday.*

---

exercise  **Rapid Oral Practice.** For each of the following, give a phrase using *as* or *than*. With positive adjectives and adverbs, use *as*. With comparative forms, use *than*.

examples: hot

as hot as

hotter

hotter than

1. quickly
2. easier
3. less difficult
4. friendly
5. more complex

6. harder
7. beautiful
8. angrily
9. brilliant
10. fewer

 Complete the following passage by adding *than* or *as*. The first one is done as an example.

THE SUN AND WEATHER

Four main factors determine weather: temperature, pressure, humidity, and wind. The sun, more <u>than</u> our own earth, has the greatest effect on these
1
factors. The earth receives less _____ two-billionths of the sun's total energy,
2
yet it receives more energy in one minute _____ we can produce in an entire
3
year through power plants.

The earth loses _____ much energy _____ it absorbs because of
4   5
reflection from cloud tops, ice fields, and snow. In addition, water vapor in our atmosphere shields the earth because it absorbs more energy _____ it
6
allows to pass through. When the water vapor absorbs more energy _____ it
7
can hold, it begins to condense and form clouds. In this way, the cycle of rainfall begins again.

The sun, then, ultimately causes all weather. The sun determines why parts of Hawaii receive _____ much rain in one month _____ parts of Chile have
8   9
gotten in sixty years.

exercise 3 Many comparisons are "understood." Complete the shortened comparisons in the following sentences by adding *as* or *than* and the understood comparison. Then change each comparison to use *than* instead of *as* or *as* instead of *than*.

example: Southwestern Canada has pleasant weather. The weather in northern Canada is much colder (than the weather in southwestern Canada is).

Southwestern Canada isn't as cold as northern Canada is.

1. British Columbia has a lot of mountains. Alberta is much flatter.
2. Manitoba is filled with lakes. Alberta doesn't have as many.
3. Edmonton has harsh winters. The winters in Vancouver aren't as severe.
4. Last year, eastern Canada got a lot of snow. This year it didn't get as much.
5. Toronto is usually quite windy in the winter. Last winter it wasn't as windy.
6. Montreal is humid, but Quebec City is often much more humid.

 The following sentences compare nouns. Complete them by using *fewer* or *less*.

example: Small towns generally have _____*fewer*_____ cars than large cities do.

1. Small towns normally have _____ pollution than large cities because they have _____ traffic.

2. In general, towns with _____ factories have _____ problems with pollution.

3. Despite pollution, people continue to move to areas like southern California, which has _____ bad weather than most parts of the country.

4. Southern California gets _____ inches of rain in one year than Vancouver, British Columbia, gets in one month.

5. Southern California has _____ windy days than British Columbia does.

6. Southern California gets _____ snow than British Columbia does.

Rephrase the following sentences, changing clauses of opposition to clauses of comparison. Give at least two new versions for each.

example: Al Aziziyah, Libya, has reached 136° F, while Death Valley, California has reached 134° F.

Two of the hottest places in the world are Al Aziziyah, Libya, and Death Valley, California. Death Valley has not gotten quite as hot as Al Aziziyah has.

Al Aziziyah has reached even higher temperatures than Death Valley has.

1. While Oymyakon, in the former Soviet Union, has reached –96° F, Vostok, Antarctica, has reached –128.6°.

2. Tutunendo, Colombia, gets 463 inches of rain annually, while Mt. Waialeale, Hawaii, gets 450 inches per year.

3. While Death Valley, California, gets around 1.7 inches of rain per year, parts of the Atacama Desert in Chile receive no measurable precipitation annually.

4. While winds at Mt. Washington, New Hampshire, have reached 231 mph, winds during a tornado in Wichita Falls, Texas, reached 280 mph.

Using What You've Learned

Imagine that you could "custom-design" the perfect place to live. For you, what would it be like? It doesn't have to be a place that already exists, but if you know of a perfect place, you can describe it. Write a short composition describing your perfect place. Be sure to describe the climate, the geography, and so on. Later, share your description with your classmates.

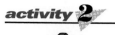

Play a game with comparisons. First, everyone should stand up. Then, go around the room in a chain, giving adjectives or adverbs and making sentences from them. Choose any adjective or adverb. Your teacher will judge if the sentence is correct. If it is not, you must sit down. The last person standing wins.

example: A: exciting
B: **New York is much more exciting than here.**
B: beautiful
C: **No one is as beautiful as you are!**

Work in pairs, and use the following chart to help you create sentences using comparatives. Create as many sentences as you can

examples: **Of the first two bridges, the Golden Gate Bridge in San Francisco is shorter.**

The Verrazano-Narrows Bridge in New York City is longer.

The Verrazano-Narrows Bridge in New York City is longer than the Golden Gate Bridge.

The Golden Gate Bridge is not quite as long as the Verrazano-Narrows Bridge.

Bridges	Verrazano-Narrows Bridge in New York City	4,260 feet long	Golden Gate Bridge in San Francisco	4,200 feet long
	Bendorf Bridge on the Rhine River	3,378 feet long	Bosphorus Bridge in Istanbul	3,524 feet long
Buildings	Sears Tower in Chicago	1,454 feet tall	World Trade Center in New York City	1,368 feet tall
	Bank of China in Hong Kong	1,001 feet tall	Eiffel Tower in Paris	984 feet tall
Deserts	Gobi Desert in Mongolia and China	500,000 square miles	Libyan Desert in North Africa	450,000 square miles
Lakes	Lake Baikal in southern Siberia	5,315 feet deep	Lake Tanganyika in Tanzania and Zaire	4,823 feet deep
Mountains	Mount McKinley in Alaska	20,320 feet tall	Mount Kilimanjaro in Tanzania	19,340 feet high

Look at the chart from Activity 3 again. Do some research and find another item to add to each group. Then, working in pairs, use each other's research to create new sentences with comparatives and superlatives. Create as many correct sentences as you can. The pair with the most new sentences wins!

TOPIC **five**

Clauses of Result

Setting the Context

What are some examples of technology used for or with water? Are there any such examples near the place you are living now?

Technology and Water

In order to manage its water, the United States has rearranged its landscape considerably. The country has spent billions of dollars to construct 20 million dams, to irrigate 60 million acres of land, and to build canals that carry one-fifth of intercity freight. This massive alteration has created extraordinary situations.

5 For example:

1. Dams control the Tennessee River so tightly that its water flow can be turned on and off like a faucet.
2. The direction of the Chicago River has been reversed so that it flows away from Lake Michigan; thus, it carries sewage away from the center of the city
10   instead of toward it.
3. Texans have pumped so much water from the ground beneath Houston that parts of the city have sunk several feet.
4. The Southwest uses such great quantities of water from the Colorado River that the river actually dries up before it ever reaches the ocean.

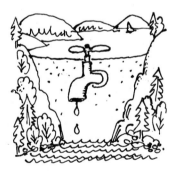

What water-management projects—dams, desalinization systems, sewage treatment—exist in your area or country? Are there any problems that you know of with these systems?

Adverb Clauses and Related Structures Showing Result

Clauses with *that* can be used to show the results or effect of a situation. See page 380 for transitions often used to show result.

	examples	notes
so . . . (*adjective/adverb*) **. . . that**	Dams control the Tennessee River **so tightly that** it can be turned off like a faucet.	*So* may be followed by an adjective or an adverb. *So* often replaces *very* when two sentences are joined.
so many **so much** . . . (*noun*) **so few** . . . **that** **so little**	**So much water** has been pumped from beneath Houston **that** parts of the city are sinking. **So many wells** are dry now **that** the city is worried about its water supply.	*So much* or *so little* is used with a noncount noun. *So many* or *so few* is used with a count noun.
such (a/an) . . . (*noun*) **. . . that**	**Such great quantities** of water are used **that** the Colorado River dries up before it ever reaches the ocean.	*Such* is used with nouns. Remember to use *a* or *an* with a singular count noun. Plural and noncount nouns do not use an article.

exercise 1 First, identify the noun, adjective, or adverb to be emphasized. Then combine each pair of sentences with *so . . . that*. Change or omit words when necessary.

example: In parts of the world, rainfall is (sparse.) People in those areas constantly conserve water.

In parts of the world, rainfall is so sparse that people constantly conserve water.

1. In other parts of the world, rainfall is plentiful. Little effort is made to conserve water.

2. People in these countries practice very little water conservation. A drought can have disastrous consequences.

3. For example, from May 1975 to August 1976, European rainfall was very far below normal. Reservoirs dried up, crops failed, and water had to be rationed.

4. During the 1980s, it was extremely dry in California. Fires spread out of control, gardens died, and even restaurants stopped serving water.

5. In many parts of the world, droughts are common. They are a daily "fact of life."

6. Some droughts, such as in recent years in north-central Africa, are long and severe. They can devastate entire populations.

Before working with *such . . . that,* review the use of articles with count and noncount nouns by completing the passage below. Use *a, an,* or *X* to indicate that no article is needed.

ALTERING THE ENVIRONMENT

_____ surface fresh water—_____ water in _____ lakes, _____ streams, and
$\quad$1$\qquad\qquad\qquad\qquad$2$\qquad\qquad$3$\qquad\qquad$4
_____ rivers—is replenished about once _____ week. _____ groundwater—
$\quad$5$\qquad\qquad\qquad\qquad\qquad\qquad$6$\qquad\qquad$7
_____ water underground— is replenished much more slowly. Because _____
$\quad$8$\qquad\qquad\qquad\qquad\qquad\qquad\qquad\qquad\qquad\qquad$9
rainfall is not dependable, _____ people dig wells to get _____ constant supply
$\qquad\qquad\qquad\qquad$10$\qquad\qquad\qquad\qquad$11
of _____ fresh water.
$\quad$12

Because of _____ well digging, _____ parts of the United States are like
$\qquad\qquad$13$\qquad\qquad$14
_____ pincushion. Over 150,000 wells have been dug to tap the Ogallala
$\quad$15
aquifer, _____ underground reservoir beneath _____ eight states. It has taken
$\qquad$16$\qquad\qquad\qquad\qquad$17

Contaminants can enter groundwater from
many sources on the surface. They form a
"plume" of pollution that is hard to detect.

Factory

Pesticide

Garbage
dump

Farm

Liquid
waste

Well

Hazardous
waste storage

Plume of contaminated water

Test drilling does
not detect pollution

AQUIFER

Impermeable underground layer

nature at least 25,000 years to fill this aquifer, and it is taking _____ humans
only _____ few decades to empty it.
18

19

Rewrite the following sentences to use *such . . . that* instead of *because*. Use the example as a model.

example: Because there is a strong relationship among all living things, damage to one part of an ecosystem will hurt another part.

There is such a strong relationship among all living things that damage to one part of an ecosystem will hurt another part.

1. Because wetlands—marshes and swamps—were considered useless places, millions of acres worldwide have been filled.
2. Because large numbers of wetlands are being drained, the United States loses over 300,000 acres annually.
3. Because wetlands are a critical source of oxygen, we must protect them at all cost.
4. Because the plants in wetlands form strong filters, they are natural water purifiers.
5. Because wetlands capture large amounts of carbon in the form of peat, they protect the atmosphere.
6. Because wetlands are feeding and breeding grounds for fish, they provide the United States with over half its saltwater fish and shellfish each year.

Until recently, this area in the Florida Everglades was a home for countless kinds of wetlands plants and wildlife.

Review. Before working with *so . . . that,* review the use of *few, little, many,* and *much.* First identify the nouns as count or noncount. Then complete the sentences with *few, little, many,* or *much.*

1. The Los Angeles basin has so _____ natural water that it can supply only about 200,000 people.

2. With so _____ people (around 8 million living in the basin alone), Los Angeles has to import large quantities of water.

3. Los Angeles gets as _____ as 80 percent of its total water supply through an aqueduct from the Owens Valley in east-central California.

4. Most of this water is from surface streams, but at times as _____ as 30 percent comes from groundwater pumping.

5. _____Owens Valley residents say that Los Angeles is turning their valley into a desert.

6. They claim that Los Angeles leaves them so _____ ground and surface water that it is destroying the environment of the valley.

7. For example, between 1900 and 1920, Los Angeles pumped so _____ gallons of water that it dried up 100-square mile Owens Lake.

8. _____ of the land is now covered with sagebrush, and _____ crops can grow.

Combine the following sentences with *so much . . . that* or *so many . . . that.*

examples: Government departments are involved in water management. Water use is almost impossible to control.

So many government departments are involved in water management that water use is almost impossible to control.

Government bureaucracy is involved in water management. Water use is almost impossible to control.

So much government bureaucracy is involved in water management that water use is almost impossible to control.

1. Water used to leak from pipes beneath Berwyn, Illinois. The city was losing 1 million gallons of water a day.
   The water pipes beneath Berwyn had leaks. The city was losing 1 million gallons of water per day.

2. Wells have become polluted. It is becoming a severe national problem.
   Groundwater has become polluted. It is becoming a severe national problem.

3. Homes get high levels of radiation from naturally occurring radon in the water and soil. United States health officials are worried about the situation.
   Radiation is emitted from radon, which occurs naturally in the water and soil near many homes. United States health officials are worried about the situation.

 **exercise 6**   **Review.**   Combine the following sentences, using a variety of connecting words and phrases. Change or omit words and add punctuation when necessary.

example: It doesn't rain frequently in the desert. Occasionally, rain comes down in torrents.

Although it doesn't rain frequently in the desert, rain occasionally comes down in torrents.

FLASH FLOODS

1. Vegetation in the desert is very sparse. The desert ground is often very hard. The water from a heavy rain does not soak in.
2. Very little water is absorbed. Most of it runs off into dry riverbeds.
3. These riverbeds or gullies are very common in dry lands. Most languages have a name for them.
4. *Arroyo* and *wadi* are words from foreign languages. These names are also used in English to describe dry riverbeds or gullies.
5. The sandy bed of the arroyo may absorb some rainwater. Most of the rainwater begins to flow forward. The rainwater quickly picks up speed.
6. The arroyo acts as a funnel. The rainwater rushes faster and faster. The rainwater often builds a wall of water several feet high.
7. It is difficult to imagine the speed and force of a flash flood. Automobile-sized boulders in a dry arroyo demonstrate a flash flood's carrying power.
8. The carrying power of a stream increases dramatically with speed. Even a small flood can pull very heavy objects along with it.
9. Heavy rains fall quickly and unpredictably in the desert. Desert travelers should watch weather signs. They should move to high ground at any sign of rain.
10. Flash floods can be devastating. Damage seldom occurs on higher ground.

 **exercise 7**   **Review.**   Combine the following ten sentences, using a variety of connecting words and phrases. Change or omit words and add punctuation when necessary.

TSUNAMI

Tsunami is a Japanese word that means "large waves in harbors." It is appropriate because only a major disturbance can produce large waves in sheltered bays.

1. In the United States, tsunami are often called "tidal waves." The name "tidal wave" is incorrect.
2. Tsunami have nothing to do with tides. The approach of tsunami on an open coast may look like a rapid rise of the tide.
3. Almost all tsunami have followed tremendous earthquakes. Some scientists believe a sudden lift or drop in the ocean floor produces these giant waves.
4. An alternative explanation is that huge submarine landslides produce them. There is no good proof of the idea of submarine landslides.
5. Tsunami move at enormous speeds in the open ocean. Tsunami can average 450 miles per hour.

6. Their height in the open ocean is small. They may have no effect on the deep-sea floor. Along a coast, they become very destructive.
7. A major earthquake shook Alaska in 1946. A tremendous tsunami hit Hawaii several hours later.
8. The waves took only four hours to reach Hawaiian shores after the earthquake. Then the shallow waters off Hawaii slowed them down.
9. The waves slowed very much. The waves moved at a rate of only about 15 miles per hour near the coast.
10. Their depth was limited in the shallow water. They grew in height to the size of a three-story wall.

Tree that was uprooted during a tsunami

Using What You've Learned

activity 1

Think about yourself and your reactions to a disaster situation. You may have experienced a flood, an earthquake, a typhoon, a blizzard. In small groups, describe the disaster and talk about how you felt and what you did.

example: **When the earthquake hit Caracas, the buildings shook so much that I thought everything would fall. I was so frightened that I could hardly breathe.**

activity 2

Individually or in pairs, use your sentences from Exercises 6 and 7 to write short paragraphs. If you have other knowledge about these phenomena, add it to your composition.

activity 3

Play another "chain" game, this time with *so . . . that* and *such . . . that*. First, everyone should stand up. Then, go around the room in a chain. The first student should give an adjective, adjective + noun, or adverb. Then, the next student makes a sentence using the word(s). Choose any adjective, noun, or adverb. Your teacher will judge if the sentence is correct. If it is not, you must sit down. The last person standing wins.

example: A: exciting class
           B: **This is such an exciting class that I don't want to have a break!**

           A: intelligent
           B: **You are so intelligent that I'm sure you'll get 650 on the TOEFL.**

activity 4   Test your knowledge of water trivia. How much water do you think it takes to do the following? Write your own answers. Outside of class, ask two people who are not classmates to give theirs. Afterward, analyze your data. Who guessed the most correct answers? The fewest?

Then bring your data back to class and in groups of three, compare answers. Again, analyze the data. (The correct answers are at the bottom of page 419.)

IN THE UNITED STATES, HOW MANY GALLONS OF WATER ARE USED . . .	YOUR NAME	NAME	NAME
1. In an average household each year?			
2. By an average person daily?			
3. To flush a toilet?			
4. To take a shower?			
5. To brush your teeth (with the water running)?			
6. To shave (with the water running)?			
7. To wash dishes by hand?			
8. To run a dishwasher?			
9. To run a washing machine?			
10. To produce a quart of milk?			
11. To produce one tomato?			
12. To produce the nation's newspapers for a day?			
Extra Question What percentage of the world's population does not have clean water?			

Use of Adverb Clauses and Phrases

Adverb phrases and clauses are frequently tested on standardized English proficiency exams. Review these commonly tested structures and check your understanding by completing the sample items below.

Remember that . . .

- Clauses follow subordinating conjunctions.
- Phrases follow prepositions.
- In formal English, *so that* (not *so*) must be used to express purpose.
- A modal auxiliary is generally used in clauses with *so that*.

Part 1: Circle the correct completion for the following.

example: _____ appears happy with his work, he often complains about the schedule.
- **a.** In spite of
- **b.** Despite
- **c.** Even
- **d.** Even though

1. The geologist was gathering rock samples _____ he could locate a site for drilling.
   - **a.** that
   - **b.** so that
   - **c.** so
   - **d.** such that

2. It was _____ polluted well that we couldn't use water from it.
   - **a.** so
   - **b.** such
   - **c.** such a
   - **d.** so many

3. Surface winds are rare at the equator _____ the earth and the atmosphere rotate at the same speed there.
   - **a.** because
   - **b.** so
   - **c.** because of
   - **d.** due to

Part 2: Circle the letter below the underlined word(s) containing an error.

example: <u>Overseas</u> travelers frequently experience culture shock <u>even</u>
        A   Ⓑ
they <u>may have spent</u> <u>a good deal of</u> time in foreign countries.
         C   D

1. The Great Lakes in <u>North America</u> form <u>the large</u> body of fresh
   A   B   C
water in <u>the</u> world.
       D

2. In English, the expression *tidal wave* <u>is often used</u> <u>despite</u> these
                                 A   B
giant waves, <u>which</u> are most likely caused by lifts or drops in the
        C
ocean floor, <u>have nothing to do</u> with tides.
            D

3. <u>Naturally occurring</u> radon emits <u>so large</u> quantities of radiation
      A   B
<u>that it</u> poses one of the <u>most worrisome</u> environmental problems
  C   D
in the United States today.

Answers:

Extra 30 percent

1. 107,000 gallons
2. 5 to 7 gallons
3. 25 to 50 gallons
4. 2 gallons
5. 10 to 15 gallons
6. 10 to 15 gallons
7. 20 gallons
8. 10 gallons
9. 30 gallons
10. 4 gallons
11. 8 gallons
12. 300 million gallons

Together on a Small Planet

Introduction

In this chapter, you will study some of the uses of noun clauses, including reported speech and embedded questions. You will also study how to reduce these clauses to phrases. Finally, you will review a variety of clauses and other structures covered in the text.

The following passage was written by the noted anthropologist, Margaret Mead, many years ago, yet its message holds true today. This passage introduces the chapter theme, Together on a Small Planet, and raises some of the topics and issues you will cover in the chapter.

Margaret Mead Speaking on the Future of Humanity

I am optimistic by nature. I am glad that I am alive. I am glad that I am living at this particular very difficult, very dangerous, and very crucial period in human history.

To this extent my viewpoint about the future reflects a personal tempera-
5   mental bent—something that must always be taken into account. But, of course, unsupported optimism is not enough.

I support my optimism with my knowledge of how far mankind has come. Throughout the hundreds of thousands of years that human life has evolved, at first physically and later culturally, human beings have withstood tremendous
10   changes and have adjusted to radically new demands. What we have to realize, I believe, is that human ingenuity, imagination, and faith in life itself have been crucial both in initiating changes and in meeting new demands imposed by change.

As an anthropologist I also have seen how a living generation of men born
15   into a Stone Age culture has moved into a modern world all at once, skipping the many small steps by which mankind as a whole moved from the distant past into the present.

I find these things encouraging. An earlier generation invented the idea of invention. Now we have invented the industrialization of invention—a way of
20   meeting a recognized problem by setting hundreds of trained persons together to work out solutions and, equally important, to work out the means of putting solutions into practice.

This is what made it possible to send men to the moon and to begin the ex-
ploration of outer space. This should give us reason to believe also that we can
25   meet the interlocking problems of runaway populations, war, and the pollution of the earth on which we depend for life. None of these problems is insoluble.

What we need is the will to demand solutions and the patience to learn how to carry them out.

Margaret Mead

discussing
ideas

What do you believe about the future of our world? Are you optimistic, as Mead was? Or are you pessimistic? Why?

TOPIC **one**

Clauses with that

Setting the Context

previewing
the
passage

What are the three most important things in your life? As you read the following passage, compare your own ideas to those of the author.

On Friendship

If someone asked me to list the three most important things in my life, I'd have to tell the person my health, my family, and my friends. And, I'd say that I worked very hard at all three of them. I know that you can't choose your family, and I realize sometimes you can't guarantee your health. But I believe that you are responsible for your friends. You make them and you keep them. Or, you lose them. Someone once said that a true friend was the best possession, and that's a proverb I believe in. I believe that you have to treat your friends accordingly. Treat them with care and affection just as you would your most valuable possession.

5

Edward Sonnenberg

discussing
ideas

Do you agree with Sonnenberg on this three choices? Would you add any others?

A. Clauses with *that*

Noun clauses may replace nouns or pronouns as subjects, objects, or complements. These clauses often begin with the subordinating conjunction *that*. In conversational English, *that* is frequently omitted.

	examples	notes
Noun or Pronoun Object	I know **something**.	Noun clauses often follow such verbs as *agree, believe, feel, find, hope, know, mention, notice, realize, regret, remark, say, tell, think, understand*, and *wish*.
Noun Clause Object	I know **(that) friends are important**.	

 Answer the following questions in your own words. Use noun clauses after *learn, realize, know, regret,* and *believe.*

1. What have you learned about people in general during this class?
2. What are the three most important things about other cultures that you have learned during this class?
3. What have you realized about your own culture?
4. What are five new things that you now know about English?
5. Is there anything that you regret about your work in English?
6. What do you think is the most valuable thing about your experience here?

 In small groups, discuss some of your answers to the questions in Exercise 1. Then choose one member to give a brief report for the class. In your report, use "reporting clauses" such as *We (all) agree (believe, think) that . . .* , *Several of us feel that . . .* , *Some of us have found that . . .* , and so on.

B. Quotations and Reported Speech

Quotations are the exact words that someone says. They are used with quotation marks, and a comma often precedes or follows the quote. Reported speech gives the ideas, but *not necessarily* the exact words, of the original speaker or writer. Reported speech does not generally require commas or quotation marks.

	examples
Quotation	Ralph Waldo Emerson once said, "The only way to have a friend is to be one."
Reported Speech	Ralph Waldo Emerson once said that the only way to have a friend was (is) to be a friend to someone.

C. Sequence of Tenses in Reported Speech

Verbs and certain modal auxiliaries may shift to past forms in reported speech. These shifts most often occur when the report is being given at a different time or place from the action. If the information is still true at the moment of speaking, the shift from present to past may be optional. The changes must be consistent, however. *That* is also optional in most of these sentences.

Changes in Verb Tense

quotations	reported speech	notes
"Max is at home."	Molly said Max was at home.	In reported speech, when the verb in the main clause (e.g., *Molly said, he mentioned*) is in the past, the verb in the noun clause is often in a past tense. The verb in the noun clause may shift from present to past or present perfect to past perfect.
"Max is studying."	She mentioned that he was studying.	
"He is going to study all day."	She remarked that he was going to study all day.	
"He has a lot of work."	She said he had a lot of work.	
"He hasn't finished yet."	She added he hadn't finished yet.	
"He started yesterday."	She said he started (had started) yesterday.	The shift of simple past and past continuous tenses in the noun clause to perfect forms is often optional.
"He was working very hard."	She said he was working (had been working) very hard.	

Note: In some cases, use of the past perfect or past perfect continuous changes the meaning. It can indicate that a situation is finished or is no longer true. Compare: *He said that he wanted to go.* (Perhaps he still wants to). *He said that he had wanted to go.* (He no longer wants to or he can't go.)

Changes in Modal Auxiliaries

quotations	reported speech	notes
"Max can't go."	She said that Max couldn't go.	*Can* often shifts to *could*.
"Max may go later."	She remarked that he might go later.	*May* often shifts to *might*.
"He will tell us."	She added he would tell us.	*Will* often shifts to *would*.
"He must finish his work."	She stressed that he had to finish his work.	*Must* is sometimes changed to *had to* when need is expressed.

Note: In reported speech, modals are changed less frequently than other verbs or auxiliaries because of the problems of differences in meaning.

Changes in Commands

quotations	reported speech	notes
"Let's leave at 8:00." "Be on time."	She said that we should leave at 8:00. She told me very firmly that I must be on time.	In reported speech, an appropriate noun or pronoun is added to a command. *Should* or other modal auxiliaries are used, depending on the strength of the original command.

 **exercise 3** Even good friends have problems, and one way to save friendships is by talking things over. In the following conversation, a group of roommates is trying to resolve a common problem, housework. Retell the conversation in reported speech by completing the sentences below. Be sure to use appropriate verb forms in your new sentences.

STEVE: We're all good friends, but we've been having a lot of problems lately.

TOM: Well, in my opinion, the biggest problem is cleaning. The apartment is a mess. Nobody cleaned last week or the week before. We must find a way to keep things cleaner.

JOHN: We can make a list of jobs to do, and each person can sign up for a job.

PETER: I'll be responsible for the kitchen area.

TOM: I'll do the living room, but we need a vacuum cleaner!

STEVE: I'm going to check the newspaper. I may be able to find a good used one.

example: Steve said that they <u>should talk things over</u> .

1. Steve remarked that they _____ but that they

   _____.

2. Tom felt the biggest problem _____ and the apartment

   _____.

3. He added that nobody _____ and that they

   _____.

4. John remarked that they _____ and that each person

   _____.

5. Peter stated that he _____.

6. Tom added that he _____ but that they

   _____.

7. Steve mentioned that he _____.

8. He added that he _____.

D. *say* Versus *tell*

examples	notes
Molly **said** that Max had to work.	In general, *say* is used when the listener is *not* mentioned.
Molly **told me** that Max had to work.	*Tell* is used when the listener *is* mentioned. (We say something, but we tell *someone* something.)

exercise 4 Reread the conversation in Exercise 3. Then complete the following with the past form of *say* or *tell*. The first one is done as an example.

1. Steve ____said____ that they'd been having a lot of problems lately.

2. Tom _____ his roommates that cleaning was their biggest problem.

3. John _____ that they could each choose a job to do.

4. Peter _____ that he would clean the kitchen.

5. Tom _____ everyone that he would take care of the living room.

6. Finally, Steve _____ the others that he would try to find a vacuum cleaner.

E. Pronoun and Adverb Changes in Reported Speech

In reported speech, pronouns are changed to show a change in speakers. Adjectives and adverbs are sometimes changed too. The use of *this, that, these, those, now, then, here,* and *there* depends on the time and place of the reported speech. *Today, tomorrow,* and *yesterday* may also change according to the time of the reported speech. Remember to be consistent. If you make the change in one place, you must make it in all cases.

	quotations	reported speech
Pronouns	Mary said, "I need your help."	Mary said that she needed my help.
	Mary said, "We must finish soon!"	Mary said we had to finish soon.
	Erik said, "You have to finish immediately."	Erik said that we had to finish immediately.
Demonstrative Pronouns and Adjectives	Mary said, "This is important."	Mary said that was important.
	Mary said, "These papers are important."	Mary said those papers were important.
Adverbs	Mary said, "I need them now."	Mary said she needed them then.
	Mary said, "The papers are here."	Mary said that the papers were there.

 **exercise 5** The following quotations are students' responses to various questions. Change each quotation to reported speech. Make all necessary changes in verb tenses, pronouns, and so on. Note that you do not need to use a "reporting clause" with every sentence; however, you do need to be consistent in all changes.

example: "I've really learned a lot here. I even learned how to surf!"
—Noriko, female, Japan

Noriko said that she had really learned a lot there. She'd even learned how to surf.

1. What has been the best part of your stay in California?
 a. "I've made wonderful new friends during my visit. I hope some of them will come to see me in Japan." —Masahiko, male, Japan
 b. "I got married." —Walter, male, Poland

2. What do you like best about Boston?
   a. "I really enjoy the variety of people here." —Odelmo, male, Venezuela
   b. "I can do almost anything here. This afternoon I may see a movie; there are at least ten good ones to pick from. Or I may go to a museum; there are several excellent ones." —Frank, male, Switzerland
3. How did you like the experience of spending a winter in Wisconsin?
   a. "We were extremely cold at first! We weren't used to cold weather at all. Little by little, my family is learning to adapt to it." —Lijia, female, Nicaragua
   b. "It was difficult at the beginning. Some days I almost froze while I was walking home. I'm finally getting used to it." —Bedi, male, Mauritania

F. Verbs and Modal Auxiliaries That Do Not Change in Reported Speech

	quotations	reported speech	notes
No Tense Changes	Molly says, "Max is at home." Molly adds, "He hasn't finished his work yet."	Molly says Max is at home. Molly adds that he hasn't finished his work yet.	In reported speech, no tense change occurs when the verb in the main clause is in the present tense.
Optional Tense Changes	Molly said, "Max is a hard worker." Molly said, "He works very hard."	Molly said Max was (is) a hard worker. Molly said he worked (works) very hard.	When the noun clause gives factual information that is true in general, either present or past forms may be used.
No Change in Modal Auxiliaries	Molly said "Max should finish soon." Molly added, "He must be tired." She remarked, "He ought to have started sooner."	Molly said Max should finish soon. Molly added that he must be tired. She remarked that he ought to have started sooner.	*Could, might, ought to, should,* and *would* are not generally changed in reported speech. *Must* does not change when it expresses probability. Perfect modals are not changed in reported speech.

exercise 6 **Error Analysis.** Many of the following statements have errors in their use of reported speech. Note that most of these statements can be true at any time, so certain changes will be optional. As you find the various errors, remember to be consistent in your corrections.

> example: Ralph Waldo Emerson ~~says~~ *said* that the only way to have a friend <u>was</u> to be one.   Either <u>was</u> or <u>is</u> is correct.

1. Charles Colton once wrote that true friendship was like good health. The value of it is seldom known until it is lost.

2. Elbert Hubbard remarked that your friend is the person who knows all about me and still liked me.

3. In her book *Emma,* Jane Austen wrote that business might bring money, but friendship hardly ever did.

4. Ned Rorem once commented that sooner or later you've heard all my best friends have to say. Now came the tolerance of real love.

5. In his journals, Emerson remarked that one of the blessings of old friends was that you can afford to be stupid with them.

6. Kurt Vonnegut wrote that love was where you find it. It was foolish to go looking for it.

7. In the first century, a Roman author comments that the friendship that can come to an end had never really begun.

8. La Rochefoucauld wrote in his *Maxims* that however rare true love may be, it is less rare than true friendship.

exercise 7 Ann Landers gave the following advice on love and friendship. Read her advice and make five statements in your own words, using reported speech. Begin your sentences with a variety of openers: *She said, stated, mentioned, wrote,* and so forth. Use *should, ought to, have to, had better,* or *must* in the noun clause, depending on the strength of the advice.

TO HELP YOU IMPROVE THE QUALITY OF LIFE

On this day—
Mend a quarrel,
Search out a forgotten friend,
Dismiss a suspicion and replace it with trust,
Write a letter to someone who misses you,
Encourage a youth who has lost faith,
Keep a promise,
Forget an old grudge,
Examine your demands on others and vow to reduce them,
Fight for a principle,
Express your gratitude,

Overcome an old fear,
Take two minutes to appreciate the beauty of nature,
Tell someone you love him.
Tell him again,
And again,
And again.

Ann Landers, *The Ann Landers Encyclopedia*

example: **Ann Landers said that I (we, people) should mend a quarrel.**

 Answer the following questions in your own words, using reported speech where appropriate.

1. When did you last talk to your best friend or another friend whom you hadn't seen for a while? What did you talk about? What news did your friend tell you? What did you say about that? What news did you tell your friend?
2. Have you made a promise lately? To whom did you make the promise? What did you promise?
3. Have you had an argument lately? What was it about? Whom did you argue with? What did you say to each other? How did you settle the argument?
4. Have you had to make a decision or solve a problem lately? What was the situation? Did you discuss it with anyone? What did you talk about? What advice did the person give you?

 Look back at the opening passage by Margaret Mead. Then use the following cues to help you paraphrase her ideas. Use reporting clauses to begin at least some of your sentences. *Note:* Because Margaret Mead is now dead, any quotations about her *must* be changed to past forms. The changes are optional for more general quotations.

- Margaret Mead said . . .
- She told us . . .
- She mentioned . . .
- She believed . . .

example: optimistic by nature

Margaret Mead said that she was optimistic by nature.

1. glad to be alive
2. glad / live
3. support / optimism
4. human beings / withstand tremendous changes
5. human ingenuity, imagination, and faith in life / crucial to change
6. see Stone Age cultures / move into the modern world in one generation
7. mankind as a whole / move by small steps into the present
8. be encouraged by these things
9. people / can solve the problems of population, war, and pollution
10. need the will and patience to find and carry out solutions

Using What You've Learned

activity 1 In pairs or small groups, take turns asking each other questions similar to those in Exercise 5. Then briefly tell the whole group what your classmates said. Use reported speech when you talk to the whole group.

activity 2 Reread the comments on friendship in Exercise 6. Then, in small groups or as a class, share your own ideas. Do you agree with some or all of the statements? Do you disagree with any? Can you add any other sayings about love or friendship from your own culture?

activity 3 Reread the advice from Ann Landers in Exercise 7. Do you have any other suggestions to add? Share your ideas in a small-group discussion or in a brief composition.

activity 4 In small groups, discuss the following quotations about friendship. After you have finished your discussion, choose a spokesperson to give a brief report to the class. Be sure to use reported speech in the summary of your discussion.

> "No man is an island . . . ; every man is part of the main. . . . Any man's death diminishes me because I am involved in mankind, and therefore never send to know for whom the bell tolls; it tolls for thee." —*John Donne*

> "He who has a thousand friends has not a friend to spare, And he who has one enemy will meet him everywhere." —Ali ibn-Abi-Talib, *A Hundred Sayings*

> "I wish that people who are conventionally supposed to love each other would say to each other when they fight, 'Please—a little less love, and a little more common decency.'" —Kurt Vonnegut, *Slapstick*

TOPIC **two**

Clauses with if, whether, and Question Words

Setting the Context

*previewing
the
passage*

How do we learn? How can we best put our knowledge to use? The following quotes look at learning and knowledge. As you read them, what are your reactions?

Education, Learning, and Knowledge

"**E**ducation is an admirable thing, but it is well to remember from time to time that nothing that is worth knowing can be taught."

—Oscar Wilde, *"The Critic as an Artist," Intentions*, 1891

5 "Experience is not what happens to you; it is what you do with what happens to you." —Aldous Huxley, *Reader's Digest*, March 1956

"I am convinced that it is of primordial* importance to learn more every year than the year before. After all, what is education but a process by which a person begins to learn how to learn? —Peter Ustinov, *Dear Me*, 1977

10 "It is not a question of how much a man knows, but what use he makes of what he knows. Not a question of what he has acquired and how he has been trained, but of what he is and what he can do." —J. G. Holland

*discussing
ideas*

Do you agree or disagree with the various ideas on education? Is formal education really valuable? Is it really possible to put all of our knowledge to use? Aren't there certain things that we want to learn about simply for the sake of learning?

---

primordial   fundamental, primary

A. Clauses with *if* and *whether*

yes/no questions	examples	notes
Is he going?	I wonder **if** he is going.	Yes/no questions may be changed into noun clauses by using *if* and *whether*. The subject must come *before* the verb in the noun clause. Noun clauses with *if* and *whether* are often used in polite requests.
Has he left yet?	Do you know **whether** he has left yet?	
Can he go?	I wonder **whether** he can go.	
Does he want to go?	Could you tell me **if** he wants to go?	
Did he leave?	I would like to know **whether** he left.	

 exercise 1   Do you have an assignment or test in the next few days? Take this opportunity to ask your teacher for more information. Change the following direct questions to noun clauses. Be sure to use correct word order. Begin your questions with the following: *Could you tell me . . . ? I would like to know . . . .*

example: Will there be any more homework this session?

I would like to know whether (if) there will be any more homework this quarter.

1. Will there be a final test in this class?
2. Do I have to take a proficiency exam?
3. Is it necessary to study for the proficiency test?
4. Have I completed all of the assignments for this class?
5. Am I going to pass this course?
6. Could I talk to you about my progress?
7. Will we have a class party?
8. Does anyone want to plan a party?

B. Clauses with Question Words

information questions	examples	notes
Where is the library?	I would like to know **where the library is.**	Information questions may also be changed to noun clauses. Question words are used to introduce them. The subject must come *before* the verb in noun clauses. These clauses are often used in polite requests.
How can I find it?	Please tell me **how I can find it.**	
When does it close?	Do you know **when it closes?**	

Imagine that you have to write a term paper for a class. Change the following questions about the assignment to noun clauses. Be sure to correct word order. Begin your new sentences with the following:

- Could you tell me . . . ?
- I would like to know . . .
- I wonder . . .
- I don't know . . .

example: When is the paper due?

Could you tell me when the paper is due?

1. How long should the paper be?
2. How many sources should I use?
3. Where can I get information on the topic?
4. Which section of the library should I check?
5. When could I discuss this with you?
6. Where can I find someone to type it?

The following is an excerpt from an interview with Meredith Pike, an educational consultant to the San Francisco public schools. The interviewer is Martha Brown.

First read the interview for meaning. Then paraphrase the discussion by completing the sentences below. Remember to use reported speech, and try to simplify ideas whenever possible.

MARTHA BROWN: What is the greatest problem facing the public schools?

MEREDITH PIKE: The greatest problem is class size. The average public school class has twenty-eight students. When class size is too big, teachers can't help students individually.

BROWN: What's the solution?

PIKE: The solution is to develop strategies that help students learn in large groups. Cooperative learning is one of these strategies.

BROWN: What does it involve?

PIKE: Cooperative learning involves dividing the class into smaller groups. Teachers' jobs become easier because they deal with the groups instead of individuals. The students learn more because each one in the group has a responsibility—for example, the stronger students help the weaker ones. The students learn the material and, at the same time, learn cooperation, an important life skill.

BROWN: How realistic is this solution?

PIKE: It's very realistic, but it takes times and commitment because teachers and administrators have to be trained in new methods.

example: Martha Brown began by asking what . . .

Martha Brown began by asking what the greatest problem facing the public schools was.

1. Pike stated . . .
2. She explained that the average public school . . . and that . . .
3. Next, Brown asked . . .
4. Pike answered that . . .

5. She said that cooperative learning . . .
6. Brown then asked . . .
7. Pike responded that . . .
8. She stated that teachers' jobs . . . and that the students . . .
9. She added that the students . . .
10. Finally, Brown asked . . .
11. Pike said . . .
12. Pike also noted, however, . . .

exercise 4   Individually, in pairs, or in small groups, combine the following pairs or groups
of sentences. Many variations are possible; above all, try to vary your sentence
structures and to eliminate unnecessary words.

example: The greatest puzzle of education is a question.
How can a child learn best?

The greatest puzzle of education is how a child can learn best.

HOW CAN PEOPLE LEARN BEST?

1. People everywhere agree on an idea.
Education is important.
Few people agree on something.
How should we provide education?

2. Does a child learn well in these ways?
Information is taught by practice.
Information is taught by repetition.
Information is taught by memorization.

3. Does a child learn better in other ways?
The teacher stimulates the child's curiosity.
The teacher makes learning fun.
The teacher makes learning pleasant.

4. Are there certain subjects?
These subjects must be memorized.
These include the alphabet and numbers.
These include the rules of spelling.
These include the multiplication tables.

5. Memorization is a part of education.
Repetitive drill is a part of education.

6. Does this mean something?
Can most learning be taught in that way?
Should most learning be taught in that way?

7. Should learning be fun for the student?
Is schooling very hard work?
The student must be forced to do it.

8. Someday we may be able to answer these questions.
Then we may be able to learn the secret of a truly good education.

Using What You've Learned

activity 1
Reread the quotations at the beginning of this section, page 433. How do these ideas apply to the process of learning a language? Give your ideas and opinions in a brief composition about language learning.

activity 2
Find someone outside your class to interview about education. You may want to ask about language learning, or you can look at a different field. You can look at formal learning (in schools and universities, for example), or you can ask about informal learning (through experience).

First, prepare four to five good questions to ask your interviewee. Tape-record your interview or take notes as the person talks. Later, write a report on the interview. Use reported speech. Finally, share your information with your classmates.

activity 3
What is your reaction to the following quotation? Think about your own education experience and use your ideas to complete the sentences to form a short paragraph. You may want to add or omit some lines. Then present it to the class.

"I am always ready to learn, but I am not always ready to be taught."
—Winston Churchill

1. I agree / disagree with Churchill's idea because . . .
2. I believe that . . .
3. I remember a time when . . .
4. While I was . . .
5. After I had . . .
6. As a result . . .
7. If I hadn't . . .
8. Nevertheless . . .

activity 4
Organize a debate on the merits of education and experience. Let half the class argue in favor of formal education and the other half in favor of experience. If you want, have your debate center on the process of language learning: Can you really learn a language in a classroom? Without a class and a teacher, do people have enough discipline to learn a language well?

activity 5
Imagine that you have the opportunity to question today's world leaders on their policies. In small groups, prepare a list of at least ten issues that you would like these leaders to address. Use the following expressions in your questions: *We would like to know . . . We would like to ask you . . . Could you please explain to us . . . ? We don't understand . . . Could you tell us . . . ?* Then take turns role-playing world leaders. You may want to organize a panel that will answer questions in a "Face the Nation (the World)" format. The rest of the class will ask questions to those who are role-playing the leaders.

TOPIC **three**

Clause to Phrase Reduction

Setting the Context

previewing the passage

Do you believe that world peace is possible? Or, do you believe that there will always be war?

Thoughts on War and Peace

The French statesman George Clemenceau once said, "I don't know whether war is an interlude during peace, or peace is an interlude during war." Given the political changes of the past decades, perhaps we can create a very long interlude of peace. Perhaps, we can even create a lasting peace. The question is not whether to try, but rather how to achieve it.

5

discussing ideas

What is your opinion on the quote by Clemenceau? Do war and peace necessarily alternate, or can one exist without the other?

A. Reduction of Commands

Commands can be reduced to infinitive phrases in reported speech. The infinitive expresses the same meaning as *should* + infinitive. The verbs *advise, beg, command, direct, encourage, order, urge,* and *warn* follow the same pattern as *tell* in infinitive phrases. The indirect object must be used.

	reported speech with noun clauses	reduction to infinitive phrases
QUOTATIONS WITH COMMANDS		
She said, "Come early."	She said **that we should come** early.	She said **to come** early.
She told us, "Come early."	She told us **that we should come** early.	She told us **to come** early.
		She advised (urged) us **to come** early.

exercise 1   The military is an institution that uses many commands. Change the following commands first to noun clauses and then to infinitive phrases. Remember to add modal auxiliaries and nouns or pronouns when necessary.

> **example:**   The sergeant said, "Stand up."
>
> **The sergeant said that we should stand up.**
>
> **The sergeant said to stand up.**

1. The officer ordered, "March."
2. The officer said, "Do not talk."
3. The commander said, "Halt, soldier."
4. The major advised, "Do not relax."
5. The soldier begged, "Give us some water."
6. The officer warned, "Be quiet."
7. The sergeant commanded, "Salute the general."
8. The general said, "Stand at ease, soldiers."

B. Reduction of Requests for Action and for Permission

Requests with *Will you . . . , Can you . . . , Would you . . . ,* and *Could you . . .* can be reduced to infinitive phrases. The indirect object *must* be used with the infinitive phrase. Requests with *May I . . . , Could I . . . ,* and *Can I . . .* can also be reduced to infinitive phrases, but *no* indirect object is used.

	reported speech with noun clauses	reduction to infinitive phrases
QUOTATIONS WITH REQUEST FOR ACTION		
She asked (us), "Will you come early?"	She asked (us) **if we would come** early.	She asked us **to come** early.
She asked (us), "Could you help me?"	She asked (us) **whether we could help** her.	She asked us **to help** her.
QUOTATIONS WITH REQUEST FOR PERMISSION		
She asked (me), "Could I speak to John?"	She asked (me) **if she could speak** to John.	She asked **to speak** to John.

**exercise 2** First, change the quotations to reported speech using noun clauses. Then reduce the noun clauses to infinitive phrases. Remember to add nouns or pronouns when necessary.

> **example:** She asked, "Could I help you?"
>
> **She asked if she could help me.**
> **She asked to help me.**

1. She asked, "Could you tell me the time?"
2. He asked, "May I use your phone?"
3. They asked their lawyer, "Would you please read this?"
4. The little boy asked his mother, "Can I go to Martin's house?"
5. The policewoman asked, "May I see your driver's license?"
6. I asked, "Could you give me some change?"

C. Reduction of Embedded Questions

Yes/no questions with modal auxiliaries can be reduced to infinitive phrases. *Whether (or not)* is always used with an infinitive form. Information questions (with *how, what, when,* and *where*) may also be reduced. With both types of questions, the speaker and the subject of the question *must* be the same person(s). Indirect objects are not necessary with either type of reduced question.

	reported speech with noun clauses	reduction to infinitive phrases
QUOTATIONS WITH YES/NO QUESTIONS		
We asked (her), "Should we leave now?"	We asked (her) **if we should leave then**.	We asked (her) **whether (or not) to leave them**.
We asked (her), "Should we come at six or at seven?"	We asked (her) **whether we should come** at six or at seven.	We asked (her) **whether to come** at six or at seven.
QUOTATIONS WITH INFORMATION QUESTIONS		
We asked (her), "How can we get to your house?"	We asked (her) **how we could get** to her house.	We asked (her) **how to get** to her house.
We asked (her), "Where should we park?"	We asked (her) **where we should park**.	We asked (her) **where to park**.

 First, change the quotations to reported speech using noun clauses. Then reduce the noun clauses to infinitive phrases.

> example: He asked, "Where can I park nearby?"
>
> **He asked where he could park nearby.**
>
> **He asked where to park nearby.**

1. She asked, "What can I do about that?"
2. He wondered, "Where should I get off the bus?"
3. They asked, "Should we buy that house?"
4. I wondered, "Should I call him?"
5. They asked the officer, "How do we get to the library from here?"
6. We asked, "When should we leave for the play?"

 First, change each quotation to reported speech using noun clauses. Then reduce the noun clauses to infinitive phrases.

> example: Our teacher warned us, "Do all the homework."
>
> **Our teacher warned us that we should do all the homework.**
>
> **Our teacher warned us to do all the homework.**

1. Our teacher reminded us, "Study for the test!"
2. He told us, "Review the entire chapter."
3. He said, "Go over the information several times."
4. John asked the teacher, "Would you repeat the assignment, please?"
5. Mary asked the teacher, "Could you explain noun clauses again?"
6. Nancy asked the teacher, "How much time should I spend reviewing?"
7. The teacher said, "Don't spend more than two hours."
8. Harry asked, "When should I come for the test?"
9. Susan asked, "What should I bring?"
10. She asked, "May I use a dictionary?"
11. The teacher told her, "Don't bring a dictionary."
12. The teacher added, "Don't worry too much!"

 Much of the education process involves giving commands and asking and answering questions. What are some other typical classroom commands, questions, and answers? Write at least three. After your teacher has checked your paper, exchange it with another classmate. Change your classmate's sentences first to reported speech and then to infinitive phrases.

 **Review.** First read the passage on the next page for meaning. Then complete it by adding appropriate connecting words. Choose from the following: *although, and, as, because, because of, despite, how many, that, when, where.* The first one is done as an example.

OUR PLANET

Although it's often hard to remember, the world _____
we live in is only a fragment in history and in the universe. And

_____ our different countries and languages, we are _all_ part of this
same small fragment of life.

Sometimes it takes an extraordinary event or point of view to remember
_____ there is a larger picture beyond our world. For astronaut
Russell Schweikert, this came in 1969 _____ he looked at the
earth from space in the Apollo IX Lunar Module. Said Schweikert,
"_____ you go around it (the earth) in an hour and a half, you begin
to recognize _____ your identity is with that _whole_ thing. And that
makes a change.

"You look down there, _____ you can't imagine _____
borders and boundaries you cross, again and again and again, _____
you don't even see them. There you are—hundreds of people killing each other
_____ some imaginary line _____ you're not even aware
of _____ you can't see it. From _____ you see it (the
earth from a spacecraft), the thing is a whole, _____ it's so beautiful. You wish _____ you could take one (person) in each hand and
say, 'Look at it from this perspective. What's important?'

"You realize _____ on that small spot, that little blue and white
thing, is everything _____ means anything to you. All of history and
music and poetry and art and birth and love: tears, joy, games. All of it on that
little spot out there _____ you can cover with your thumb."

Using What You've Learned

Only a few months before his death in 1963, John F. Kennedy talked about our
world during a commencement address at American University. Kennedy very
eloquently said:

> We can help make the world safe for diversity. For, in the final analysis,
> our most basic common link is that we all inhabit this small planet. We all
> breathe the same air. We all cherish our children's future. And we are all
> mortal.

In a discussion with your classmates or in a brief composition, describe some of the bonds that you now share with others because of your English studies. What have you learned about other peoples and other cultures? How has this affected you?

Poetry is a beautiful form of expression in any language, but it is often difficult to write. In poetry, every word plays an important role, so each must be chosen with care. Interestingly, it is sometimes easier to write poetry in a second or foreign language. A language learner can bring different perspectives and ideas to poetry and thus produce unusual combinations of words and images. Individually, in small groups, or as a class, use the following directions to help you write short poems. You may choose your own topic or select from the suggestions below.

1. Choose the name of another classmate and write a poem about your classmate.
2. Write a poem about English (grammar, composition, and so on).
3. Write about an emotion or idea: love, friendship, homesickness, curiosity.
4. Write about a favorite place.
5. Write about your home area or country.

GUIDELINES

You need not follow these strictly.

Line 1: Write a sentence of three to five words about your topic.
Line 2: Take a noun from line 1 and describe it.
Line 3: Add movement to the idea in line 2.
Line 4: Pick a word in line 3 and compare it to something (*X is like* . . .).
Line 5: Take the idea in line 4 and describe it or add more action.
Line 6: Take the idea in line 5 and compare it to something (*X is* . . .).
Line 7: Make the idea in line 6 either very big or very small.
Line 8: Describe the idea in line 7.
Lines 9 to 10: Make a final statement (your opinion, and so on).

A SMALLER WORLD

We came from so many places,
Gentle, crowded, warm, noisy, icy places,
Excited travelers, nervous and naive,
Like newborns entering a new world.
Babbling and blundering our way to English,
Like babies learning to talk.
Mountains of words, ideas, customs to climb,
A struggle for understanding.
Yet our world has become smaller
Because we have known each other.

The earth rising above the moon's horizon

Class poem written by students from Mexico, Brazil, Japan, Colombia, Kuwait, Honduras, Switzerland, and Indonesia

Use of Noun Clauses

Noun clauses are frequently tested on standardized English proficiency exams. Review these commonly tested structures and check your understanding by completing the sample items below.

Remember that . . .

- In reported speech, you must be consistent in changes in verb tenses, modal auxiliaries, pronouns, and adverbials.
- In questions used as noun clauses, the subject comes before the verb.
- You *tell someone something,* but you *say something to someone.*

Part 1: Circle the correct completion for the following.

example: I don't know _____ unhappy with his work schedule.
      a. why is John
      b. why does John
      c. why John is
      d. is John

1. The instructor _____ that the test would cover the last four chapters of the book.
      a. said the class
      b. told
      c. told to the class
      d. said to the class

2. Our new neighbors wanted to know _____.
      a. where the nearest store had been
      b. where the nearest store was
      c. where was the nearest store
      d. where is the nearest store

3. We were wondering how _____ to the concert on time.
      a. could we get
      b. are we going to get
      c. we could get
      d. can we get

Part 2: Circle the letter below the underlined word(s) containing an error.

example: <u>Overseas</u> travelers frequently experience culture shock <u>whether</u>
      A   B
<u>or not</u> <u>have they</u> already done <u>a good deal</u> of traveling.
      C   D

1. Could you please <u>tell</u> <u>me</u> how many countries <u>are</u> there in the
                 A B   C
   United Nations <u>at this time</u>?
                        D

2. Educators <u>often</u> debate <u>whether or not</u> is rote memorization a
                    A   B   C
   valuable way <u>of learning</u>.
                  D

3. Margaret Mead, <u>the</u> <u>noted</u> anthropologist, once <u>told</u> that humanity's
                      A B   C
   greatest attributes <u>are</u> ingenuity, imagination, and faith.
                        D

TOPIC **four**

Review: Chapters Nine to Twelve

Review. Complete the following exercise with appropriate past tense forms—active or passive voice—of the verbs in parentheses. The first one is done as an example.

TURNING POINTS IN HUMAN HISTORY

1. A form of writing <u>was developed</u> by the Sumerians during the fourth
                               (develop)
   century B.C.

2. The Egyptian pyramids _____ over 4,000 years ago.
                                     (build)

3. By about 100 B.C., the Chinese _____ an Imperial University,
                                       (build)
   _____ irrigation methods and water clocks, and
   (develop)
   _____ sundials and seismographs.
   (invent)

4. By about 300 A.D., the Mayans _____ the "Long Count," a
                                     (use)
   complex calendar that _____ extremely accurate. The Mayans
                             (be)
   _____ a complex arithmetic and _____ the first
   (develop / also)   (be)
   humans to use a symbol for zero.

5. In 1456, Johannes Gutenberg and his associates _____ the first
(print)

book, the Latin Bible, which _____ of 643 leaves of paper.
(compose)

6. Around 1590, William Shakespeare _____ in London and
(arrive)

_____ writing his first plays, the three parts of *Henry VI*.
(begin)

7. During the 1770s, James Watt _____ the steam engine, which
(develop)

_____ the beginning of the Industrial Revolution.
(signal)

8. Not long before his death in 1827, Ludwig van Beethoven

_____ his Ninth Symphony, which _____ the first
(compose)   (be)

symphony to use singers and a chorus. At that time, Beethoven

_____ completely deaf.
(become / already)

9. The daguerreotype photography process _____ in 1837 by Louis
(invent)

Daguerre. While Daguerre _____ his process, William Talbot
(perfect)

_____ the process of making negatives. In 1839, it
(develop)

_____ possible to make multiple copies of a picture.
(become)

10. In 1872, Yellowstone National Park _____. It _____
(found)   (be)

the first of its kind in the world and _____ an example for
(set)

countries everywhere to follow.

11. Orville and Wilbur Wright _____ the first sustained flight of a
(make)

powered aircraft in 1903. Before then, Otto Lilienthal _____
(make / already)

many flights in gliders.

12. The special theory of relativity _____ by Einstein in 1905.
(publish)

13. Alexander Fleming _____ the life-saving properties of penicillin
(discover)

in 1928.

14. On July 21, 1969, Neil Armstrong _____ the first human to walk
(become)

on the surface of the moon. Numerous satellites _____ before
(launch)

then, and astronauts _____ the moon, but no one
(orbit)

_____ the surface until that day.
(touch / ever)

Review. Complete the following exercise with appropriate present and future forms—active or passive voice—of the verbs in parentheses. The first two items are done as examples.

THE STATE OF OUR EARTH

How __is__ our earth __doing__ these days? Many critics
   1 (be)   2 (do)

_____ that we _____ a disaster of horrible proportions.
   3 (say)   4 (approach / fast)

Others _____ that while we _____ by very serious
   5 (claim)   6 (face)

problems, numerous healthy signs _____.
   7 (exist)

What _____ some of the worst crises that _____ us?
   8 (be)   9 (face)

- All three major sources of food—ocean fisheries, rangelands, and

  croplands—_____ in trouble. Much of our existing land
     10 (be)

  _____ or _____.
     11 (overgraze)   12 (overfarm)

- World per capita grain production _____, yet worldwide
     13 (fall)

  demand for it _____, in large part because of the demand for
     14 (increase)

  beef. Seven pounds of grain _____ to add one pound to a steer.
     15 (need)

- Of all 9,600 species of birds, 6,500 _____ in decline, and 1,000
     16 (be)

  of these _____ by extinction.
     17 (threaten)

- Sixty to seventy percent of the coral reef systems in Southeast Asia

  _____ from dynamite fishing, coral mining, and coastal
     18 (degrade)

  development.

- Hundreds of acres of tropical rainforest _____ each day.
     19 (cut)

  What _____ some of the positive signs? Consider the following:
     20 (be)

- Child mortality _____ worldwide.
     21 (drop / currently)

- Production of CFCs, which _____ holes in the ozone layer,
     22 (create)

  _____.
     23 (decrease)

- Recycled paper _____ in over 60 percent of the U.S. paper
     24 (use)

  output.

- Use of wind power _____, especially in Europe.

25 (rise / rapidly)

- The world _____ three times more bicycles than cars.

26 (produce)

- In the United States, the number of commuters who _____ to

27 (bicycle)
  work _____ during the last 7 to 8 years. (It's now over 4 million.)

28 (double)

- New genetic techniques _____ it possible to create high-yield,

29 (make / soon)
  drought- and insect-resistant plants of all types.

- Robots _____ humans in a variety of jobs that _____

30 (replace / now) 31 (be / traditionally)
  dangerous or hazardous to health.

- Computer networks _____ over 30 million people worldwide,

32 (link / currently)
  and in theory, through the use of fiber optics, one-half of the world

  _____ able to talk directly with the other half!

33 (be / someday)

Review. Complete the following exercise with appropriate active or passive forms of the verbs in parentheses. In some cases, you will need to add modal auxiliaries. Some items may have more than one correct answer. The first one is done as an example.

LIFE ON EARTH

Life on earth ___developed___ because the conditions _____

1 (develop) 2 (be)
suitable for it. If the earth _____ smaller or colder, for example, life

3 (be)
_____ different forms. If the conditions _____ suitable,

4 (have) 5 (not be)
no living organisms _____ on earth at all.

6 (develop)

The simplest living creatures _____ of a single living unit, the

7 (consist)
cell. More complex creatures _____ up of hundreds and even mil-

8 (make)
lions of cells. However, all living organisms _____ certain charac-

9 (share)
teristics. These _____ reproduction, response, growth, and use of

10 (include)
energy. Plants and animals _____ different only in the way that the

11 (be)
basic activities of life _____ out by each organism.

12 (carry)

Of all the creatures alive on earth, humans _____ the greatest

13 (have)
impact. The impact of humans _____ because we _____

14 (come / often) 15 (be)

able to think. The power to think _____ us ways both to create and
16 (give)
to destroy.

In the past, humans _____ less impact, especially on the
17 (have)
environment. Because early humans _____ from place to place,
18 (move)
their movement _____ nature a chance to recover. For example,
19 (give)
even though humans _____ trees, forests _____ to
20 (cut)   21 (return / soon)
their former size after the humans _____ on.
22 (move)
Today, nature _____ a chance to recover. Our demands on the
23 (give / seldom)
earth _____ steadily. All human activity _____ to require
24 (increase)   25 (seem)
more and more land and more and more resources. Humans _____
26 (share)
this earth with millions of other animals and plants, yet we _____
27 (act / often)
without ever thinking about our impact on our world.

 **Review.**   Complete the following exercise with *a, an, the,* or *X* to indicate that no
article is necessary. The first item is done as an example.

THE MASS MOVEMENT OF PEOPLES

Across _the_ globe, _____ people are moving to _____ degree never before
    1   2   3
seen in _____ history of _____ world. Today, at least _____ 100 million people
        4   5   6
live outside of _____ country where they were born. This includes approxi-
              7
mately 30 million who have moved to _____ America or _____ Western Europe
                                    8   9
since _____ 1980. In fact, _____ 1980s were _____ years of _____ incredible
     10   11   12   13
movement and _____ change _____ worldwide.
            14   15

_____ largest migrations of _____ people have not been from _____ country
16   17   18
to _____ country, however. Most migration has been from _____ rural to _____
  19   20   21
urban areas. Each year 20 million to 30 million people move from _____
                                                          22
countryside to _____ urban area. And _____ most of this movement is in _____
             23   24   25
Third World. By _____ year 2000, 17 of _____ world's 20 largest cities will be
              26   27
in _____ third-world countries. _____ Mexico City is expected to grow to over
  28   29
25 million people, and São Paulo to over 22 million. _____ New York, which
                                              30

was _____ biggest city in _____ world in _____ 1950, will be _____ number 5
       31   32   33   34
in 2000, but _____ London (number 2 in 1950) and Paris (number 4 in 1950)
              35
won't even be in _____ top largest cities in _____ world in 2000.
                  36   37

    In _____ past, most migrants were _____ men. Today, however, almost
            38   39
_____ half are _____ women or _____ young girls, looking for _____ work and
  40   41   42   43
_____ ways to send _____ money back _____ home.
  44   45   46

Adapted from "Focus on Change," *U.S. News and World Report,* 1994

Review. Choose the correct forms of the words in parentheses. An *X* indicates that no word is necessary. The first one is done as an example.

LIVING TOGETHER ON A SMALL PLANET

    The environment is (*X* / (the)) world (that / who) all living things share. It
                                    1   2
is what is—air, fire, wind, water, life, and sometimes (the / *X*) culture. The
                                                          3
environment consists of all the things that act and (is / are) acted upon. Living
                                                       4
creatures (is / are) born into the environment and (are / were) part of it too.
           5   6
Yet there is (no / none) creature (who / whom) perceives all of what is and
               7   8
what happens. A dog perceives things (that / what) we can't, and we perceive
                                         9
and understand (much / many) things beyond (its / it's) world. For a dog, a
                  10   11
book isn't much different from a stick, (while / on the other hand) for us, one
                                           12
stick is pretty much like every other stick. There is no world (that / who) is
                                                                  13
experienced (by / from) all living creatures. (Despite / Although) we all live in
              14   15
the same environment, we create many worlds.

    We actually know very (little / few) of the world, even of what (does
                             16
surround / surrounds) us every day. It is worth (to take / taking) the time
17   18
(to think / thinking) of the variety of ways in (that / which) the environment
 19   20
could be structured and (to discover / discovering) how (*X* / do) different
                           21   22
living things actually structure it. We are all collections of atoms, specks in
(*X* / the) universe, just the right size in our own worlds, giants to fleas,
 23
midgets to whales. Our view of the world is only one of (many / much). It
                                                          24

enriches (our / us) understanding of ourselves to move away from familiar
                        25
worlds and attempt to understand the experience of others . . . . The respect

for life we can (gain / to gain) from these efforts (might / might have) in
                              26   27
some small way help us work toward (preserving / to preserve) the world
                                                            28
we share.

Adapted from Judith and Herbert Kohl, The View from the Oak

 **exercise 6**   **Review.**   Work in pairs and review a variety of questions and statements. Each pair can choose a set of charts: charts 1A and 1B, charts 2A and 2B, or charts 3A and 3B. In your pairs, take turns asking and answering questions in order to complete the following charts. Do not look at each other's charts.

After you have completed your set of charts, join with another pair with different charts. Take turns telling some of the information you learned from the charts.

The State of the Earth
Chart 1A: Selected Countries of the World

Country		Czech Republic	Egypt		
Capital	Santiago			Libreville	Seoul
Population (1992)	13.5 million			1.2 million	
Per capita GDP* (1990)		$7,700			$6,300
Primary products		machinery, oil products, iron and steel, wheat, sugar beets, potatoes, rye, corn	textiles, chemicals, petrochemicals, food processing, cotton, rice, beans, fruit, grains		electronics, ships, textiles, clothing, motor vehicles, rice, barley, vegetables, wheat
Literacy rate	92%			70%	
*GDP gross domestic product					

The State of the Earth
Chart 1B: Selected Countries of the World

Country	Chile			Gabon	South Korea
Capital		Prague	Cairo		
Population (1992)		10.5 million	56.5 million		44.2 million
Per capita GDP* (1990)	$2,200		$720	$4,400	
Primary products	fishing, wood products, iron, steel, grain, onions, beans, potatoes			oil products, cocoa, coffee, rice, peanuts, palm products, cassava, bananas	
Literacy rate		99%	44%		96%

*GDP gross domestic product

The State of the Earth
Chart 2A: Endangered Species

Common name	blue whale	giant panda			tiger
Location	polar seas		Japan	Indonesia	
Description		a bearlike mammal, a member of the raccoon family, growing 4–5 feet tall and weighing up to 250 pounds	one of the oldest and largest on earth, a magnificent long-necked marsh bird up to 5 feet tall		
Diet				herbivorous, browsing on low shrubs and trees in grasslands	carnivorous, eating birds, deer, cattle, and reptiles
Cause of endangerment	overhunting	loss of habitat	hunting, loss of habitat		
Current status			fully protected today, its population is slowly increasing, 33% of which is in zoos	currently protected, although only about 50 remain and are still threatened by poachers	

The State of the Earth
Chart 2B: Endangered Species

Common name			Japanese crane	Javanese rhinoceros	
Location		China			Asia
Description	largest animal, up to 90 feet in length and 125 tons in weight			massive horned and hoofed mammal weighing up to 7,000 pounds (3.5 tons)	large, powerful, nonclimbing striped cat up to 650 pounds in weight and 10–13 feet in length
Diet	krill (a small shrimp-like saltwater animal)	vegetarian (preferring bamboo) although they may eat fish or small rodents	omnivorous, eating wild fruit, seeds, water plants, insects, frogs, and reptiles		
Cause of endangerment				hunting	loss of habitat, trophy hunting
Current status	currently protected, although possibly too late	currently protected in Sichuan, China, where fewer than 1,000 remain			currently protected in India, where the tiger population is increasing slowly

The State of the Earth
Chart 3A: International Organizations

Organization		International Bank for Reconstruction and Development (The World Bank)	International Red Cross	United Nations Children's Fund (UNICEF)	
Headquarters	Rome, Italy			New York, New York, U.S.A.	Geneva, Switzerland
Year founded			1863		1948
Purpose	to increase production from farms, forests, and fisheries; improve distribution and nutrition in rural areas	to provide loans and technical assistance for economic development projects in developing countries			to collect and share information in medical and scientific areas; to promote international standards for drugs and vaccines

The State of the Earth Chart 3B: International Organizations				
Organization	Food and Agricultural Organization (FAO)				World Health Organization
Headquarters		Washington, D.C., U.S.A.	Geneva, Switzerland		
Year founded	1943	1944		1946	
Purpose			to lessen human suffering through disaster relief and neutral aid to war victims	to give aid and development assistance to pro-grams for children and mothers in developing countries	

focus on testing

Review of Problem Areas: Chapters Nine to Twelve

A variety of problem areas are included in this test. Check your understanding by completing the sample items below.

Part 1: Circle the correct completion for the following.

example: John said that when he _____ satisfied with his work, he would submit the project.
- **a.** will be
- **b.** is
- **c.** would be
- **d.** was ⟵(circled)

1. The doctor urged _____ a vacation.
   - **a.** her patient take
   - **b.** her patient taking
   - **c.** to take
   - **d.** her patient to take

2. Could you tell me how long _____ to get there by bus?
   - **a.** it should take
   - **b.** should it take
   - **c.** does it take
   - **d.** it should have take

3. If she had known the consequences, she _____ that.
   a. probably would not do
   b. would not do probably
   c. would probably not have done
   d. would not have probably done

4. _____ problems with the computer, we weren't able to complete the report on time.
   a. Because
   b. Due to
   c. Although
   d. Since

5. It was _____ that I fell asleep before the end.
   a. so boring movie
   b. such boring movie
   c. such boring a movie
   d. such a boring movie

Part 2: Circle the letter below the underlined word(s) containing an error.

example: Many <u>individuals</u> experience culture shock <u>whether or not they</u>
                   A   B

            <u>fluently speak</u> the language of the country <u>where do they live.</u>
            C   Ⓓ

1. Winston Churchill <u>says</u> that <u>although</u> he <u>was always</u> ready to learn,
                    A   B   C

    he <u>was not</u> always ready to be taught.
          D

2. The Great Pyramid in Egypt, <u>that</u> has stood for over four <u>thousand</u>
                            A   B

    years, <u>was built</u> without use of <u>the wheel.</u>
            C   D

3. Worldwide demand for grain <u>has increased</u> <u>dramatically,</u> in large
                                  A   B

    part <u>because</u> the demand for <u>more</u> beef production.
            C   D

4. If inventors <u>such as</u> James Watt <u>didn't develop</u> engines, the Indus-
                  A   B

    trial Revolution <u>could</u> never <u>have occurred.</u>
                 C   D

5. Flash floods have <u>so</u> tremendous <u>carrying</u> power <u>that</u> <u>even</u> a small
                     A   B   C D

    flood can move rocks the size of cars.

Appendixes

Spelling Rules

Spelling Rules for *-s, -ed, -er, -est,* and *-ing* Endings

This chart summarizes the basic spelling rules for endings with verbs, nouns, adjectives, and adverbs.

rule	word	-s	-ed	-er	-est	-ing
For most words, simply add *-s, -ed, -er, -est,* or *-ing* without making any other changes.	clean cool	cleans cools	cleaned cooled	cleaner cooler	cleanest coolest	cleaning cooling

Spelling changes occur with the following.

rule	word	-s	-ed	-er	-est	-ing
For words ending in a consonant + *y,* change the *y* to *i* before adding *-s, -ed, -er,* or *-est.* Do *not* change or drop the *y* before adding *-ing.*	carry happy lonely study worry	carries studies worries	carried studied worried	carrier happier lonelier worrier	happiest loneliest	 carrying studying worrying
For most words ending in *e,* drop the *e* before adding *-ed, -er, -est,* or *-ing.* *Exceptions:*	dance late nice save write agree canoe		danced saved	dancer later nicer saver writer	latest nicest	dancing saving writing agreeing canoeing
For many words ending in one vowel and one consonant, double the final consonant before adding *-ed, -er, -est,* or *-ing.* These include one syllable words and words with stress on the final syllable.	begin hot mad plan occur refer run shop win		 planned occurred referred shopped	beginner hotter madder planner runner shopper winner	hottest maddest	beginning planning occurring referring running shopping winning

rule	word	-s	-ed	-er	-est	-ing
In words ending in one vowel and one consonant, do *not* double the final consonant if the last syllable is not stressed.	enter happen open travel visit		entered happened opened traveled visited	opener traveler		entering happening opening traveling visiting
Exceptions: including words ending in *w, x,* or *y*	bus fix play sew	buses	bused fixed played sewed	fixer player sewer		busing fixing playing sewing
For most words ending in *f* or *lf,* change the *f* to *v* and add *-es.*	half loaf shelf	halves loaves shelves	halved shelved	shelver		halving shelving
Exceptions:	belief chief proof roof safe	beliefs chiefs proofs roofs safes				
For words ending in *ch, sh, s, x, z,* and sometimes *o,* add *-es.*	church wash class fix quiz tomato zero	churches washes classes fixes quizzes tomatoes zeroes				
Exceptions:	dynamo ghetto monarch piano portfolio radio studio	dynamos ghettos monarchs pianos portfolios radios studios				

Irregular Noun Plurals

person	people	foot	feet	deer	deer	series	series
child	children	tooth	teeth	fish	fish	species	species
man	men			goose	geese		
woman	women			ox	oxen		

Nouns with Foreign Origins

-is	changes to -es	-on or -um	changes to -a
analysis	analyses	bacterium	bacteria
basis	bases	criterion	criteria
crisis	crises	curriculum	curricula
hypothesis	hypotheses	datum	data
oasis	oases	medium	media
parenthesis	parentheses	memorandum	memoranda
synthesis	syntheses	phenomenon	phenomena
thesis	theses		

-us	changes to -i	other	
cactus	cacti or cactuses	formula	formulae or formulas
nucleus	nuclei		
radius	radii	appendix	appendices or appendixes
stimulus	stimuli		
syllabus	syllabi or syllabuses	index	indices or indexes

Nouns with No Singular Form

binoculars	pajamas	police	shears	scissors
clothes	pants	premises	shorts	tongs
glasses	pliers	scales	slacks	tweezers

Irregular Verbs

simple form	past	past participle
arise	arose	arisen
awake	awoke/awaked	awaked/awoken
be	was/were	been
bear	bore	borne/born
beat	beat	beat
become	became	become
begin	began	begun
bend	bent	bent
bet	bet	bet
bite	bit	bitten
bleed	bled	bled
blow	blew	blown
break	broke	broken
breed	bred	bred
bring	brought	brought
broadcast	broadcast	broadcast
build	built	built
burst	burst	burst
buy	bought	bought

simple form	past	past participle
cast	cast	cast
catch	caught	caught
choose	chose	chosen
cling	clung	clung
come	came	come
cost	cost	cost
creep	crept	crept
cut	cut	cut
deal	dealt	dealt
dig	dug	dug
do	did	done
draw	drew	drawn
drink	drank	drunk
drive	drove	driven
eat	ate	eaten
fall	fell	fallen
feed	fed	fed
feel	felt	felt
fight	fought	fought
find	found	found
flee	fled	fled
fly	flew	flown
forbid	forbade	forbidden
forget	forgot	forgotten
forsake	forsook	forsaken
freeze	froze	frozen
get	got	got/gotten
give	gave	given
go	went	gone
grind	ground	ground
grow	grew	grown
hang	hung/hanged	hung/hanged
have	had	had
hear	heard	heard
hide	hid	hidden
hit	hit	hit
hold	held	held
hurt	hurt	hurt
keep	kept	kept
know	knew	known
lay	laid	laid
lead	led	led
leap	leapt	leapt
leave	left	left
lend	lent	lent
let	let	let

simple form	past	past participle
lie	lay	lain
light	lit/lighted	lit/lighted
lose	lost	lost
make	made	made
mean	meant	meant
meet	met	met
overcome	overcame	overcome
pay	paid	paid
prove	proved	proved/proven*
put	put	put
quit	quit	quit
read	read	read
ride	rode	ridden
ring	rang	rung
rise	rose	risen
run	ran	run
say	said	said
see	saw	seen
seek	sought	sought
sell	sold	sold
send	sent	sent
set	set	set
shake	shook	shaken
shoot	shot	shot
show	showed	showed/shown*
shut	shut	shut
sing	sang	sung
sink	sank	sunk
sit	sat	sat
sleep	slept	slept
slide	slid	slid
slit	slit	slit
speak	spoke	spoken
spend	spent	spent
spin	spun	spun
split	split	split
spread	spread	spread
spring	sprang	sprung
stand	stood	stood
steal	stole	stolen
stick	stuck	stuck
sting	stung	stung
strike	struck	struck/stricken*
strive	strove	striven

*These participles are most often used with the passive voice.

simple form	past	past participle
swear	swore	sworn
sweep	swept	swept
swim	swam	swum
swing	swung	swung
take	took	taken
teach	taught	taught
tear	tore	torn
tell	told	told
think	thought	thought
throw	threw	thrown
thrust	thrust	thrust
understand	understood	understood
upset	upset	upset
wake	woke/waked	woken/waked
wear	wore	worn
weave	wove	woven
wind	wound	wound
withdraw	withdrew	withdrawn
write	wrote	written

APPENDIX **two**

Formation of Statements and Questions

The Simple Present and Past Tenses and *have* as a Main Verb*

	question word	auxiliary verb	subject	auxiliary verb (and negative)		main verb	auxiliary verb	pronoun
Affirmative Statements			You (I, We, They)			study.		
			Ted (He, She, It)			studies.		
			She (We, They, etc.)			studied.		
Negative Statements			You	don't	(didn't)	study.		
			Ted	doesn't	(didn't)	study.		
Tag Questions			You			study,	don't	you?
			You	don't		study,	do	you?
			Ted			studies,	doesn't	he?
			Ted	doesn't		study,	does	he?
Yes/No Questions		Do(n't)	you			study?		
		Does(n't)	Ted			study?		
		Did(n't)	she			study?		
Short Responses		Yes,	I	do (did).				
		No,	I	don't (didn't).				
		Yes,	he	does (did).				
		No,	he	doesn't (didn't).				
Information Questions	Where	do	you			study?		
	When	does	Ted			study?		
	Who					studied?		

Have as a main verb forms statements and questions in the same way as other simple present and past tense verbs.

464

Mosaic One • Grammar

The Continuous and Perfect Tenses, the Modal Auxiliaries, and *be* as a Main Verb*

	question word	auxiliary verb	subject	auxiliary verb (and negative)	main verb	auxiliary verb	pronoun
Affirmative and Negative Statements			Ted	is (was) (not)	studying.		
			Ted	should (may, etc.) (not)	study.		
			Ted	has (had) (not)	studied.		
Tag Questions			Ted	is	studying,	isn't	he?
			Ted	isn't	studying,	is	he?
			Ted	should	study,	shouldn't	he?
			Ted	shouldn't	study,	should	he?
			Ted	has	studied,	hasn't	he?
			Ted	hasn't	studied,	has	he?
Yes/No Questions		Is(n't)	Ted		studying?		
		Should(n't)	Ted		study?		
		Has(n't)	Ted		studied?		
Short Responses		Yes,	he is.	No, he isn't.			
		Yes,	he should.	No, he shouldn't.			
		Yes,	he has.	No, he hasn't.			
Information Questions	Where	is	Ted		studying?		
	What	should	Ted		study?		
	How long	has	Ted		studied?		
	Who			is	studying?		

Be as a main verb forms statements and questions in the same way as the auxiliary *be* does.

Summary of Modal Auxiliaries and Related Structures

Present/Future Time Frame

modal auxiliary	function	examples
can	ability	**Can** you touch your toes without bending your knees?
	informal request	**Can** you teach me to swim?
could	request	**Could** I make an appointment with Dr. Horiuchi?
	possibility	Perhaps Noriko **could** take you to the dentist.
may	request	**May** I leave now?
	permission	Yes, you **may**.
	possibility	Sulaiman **may** be sick.
might	possibility	He **might** have the flu.
must	probability	He **must** be at the doctor's because he isn't at home.
	need	You **must** take this medicine on an empty stomach.
must not	strong need not to do something	You **must not** drive while you are taking this medicine.
ought to	advice	She **ought to** get more rest.
	expectation	The doctor **ought to** be here soon.
shall	request	**Shall** I get a bandage?
	intention	We **shall** probably go to the hospital later today.
should	advice	He **should** give up smoking.
	expectation	The swelling **should** go down in a few hours.
will	intention	I **will** get more exercise from now on!
would	request	**Would** you get me a bandage, please? **Would** you mind getting me a bandage?
	preference	**Would** you like soda pop? I **would rather** have juice than soda pop.
be able to	ability	**Are** you **able to** swim three miles?
had better	advice	You **had better** not swim so soon after lunch.
have to (have got to)	need	I **have to (have got to)** lose weight.
don't/doesn't have to	lack of need	We **don't have to** get X rays.

Past Time Frame

modal auxiliary	function	examples
could	ability	I **could** not swim until last year.
could have	possibility	I **could have** taken lessons sooner.
may have	possibility	They **may** already **have** gone to the hospital.
might have	possibility	Juan **might have** injured his back when he fell.
must have	probability	He **must have** been in a lot of pain.
ought to have	advice not taken	He **ought to have** been more careful.
	expectation	The doctor **ought to have** called us by now.
should have	advice not taken	**Should** we **have** waited for help?
	expectation	Someone **should have** arrived by now.
would	habits	When I was younger, I **would** always faint at the sight of blood.
would have	preference	I **would have liked** to visit her. She **would rather** not **have** visited the hospital.
	intention not completed	Under other circumstances, **would** you **have** had that operation?
be able to	ability	Nadia was **able to** run two miles.
didn't have to	lack of need	We **didn't have to** practice on Monday because of the rain.
had to	need	We **had to** practice twice as long yesterday because we missed practice on Monday.
used to	habits	We **used to** eat a lot of sugar, but we don't anymore.

the with Proper Nouns

with *the*		without *the*	
The is used when the class of noun (continent, country, etc.) comes before the name: *the* + class + *of* + name.	the continent of Asia the United States of America the U.S.A.	*The* is not used with names of planets, continents, countries, states, provinces, cities, and streets.	Mars Africa Antarctica Russia Ohio Quebec Austin State Street
The is used with most names of regions. *Exceptions:*	the West the Midwest the equator New England southern (northern, etc.) Ontario	*Exceptions:*	(the) earth the world the Netherlands the Sudan the Hague the Champs-Élysées
The is used with plural islands, lakes, and mountains.	the Hawaiian Islands the Great Lakes the Alps	*The* is not used with singular islands, lakes, and mountains.	Oahu Fiji Lake Superior Mt. Whitney Pikes Peak
The is used with oceans, seas, rivers, canals, deserts, jungles, forests, and bridges.*	the Pacific Ocean the Persian Gulf the Mississippi River the Suez Canal the Sahara Desert the Black Forest the Golden Gate Bridge	*Exceptions:*	the Isle of Wight the Great Salt Lake the Matterhorn (and other mountains with German names that are used in English)
The is generally used when the word *college, university,* or *school* comes before the name: *the* + . . . + *of* + name.	the University of California the Rhode Island School of Design	*The* is not used when the name of a college or university comes before the word *college* or *university.* *Exception:*	Boston University Amherst College the Sorbonne

*The class name is often omitted with well-known oceans, deserts, and rivers: *the Atlantic, the Nile.*

with *the*		without *the*	
The is used with adjectives of nationality and other adjectives that function as nouns.	the Germans the Japanese the rich the poor the hungry the strong	*The* is not used with names of languages. *Note: The* is used with the word *language: the German language.*	German Japanese
The is used in dates when the number comes before the month.	the twenty-eighth of March	*The* is not used in dates when the month begins the phrase.	March 28
The is used with decades, centuries, and eras.	the 1990s the 1800s the Dark Ages	*The* is not used with specific years.	1951 1890
The is used with names of museums and libraries.	the Museum of Modern Art the Chicago Public Library		

Summary of Gerunds and Infinitives

Verbs Often Followed by Gerunds

admit	She **admitted** stealing the money.
anticipate	We **anticipate** arriving late.
appreciate	I really **appreciated** getting your card.
avoid	She **avoids** stepping on cracks—a superstition.
be worth	I am sure it **is** worth waiting.
can(not) help	He **can't help** getting upset about that.
consider	Have you **considered** moving?
delay	They **delayed** starting the game because of the rain.
deny	He **denied** speeding.
dislike	He really **dislikes** getting up early.
dread	She **dreads** going to the dentist.
enjoy	We always **enjoy** traveling.
escape	We narrowly **escaped** hitting the other car.
finish	Have you **finished** writing that paper?
forgive	I can **forgive** his cheating, but I can't **forgive** his lying.
imagine	Can you **imagine** living in Bogotá?
involve	This job **involves** meeting a lot of people.
keep (on)	**Keep on** working until I tell you to stop.
mention	Did she **mention** quitting her job?
miss	I **miss** hearing your voice.
postpone	Will they **postpone** calling a meeting?
practice	A good tennis player has to **practice** serving.
recommend	I **recommend** taking some aspirin.
regret	I **regret** saying that.
risk	She **risked** losing all her money in that deal.
spend (time)	Do you **spend** much **time** doing your homework?
suggest	They **suggested** having a picnic.
tolerate	I can't **tolerate** listening to rock music.
understand	Do you **understand** his not calling?

Verbs Often Followed by Infinitives

subject + verb + infinitive

afford	We can't **afford** to go.
agree	They **agreed** to help.
appear	She **appeared** to be calm, but she was quite nervous.
be	We **were** to do the homework in Chapter 3.
be able	**Were** you **able** to finish the work?
be supposed	You **were supposed** to do it yesterday.
care	I don't **care** to go.
decide	He **decided** to stay.
deserve	She **deserves** to get a high grade.
fail	They **failed** to make the announcement.
forget	I **forgot** to buy eggs.
happen	Did he **happen** to stop by?
have	I **have** to leave.
hesitate	Don't **hesitate** to call!
hope	We **hope** to visit Rome next spring.
intend	I **intend** to stop there for several days.
know how	Do you **know how** to play squash?
learn	She is **learning** to play tennis.
manage	Somehow he **managed** to finish the race.
offer	They **offered** to help us.
plan	We **planned** to leave earlier.
prepare	They **prepared** to get on board the plane.
pretend	He **pretended** not to notice us.
refuse	I **refuse** to get up at 5:00 A.M.!
seem	He **seems** to be upset.
tend	She **tends** to forget things.
threaten	The employee **threatened** to quit.
volunteer	Several people **volunteered** to help us.
wait	She **waited** for the letter carrier to come.
wish	We **wished** to go, but we couldn't.

ask	We **asked** to come. We **asked** them to come.
beg	He **begged** to go. He **begged** us to go.
dare	I **dared** to go. I **dared** him to go.
expect	I **expect** to finish soon. I **expect** them to finish soon.
need	I **need** to go. I **need** you to go.
promise	She **promised** to help. She **promised** her mother to help.
want	They **want** to leave. They **want** us to leave.
would like	He **would like** to stay. He **would like** you to stay.
use	They **used** to live there. (habitual past) They **used** a hammer to fix the table. (method)

advise*	The doctor **advised** me to rest.
allow*	He won't **allow** you to swim.
cause*	The accident **caused** me to faint.
convince	She **convinced** us to try again.
encourage*	I **encourage** you to study languages.
force	The hijacker **forced** them to land the plane.
get	He **got** them to pay ransom.
hire	We **hired** you to do the job.
invite	They **invited** us to come.
order	I **am ordering** you to stop!
permit*	Will they **permit** us to camp here?
persuade	Perhaps we can **persuade** them to let us go.
remind	Did you **remind** her to buy milk?
require	The school **required** us to wear uniforms.
teach*	He **taught** me to play tennis.
tell	I **told** him not to come.
urge	We **urge** you to change your mind.
warn	I **am warning** you to stop!

*These verbs are followed by gerunds if no noun or pronoun object is used after the main verb.

verb + gerund or infinitive (*same meaning*)

begin	She **began** to work (working) on the project.
can't bear	I **can't bear** to see (seeing) her work so much.
can't stand	She **can't stand** to stay (staying) alone at night.
continue	They'll **continue** to practice (practicing) several days more.
hate	He **hates** to play (playing) golf.
like	I **like** to play (playing) tennis.
love	Mary **loves** to read (reading) novels.
neglect	We **neglected** to tell (telling) her about that.
prefer	I **prefer** to go (going) alone.
start	We **started** to worry (worrying) about the situation.

verb + gerund or infinitive (*different meanings*)

mean	I **meant** to finish the project sooner. This **means** delaying the project.
quit (stop)	He **quit (stopped)** to take a long break. We **quit (stopped)** taking breaks in order to leave work earlier.
remember	Did you **remember** to tell her? I **remember** telling her about it, but she forgot.
try	We **tried** to call you, but the phone was out of order. I **tried** calling, and then I decided to write you a note.

(continued from page ii)

Index

F

few, 194, 196, 197
Focus on Testing
  review of problem areas, 144,
    307, 454
  types of standardized tests, 62
  use of adjective clauses and
    phrases, 343
  use of adverb clauses and
    phrases, 418
  use of conditional and sub-
    junctive forms, 371
  use of modal auxiliaries, 139
  use of noun clauses, 444
  use of passive voice, 177
  use of singular and plural forms,
    203
  use of verb forms, 261
  use of verbs, 101
for, 8, 56, 58, 96, 266, 269, 270,
  380
fragments, 299

G

gerunds
  forms and functions of, 219
  and parallel structures, 224, 261
  and phrases of concession, 386
  following prepositions, 221, 222,
    261
  used to +, 88n
  verbs followed by, 231, 237,
    239n, 245, 248
  would you mind +, 113
get, 253, 254, 256
going to, 83, 90

H

had better (not), 126
had/have to, 121, 124, 125
have, 34, 53, 78, 162, 253
hope versus *wish,* 348, 371
how (long / many times / often),
  36, 37, 46, 56, 77, 194, 195,
  227, 440
however, 270, 386

I

if, 266, 278, 288, 296, 354, 364,
  365, 434
*in (fact / addition / contrast /
  order to / spite of),* 270, 378,
  388, 386

infinitives
  following adjectives, adverbs,
    and nouns, 227
  causative verbs followed by,
    254
  forms and functions of, 224
  modals +, 116
  as principal part, 19
  to used in, 222
  verbs followed by, 231, 238,
    245, 248
it, anticipatory, 158

J

just, 71, 78, 94, 196, 282

L

least, 395, 396
less (. . . than), 395, 396, 406
little, 193, 195, 196, 197
lots (of), 193

M

many, 193, 194, 197, 406n
may (not)
  as modal auxiliary, 19, 358,
    378
  in passive voice, 171
  requesting permission, 114
  expressing possibility, 132
  and reported speech, 425, 439
might (not)
  in imaginary conditions, 354
  as modal auxiliary, 19, 353, 358,
    378
  in passive voice, 171
  expressing ability, 132
  in reported speech, 425, 429
modal auxiliaries
  requesting action, permission,
    113, 114
  and adverb clauses of time,
    condition, 296, 295
  in clauses with *if, so that,* 371,
    378, 418
  expressing expectation, prefer-
    ence, need, advice, possibility,
    probability, 109, 116–117, 121,
    124–125, 126, 128, 132, 135
  introduction to, 106
  as main verbs, 34
  with passive voice, 171, 177
  perfect, 139, 358, 360, 364

in reported speech, 425, 426, 429,
  440, 444
simple forms of, 19, 20, 365
modifiers, 196–197, 312, 343
more (. . . than), 395, 396, 406
most, 395, 396
much, 195, 197, 406n
must(n't)
  as modal auxiliary, 19, 358
  expressing need, 121
  in passive voice, 171
  expressing probability, 135
  and reported speech, 425, 429

N

need, 253, 254
negatives, 34, 36, 106
never, 78, 94
nevertheless, 386
no/no sooner, 94, 193
none, 193, 198
nor, 8, 266
not (ever/yet/many/much/enough),
  78, 194, 195, 219, 224, 227, 282
nouns
  abstract and concrete, 182
  modified by adjectives, adjective
    clauses, 12, 314, 318, 322, 341
  with adverb clauses of result, 411
  and appositives, 338
  by +, 155
  with causative verbs, 253, 254
  collective, 186, 187, 203
  as complements, 6
  count/noncount, 182, 183–184,
    186, 188–189, 193, 194, 195,
    196–197, 203, 205, 206, 207
  each +, 198
  gerunds as, 219
  + infinitives, 227, 239, 245
  modals +, 116
  as parts of speech, 4
  possessive, 39, 219
  proper, 155, 208
  singular and plural, 182, 186, 187
  as subjects, 5, 224
numbers, ordinal, 206

O

objects
  direct, indirect, 6, 12, 13, 153,
    438, 439, 440
  noun clauses as, 424
  of prepositions, 221, 224, 333